CHANGING ENVIRONMENTS

AS level Geography *for* Edexcel B

Series editors:
Sue Warn and Michael Naish

Authors:
Sue Sleep
Steve Frampton
Bob Hordern
David Flint

Longman

Edinburgh Gate
Harlow, Essex

Pearson Education Limited
Edinburgh Gate
Harlow
Essex
CM20 2JE
England

ISBN 0582 429 811

First published 2000
Printed in Italy by G. Canale & C.S.p.A. Borgano T.se - Turin
Designed by Amanda Easter
Illustrated by Oxford Design and Illustrators
Picture research by Louise Edgeworth

The Publisher's policy is to use paper manufactured from sustainable forests.

Contents

Acknowledgements

We are grateful to the following for permission to reproduce **copyright material**:

Bradford & District Newspapers for the articles 'Gloomy Picture of Rural Living' and 'Stainforth Post Office' in CRAVEN HERALD June and September, 1999; Guardian News Service Ltd for extracts from the articles 'Greens and Tories unite to oppose new town?' in THE GUARDIAN 17.12.97, 'The Shutters are ...' in THE GUARDIAN 19.5.98 and '£1m a mile needed to make bus lines work' by Paul Brown in THE GUARDIAN 7.1.99; Independent Newspapers (UK) Ltd for the article 'New homes in Lake District to be sold solely to locals' by Mark Rowe in INDEPENDENT ON SUNDAY 10.5.98; News International Syndication for the article 'The day the tide cam in to stay' by Simon de Bruxelles in THE TIMES 27.10.97 © Times Newspapers Limited 1997; Professor Orrin H Pilkey for extracts from 'A Time for Retreat' in the CITIES ON THE BEACH Conference 16.1.85; Stourbridge News & County Express for an extract from the article 'Avalanche of crime' in STOURBRIDGE NEWS 11.11.99; Westmorland Gazette Newspapers for the article 'Top Award for Rosthwaite Housing' from WESTMORLAND GAZETTE; Weymouth & Portland Borough Council for abridged extracts from case study 2 'Chesil Beach and the Fleet' in PORTLAND GEOGRAPHY FIELDWORK GUIDE: PORTLAND. "It's Living Geography".

We have been unable to trace the copyright holder of 'The Retreat Alternative in the Real World' by R. Sturza in CITIES ON THE BEACH Conference 16.1.1985 and would appreciate any information which would enable us to do so.

We are grateful to the following for permission to use **photos** and other copyright material:

Aerofilms 24 top; Albemarle-Pamlico, Estuarine Study 105; Barnabys Picture Library 232; Brian Dicks 147; Digital Vision Ltd 1, 125; Ecoscene 172(Chinch Gryniewicz); Mary Evans Picture Library 190; Steve Frampton 61, 62, 71, 74, 76, 78, 79, 84, 85, 91, 93, 96, 98, 101; GeoScience Features Picture Library 14 top, 24 bottom; Geoslides Photography 14 bottom left; Bob Hordern 127, 130, 131, 137, 151, 152, 153, 156, 169; Intermediate Technology 177, 178 top; Colin MacFarlane 99; Mountain Camera 14 bottom right(John Cleare); Nature Conservancy Council 83; Network 185 right(P Ginter/Bilderberg); Orange Personal Communications Services 1998 129 top; Maps reproduced from Ordnance Survey Mapping with the permission of the Controller of Her Majesty's Stationery Office, Crown Copyright 150, 204; PA News 32; Panos Pictures 126 right(Giacoma Pirozzi), 178 bottom(David Constantine), 242 centre(Roderick Johnson); Photofusion 201(Robert Brook), 202 bottom(Mark Campbell); Pictor International 126 centre, 191, 202 top, 203, 216, 242 right; Popperfoto 48; Rail Track 1999 129 bottom; Rex Features 2(Dale Cherry); Science Photo Library 8(James King-Holmes); Sealand Aerial 185 left; Skyscan Photolibrary 17(John Farmar), 196(William Cross); Sue Sleep 37, 38; Still Pictures 135(Mark Edwards), 186 left(Paul Harrison), 186 right(David Drain), 193(Edward Parker), 197(Nigel Dickinson), 206(Mikkel Ostergaard), 212(John Maier), 213 top(Ron Giling), 242 left(Chris Caldicott); Stone 213 bottom(Peter Seaward); TRH Pictures 155.

UNIT ONE

Changing landforms and their management

Chapter One: River Environments

1 Water: Too much or too little?

There is a common assumption that the world's water supply is virtually inexhaustible. This assumption is false. Fresh water represents less than half of one per cent of the total; the rest is either sea water or locked up in ice caps or soil. Worldwide, the consumption of water is doubling every 20 years – more than twice the rate of increase in population, placing enormous pressures on aquatic ecosystems. By the year 2025, as much as two thirds of the world's population will be living under conditions of severe water shortage.

Figure 1.1   *Worldwide water.*
Source: *The Ecologist,* June 1999.

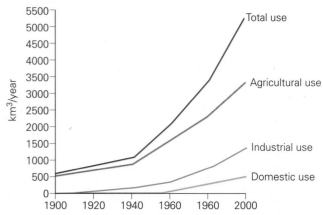

Figure 1.2   *Water use increased dramatically during the last century.*   Source: *Ambio,* 27, Sept. 1998.

Water is an essential requirement for life on earth. Our very existence depends on it, yet in the developed world especially, it is a resource that we take very much for granted. We depend on it not only for drinking and domestic use, for industry and agriculture, but increasingly as an amenity for recreational use too. As Figure 1.2 shows, global water use has increased nearly tenfold over the last century. As demand for water continues to escalate, water resource management will become critical for governments the world over if they are to avoid the problems brought about by water shortages. Global warming and rising sea levels add a further dimension to these management difficulties. Changing climate patterns will not only lead to global increases in temperature, but to less **precipitation** for some regions of the Earth and more for others.

Humans have always been attracted to river environments in their search for plentiful supplies of fresh water. These environments include the river itself, the land it flows over, and the **ecosystems** that the river supports. However, this attraction to water may also expose people to the hazards of too much water, which can have catastrophic effects both on the people and their built environment. In 1998 for example, many lowland parts of England and Wales suffered from widespread flooding (Figure 1.3). In 2000, disastrous floods in Mozambique caused thousands of deaths and made many people homeless.

In many countries, one response to the problems of too much or too little water has been to try to control rivers, for example by building dams or altering their courses. This has not always been successful as we shall investigate further during the course of this chapter.

ACTIVITIES

1 Analyse the data shown on the graph in Figure 1.2. At the end of the 20th century, which type of activities had the largest demand for water?

2 How are demands for water likely to change in the future?

3 Too much water or too little water: these are difficulties that people all over the world have to cope with. Some countries, such as the UK, suffer both problems at different times of the year. Produce two star diagrams to show the impacts of these extremes, too much water and too little water, for people and their activities. Remember to consider the problems that may be encountered in parts of the world other than the UK. You might find it useful to brainstorm your ideas with other class members. Once you have produced your diagram, colour code it to identify those problems that are likely to be short lived, and those that may become long-term problems.

Figure 1.3   *Floods in Northampton, UK.*

The global hydrological cycle – what is it and how does it work?

We are all familiar with systems that we use every day such as the braking system of a car, the hi-fi system in our home, or even our own digestive systems! These systems all have one thing in common, they are simply a collection of component parts that work together in order to do a specific job. They usually have inputs that allow them to function, processes and stores within them, and a final output.

We can use a systems approach to study natural systems at work in the environment around us, for example the hydrological system.

When seen from space, it is apparent that the Earth's surface is predominantly covered in water. Unlike the other planets in our solar system, temperature conditions on Earth allow water to be present in all its states, that is as a gas (water vapour), a solid (ice), and a liquid.

This water on the Earth's surface and in its atmosphere is not lost into space, and neither is it added to from outside the atmosphere. We refer to this as a closed system, as no gains or losses from outside the global system are necessary for the system to function. Instead, the water is continuously cycled between the oceans, the land, and the atmosphere in a series of processes known as the global **hydrological cycle**. As part of this cycle, the water also enters the biosphere, that is the plants and animals that are found in the ecosystems on land (terrestrial) and in water (aquatic). The main features of the global hydrological cycle are shown in Figure 1.4.

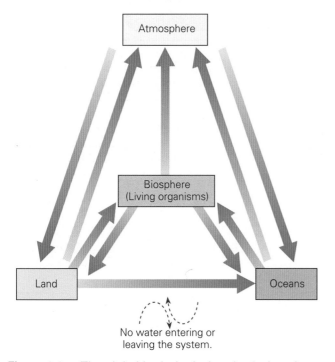

Figure 1.4   *The global hydrological cycle: A closed system.*

ACTIVITIES

1   Draw a large copy of the global hydrological cycle shown in Figure 1.4. Label the arrows to show the processes involved at different stages in the system.

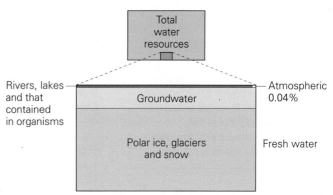

Figure 1.5   *Global water supplies may be large but only a small proportion is fresh water.*
Source: *Hydrology and the River Environment*, Clarendon Press, 1994.

Despite the large amount of water on Earth, humans are dependent on only a very small proportion of it for their survival. More than 97 per cent of the Earth's water is salt water and only a fraction of the fresh water supply is in a liquid state (Figure 1.5). The hydrological cycle is essential to life on Earth as it provides a continuous (though unevenly distributed) supply of fresh water in the form of precipitation (e.g. rain, snow, dew) onto the land. (Figure 1.7).

Water can be stored in any of these component parts as a liquid, a gas, or a solid, for varying degrees of time (Figure 1.6). Water stored as ice, for example, may remain trapped for many thousands of years, whilst water in the atmosphere may stay there for only a few days.

Storage component	Average water storage time
Atmosphere	8–10 days
Oceans and seas	4000 years +
Lakes and reservoirs	Up to two weeks
Rivers	Up to two weeks
Wetlands	Years
Biological water (as part of plants or animals)	One week
Soil water	Two weeks to one year
Ground water	Days to thousands of years
Ice	Tens to thousands of years

Figure 1.6   *Average storage times for water molecules in the different components of the hydrological cycle.*
Source: *Hydrology and the River Environment*, Clarendon Press, 1994.

Water moving through the hydrological cycle does not necessarily pass through all of the components of the cycle, but may enter very localised, short cycles. In warm atmospheric conditions, for example, rainfall may evaporate before reaching the ground, so the water immediately cycles back into the atmosphere. Cycling times may be longer where the water falls over land surfaces, especially if the water enters a storage component such as a lake or glacier.

Infiltration: Water soaking into the soil from the surface.

Throughflow: Water moving downhill through the soil layers. It will generally move slowly, but flow may concentrate along the line of roots or soil weaknesses and form natural pipes; the flow in these will be much faster.

Groundwater flow: Water moving within rocks below the ground.

Precipitation: Water deposited on the ground as a liquid or as a solid, for example rain, hail, snow, or even fog.

Channel flow: Water moving downhill within rivers.

Overland or surface flow: Water moving across the surface of the ground. This may happen when the rain cannot soak quickly enough into the ground, for example where there are tarmac surfaces or hard-baked soil, or even during very heavy rainfall. Saturated overland flow is more common and occurs when the soil is saturated and infiltration cannot take place.

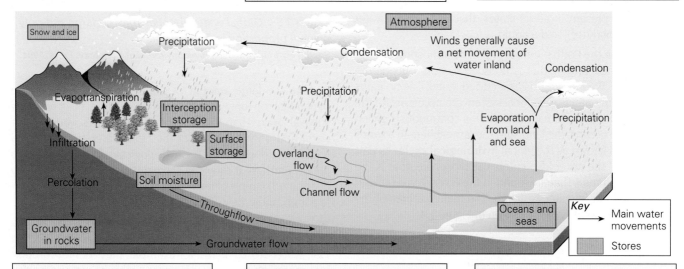

Evapotranspiration: The combined processes of evaporation and transpiration that result in the loss of water from the leaf. Transpiration is the loss of water through the tiny holes called stomata in the leaf surface. In practice it is very difficult to calculate the two amounts separately, so they are often grouped together.

Interception: Plants trap some of the precipitation so it may not immediately pass to the ground. Some may drip to the ground as throughfall; some may flow down the stem as stemflow. Alternatively, the precipitation may evaporate directly off the leaf surface and never reach the ground.

Percolation: Water moving from the surface layers of soil into deeper layers of soil and rock.

Evaporation: Water changing from its liquid form to a gas (water vapour) and returning to the atmosphere.

Figure 1.7   *The global hydrological cycle showing the main components and movements.*

ACTIVITIES

1   Carefully study the processes at work in the hydrological cycle. Construct your own flow diagram to show how various parts of the hydrological cycle are connected. The boxes on the right show the stores in the cycle. Make your own copy of these boxes, arranging them in a suitable way, and draw labelled arrows between the boxes to show the hydrological processes linking them.

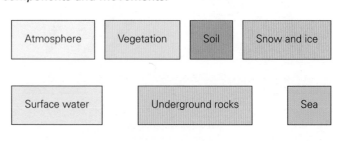

The drainage basin as part of the hydrological system

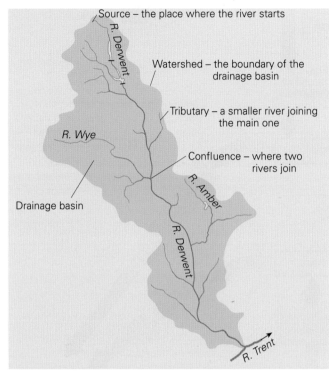

Figure 1.8 *The drainage basin of the River Derwent in Derbyshire. The features of the drainage basin are named.*

A **drainage basin** is an area of the land's surface from which a river receives its supply of water; in much the same way as a catchment area of a college or school is the area from which it receives students. For this reason, catchment is an alternative word for drainage basin. The edge of a drainage basin can be marked by an imaginary line called the **watershed**. The other main features of a drainage basin are shown in Figure 1.8.

Sometimes we may need to study only a small part of a drainage basin, for example, if we are observing the impacts of localised land-use changes on river flow, we may concentrate on the catchment of a single tributary within the drainage basin; we refer to this as a sub-catchment. Figure 1.8 shows the River Derwent drainage basin, which includes the River Wye, a tributary of the River Derwent. The Wye has its own catchment, which is a sub-catchment of the larger River Derwent drainage basin. Increasingly, catchment areas are being used as the major planning unit by the environmental or river management agencies.

Unlike the global hydrological cycle, a drainage basin works as an open system requiring inputs from outside in order to function. As a result, it is linked to other systems as Figure 1.9 shows. The drainage basin relies on the atmosphere for its input of water, whilst water that passes through the drainage basin leaves the system either to return to the atmosphere or to become an input into the coastal and ocean systems. A single drainage basin is one part of the whole hydrological cycle, but the hydrological processes taking place within it are mostly the same as those operating at the global scale (Figure 1.10).

ACTIVITIES

1 Referring to Figure 1.10 as a guide, describe three different routes that water entering the drainage basin as precipitation could take to reach the river channel.
2 Explain in detail why not all of the water will reach the river. If water does reach the river and then leaves the drainage basin, where can it go? Remember the information that you were given in Figure 1.9.
3 Apart from water, what else will the river transport out of the drainage basin and into the coastal system? Present your ideas as a list, indicating where each item on your list is likely to have come from. Remember that natural processes and human activities will add materials to the river.

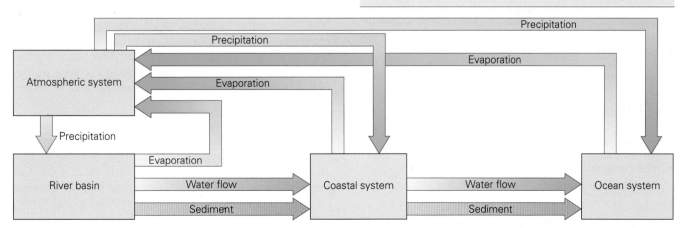

Figure 1.9 *A drainage basin is an open system linked to other systems by its inputs and outputs.*

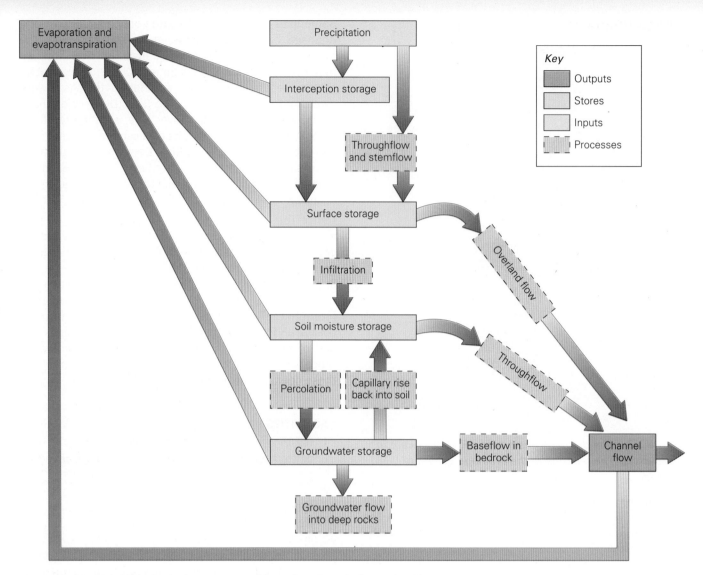

Figure 1.10   *The hydrological processes taking place in a drainage basin.*

When we study a drainage basin it is relatively easy to measure inputs of precipitation and the output of water in a river channel. Measurements of some of the other flows and stores are less easy to collect. The following written equation is often used to summarise the water balance of a drainage basin:

runoff = precipitation – evaporation ± changes in storage

In other words, the river flow out of the drainage basin is determined by:

- the amount of precipitation
- the losses in evaporation or evapotranspiration
- the gains or losses from the storage areas: surface storage, soil moisture, and groundwater storage.

The amount of water stored in soil and rock varies – what impact does this have?

The flows of water above and below ground directly affect how much water is stored within the drainage basin as groundwater storage or soil moisture storage. Plants depend on soil moisture content for their water supply, and soil moisture content varies during the year, as the fading green of many lawns in eastern and southern Britain in summer will testify.

Using climate, soil moisture and channel flow data, with estimates of evapotranspiration, it is possible to construct a water budget graph or model. A water budget graph allows us to understand in a little more detail the processes at work in the drainage basin and the balance of these processes over the year. It also allows us to compare basins in different areas. Figure 1.11 shows two examples of water budget graphs.

(a)   Birmingham, UK

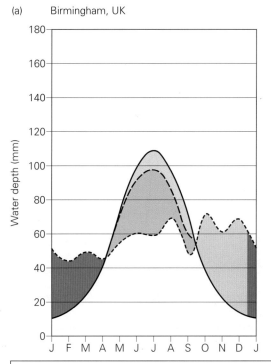

(b)   Athens, Greece

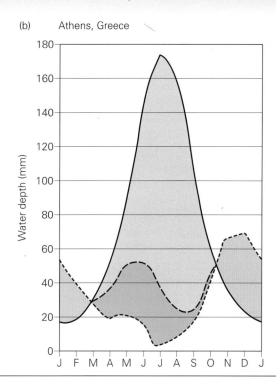

Key

� Water deficiency	- - - - Precipitation
▦ Soil moisture use	—— Potential evapotranspiration: (the amount of evapotranspiration that would take place if there were always plentiful supplies of water in the soil)
▨ Soil moisture recharge	
■ Water surplus	- - - Actual evapotranspiration: (the amount of evapotranspiration that actually takes place because of limitations imposed by lack of rainfall and reduced soil water content)

Although the rainfall in Birmingham is relatively constant during the year, higher temperatures in summer increase evapotranspiration and as a result the soil suffers a water deficit in summer. Lower temperatures in the autumn along with increasing rainfall soon recharge the soil water.
At what time of the year is surface run-off likely to be the greatest?

High summer temperatures cause high rates of evapotranspiration in summer and there is a very large soil water deficit. Although this is reduced in winter, rainfall is not sufficient to create a water surplus in the soil.
How will surface run-off be affected?

Figure 1.11 *Water budget graphs for* (a) *Birmingham, UK and* (b) *Athens, Greece.* Source: *General Climatology*, Prentice Hall, 1983.

In both water budget graphs it is possible to see times of the year when precipitation is greater than evapotranspiration. The excess water replaces water lost from the soil moisture store during drier periods. This is referred to as **recharge**. More water will also be available for overland flow and channel flow. When the soil moisture store is full, there will be a water surplus and there will be more percolation into groundwater stores.

During drier periods evapotranspiration is greater than precipitation. The store of soil moisture will decline and eventually will be used up, leaving a water deficit. A water deficit will directly affect plants dependent on this moisture reserve and also the activities of, for example, farmers trying to maintain the growth of their crops. Channel flow may also be reduced or fail completely.

The moisture content of a soil is determined by a number of factors:

Variations of inputs and outputs

- The input of moisture into the soil from precipitation, infiltration, or throughflow.
- The loss of moisture from the soil as evaporation, throughflow, percolation, plant uptake, and evapotranspiration.

The characteristics of the soil

- Large amounts of organic matter help to hold water, acting rather like a sponge.
- Smaller soil particles help to retain water in the small pores or spaces between them. Clay soils, for example, tend to be wetter, and slow to dry out.
- Larger particles tend not to fit so closely together and as a result water can drain quickly through. Sandy soils, for example, often suffer from low moisture content in summer because of this.

Groundwater stores also reflect the changes in soil moisture content, and the level of water in the rock, referred to as the water-table, will fluctuate during the year. Figure 1.12 shows such variations for a borehole in the Peak District.

ACTIVITIES

1 During dry periods when there are soil moisture deficits, many rivers maintain their flows, though at much lower levels. Where is the water likely to come from in this case?
2 Explain why the water-table in the Alstonfield borehole changes in a regular pattern. Suggest why this pattern may have changed in 1996 and 1997.
3 Compare the water-table in the Alstonfield borehole with data from a different region of the UK. Use the Institute of Hydrology website listed at the end of this unit to gain access to these.

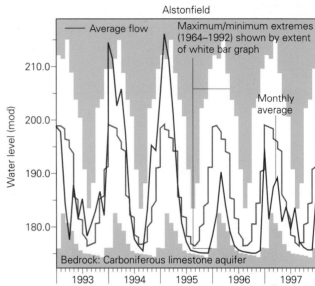

Figure 1.12 *Water-table variations in the Alstonfield borehole, north Peak District.*

Source: Institute of Hydrology and British Geological Survey, 1998 Yearbook

River flows and flood hydrographs

River channels provide a swift, surface-flow route for water out of the drainage basin. A great many factors cause channel flow to vary, but rivers tend to fall into one of three main types (Figure 1.13).

River type	Flow characteristics
Permanent or perennial channels	These channels flow throughout the whole year though there may still be great variations in the rate of flow during the year.
Intermittent channels	River flow may dry up during periods of low rainfall or high temperatures. This is most likely to occur where bedrock is permeable and rainfall relatively low or very seasonal, for example, in chalk areas of southern England.
Ephemeral channels	These channels carry water only very occasionally, for example those in desert areas where rainfall is rare.

Figure 1.13 *River types and their flow characteristics.*

The routes that water may take in the drainage basin to reach the river channel are shown in Figure 1.16, though the importance of each process will vary both within the drainage basin and between drainage basins. The water flowing in a river channel is referred to as its discharge and

is measured by calculating the total volume of water in the channel passing a particular point every second. It is therefore a function of both velocity and volume. Measurements are usually made in cubic metres per second, written as cumecs or m³/sec. The weir shown in Figure 1.14 has been built to allow such measurements to be taken, and with the use of continuous recording equipment, the changing flow patterns of the river can be analysed.

The **discharge** of a river at any point can be plotted on a **hydrograph**. A storm, or flood, hydrograph shows the river's response to a single rainfall event. An annual hydrograph indicates the yearly pattern of flow. Both types of hydrograph are useful tools as they allow us to study drainage basin processes and river channel response.

Figure 1.14 *An artificial weir allows continuous measurement of river flows.*

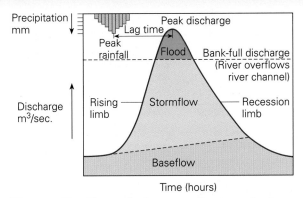

Figure 1.15 *The main features of a storm hydrograph.*

The main features of a storm hydrograph are shown in Figure 1.15; river discharge is shown in relation to precipitation. When the precipitation first starts, there is initially little increase in discharge, as only a small amount of rain will fall directly into the channel. Instead, rain is being intercepted by vegetation, or infiltrating into the ground where it may be refilling the soil moisture store if there was a deficit. As the soil becomes saturated, overland flow and throughflow start to reach the river and the discharge increases; this is shown by the rising limb in Figure 1.15. In the early stages of the rainfall event water reaches the river channel mainly from direct precipitation and overland flow, with gradually increasing amounts from throughflow taking place in the upper soil layers. The speed at which the river discharge increases will vary greatly and the time between peak rainfall and peak discharge, known as the **lag time**, can be used to measure this.

The recession limb on Figure 1.15 shows the rate at which the river discharge declines. It is usually not as steep as the rising limb, in other words it takes longer for the river to fall than it does to rise. This is because water is still reaching the river from slower, throughflow routes and from groundwater flow. The contribution that groundwater makes to the discharge is usually estimated and is shown on the hydrograph as base flow. Although the base flow may appear to be a rather insignificant part of the storm hydrograph, it is an important component of river discharge. It is the groundwater store that supplies much of the river discharge between storm events and keeps rivers flowing during periods of drought.

Factors which influence storm hydrographs

Figure 1.16 shows some of the factors that may affect flow routes:

*   vegetation cover
*   rock type
*   presence of lakes and reservoirs
*   climate
*   slope characteristics of the basin
*   soil type and depth
*   rainfall intensity and duration
*   land use, including the amount of urbanisation.

The balance of these factors in any one drainage basin will affect both the pattern of river flow over the year and a river's response to a single rainfall event as shown in a hydrograph. The shape, size, and drainage density of the drainage basin will also be important. A change in any one of these factors will have an impact (Figure 1.17).

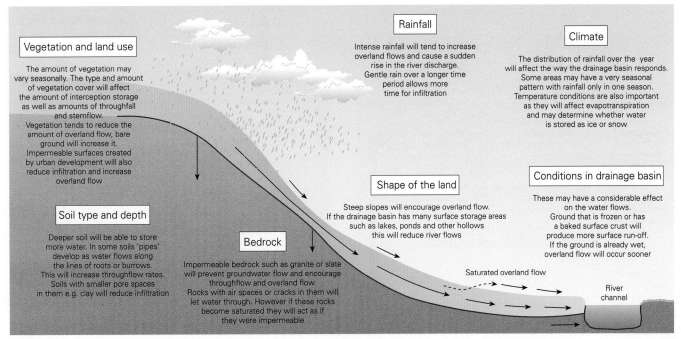

Figure 1.16 *Factors that influence water flows within a drainage basin.*

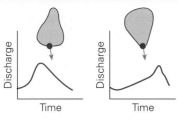

Drainage basin shape
Where the rain falls closer to the gauging station the river's rise in discharge will be noted sooner. In a catchment where the precipitation falls mainly in the upper area close to the source it will take longer to flow to the gauging station (or river mouth)

Drainage basin size
In a smaller drainage basin water will reach the river more quickly as there is less distance to travel. In a larger drainage basin the time lag will be longer, the quantity of water will also be greater

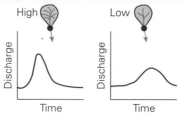

Drainage density
Water flows more slowly over the surface, in the soil or in the underground rock than it does in a river channel. In a high drainage density basin water reaches a channel more quickly and so flows out of the drainage basin more quickly

Surface characteristics: the storm hydrograph for Tokyo, Japan has changed as urbanisation has increased.

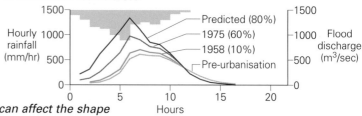

Figure 1.17   *How the characteristics of a drainage basin can affect the shape of a storm hydrograph.*   Source: *Drainage Basin Form and Process*, Arnold, 1973.

ACTIVITIES

1 Write a report to describe the impact of urbanisation on the Tokyo storm hydrograph (Figure 1.17). Your report should contain three parts:

   a *Before urbanisation*: Explain how the river responded to the storm before any development took place in the area. Make sure that you include details such as the peak discharge and the length of the lag time.

   b *After urbanisation*: What impact has urbanisation had on the storm hydrograph, including the size and timing of the peak discharge?

   c What problems might be caused for people living in western Tokyo by these changes in the way the river responds to rainfall?

How does the drainage basin system respond to changes in inputs?

In any system, including a drainage basin, processes at work help to regulate the system and keep it in a state of balance or equilibrium. A period of heavy rainfall, for example, may result in increased overland flow and channel flow above the surface and greater throughflow and groundwater flow below the surface. These processes help remove extra water from the drainage basin and return it to its normal state. Regulating processes like these are referred to as negative feedback Figure 1.18.

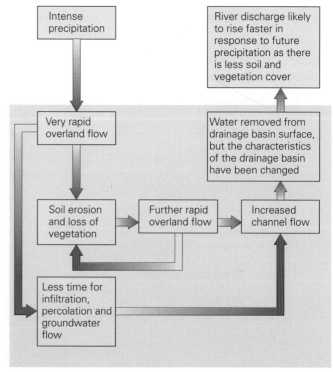

Figure 1.18   *Negative feedback.*

Figure 1.19   *Positive feedback.*

In some situations, perhaps if the rainfall is particularly heavy or lasts a long time, the usual feedback processes may not be able to work effectively. Instead, the changes have a 'knock-on' or 'snowballing' effect which can cause permanent or long-term changes in the system. This is referred to as positive feedback. An example in a drainage basin, illustrated in Figure 1.19, might be a severe storm causing soil **erosion** and loss of vegetation on hillsides. This lack of soil and vegetation may cause the river to rise more quickly during future storms. Events of this type may have long-term impacts on the way the drainage basin will function as it will take a long time for the soil and vegetation to develop again.

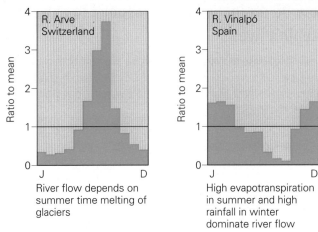

River flow depends on summer time melting of glaciers

High evapotranspiration in summer and high rainfall in winter dominate river flow

Figure 1.20 *Contrasting simple river regimes.*
Source: *Hydrology in Practice*, Chapman and Hall, 1994

ACTIVITIES

1 Systems diagrams like those illustrated in Figures 1.18 and 1.19 are a useful way of presenting and summarising the processes at work within a drainage basin. Draw your own diagrams to show how a drainage basin system will be affected by:
   a cutting down a large area of forest
   b the development of a city like Tokyo.

River regimes

The regime of a river is the expected seasonal pattern of discharge over the year at one particular point. It is based on average monthly discharge figures collected over at least 20 years, so that small year-to-year variations are ironed out, although in some rivers the variability of the discharge is a key feature of the regime.

The **river regime** may be linked to the pattern of rainfall during the year, with high river discharges corresponding to seasons of high rainfall and low flows occurring in drier seasons. Temperature is also important, for high temperatures will increase rates of evapotranspiration. This will obviously affect the amount of water flowing into the river.

The nature of the precipitation can also be important, because if most of the winter precipitation falls as snow it may only contribute to river discharge with seasonal melting in spring or summer. The River Arve in Switzerland (Figure 1.20), for example, depends mainly on glacial meltwater for its flow in summer. This is typical of a simple river regime where high discharges are confined to one period of the year. The River Vinalpó in Spain also has a simple regime with peak discharges in the winter coinciding with the periods of highest rainfall, and reduced river discharge in summer due to high rates of evapotranspiration.

Some rivers exhibit more complex flow patterns, where discharge relies on a number of causes. Rivers that have such regimes are likely to have very large drainage basins. As a result the river may pass through a variety of terrain, over different types of bedrock, and through more than one climate zone. This is the case with rivers such as the Amazon, the Nile, the Mississippi, and the Rhône (Figure 1.21).

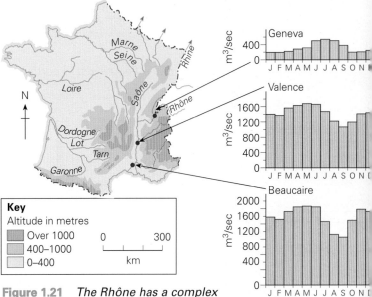

Figure 1.21 *The Rhône has a complex regime. The annual pattern of flow close to the source is very different from that near its mouth.*
Source: Edexcel, Module 6211 Resource Booklet, 1999.

ACTIVITIES

1 Explain how and why the regime of the Rhône changes so much between its source near Geneva and its mouth near Beaucaire. In your answer, mention the size of the discharges as well as the seasonal distribution of flow.

How do drainage basins respond to extreme rainfall events and what are the effects on people's lives?

People living close to rivers can adapt to the seasonal pattern of river flows, even if it means adjusting to an annual flood. It is extreme events, usually those that happen with little warning, that provide the greatest challenges for these people.

On the night of 27–28 October 1990, north-east Ireland suffered intense precipitation over a few hours. This led to high discharges in local rivers and flooding at Ballycastle, Cushendun, and Knocknacarry.

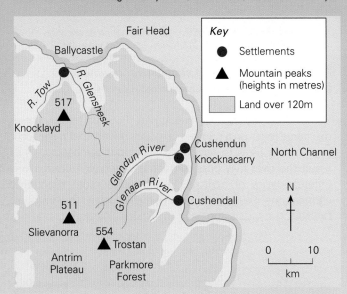

Figure 1.22 *The location of the flood event in north-east Ireland, 27–28 October 1990.*

Source: *Geography* 84, July 1999.

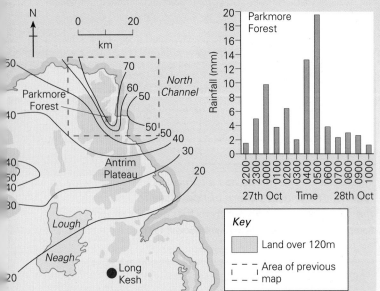

Figure 1.23 *Total precipitation shown as isohyets for the north-east of Ireland and the hourly rainfall totals for Parkmore Forest, 27-28 October, 1990.*

Source: *Geography* 84, July 1999.

A low pressure system (depression) passing over Ireland produced intense rainfall at a time when the area had already received more than 125 per cent of its normal October rainfall. The rainfall totals shown as **isohyets** in Figure 1.23 indicate the intensity of the storm, though in fact most of this rain fell in just six hours between 00.00 hours and 06.00 hours on 28 October 1990. Rainfall of this magnitude would be expected only every 270 years.

The main rivers in the region have small, steep-sided catchments and include part of the Antrim Plateau where there are no trees, only a covering of blanket peat. It was the sudden increase in discharge of these rivers that caused flooding in the region. In 1990 there were no **gauging stations** to measure the flows of these rivers, so flood hydrographs could not be drawn. The Department of Agriculture for Northern Ireland estimated that the discharge of the River Tow at Ballycastle reached a peak discharge of approximately 50m³/sec. in the early hours of 28 October 1990.

In Ballycastle it was the River Tow that caused most of the flooding problems, though the town also received surface run-off directly from the steep slopes of nearby hills to the south-east, where drainage ditches could not cope. Many houses that were not affected by the rising river levels were flooded by this surface run-off.

The Tow has a drainage basin covering an area of 24.35 km². Ballycastle itself covers an area of 1 km² but because of its location near the mouth of the River Tow it has little impact on peak discharges. To the west of the river, which cuts the drainage basin in half, is relatively flat agricultural land. To the south-east lies land that rises steeply to the peak of Knocklayd (Figure 1.22). These steep slopes and rapid overland flow, combined with heavy rainfall, caused the discharge in the Tow to increase very quickly and it flooded its banks. One person died in Ballycastle and the flooding affected several houses. The floodwater also disrupted transport networks in the region as some roads were blocked and bridges washed away. In some areas top-soil was eroded by the fast-flowing water and in others, sediment was deposited on top of agricultural land.

Since this flood, changes have been made to the river channels at Ballycastle and Cushendun to reduce the future impact of floods. The hydrological monitoring system for the area has also been improved; the river Tow now has a gauge to measure stream flow in Ballycastle and the river Glendun has a similar gauge in its upper course.

ACTIVITIES

1 Use an atlas to find out about the geology of the Antrim Plateau. How are its characteristics likely to have increased the problems of flooding?
2 Draw your own annotated flood hydrograph for the river Tow at Ballycastle covering the same period as the rainfall graph in Figure 1.23. Assume for the purposes of this exercise that the peak discharge occurred at 02.00 hours on 28 October 1990 and that normal river flow on the Tow at this time of year is 5 m³/sec. Calculate the lag time and mark it on your hydrograph.

ACTIVITIES

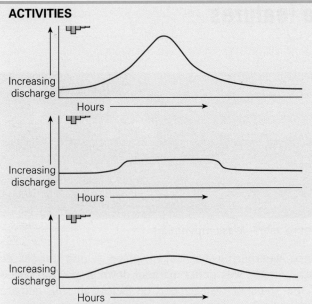

Figure 1.24 *Three different types of hydrograph. The blue bars show precipitation.*

1 Look at the three simple hydrographs in Figure 1.24.

 a Which of them shows a river that is:
 • controlled by a water storage dam
 • flowing out of a drainage basin where the land is used mainly for coniferous forestry plantations
 • flowing out of the same drainage basin after most of the trees have been felled?

 b Explain the reasons for your choices.

 c Draw your own pairs of simple hydrographs to show the river discharges you would expect from:
 • a short but heavy rainstorm compared with a longer period of light rainfall
 • rain falling on already saturated ground compared with rain falling on relatively dry ground.

 d Explain what your hydrographs show.

2 Surface run-off varies greatly between different parts of the UK as shown in Figure 1.25. Explain the reasons for this variation. You will find it useful to consult atlas maps, particularly those showing the relief, geology, rainfall distribution, and temperature variations within the UK.

3 **a** Search the Institute of Hydrology website listed at the end of this unit and find river flow data for rivers in different parts of the UK. There is a map showing the location of all the gauging stations.

 b Choose at least five rivers flowing in areas of high surface run-off, and five rivers flowing in areas of low surface run-off. For each river, find out the precipitation total received in its drainage basin and the run-off total in millimetres. It will also be useful to study the catchment description for each river to see if there are any special characteristics of the drainage basin that affect run-off. Present your findings in a table.

 c State whether your findings support the conclusions you came to in Question 1.
   Are there any rivers where the run-off is a lot higher or lower than you expected? Try to explain the reasons in each case.

4 Carry out fieldwork in your local environment, perhaps within the school grounds, to investigate the factors that cause infiltration rates to vary in different areas. Use either a real infiltration ring or improvise with a piece of plastic piping or metal tube. This tube will need to be at least 40 cm long and preferably about 20 cm in diameter. Inside one end of the tube tape a plastic ruler. This will allow you to measure the infiltration rate. Figure 1.26 shows how to use this apparatus.

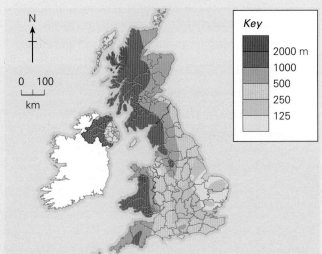

Figure 1.25 *Surface run-off variations across the UK.*
Source: *British Rivers* Allen and Unwin 1998.

Key
2000 m
1000
500
250
125

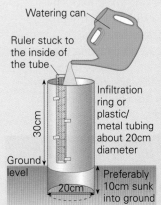

Add water up to the 20cm mark. You will need to work quickly. Measure the fall in water level at the end of each minute.
   At the end of each minute quickly top the water back up to 20cm (if the water level is allowed to fall too low this on its own will affect the infiltration rate).
   If necessary, you may need to top up more frequently, noting each time the amount of water added and how high you filled it.
You will then be able to use your figures to plot a graph showing infiltration rate in millimetres per minute.

Location: flowerbed	Height of water	Amount of water added	New water level
0	20	–	–
After 1 minute	13	7	20
After 2 minutes	14	6	20
After 3 minutes	16	4	20

Figure 1.26 *Calculating infiltration rates.*

2 River processes and landscape features

So far we have studied hydrological activity within the drainage basin, but have paid little attention to the geomorphological activity that takes place there. **Geomorphology** is the study of landforms and in particular, their structure, origin, and development through time.

Within a drainage basin the processes of **weathering, erosion, transport**, and **deposition** are responsible for the landscape features found there. The shape of the river valley for example is partly due to erosion by the river but is mainly the result of slope processes, including weathering, and the transport of the weathered material.

Weathering is the breakdown of rock *in situ*, i.e. where it is (Figure 1.27); the end product being a layer of rocky particles or **regolith**. This layer may vary in thickness and contain particles of different sizes, some of which may have been chemically altered. This weathered layer is the first stage in soil formation.

There are three main types of weathering:

- **Mechanical weathering** is the physical breakdown of rock, for example by the action of water freezing and opening up cracks (freeze-thaw weathering), or the continuous heating and cooling of rocks that weakens them so that outer layers fall off (exfoliation).
- **Chemical weathering** occurs when rocks are exposed to water. Rainfall is naturally acid because of the carbon dioxide which is dissolved in it. Chemical reactions taking place between the water and the rocks cause the rock to break down. It happens especially where rocks are alkali and permeable so that water can easily penetrate the rocks.
- **Biological weathering** is caused by living organisms. Lichens living on rocks or plant roots in the soil release chemicals that increase the rate of rock breakdown. Plant roots can also help to open up joints and thus weaken rocks.

Figure 1.28   *Mass movement.*

Once weathering has taken place, slope processes transport the weathered material down slope. The speed of this transport will depend on factors such as climate and vegetation cover.

- Extreme events such as landslides or rock falls are called **mass movements** (Figure 1.28). They are caused by the weight of the weathered material and gravity. Slower, but more continuous processes such as soil creep produce sets of small terraces across the slope that gradually 'creep' downhill.
- **Slope-wash** processes depend on water on or close to the surface as the erosive force. Raindrops hitting the ground throw up material and may increase its speed of movement down the slope. Once water is moving across the surface, it may wash off surface material on a large area of slope (sheet wash), or it may start to flow in small channels down the slope. It is then more efficient at eroding material and small rills or deep gullies may form (Figure 1.29). Material may also be removed from the slope in **solution**, especially where the climate is very hot and humid so that the rate of chemical weathering is high.

These slope processes are summarised in Figure 1.30.

Figure 1.27   *Rock weathering.*

Figure 1.29   *The effects of slope-wash.*

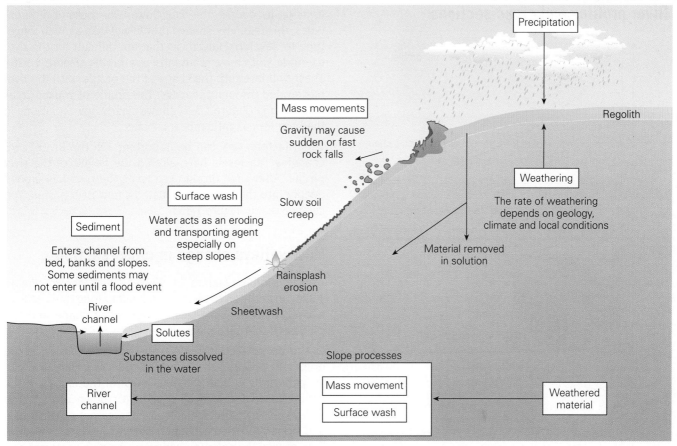

Figure 1.30 *A summary of the slope processes that contribute to landform development in river valleys.*

ACTIVITIES

1 Make a list of factors that affect the rate of weathering of rocks.
2 Consider the slope shown in Figure 1.30 as an open system. List the inputs and outputs of this slope system.
3 What types of human activity could **a** speed up or **b** slow down the transport of material from this slope system? Draw an annotated diagram or flow diagram to show these activities and the impact you think they might have.

The sediment that enters the river channel may be carried downstream by the force of moving water. Although additional material may be eroded from the bed and banks as the river flows towards the sea, a lot of the sediment carried by the river is that supplied in the upper sections of the drainage basin, especially if this is in a mountainous area. The sediment passes downstream and in the lower reaches of the river, closer to the mouth, it may be deposited. This generalised pattern or model suggested by Stanley Schumm is shown in Figure 1.31 and provides a useful starting point for the study of river processes and landforms. (It is important to remember that a model is only a simplification of reality and local conditions may not fit into this pattern.)

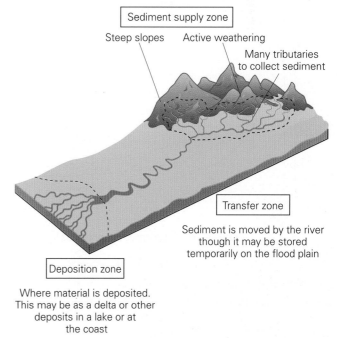

Figure 1.31 *Sediment production, transport, and deposition in a drainage basin.*

Source: *The Fluvial System* Wiley, 1997.

River profiles and cross-sections

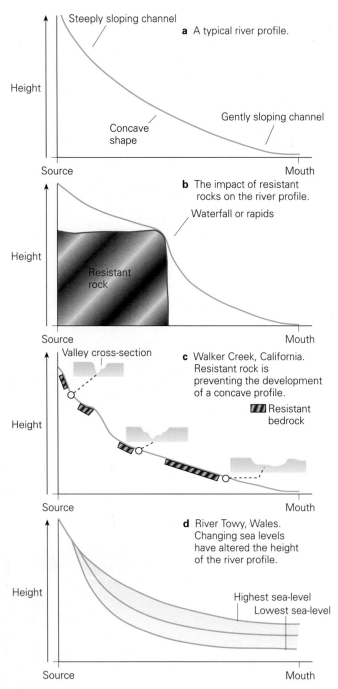

a A typical river profile.

b The impact of resistant rocks on the river profile.

c Walker Creek, California. Resistant rock is preventing the development of a concave profile.

d River Towy, Wales. Changing sea levels have altered the height of the river profile.

Figure 1.32 *The shape of a typical long profile and how this can vary.*

The changing height of a river channel as it passes from source to mouth is known as the **long profile**. As a river erodes into its river valley in some places, and drops or deposits material in others, the profile that develops is often concave in shape. Figure 1.32a shows the shape of a typical long profile once the irregularities in the landscape have been removed by erosion and deposition.

If, along its course, the river flows over rocks of different types, this regularly-shaped profile will take a much longer time to develop. Hard rocks that are difficult for the river to erode will create waterfalls and rapids (Figure 1.32b). These will interrupt the shape of the profile until the river has eroded through the rocks. The profile of Walker Creek in California (Figure 1.32c) shows clearly how variations in the bedrock can influence its shape.

Other factors, too, can be important. On the River Towy, changing sea levels have altered the height of the river profile. After each drop in sea level, the river has eroded deeper into the valley and created a new river profile. You can see this in Figure 1.32d.

How valleys change in cross-section

As the profile diagram of Walker Creek shows (Figure 1.32c), in addition to changes in height along the profile of a river, there are changes in the valley shape and the processes that take place there.

In the upper sections of a river or where erosion is the dominant process, the valley cross-section is typically v-shaped and very narrow. Here much of the energy of the river is used for vertical erosion (or downcutting). The valley sides are subjected to various weathering processes and slope processes as already shown on pages 14 and 15. This causes the valley to widen as the slopes retreat and produces the characteristic valley shape. Local factors such as geology, climate, and human activities may also affect the exact shape of the valley.

It is important to remember that although erosion is the dominant process in the upper sections of a river, deposition can also take place if local conditions are suitable. If, for example, a river enters an upland lake or tarn, the water flow slows and deposition will take place. Similarly, although deposition becomes increasingly important as the river approaches its mouth, erosion also still has an important part to play.

The Gordale Beck: Limestone, till, and more than a little melting ice!

The Gordale Beck flows in the Yorkshire Dales. Here, different rock types have strongly influenced the appearance of the landscape. The main rock type is Carboniferous Limestone; a hard but permeable rock that allows water to pass through the joints. Slate, an impermeable rock, is also found in the area, where it is covered with till. Till is an easily eroded deposit left by glaciers as they melted. It is made up of various stones and smaller rock particles. Figure 1.33 shows the geology of the Gordale area and some of the landforms that can be seen there.

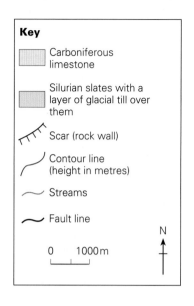

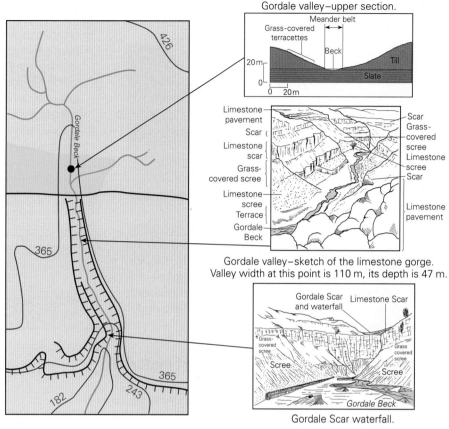

Figure 1.33   *Geology and landscape features at Gordale, Yorkshire Dales.*

Source: *Practical Foundations of Geography* Allen and Unwin, 1981.

The valley features at Gordale may appear to be shaped by river and slope processes at work today, but those processes operating 12,000 years ago are likely to have been more important. The limestone gorge is thought to have been formed at the end of the last ice age by large amounts of water from the melting glaciers. This water may have flowed over frozen ground and so been unable to percolate down into the limestone. Instead, it eroded the limestone at the surface and formed the deep gorge. The present Gordale Beck is certainly too small to have formed the gorge in recent times.

ACTIVITIES

1   Use the information shown in the sketch of the limestone gorge at Gordale to draw an annotated cross-section of the valley.
2   Compare your cross-section of the valley at this point with that of the upper section of the Gordale valley where till is found over slate. Describe and account for the differences.
3   Explain what has caused the development of a waterfall at Gordale Scar and how this feature will affect the long profile of the river.

Rivers and floodplains

Where rivers flow over much more gently sloping land, typically in the lower sections of their profile, they use more energy eroding sideways (lateral erosion) than vertically. The river valley in the lower sections tends to be much wider and flatter as a result. The rate of deposition is greater than erosion rates, and each time the river floods, a thin layer of sediment is deposited across the flat valley floor or **floodplain**. Heavier particles are deposited closer to the river and gradually embankments called **levees** build up along the banks. Figure 1.34 shows a river flowing across its floodplain. The main features of the floodplain system are also shown in Figure 1.35.

Figure 1.34   *The River Frome in its floodplain.*

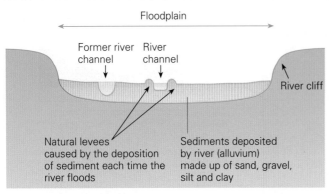

Figure 1.35   *A cross-section through a typical floodplain.*

The floodplain is not a stable set of landforms, but rather a dynamic environment where deposition and erosion are constantly changing the river channel and the floodplain, even in the short term. As we will see in Section 1.5, because of their dynamic nature, rivers in their floodplain stages have sometimes proved to be very difficult for humans to manage.

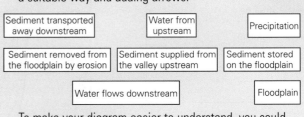
How does a river erode and transport material?

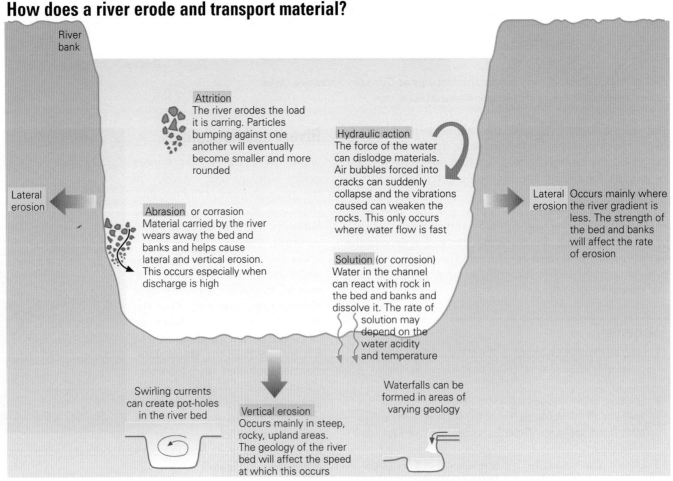

Figure 1.36   *There are four main types of erosion that take place in a river channel; attrition, abrasion, hydraulic action and solution.*

The processes of erosion that take place within the river channel are summarised in Figure 1.36. These processes allow the river to erode back into the slopes near its source (headward erosion), as well as sideways (lateral erosion) and downwards (vertical erosion).

The material that is eroded may then be transported by the river, again in a number of different ways, according to the type and speed of the water flow and the size of the particles (Figure 1.37).

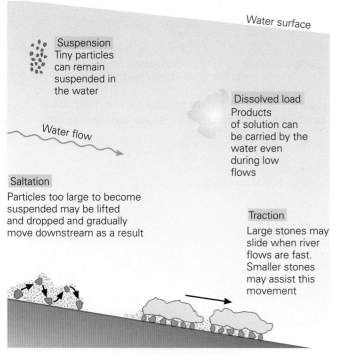

Suspension
Tiny particles can remain suspended in the water

Dissolved load
Products of solution can be carried by the water even during low flows

Water flow

Water surface

Saltation
Particles too large to become suspended may be lifted and dropped and gradually move downstream as a result

Traction
Large stones may slide when river flows are fast. Smaller stones may assist this movement

Figure 1.37   *A river can transport its load in different ways.*

The material carried by the river is called its **load**. It is made up of sediments of different sizes – from the smallest clay particle up to large pebbles and even boulders. As we have already seen, the amount of sediment input into a river is decided not only by the amount of erosion in the river channel itself, but also by the weathering and slope processes taking place in the river valley.

Once the sediment enters the river channel, the size of an individual particle and the speed of the water flow will determine whether or not the particle is transported. This is shown in Figure 1.38 on the Hjulström Curve. Note that all sizes of particles require more energy to start them moving than they do to keep them moving. The larger the particle, the greater the energy required to move it. However, very tiny particles, for example clay, require larger amounts of energy to move them than might be expected, as they have a tendency to stick together and to behave like larger particles.

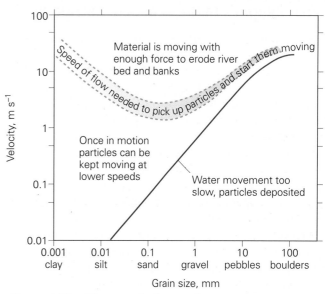

Figure 1.38   *The speed of water flow and its relationship with erosion and deposition. The Hjulström Curve.*
Source: *Bulletin of the Geological Institute of Uppsala* 25, 1935.

During flood events, when discharge and velocity increase in the river channel, the total amount of load carried by the river, referred to as its **capacity**, will change. This can be seen in the hydrograph for the Rhine which shows sediment concentration during the winter floods of 1993–94 (Figure 1.39).

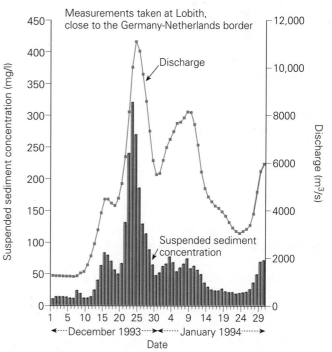

Figure 1.39   *Suspended sediment concentration during the Rhine floods in 1993–94.*
Source: *Earth Surface Processes and Landforms* 23, 1998.

What happens to the sediment carried by rivers?

For a greater understanding of the inputs, transport, and outputs of sediment in a river we need to take into account storage that may take place. If the water flow is not fast enough to move particles. they will be stored as deposits either within the channel or on the floodplain. Storage times may vary, but the very largest boulders may only be transported during the high velocities associated with extreme flood events and as a result they may be stored for many tens or even hundreds of years.

If storage times and amounts can be calculated (not an easy task) it is possible to work out the balance between erosion and deposition of sediment in a catchment. An example of such a sediment budget is shown in Figure 1.40. In this case little more than a quarter of the sediment produced as a result of soil erosion actually leaves the catchment. The remainder is stored mainly on the floodplain.

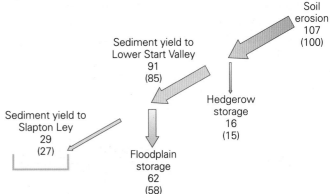

Sediment figures are in tonnes/km²/year.
The percentages of the total sediment budget are shown in brackets

Figure 1.40   *A sediment budget for the River Start catchment in south Devon.*   Source: *Geography* 82, 1997.

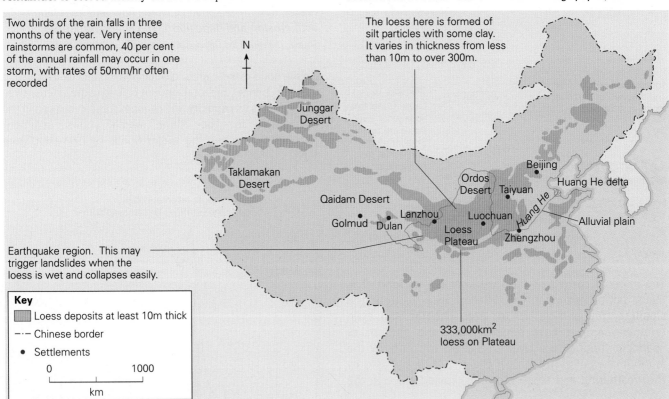

Two thirds of the rain falls in three months of the year. Very intense rainstorms are common, 40 per cent of the annual rainfall may occur in one storm, with rates of 50mm/hr often recorded

The loess here is formed of silt particles with some clay. It varies in thickness from less than 10m to over 300m.

N

Junggar Desert

Taklamakan Desert

Qaidam Desert

Golmud   Dulan   Lanzhou

Ordos Desert   Taiyuan   Beijing

Huang He delta

Luochuan   Huang He

Loess Plateau   Zhengzhou   Alluvial plain

Earthquake region. This may trigger landslides when the loess is wet and collapses easily.

333,000km²
loess on Plateau

Key

▦ Loess deposits at least 10m thick

–·– Chinese border

• Settlements

0 ———— 1000
km

Figure 1.41   *The course of the Huang He in relation to the Loess Plateau of central China.*
Source: *Process Models and Theoretical Geomorphology,* Wiley, 1994.

Rivers vary considerably in their capacity to transport and store sediment. The Huang He is the second largest river in China and is well known for its exceedingly high sediment load. The average sediment concentration is 37 kg/m³, this is eight times greater than the average sediment concentration in the Ganges and 26 times greater than that in the Nile. During peak flows it is estimated that the sediment content of the river may reach 900 kg/m³ or approximately 40 per cent by weight.

The reason for this high sediment content is that the Huang He flows through the Loess Plateau of central China. Loess is a wind-blown deposit that is very fertile but it can also be easily eroded by water. The Huang He and its tributaries have cut deep valleys through the loess and the yellow-brown sediment that they collect flowing through this plateau area has given the Huang He its alternative name, the Yellow River.

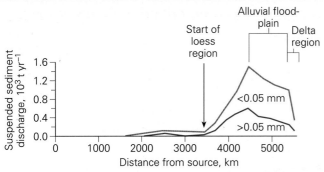

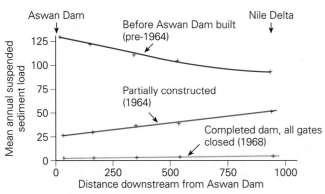

Figure 1.42 *Downstream variations in the sediment load of the Huang He.* Source: *Journal of Geology,* 91, 1983.

Figure 1.43 *Change in the suspended sediment load downstream of the Aswan dam on the Nile.* Source: *The variability of large alluvial rivers,* American Society of Civil Engineers, *1994.*

The large sediment load of the Huang He has created problems for dam and reservoir management downstream and for people living in the flat, floodplain area where deposition of sediment in the river channel has made flooding more common. Only 24 per cent of the enormous sediment load of the Huang He reaches the sea because 33 per cent is deposited on the floodplain and 43 per cent in the delta area.

The sediment budget of the Nile is very different from that of the Huang He. The Nile does not flow through areas of such easily eroded material and its average sediment load is only 1.4kg/m³. Before the dam, a total of 130 million tonnes of silt was carried in the Nile, 10 per cent of it being deposited on the floodplain whilst the majority (90 per cent) was either deposited in the delta area or flowed into the Mediterranean Sea. Here the fertile silt helped to support a productive fishing industry. This silt is now collecting behind the Aswan Dam and as Figure 1.43 shows, the amount of sediment carried by the Nile is now very much reduced.

ACTIVITIES

1 Explain the reasons why the sediment budgets of the Nile and the Huang He are very different.

Hydraulic geometry and patterns in rivers

Hydraulic geometry is the study of channel measurements and how they change over the course of a river. Measurements of depth, width, discharge, velocity, and sometimes load are taken. Figure 1.44 shows how some of these variables change along a river's course.

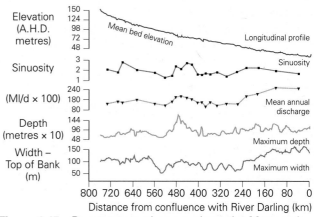

Figure 1.44 *The Bradshaw model showing downstream changes in river characteristics.* Source: *The Earths changing Surface,* Hodder and Stoughton, 1978.

Figure 1.45 *Downstream changes along the Murray river in south-east Australia.*

Source: *The variability of large alluvial rivers* American Society of Civil Engineers, 1994.

The velocity of a river depends on how steep the land and river channel are, as well as their shape and roughness. How efficiently a river erodes or transports material will depend on this velocity.

Where the water is in contact with the bed and banks (called the wetted perimeter), friction will slow the water down. Figure 1.46 indicates how this wetted perimeter will vary with channel shape and the influence this friction has on the speed of the water flow. Most of the river's energy is spent overcoming the friction of the bed and banks, so rivers with rough beds and banks will have larger wetted perimeters, flow more slowly and be less efficient.

The **hydraulic radius** is a measure of this efficiency and is calculated by comparing the size of the wetted perimeter with the cross-sectional area of the river, as shown in Figure 1.46.

River A

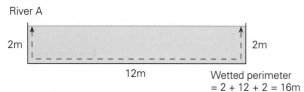

12m

Wetted perimeter
= 2 + 12 + 2 = 16m

More water is in contact with bed and banks. This friction decreases the velocity of the water flow.

River B

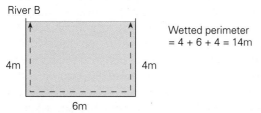

Wetted perimeter
= 4 + 6 + 4 = 14m

6m

Less water is in contact with bed and banks. Friction is less so the water velocity will be higher.

It is possible to compare channel efficiency between rivers by calculating the hydraulic radius. This calculation allows us to compare the volume of water with the amount of friction in a river. The higher the value the more efficient the river will be.

Hydraulic radius =

Amount of water in cross section of channel ÷ wetted perimeter
(width × average depth)

River A hydraulic radius = $\frac{24}{16}$ = 1.50

River B hydraulic radius = $\frac{24}{14}$ = 1.71

Figure 1.46   *Channel shape and hydraulic radius.*

The efficiency of a river will vary along its length. An efficient river will have more energy remaining for erosion or transport. Where the river is less efficient, deposition will occur. This may happen where:

- the discharge of a river is reduced
- the speed of flow is less
- the load increases.

ACTIVITIES

1 **a** Study the Bradshaw model (Figure 1.44). Describe and suggest reasons for the downstream changes in discharge, load quantity, and load particle size.

   b It might seem surprising at first that velocity increases downstream even though the gradient of the river channel has decreased. Using evidence from the model and your knowledge of hydraulic geometry explain this change in velocity.

   c Assess how well the data from the Murray river (Figure 1.45) fits the Bradshaw model. Explain the reasons for any differences that you find.

Landforms associated with changing river channels

The plan of a river at any point tends to fall into one of three basic types, known as river traces (Figure 1.47). River channels tend to develop winding or sinuous courses rather than straight ones. The index of sinuosity is used to indicate how winding a river is and allows us to compare rivers. The method of calculation is shown in Figure 1.47.

River traces

Rivers usually fall into one of three main types:

1 Straight
A river is usually only straight for short stretches unless it has been altered by humans.

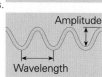

2 Meandering
The River Dove in Derbyshire shows typical meanders. They are often very regular.

3 Braided
A braided river divides into multiple channels separated by islands or gravel deposits, e.g. Fraser River, Canada.

Calculating the index of sinuosity

$$index = \frac{distance\ measured\ along\ river\ channel\ A–B}{straight\ line\ distance\ between\ A\ and\ B}$$

An index of >1.5 indicates a meandering channel

Figure 1.47   *Sinuosity in rivers and how the index of sinuosity is calculated.*

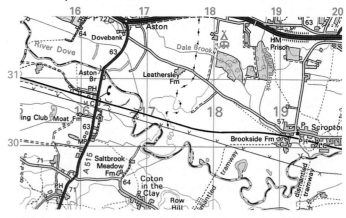

Figure 1.48   *A section of the River Dove on the Staffordshire–Derbyshire border.*

ACTIVITIES

1 Use the index of sinuosity to compare the sinuosity of the River Dove from grid reference 152315 to 167304, with the section between 167304 and 192296.

2 Suggest possible reasons why the section of river close to the bridge at 164312 is less sinuous.

Changing channels and the floodplain

In areas of steep slopes, rivers use a large amount of energy to erode vertically. Consequently, the river channel tends not to alter its position as much as a river flowing over more gentle gradients, where lateral erosion is more significant. In both straight and meandering channels, pools and riffles may develop. These can be seen in Figure 1.49. Many theories have attempted to explain their pattern, not entirely successfully. However, pools and riffles are thought to be caused by a complicated interaction between the speed of water flows, and erosion and deposition. The result is a regular pattern of shallow riffles and deeper pools. Many geographers have suggested that there is a link between these pool and riffle sequences and the development of meanders.

A river meandering across a floodplain has a constantly changing channel. Lateral erosion of the banks occurs at the outside of the bends as a result of centrifugal forces which cause the surface water to move out more towards the outer bank and create a spiralling water flow known as helical flow in the river channel. This leads to the **meander** growing wider and eroding into the valley sides. This widens the floodplain and leaves a line of river cliffs or **bluffs** Figure 1.49. The meanders also tend to migrate downstream because of the direction of greatest erosion at each bend. The combined effects of lateral erosion and migration downstream can lead to the formation of **river terraces** as shown in Figure 1.49.

In much the same way as pools and riffles are evenly spaced, meanders also tend to be regularly spaced. Only if there is an irregularity in the way the river erodes, for example if one section of the river bank is more resistant to erosion, will one meander be able to move closer to the next. Where the two meander loops are close together, the river may break through to form a **cut-off**. Deposition at the entrance to the now abandoned meander loop will silt it up and leave this as an **ox-bow** lake (Figures 1.50 and 1.51).

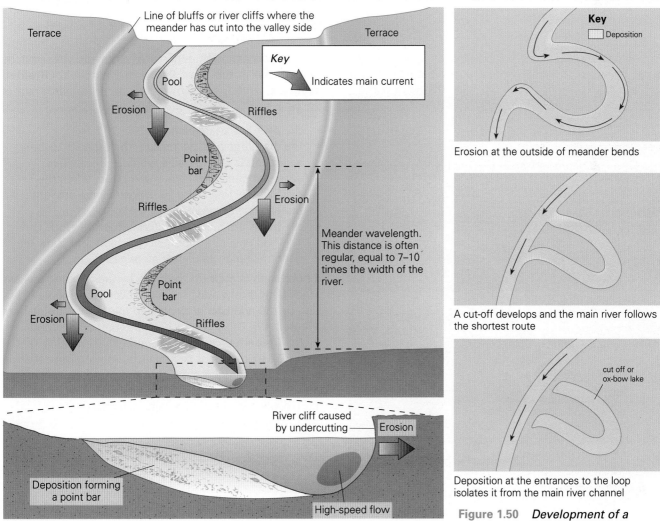

Figure 1.49 *River processes and landforms in a floodplain environment.*

Figure 1.50 *Development of a cut-off and an ox-bow lake.*

Figure 1.51   *An ox-bow lake*

Under certain circumstances, rivers no longer flow in a single channel but instead flow in shallow, multiple channels separated by deposits of sediment. These can be clearly seen in the River Rhône in Figure 1.52. **Braided channels**, as they are known, may occur for all or part of the year if:

* the river has a large load
* the discharge and, as a result, the capacity to carry sediment, is very variable, perhaps because of seasonal rainfall or high evaporation. When the discharge is low, the river deposits large amounts of material that disrupt the flow of water
* the banks are made of material that will erode easily. This will ensure a supply of sediment and allow the river to change its course more easily.

A floodplain is built up gradually by the flooding process which periodically adds sediment over the floodplain, but also by the addition of deposited material at **point bars** (Figure 1.49). This material becomes part of the floodplain as the meanders migrate towards the outsides of the bends. The process of sediment build-up or aggradation may be disrupted if the river has more energy available to cut vertically down into the floodplain. This might happen if the discharge of the river were to increase or the load of the river to decrease.

Figure 1.52   *Intricate braiding of the River Rhône, Switzerland.*

What ecosystems exist in a river environment?

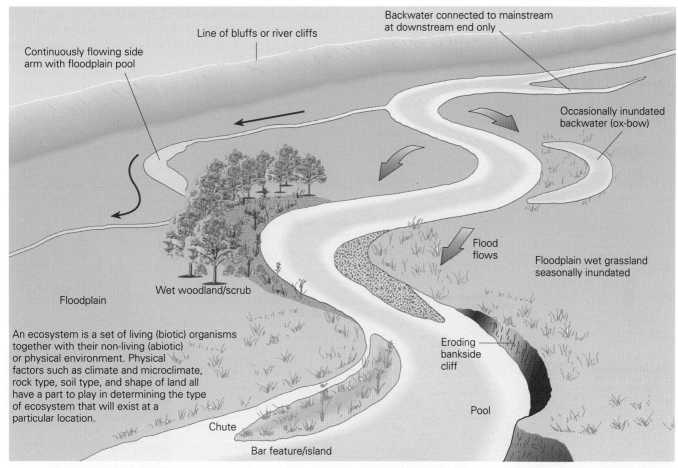

Continuously flowing side arm with floodplain pool

Line of bluffs or river cliffs

Backwater connected to mainstream at downstream end only

Occasionally inundated backwater (ox-bow)

Flood flows

Floodplain wet grassland seasonally inundated

Wet woodland/scrub

Floodplain

An ecosystem is a set of living (biotic) organisms together with their non-living (abiotic) or physical environment. Physical factors such as climate and microclimate, rock type, soil type, and shape of land all have a part to play in determining the type of ecosystem that will exist at a particular location.

Eroding bankside cliff

Pool

Chute

Bar feature/island

Figure 1.53 *Some of the different types of ecosystems found in or close to rivers.*
Source: *The New Rivers and Wildlife Handbook* RSPB, NRA and RSNC, 1994.

The plants and animals that live in rivers, along the riverbanks (riparian zone), or on the floodplain are all part of the river environment. Rivers and their floodplains support a great many ecosystem types. Some of these can be seen in Figure 1.53.

Many of these habitats are wetland ecosystems where the water-table is close to, or at the surface and where there is either regular flooding or water present all the time. These wetland ecosystems tend to have very particular soil or sediment conditions and the rich variety of plants and animals living in wetland habitats often have special adaptations to allow them to survive there. Plants in these ecosystems grow very well, i.e. they are very productive.

When we study these ecosystems we are interested in two aspects:

Their structure
* How is the ecosystem organised?
* What are the different plants and animals found there?
* Which plants and animals are most common?
* Where are the plants and animals found in the ecosystem? Are the plants arranged in a certain way?
* Which food chains are operating?

How they function
* What inputs and outputs are there?
* In what ways does energy flow through the system?
* How are nutrients cycled?
* Is the ecosystem changing?

ACTIVITIES

1 Explain why you think plants in wetland ecosystems such as those shown in Figure 1.53 grow so well.
2 How does this help animal species living in the same ecosystems?

The diagram in Figure 1.54 shows some of the main features of the structure and functioning of an ox-bow lake ecosystem on the river Wreake floodplain.

All ecosystems, including wetland and aquatic ecosystems, depend on a flow of energy from the sun in order to function. This energy is used by plants or **producers** to **photosynthesise**. The energy locked in their tissues is passed along a food chain, firstly to plant eaters (herbivores) that consume the plant material, and then to carnivores (animal eaters) that consume them. At any stage plants, animals, or their waste products may pass into the decomposer system to be used as **decomposers** for a food supply.

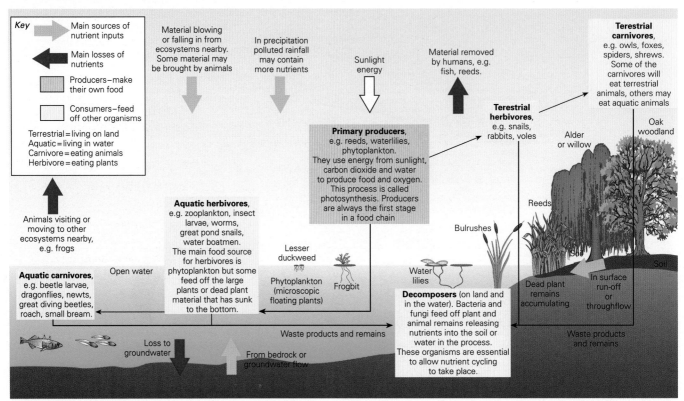

Figure 1.54 *The structure and functioning of the Wreake ox-bow lake. The way the vegetation has developed on the bank is typical of a hydrosere.*

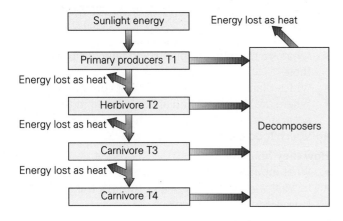

Figure 1.55 *Flow chart describing the food chain.*

Energy flows along this food chain and so passes through the ecosystem. Energy cannot be recycled and so a constant supply from the sun is essential. This is because not all of the energy that an organism takes in is passed on to the next stage, or trophic level, in the food chain. Some of the energy is used by the plant or animal itself, for example, for movement or growth, and is given off as heat. This energy cannot be re-used or recycled. In most cases not all of the plant or animal is eaten, for example the bones of fish are not digested. This means that some energy will not be passed along the food chain, though it may later pass into the decomposer part of the system. Waste materials such as urine and fæces may also be used by decomposers.

As a result, the amount of energy contained at each level of the food chain gradually decreases and food chains tend to be limited to a maximum of five trophic levels.

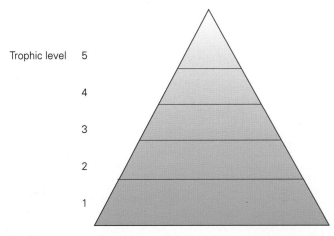

Figure 1.56 *Energy in the food chain. The width of the pyramid indicates the amount of energy at each stage of the food chain.*

Nutrients, however, are cycled within an ecosystem. The main nutrients, nitrogen, phosphorous, and potassium, along with others such as calcium, magnesium, and iron, to name only a few, are taken up by plants or **phytoplankton** from the store of nutrients in the soil, sediment, or water. They are then passed to **consumers** along the food chain. Nutrients can be returned to the store if plant or animal tissues or waste products are decomposed and the nutrients released. The nutrients may then become available for plants to use once more.

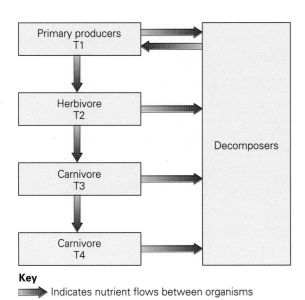

Key
➡ Indicates nutrient flows between organisms

Figure 1.57 *Cycle of the nutrients within the food chain.*

ACTIVITIES

1 Draw your own copy of the simple food chain shown in Figure 1.55. Add to it the names of plants and animals that you might expect to find at each trophic level in the ox-bow lake shown in Figure 1.54.

2 It is more accurate to show feeding relationships as a food web, because an animal may rely on more than one source of food for its survival. Use the following information to draw part of the food web for the ox-bow lake shown in Figure 1.54. Show with arrows what each animal feeds on.

Food source	Animal
Phytoplankton	Zooplankton (tiny microscopic animals), mayfly larvae
Dead remain of plants	Worms
Water plants	Tadpoles, mayfly larvae, roach
Zooplankton	Tadpoles, caddis fly, mayfly larvae
Worms	Leeches, great diving beetles, bream
Mayfly larvae	Bream, roach, dragonfly nymphs
Dragonfly nymphs	Bream, roach
Tadpoles	Great diving beetles, bream
Bream and roach	Herons

3 Describe how nutrients are lost and gained in the ox-bow lake ecosystem. Explain how human activities could alter these processes.

4 Explain how nutrient cycling within an ecosystem is different from the energy flow through an ecosystem.

5 Why are decomposers so important in an ecosystem? (Think about what would happen if they were not there.)

Wetland ecosystems under threat

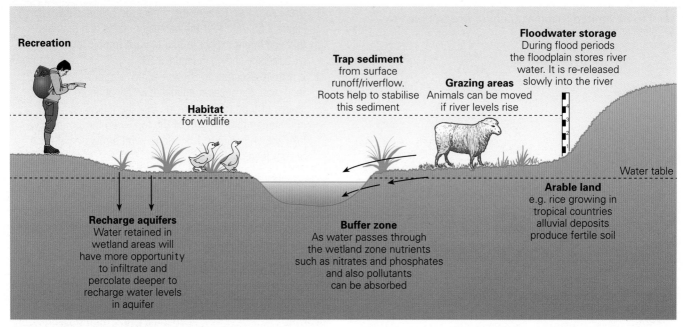

Recreation

Habitat
for wildlife

Trap sediment
from surface
runoff/riverflow.
Roots help to stabilise
this sediment

Grazing areas
Animals can be moved
if river levels rise

Floodwater storage
During flood periods
the floodplain stores river
water. It is re-released
slowly into the river

Water table

Recharge aquifers
Water retained in
wetland areas will
have more opportunity
to infiltrate and
percolate deeper to
recharge water levels
in aquifer

Buffer zone
As water passes through
the wetland zone nutrients
such as nitrates and phosphates
and also pollutants
can be absorbed

Arable land
e.g. rice growing in
tropical countries
alluvial deposits
produce fertile soil

Figure 1.58   *The functions of wetland areas.*

Wetlands comprise a variety of different habitats including marshlands, fenlands, reedbeds, water meadows, swamps, as well as those on the banks of rivers and streams.

In the absence of human interference, wetland ecosystems would naturally be found more frequently on floodplains. However, with increasing pressure to acquire land for agricultural and particularly urban land uses, many wetland areas have been drained and the specially adapted plant and animal communities lost. Changing the hydrological conditions in other ways, such as improving flood control and increasing withdrawal of water from rivers or boreholes (**abstraction**), can lower the water-table and place these habitats at risk. Pollution, whether from the air or water, can also adversely affect wetland ecosystems. The result of all of these pressures has been a very rapid global decline in wetland habitats. And it is these wetland areas that perform numerous functions that we have only recently started to appreciate. A summary of these is shown in Figure 1.58.

In an attempt to raise awareness and halt the decline in these valuable habitats, 23 countries attended a wetland convention at Ramsar in Iran in 1971. Here they signed a conservation treaty and agreed to establish sites to protect internationally important wetlands. In 1999, the UK had 126 Ramsar sites as shown in Figure 1.59. Some wetlands have also been protected in other ways, for example by being classified as Sites of Special Scientific Interest (SSSI), Special Areas of Conservation (SAC) or Environmentally Sensitive Areas (ESA).

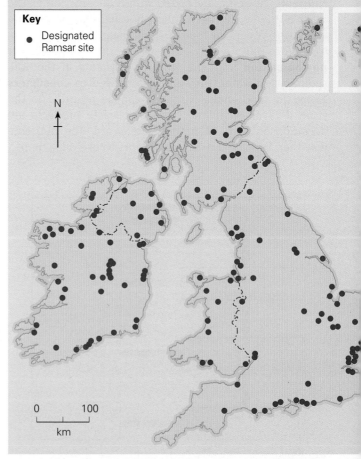

Key
● Designated
   Ramsar site

N

0   100
km

Figure 1.59   *Ramsar sites in Britain and Ireland (January 1999)*
Source: Wetlands International

http://www.wetlands.agro.nl/ramsar.wetl_ram-fig0B&1.html

ACTIVITIES

1 The table in Figure 1.60 shows information about the sediment load of selected rivers from around the world.

River	Drainage area 10^3km^2	Mean discharge 10^3km^2	Mean suspended sediment load 10^6ty^{-1}
Congo	3500	41.1	48.0
Niger	1200	4.9	25.0
Nile	3000	1.2	2.0
Huang He	752	1.1	900.0
Lena	2440	16.0	12.0
Yenisei	2500	17.6	15.0
Murray Darling	1060	0.7	30.0
Danube	817	6.5	83.0
Volga	1459	7.7	27.0
Mississippi	3267	18.4	210.0
St Lawrence	1150	13.1	5.1
Paraná	2800	15.0	80.0

Figure 1.60 *Suspended sediment loads of major world rivers.*

Source: *Fluvial Forms and Processes* Arnold, 1998.

a Locate each river on a world map. Draw a circle or bar at the mouth of each river proportional to the size of the load carried. Think carefully about the choice of scale so that all of the information will fit on your map.

b Draw a scattergraph to show the relationship between drainage area and mean discharge. To make drawing conclusions easier, make sure that you can identify which point represents which river. This scattergraph will allow you to look for a link between drainage basin size and discharge but in order to investigate how strong this link is, you should calculate the Spearman's Rank Correlation Co-efficient.

c What conclusions can you draw about the relationship between discharge and drainage area? Explain your findings.

d Draw a second scattergraph to show the relationship between mean discharge and sediment load, taking care with your choice of vertical scale. Calculate the Spearman's Rank Correlation Co-efficient.

e Does your scattergraph produce a clear pattern? How might the storage of sediment within the drainage basin help you to explain your scattergraph?

2 Make a study of a small river or stream near where you live. Investigate downstream changes in channel geometry and hydraulic radius and relate these to changes in velocity. In order to do this you will need to:

- carry out measurements at different sites along the course of your river. Consider carefully the location and number of these sites: you are more likely to be able to see clearer patterns if you collect data at a large number of well-spaced locations

- measure width, average depth, wetted perimeter, and flow velocity at each site. Record any particular conditions that could be affecting river processes or features. These could be shown on a field sketch

- calculate the hydraulic radius and discharge for each site. Present the results in graph form. Mark the downstream changes in width, average depth, and velocity on the same graph.

- assess how well your results fit the Bradshaw model of downstream changes (page 21). Explain the reasons for your answer.

You might find it interesting to compare your results with those from another river where the channel has been altered considerably by human activities, perhaps for flood control purposes. Alternatively, comparisons could be made between rivers in upland and lowland areas, or where the underlying rocks are of different geology. These and other ideas for fieldwork are shown in Figure 1.61.

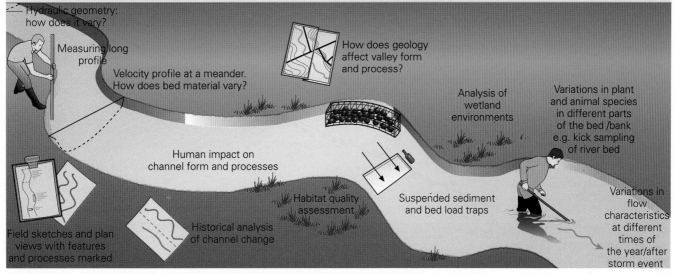

Figure 1.61 *Some ideas for fieldwork. Consult a specialist text for details of methods.*

3 How do rivers have an impact on human activities?

People have chosen to live close to rivers for various reasons for thousands of years. This means that they can reap the benefits that living by a river may bring, but they must also face the potential risk of flooding. River flooding occurs when the discharge of a river becomes too great for the capacity of the river channel. When bank-full stage is reached (i.e. the channel is full) further increases cause inundation of adjacent land. This will tend to have the greatest impact on broad, flat floodplains where the water can easily spread and where population densities are often high. Floods may cause damage to property, sometimes loss of life, and certainly disruption to human activities in varying degrees.

In some cases, especially in lowland areas, rivers may rise gradually and flood warning systems may give people hours or even days advance warning of an impending flood. However, impermeable surfaces, intense rainfall,

steep slopes, sudden snow melt, or even failure of dams or levees may allow flash floods to occur.

Flooding is very much a natural phenomenon, but it becomes a hazard when it occurs in areas occupied or utilised by humans. River valleys, especially lowland floodplains, have always attracted people, because of their advantages for transport, settlement, industry, and agriculture. Unfortunately, human activities in a drainage basin tend to increase the risks from flooding as Figure 1.62 shows.

In order to try to minimise the damage caused by river floods it useful to know how often a flood of a certain size will occur. The time between flood events of the same size is known as the **recurrence interval** or return period (Figure 1.63). For example, the 1990 river levels of the River Tow in Ballycastle had a recurrence interval of more than 200 years (page 12).

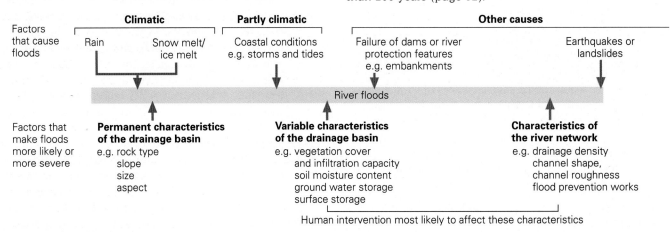

Figure 1.62 *Factors that cause floods, and factors that make them worse.*

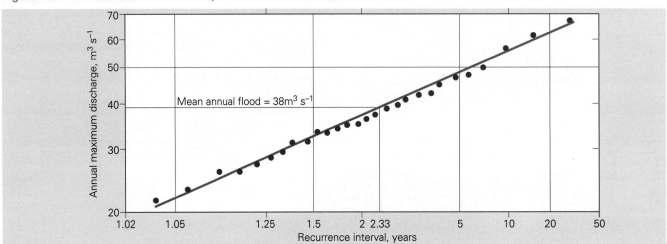

Figure 1.63 *A typical recurrence interval graph showing that larger floods are likely to be less frequent.*

Source: *Fluvial Forms and Processes* Arnold, 1998.

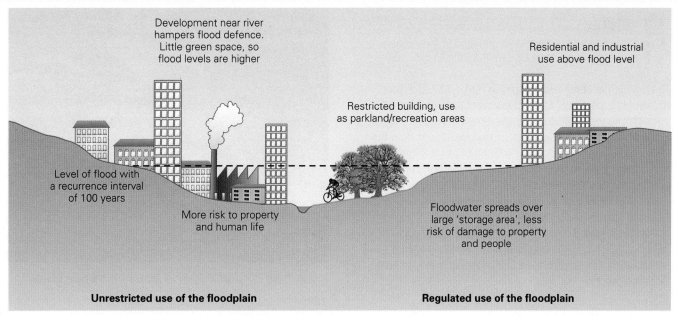

Figure 1.64 *How risk of flooding may influence land use in an urban area.*

Information about recurrence intervals can allow planners to assess the risk of flooding at a particular site and plan land use accordingly (Figure 1.64). Insurance premiums for homes and businesses are likely to be greater in zones where the recurrence interval is short. It is also possible to use information about recurrence intervals of low flows to predict drought conditions. Recurrence intervals are very important when planning water provision for the future.

ACTIVITIES

1 Make a list of human activities that could increase the risks of flooding.
2 Why do you think that despite the obvious risks, especially in floodplain areas, people still choose to live close to rivers?

Flooding on the River Derwent, North Yorkshire, March 1999

In March 1999, the River Derwent and its tributaries in North Yorkshire experienced their worst floods for 100 years. At a time when no other area of England and Wales was suffering from flood problems, North Yorkshire received a large amount of rainfall from a low-pressure area over the North Sea. Some of this rain fell onto snow. At Church Houses on the North York Moors, 229 mm of rain fell between 1 and 9 March 1999, this is more than three times the average rainfall for the whole of March (75 mm).

Run-off from the North York Moors was very high and although some of the water from the Upper Derwent was diverted along the Scarborough Cut and out to sea, overland flow from the saturated catchment soon caused the river to rise downstream of the cut. At Malton, river levels rose 20–30 mm/hour over a period of 120 hours until the River Derwent reached a record level of 4.38 m above its normal level. Problems also occurred at Pickering, Stamford Bridge, and Elvington. Many roads in the area were flooded and the York–Scarborough railway line was closed. 198 homes were flooded, 103 of them at Norton which was by far the worst affected settlement. Low-lying agricultural land throughout the floodplain was inundated, although this helped to reduce flood peaks downstream as these areas acted as water storage zones.

The Environment Agency flood incident room in York worked 24 hours a day during the flood. The first warnings of an expected flood event were given to North Yorkshire County Council on Friday, 5 March 1999 based on rainfall predictions. The Environment Agency issued nine formal flood warnings in total. These were conveyed to the public by the media, the emergency services, the AA, the local authority and the Environment Agency itself, the latter using either automatic voice messaging over the telephone, or visiting agency staff. The Environment Agency also provided and helped to operate pumps, supplied 13,000 sand bags to local authorities, and monitored river levels.

ACTIVITIES

1   Study Figure 1.66. How did the features of the River Derwent drainage basin contribute to the March 1999 flood?

2   Explain the storm hydrographs in Figure 1.67. Consider people's responses to the flood event and construct a role-play situation within your class. Create a range of typical characters, these might include representatives from the Environment Agency, North Yorkshire County Council, the emergency services, Railtrack, local residents, and farmers. The Environment Agency website listed at the end of this unit as well as on-line newspaper archives can be used as a source of additional information. The theme of your role play should be a public meeting where different groups can state their reaction to the flood. As a group, draw up a list of priorities that would help manage future flood events in the area .

Figure 1.65   *Flood waters at Stamford Bridge, March 1999.*

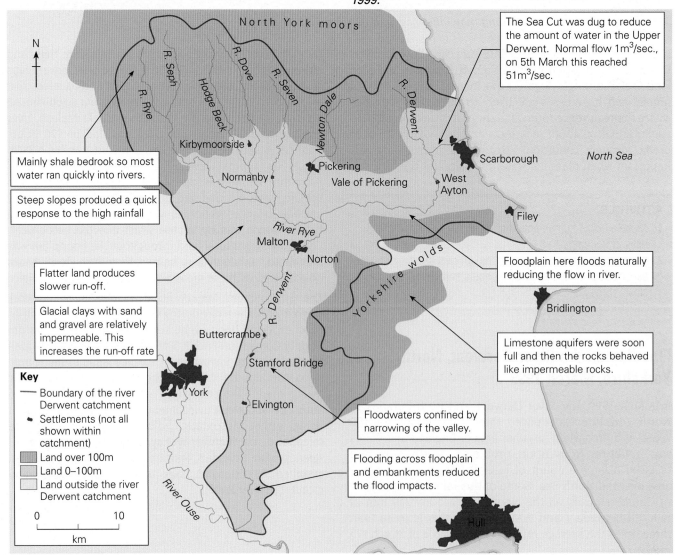

The Sea Cut was dug to reduce the amount of water in the Upper Derwent. Normal flow 1m³/sec., on 5th March this reached 51m³/sec.

Mainly shale bedrook so most water ran quickly into rivers.

Steep slopes produced a quick response to the high rainfall

Flatter land produces slower run-off.

Glacial clays with sand and gravel are relatively impermeable. This increases the run-off rate

Floodplain here floods naturally reducing the flow in river.

Limestone aquifers were soon full and then the rocks behaved like impermeable rocks.

Floodwaters confined by narrowing of the valley.

Flooding across floodplain and embankments reduced the flood impacts.

Key
— Boundary of the river Derwent catchment
• Settlements (not all shown within catchment)
▓ Land over 100m
░ Land 0–100m
░ Land outside the river Derwent catchment

0   10
km

Figure 1.66   *The physical characteristics of the River Derwent drainage basin contributed to the serious flood.*

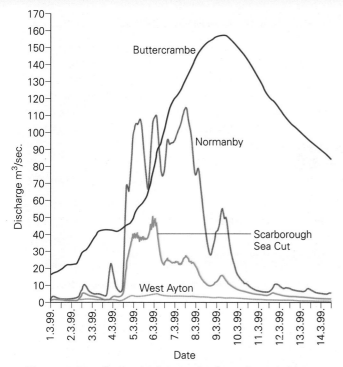

Figure 1.67 *Storm hydrographs for selected rivers during the floods of March 1999.*   Source: *The Derwent Floods 5-14 March 1999*, Environment Agency, 1999.

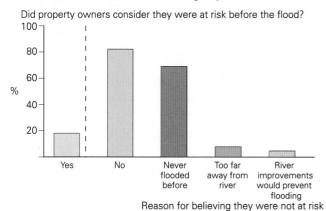

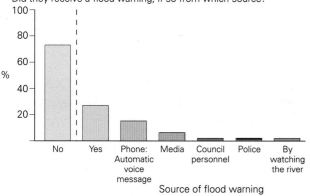

Figure 1.68 *Public responses to the floods of March 1999.*   Data From: *The Derwent Floods 5-14 March 1999*, Environment Agency, 1999.

What benefits do floods bring?

Catastrophic floods that tend to make headline news bring few benefits in comparison to the misery that they cause. However, the predictable annual rise in a river that may cause more limited flooding, referred to as the annual flood, may bring enormous benefits:

- Some of the water on the floodplain will infiltrate and help recharge groundwater supplies.
- Many plants and animals in wetland ecosystems may rely on floods to survive.
- Floodplain areas are often important for agriculture, and silt deposited on the floodplain will increase the fertility of the soil.
- Soils rich in clay or silt may provide materials for other industries, for example brick making. In the Nile delta, using the clay to make bricks has resulted in loss of important agricultural top-soil, though this practice has now been restricted on a commercial scale.

Too little rather than too much: Low flows in rivers

Many rivers have a seasonal regime with one or more periods of reduced flow. These are usually related to patterns of rainfall and evapotranspiration. When rainfall totals in England and Wales have been lower than usual, for example during the drought of 1975–76 or during the early and mid 1990s, river discharges in central and southern England have fallen in some cases to less than half their normal flow rates.

As water use in Britain has increased, these low flows have been compounded by water removal from rivers or water abstraction from groundwater supplies. Water companies can, under licence, pump water out of underground water-storing rocks (**aquifers**). The problem is that many of these licences were granted years ago, before knowledge of underground hydrology and the link with surface channel flow was particularly advanced.

The River Piddle: Maintaining the flow

The River Piddle in Dorset is one of 20 low-flow rivers in England and Wales that has been made a priority for action by the Environment Agency. Figure 1.69 shows the flow regime for the river and the influence that abstraction from four local boreholes operated by Wessex Water has on the flow. These low flows have reduced the amenity value of the river and threatened river ecosystems in the drainage basin. Fish have decreased in numbers to such an extent that the angling potential of the river has been severely reduced.

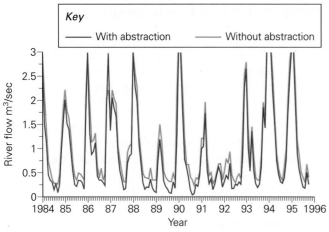

Figure 1.69 *The impact of water abstraction on the flow of the River Piddle in its middle section at Briantspuddle.*

Source: *River Piddle Low Flows, Remedial Action* EA, 1996.

ACTIVITIES

1 Write an evaluation report on water flows in the River Piddle. Explain the nature and causes of the problem and how the different aspects of the action plan outlined in Figure 1.70 will help to restore the river. Finally assess whether you think the action plan is a suitable long-term solution to the problem.

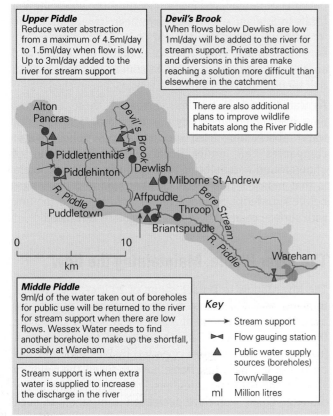

Upper Piddle
Reduce water abstraction from a maximum of 4.5ml/day to 1.5ml/day when flow is low. Up to 3ml/day added to the river for stream support

Devil's Brook
When flows below Dewlish are low 1ml/day will be added to the river for stream support. Private abstractions and diversions in this area make reaching a solution more difficult than elsewhere in the catchment

There are also additional plans to improve wildlife habitats along the River Piddle

Middle Piddle
9ml/d of the water taken out of boreholes for public use will be returned to the river for stream support when there are low flows. Wessex Water needs to find another borehole to make up the shortfall, possibly at Wareham

Stream support is when extra water is supplied to increase the discharge in the river

Key
→ Stream support
⋈ Flow gauging station
▲ Public water supply sources (boreholes)
● Town/village
ml Million litres

Figure 1.70 *Improving the flows on the River Piddle.*

Source: *River Piddle Low Flows, Remedial Action* EA, 1996.

Sediments and channel changes

The sediment carried by a river is a product of weathering and subsequent erosion in the drainage basin. As we have seen, the amount of sediment supplied to the river is also influenced by the types of human activity in the drainage basin. Once sediment has entered the river channel, the load of a river may present considerable problems for people using the river or living close to it. In some circumstances the sediment can, however, prove to be an asset.

Sediment may have an impact in different ways within the drainage basin:

- **In the river channel**

  The deposition of sediment is most likely to occur in the lower reaches of rivers. This has been well documented in the Mississippi and the Huang He. Natural levees have formed when sediments have been deposited during flooding. Gradually, because of the development of these levees and deposition of sediment on the channel bed, the rivers flow in channels raised above the level of the floodplain (see Figure 1.71). Where the rivers have been controlled further by artificial levees they have been able to flood less frequently and the accumulation of sediment on the bed has been faster. This has made the rivers much shallower and in order to prevent flooding the levees may have to be raised even higher. Unfortunately, when floodwaters break through natural or artificial levees, the impacts of the flooding are very severe as the water escapes suddenly onto low-lying land that may be several metres below the level of the river channel.

An alternative to building high artificial levees may be to remove material from the river channel by dredging. This may be beneficial in a number of ways; apart from reducing flood risk it may also provide a supply of sand and gravel for construction purposes as well as helping to maintain a navigable route along the river.

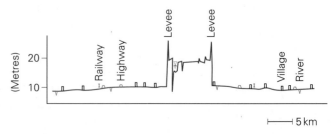

In this cross section the levees are artificial; because of deposition of sediment within the channel the river bed is now above the adjacent land

Figure 1.71 *The raised river bed of the Huang He in central China.*

Source: *The variability of large alluvial rivers* American Society of Civil Engineers, 1994.

Products originating from industry, agriculture, domestic sewage, or air pollution can be found in sediments. The Chernobyl nuclear accident in 1986 left traces of radioactive isotopes in sediments, particularly in the northern hemisphere. Heavy metals such as mercury, pesticides, and other persistent chemicals may also pose a pollution hazard and the final destination of sediments removed from the river must be planned carefully.

Dredging may have other environmental impacts too. Regular removal of sediment will reduce the habitat quality for wildlife and could affect the fish stock.

- **On the floodplain**

  The sediment can supply nutrients during the annual flood. After the Aswan dam had been built across the Nile in 1968 the floodplains downstream no longer received their annual input of nutrients and for many farmers the only alternative now is to buy artificial fertilisers to maintain crop yields.

- **In reservoirs and lakes**

  The rate of deposition, or sedimentation, behind a dam is very significant for it will not only reduce its water-storing capacity but also its ability to prevent flooding or produce electricity. Sediment may also clog irrigation ditches linked to the dam or to weirs in the river. This can have implications for farmers dependent on the water supply, especially those located at some distance from the river, as the silting up of ditches may prevent the water reaching them.

  The Sanmexia dam built on the Huang He in China in 1960 is an extreme example of the problems caused by sediment. The water of the Huang He is so sediment rich that the capacity of the reservoir was reduced by over a third by 1964. Rates of sedimentation are an important consideration when planning the location of a dam and predicting its useful life span.

- **At the river mouth**

  Where lake or coastal conditions are suitable, sediments deposited at the mouth of a river may form a delta. A reduction in the sediment load of the river will affect the sediment budget of the delta. If erosion by currents is greater than the deposition of sediment then the delta will start to decrease in size. The construction of the Aswan Dam on the Nile has caused the loss of fertile agricultural land in its delta region. Sardine catches in the eastern Mediterranean Sea have also been reduced as many nutrients formerly available to the fish are retained within the sediment behind the dam. Deltas in many other areas of the world, for example the Ganges delta (Bangladesh) and Mississippi delta (USA), have also been affected by reduction in the sediment supply. This sediment starvation can have more wide-ranging impacts too. The balance between the coastal processes of erosion and deposition can be altered, not only in the delta region, but along an extended length of coastline.

ACTIVITIES

1 Consider the options for managing sediment, particularly looking at the information given in Figure 1.72. Produce either a poster or a report analysing the advantages and disadvantages of each option.

2 As part of your analysis, decide which you think would be the best long-term solution. Explain your choice carefully and give details of how the scheme would work.

Dredging of sediment

Removal of sediment from reservoirs or river channels. Needs to be completed regularly and storage of the sediment may be a problem. An alternative is simply to loosen the sediment on the channel bed and let natural processes remove it. This may simply relocate the problem.

Reservoir flushing

Some sediments can be released by reservoir flushing. This is usually carried out by lowering the water level in the dam and opening lower sluice gates which allows water to flush out sediments. Unfortunately, if sediment levels are too deep the sluice gates may no longer open. Flushing is not always a suitable option and depends on the dam construction. The release of sediment-rich water will also have impacts downstream.

Catchment changes

Land-use changes in the drainage basin to reduce sediment supply. This may be a problem if the drainage basin is very large. It may even be managed by people living in different countries

Do nothing

This requires no action or direct expense but there will still be economic consequences due to reduced hydroelectric power production, reduced water storing capacity and the increased risk of flooding

Abandon reservoir

Every dam has a predicted economic lifespan. To prolong the life of a reservoir may require costly repairs. Some smaller dams in the USA have been abandoned. In most cases the dam must be removed. This may be very expensive and not an economic option for large dams. There will be a sudden release of sediment downstream too.

Figure 1.72   *How can the problem of sediment be reduced?*

How do river channels change with time and what impact does this have?

Rivers are dynamic systems and the channels that they flow in are constantly changing. In lowland areas where population densities tend to be greater, these changes may be highly significant. However, the changes are often predictable and take place over a long time span so people may be able to adapt their activities or even try to prevent the changes that threaten them. A river noted for the dynamic nature of its channel is the River Mississippi in the USA.

In the lower sections of the Mississippi especially, efforts to maintain the river's course and control flooding have been taking place for over 150 years. During its journey south the river meanders across the floodplain. Lateral erosion allows the meanders to migrate downstream and cut-offs to develop. As the river alters its course, land is lost and the deep-water channel used by boats tends to change, or become increasingly shallow. The increasing size of the meanders has constantly added to distances and journey times, so the river has been straightened (realigned), or widened, or deepened (resectioned) in many places (see also page 39). The river is an important routeway from the Gulf of Mexico to the interior states of the USA and so maintenance of the navigation channel is essential.

Part of the Mississippi floodplain is shown in Figure 1.73. Here at Vicksburg, 250 km north of Baton Rouge, remains of abandoned channels and old river courses are evident. In some areas, deposits left by the river in old meander loops or channels are important sources of building materials or groundwater supplies. But the deposits also pose a hazard when constructing roads, railways, and buildings, as well as flood control measures, as they may not be sufficiently stable to allow building work. It is therefore important for planners to be aware of the locations of these deposits when planning developments on the floodplain.

ACTIVITIES

1 Consider the map and cross-section in Figure 1.73.
   a Explain why the agricultural land west of Vicksburg needs protecting by levees.
   b How secure is the city of Vicksburg from the effects of river erosion?

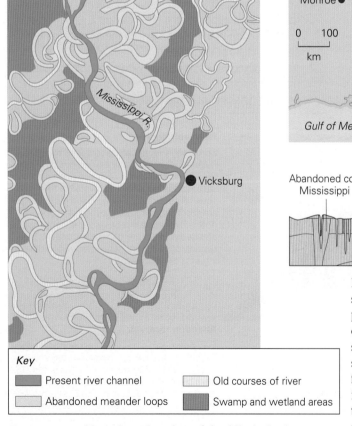

Key

- ■ Present river channel
- ▢ Abandoned meander loops
- ▢ Old courses of river
- ■ Swamp and wetland areas

Figure 1.73   *Meander migration of the Mississippi at Vicksburg.*

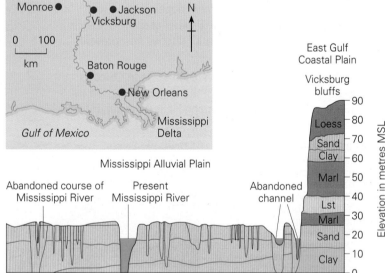

Each year along the Mississippi, millions of dollars are spent on building levees to contain the river channel and protect against flooding, on dredging the navigation channel, and on stabilising the banks to preserve settlements and farmland. This expenditure is essential if settlements and agriculture are to be preserved on the floodplain. However, recent floods on the Mississippi indicate that trying to control a river that has a natural tendency to meander may be counter-productive, for although the effects of small floods may be reduced, the larger-scale events may have a much greater impact.

4 How have humans influenced river environments?

In all drainage basins, apart from those that are very remote and inaccessible, humans alter the landscape both directly and indirectly by altering the processes that shape the landscape. The different ways that humans change their environment may be at odds with one another and conflicts may result. There will also be conflict with the physical processes at work and as human populations within drainage basins increase, these conflicts are likely to become greater. Drainage basin management, or catchment management as it is often referred to, must take into account these potential conflicts and attempt to predict and resolve them. In this section we will consider both the direct and indirect ways in which humans can affect river environments.

How have people directly altered river channels?

Over the last one hundred years particularly, river channels have been altered mainly to prevent flooding, to aid transport, and to reduce erosion. These channel modifications are known as **channelisation** and result in a river that may have been altered in cross-section, gradient, and flow characteristics. The main techniques of channelisation are shown in Figure 1.74.

Name of technique	Impact on the channel
Resectioning	The depth and/or width of the channel is altered in order to alter the amount of water it can hold (its capacity).
Re-aligning or straightening	Part of the river channel is removed creating an artificial cut-off. Removing a section of the river means that the river is shortened. As a result, the gradient of the river bed is steeper. This increases the speed of flow in this stretch of the river.
Constructing levees	Flood banks confine the river flow within a smaller area.
Bank protection	This stabilises the banks and prevents erosion. Gabions (rock baskets) or concrete liners are commonly used.
Clearing	Clearing the channel of any obstructions including sediment and vegetation.

Figure 1.74 *Channelisation techniques and their impacts.*

ACTIVITIES

1 For each of the methods of channelisation shown in Figure 1.74, suggest how they would help to prevent floods.
2 What impact do you think these methods of channelisation would have on the plants and animals that live in or close to the river?

Most major rivers have been channelised to varying degrees. The River Trent that runs from its source at Biddolph Moor, just north of Stoke-on-Trent, to the Humber estuary has been channelised along certain sections in order to prevent flooding. When the Trent reaches Nottingham, the average flow is 54.3m³/sec., though this varies considerably. During the last major flood in 1947 the average flow rose more than twenty times to 1132m³/sec., whilst in the severe drought of 1975–76 it dropped to only 18m³/sec.! The potential hazards from flooding have been made worse in Nottingham by the further growth of the urban area onto the floodplain. Figure 1.76 shows how little undeveloped floodplain remains in Nottingham. This causes more rapid surface run-off and a faster rise in river levels. However, changes made to the river channel and floodplain since 1947 have, so far, successfully reduced the impacts of flooding. See Figures 1.75 and 1.76.

Figure 1.75 *The River Trent at Trent Bridge in Nottingham where it has been widened and lined with concrete.*

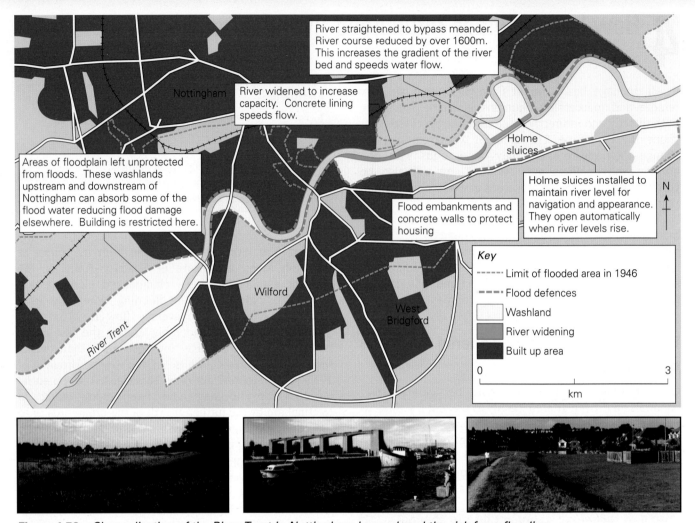

River straightened to bypass meander. River course reduced by over 1600m. This increases the gradient of the river bed and speeds water flow.

River widened to increase capacity. Concrete lining speeds flow.

Nottingham

Holme sluices

Areas of floodplain left unprotected from floods. These washlands upstream and downstream of Nottingham can absorb some of the flood water reducing flood damage elsewhere. Building is restricted here.

Flood embankments and concrete walls to protect housing

Holme sluices installed to maintain river level for navigation and appearance. They open automatically when river levels rise.

N

Wilford

West Bridgford

River Trent

Key

- - - - - Limit of flooded area in 1946

- - - - - Flood defences

☐ Washland

☐ River widening

■ Built up area

0   3
km

Figure 1.76 *Channelisation of the River Trent in Nottingham has reduced the risk from flooding.*

Regulating river flow: The use of dams

Whilst channelisation of river channels may extend over great lengths, the building of a dam takes place at a specific location. However, the impact of the dam is usually not confined solely to that location. Most dams are built in narrow, upland valleys but they can be built in lowland areas where local conditions are suitable, for example Rutland Water in the East Midlands. This site was chosen for proximity to demand, and relies on a supply of water pumped from local rivers for its water supply rather than the direct flow of a single river.

In the second half of the 19th century, the numbers of large dams (those 15 m high or more) escalated as technology developed. There are now more than 45,000 large dams worldwide. They were often, and sometimes still are, seen as prestige projects and indicators of engineering excellence. However, studies set up to evaluate the success of such projects suggest that the advantages of dam construction may no longer outweigh the disadvantages. The number of large dam projects undertaken has started to decline in the last two decades, though one particular development in China is still progressing and is attracting a great deal of interest because of the unimaginable size of the project.

ACTIVITIES

1 Dams and reservoirs are often described as being multipurpose. Make a list of the reasons why dams may be built.

2 Suggest why most dams are built in upland areas. Why might lowland locations still be considered?

The Three Gorges Dam

The largest and one of the most controversial dams being built at present is the Three Gorges Dam on the Yangtze river in central China. The dam was first proposed more than 80 years ago, construction started in 1993 and it is not expected to be finished until 2009. The final cost is expected to be around £45 billion. The scale of the resettlement programme and the possible environmental impacts of the enormous dam have caused great political and public debate both abroad and, more recently, within China itself. Pressure from environmental groups and doubts about the effectiveness of the scheme have caused some investors and foreign consultants to pull out.

A major concern is the large amount of sediment carried by the Yangtze which will be trapped behind the dam. In order to reduce sedimentation rates, it is likely that sediment-rich water which arrives mainly during the four-month flood season will be released from the dam and only water flowing into the reservoir between floods will be stored. The irony is that this will reduce its effectiveness as a flood control measure. Figures 1.77 and 1.78 give two alternative views of the project.

The Three Gorges Dam – who will benefit?

The sheer scale of the Three Gorges Dam daunts the imagination. No fewer than 1.3 million people are to be forced to leave homes which have been inhabited for centuries along the stretch of river between Chongqing and the brash new city of Yichang. Four cities, eight towns, and 356 large villages will be submerged, along with countless farms and acres of land. The dam's purpose is to control the devastating annual floods along the world's third longest river, to generate electricity for China's development and thus to cut pollution by replacing 50 million tons of raw coal combustion every year.

An enormous human tragedy is in the making as the Chinese government will almost certainly have to send in troops to get the peasants out of their ancestral homes over the next eight years.

People complained that the compensation offered for their homes was far below the amount they need to buy apartments in the blocks that are under construction. The gleaming new cities are rising all along the Yangtze above the 536ft (160m) mark to which the waters will rise.

Figure 1.77 *Extracts from 'The Three Gorges Dam – who will benefit?' by Michael Sheridan.* Source: The Sunday Times, *14 March 1999.*

Advantages of the scheme include:

- Reduced flood risk in the lower reaches of the Yangtze. Recurrence interval for floods increased from ten years to 100 years.
- The dam will generate 84.68BkW of hydro-electric power a year.
- The resettlement programme will benefit local people because of the economic development that will take place in the region.
- Relocated people will maintain and improve their standard of living.
- Navigation will be improved and there will be scenic views from the boats.
- Endangered animals such as the Chinese river dolphin will be protected in reserves.

Figure 1.78 *Wang Rushu: Senior Engineer, Three Gorges Project Development Corporation, Yichang, China.*

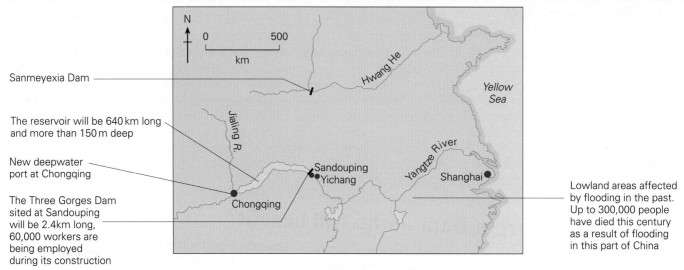

Sanmeyexia Dam

The reservoir will be 640 km long and more than 150 m deep

New deepwater port at Chongqing

The Three Gorges Dam sited at Sandouping will be 2.4km long, 60,000 workers are being employed during its construction

Lowland areas affected by flooding in the past. Up to 300,000 people have died this century as a result of flooding in this part of China

Figure 1.79 *The location of the Three Gorges Dam and reservoir.*

ACTIVITIES

1 Within your class, debate the following question: 'The Three Gorges Dam project: Essential engineering masterpiece or environmental disaster?'
You will need to divide the class into two groups to represent the alternative views. Both groups should prepare their ideas carefully to justify their side of the argument. You may wish to find out further information to support your cases by referring to some of the websites listed at the end of this unit.
After the debate you should record your own, personal views on the scheme.

How can urban areas affect river environments?

As urban areas increase in size and number, their capacity to affect hydrological processes increases too (Figure 1.80). In comparison with rural areas, the inputs of water into the urban hydrological system tend to be greater. This is partly because urban areas tend to receive slightly more rainfall due to localised climate conditions and partly because of transfers of water piped into urban areas from elsewhere in the drainage basin, or even from outside it. The surface characteristics of an urban area will also alter the hydrological processes because they tend to be smooth and impermeable, with less surface-storage capacity. Storm drains carrying run-off water from roads and pavements will speed the flow of water directly into nearby rivers. The resulting storm hydrograph shows a rapid or 'flashy' response to precipitation which is very different from that of a rural catchment.

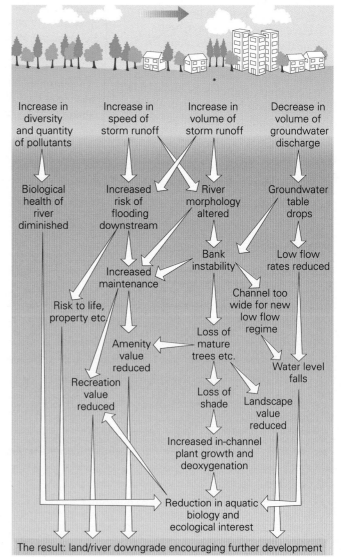

Figure 1.80 *The hydrological impacts of urbanisation.*
Source: *Geography Review* 9, January 1996.

Land use				
Date	1866–96	1933	1951	1991
Land use	Mainly agricultural	Housing development started	Increased housing development	Much of drainage basin now suburbs

Average width of channel (metres)				
Date	1866–96	1933	1951	1991
Natural channel upstream from the urban area	3.54	3.60	3.58	3.56
Natural channel downstream of the urban area	4.10	3.67	4.25	6.30

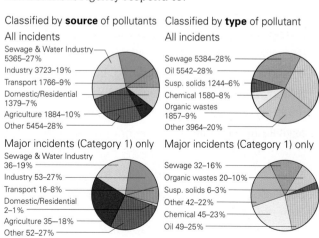

Figure 1.81   *Impacts of land-use change on the river channel of Monks Brook in southern Hampshire.*

In many urban areas, rivers have either been channelised or confined to culverts under the ground. However, increases in discharge as a result of urbanisation can also cause unintentional changes in river channels.

Monks Brook in southern Hampshire illustrates this. The stream, a tributary of the River Itchen, is located to the north-west of Eastleigh, near Southampton. Before urbanisation started in the 1930s, the area was used mainly for agriculture. Housing development in the 1950s and 1960s and again since the 1970s has increased surface run-off and peak discharges, especially around Chandlers Ford. Results from the analysis of maps dating as far back as the 1860s along with measurements of current channel dimensions are shown in Figure 1.81.

ACTIVITIES

1   Study carefully the information in Figure 1.80. Use it to help you to describe the possible consequences of increases in volume and speed of storm run-off.

2   **a**   Write a brief report on the findings shown in Figure 1.81. You will need to indicate where the channel width has changed the most and give the reasons for this.

   b   What problems might these changes to the drainage basin and the river channel cause for people?

How have people affected the quality of water in river environments?

In England and Wales the Environment Agency is responsible for responding to water pollution incidents from whatever source. Their job is to manage the incident and so reduce its environmental impact. Figure 1.82 shows the main pollution sources and types that the Environment Agency respond to.

Classified by **source** of pollutants
All incidents
Sewage & Water Industry 5365–27%
Industry 3723–19%
Transport 1766–9%
Domestic/Residential 1379–7%
Agriculture 1884–10%
Other 5454–28%

Classified by **type** of pollutant
All incidents
Sewage 5384–28%
Oil 5542–28%
Susp. solids 1244–6%
Chemical 1580–8%
Organic wastes 1857–9%
Other 3964–20%

Major incidents (Category 1) only
Sewage & Water Industry 36–19%
Industry 53–27%
Transport 16–8%
Domestic/Residential 2–1%
Agriculture 35–18%
Other 52–27%

Major incidents (Category 1) only
Sewage 32–16%
Organic wastes 20–10%
Susp. solids 6–3%
Other 42–22%
Chemical 45–23%
Oil 49–25%

Figure 1.82   *Pollution incidents classified by type and source of pollution.*   Source: *Water Pollution Incidents in England and Wales,* Environment Agency, 1998.

Although major pollution accidents may often make news headlines, it is the more frequent and smaller pollution events that are usually responsible for much of the environmental pollution. In the UK some polluting substances are quite legally pumped into streams and rivers, but only after a licence has been obtained from the Environment Agency or their equivalent in Scotland and Northern Ireland, who will then monitor the polluting activity. Registers of licences granted can be inspected at local Environment Agency offices. Similar systems exist in other MEDCs in order to try and manage pollution and its effects.

Pollution released from easily identifiable specific points or **point sources**, for example, waste water pumped into a river from a discharge pipe, is much easier to monitor and indeed regulate than **diffuse sources** of pollution. These can originate from a large area of the catchment and usually enter the river channel along the river bank. They may be washed in from the soil surface or pass into the river in throughflow or groundwater flow. Diffuse sources of pollution include, for example, agricultural pesticides or fertilisers and sewage waste from livestock farms.

The most important point sources of pollution flowing into rivers in the UK are the sewage wastes disposed of by sewage treatment works. Here, pollution problems can arise because organic sewage waste provides a nutrient source for bacterial populations living in the river. As they decompose the organic waste, the bacteria use up oxygen in the water, thus affecting the survival of aquatic life in the river. The **biological oxygen demand** (BOD) is used as an indicator of organic pollution in water bodies. Other waste products such as spillages from breweries or dairies, although seemingly harmless, can devastate aquatic ecosystems in the same way.

If it has not been effectively treated, sewage waste can also contain harmful bacteria and viruses and a worrying array of new chemicals as Figure 1.83 describes.

Nitrate and pollution from agricultural land is one of the most significant diffuse sources of pollution. Nitrates are mainly washed through the soil (leached) into water courses or into the groundwater from either artificial fertilisers or from decomposing organic matter. There is a problem of increasing levels of nitrate in groundwater supplies, mainly due to changes in agriculture. An EC maximum limit of 50 mg/l of nitrate has been placed on drinking water as nitrates are believed to pose a health risk. The body converts nitrates to nitrite which may be linked to stomach cancer and a disease known as blue baby syndrome in very young infants. Nitrates are just one of the substances monitored in drinking water as Figure 1.84 shows.

A little too much medicine?

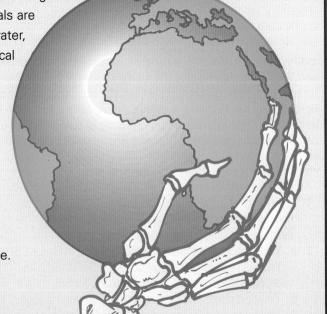

Over the past six years, a new class of water pollution has emerged. Pharmaceutical drugs given to people and domestic animals are being found in surface water, groundwater, tap drinking water, and even the oceans. German scientists report that a typical water sample contains between 30 and 60 drugs. The concentrations of some are comparable to the low parts-per-billion levels at which pesticides are typically found. To some people this is reassuring, but others are asking, 'What is the long-term effect of drinking, day after day, a dilute cocktail of pesticides, antibiotics, painkillers, tranquillisers, and chemotherapy agents?' Scientists also point out that the high quantities of antibiotics in water allow bacteria to build up resistance. Super bugs, such as E-coli, are the inevitable consequence.

Figure 1.83   *Water pollution*   Source: *The Ecologist*, November–December 1998.

Concentrations measured:

Substance	Minimum	Maximum	Mean	Maximum allowed
Fæcal bacteria (coliforms)	0	0	0	0
Nitrate	3.9 mg/l	20.6 mg/l	17.4 mg/l	50 mg/l
Aluminium	<20 µg/l	<20 µg/l	<20 µg/l	200 µg/l
Lead	1 µg/l	1 µg/l	1 µg/l	50 µg/l
Iron	<20 µg/l	<20 µg/l	<20 µg/l	200 µg/l
Tetrachloromethane (industrial solvent)	<0.3 µg/l	<0.3 µg/l	<0.3 µg/l	3 µg/l
pH	7.6	7.7	7.6	5.5–9.5
Total chlorine	0.05 mg/l	0.51 mg/l	0.25 mg/l	–
Total pesticides	<0.2 µg/l	<0.2 µg/l	<0.2 µg/l	0.5 µg/l

Figure 1.84 *Water authorities monitor chemicals and bacteria in the drinking water supply and the results can be requested by customers. The table shows a small selection of these measurements for one water supply area.*
Source: *Water Supply Zone Report* Seven Trent Water, 1999.

Nitrates can also cause a problem in rivers, lakes, and ponds. Along with phosphates derived from fertilisers or from sewage inputs, nitrates encourage the growth of green or blue-green algae. Algae are short-lived and when they die, bacteria feed off the remains and reduce the oxygen content of the water. This process is referred to as **eutrophication** or nutrient enrichment and it causes a reduction in aquatic life, especially fish, which die because of the oxygen shortage in the water. Some blue-green algae also produce toxic substances which can kill other organisms and taint the water. This is obviously serious if it occurs in a reservoir. However, it has been discovered that chemicals produced by placing barley straw in the water are a most effective way of reducing the numbers of blue-green algae.

Eutrophication is most likely to affect still water bodies such as lakes and ponds where there is little movement of the water to reintroduce oxygen. Control of the nutrient content of the rivers flowing into these water bodies is therefore of paramount importance and leads to conflicts between the requirements of agricultural land use, wildlife conservation, and drinking water provision.

The River Trent: Water quality issues

The Trent is an important East Midlands river, its drainage basin covering an area of 10,500 km². Unfortunately, it has long been renowned for its poor water quality. This poor water quality was due to the large centres of population such as Stoke-on-Trent, Nottingham, and Derby, as well as the industrial development that gradually grew within the catchment. Poor effluent and sewage treatment led to a deterioration in the quality of the river water. Since the

1960s though, improvements in effluent treatment and legislation to prevent pollution have produced a marked improvement (Figure 1.85).

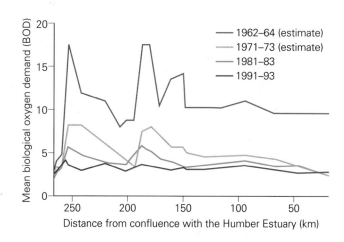

Figure 1.85 *Estimates of the biological oxygen demand (BOD) for the River Trent, 1962-92.*
Source: *Intergrated River Basin Development*, Wiley, 1999.

These improvements in water quality have led to another pressure because increasing public demand for water has made the Trent a potentially new source for abstraction. Previously, only the cleaner tributaries, the Derwent and the Dove, were considered suitable for this purpose. However, there is potentially a conflict between this abstraction and other uses of the river water, mainly because a minimum flow of water is needed to:

- dilute the sewage and industrial effluent in the river in order to protect riverine ecosystems. If water is removed, this effluent would take up a larger proportion of the river's flow
- preserve the coarse fisheries for which the Trent is famous
- maintain sufficient water for navigation
- maintain flows for recreational users, for example, sailing, rowing, riverboat cruising, and canoeing.

After research into the impact of water abstraction, abstraction for the public supply does now take place at Shardlow near Nottingham. Further abstractions are planned, including removal of river water to be pumped south to meet the demand for water in south-east England.

ACTIVITIES

1 Consult an atlas to find out the extent of the Trent drainage basin and the cities contained within it.
2 Refer to Figure 1.85 to identify which sections of the Trent improved most in terms of water quality between 1962 and 1992. Give your answer in terms of distance from the confluence with the Humber estuary. Use an atlas map to measure along the Trent and find out which settlements or tributary confluences these distances correspond to.
3 Suggest what consequences the abstraction of water at Shardlow could have for the river and users of the river. Make sure that you refer to the impacts on the river channel and sediment, the floodplain and ecosystems, the pollution concentrations in the river, the flood risk, and the amenity value of the river.

What problems can occur when too much water is removed from groundwater sources?

Some of our public water supply comes from direct abstraction of river water. The amount of water that can be withdrawn from a river without causing too much disturbance can usually be predicted and limits are normally set based on a study of the river regime and, particularly, of the incidence of low flows. However, it is less easy to predict the amounts of water that can be removed from groundwater sources without causing adverse effects. If water abstraction from an aquifer is to be maintained, then the inputs of water must equal the water removed; increasing demand for water means that this is not always the case. The results of over-abstraction are an increasing cause for concern as the case study of the River Piddle (page 32) indicates. Other impacts are also shown in Figures 1.86 and 1.87.

Worldwatch News release, Thursday, 26 August 1999.

Water tables are falling from the overpumping of groundwater in the breadbaskets and rice bowls of central and northern China, north-west India, parts of Pakistan, much of the United States, North Africa, the Middle East, and the Arabian Peninsula. Farmers in these regions are pumping groundwater faster than nature is replenishing it.

During the last three decades, as farmers sunk millions of wells, the depletion of underground aquifers has spread from isolated pockets of the agricultural landscape to large portions of irrigated land. In India, a government-commissioned study found that over-exploitation of groundwater resources is widespread across the country. As much as a quarter of India's grain production could be at risk as a result of groundwater depletion.

All told, the world's farmers are racking up an annual water deficit of some 160 billion cubic metres – the amount used to produce nearly 10 per cent of the world's grain. Water scarcity is now the single biggest threat to global food production. Only by taking action now to conserve the water supplies in our major crop-producing regions can we secure enough water to satisfy future food needs.

Figure 1.86 *Falling water tables.*
Source: *Worldwatch*, 26 August 1999.

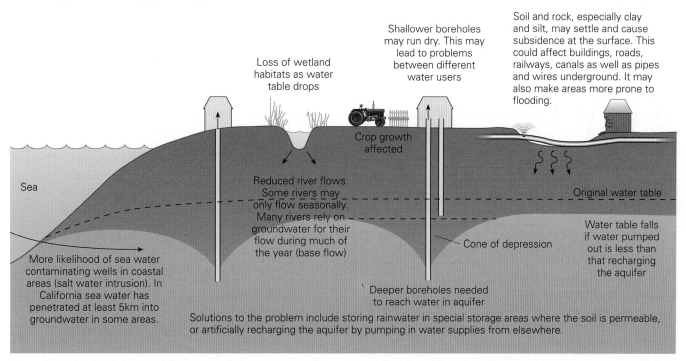

Loss of wetland habitats as water table drops

Shallower boreholes may run dry. This may lead to problems between different water users

Soil and rock, especially clay and silt, may settle and cause subsidence at the surface. This could affect buildings, roads, railways, canals as well as pipes and wires underground. It may also make areas more prone to flooding.

Crop growth affected

Sea

Reduced river flows. Some rivers may only flow seasonally. Many rivers rely on groundwater for their flow during much of the year (base flow)

Original water table

Cone of depression

Water table falls if water pumped out is less than that recharging the aquifer

More likelihood of sea water contaminating wells in coastal areas (salt water intrusion). In California sea water has penetrated at least 5km into groundwater in some areas.

Deeper boreholes needed to reach water in aquifer

Solutions to the problem include storing rainwater in special storage areas where the soil is permeable, or artificially recharging the aquifer by pumping in water supplies from elsewhere.

Figure 1.87 *The impact of over-abstraction on groundwater supplies and the environment.*

A very different problem though is starting to affect some British cities. Groundwater levels have started to rise! They are rising as a result of tighter restrictions being placed on groundwater abstraction and because of the closure of many heavy industries that were great consumers of water. There is now a fear that basements will suffer more frequent flooding and that groundwater could become more polluted as it rises closer to the surface and comes into contact with contaminated soil.

Water use	Surface water	Ground -water	Treated waste -water	Total
Domestic	46.0	170.0	0	216.0
Irrigation	350.0	313.0	52.0	715.0
Industrial	2.5	22.0	0	25.0
Total	399.0	505.0	52.0	956.0

Figure 1.88 *Water use in Jordan in 1995 (millions m³/year).* Source: *Journal of Water and Environmental Management,* 13, August 1999.

In some areas of the world, groundwater supplies are vital because they provide water for agriculture, industry, and domestic use (Figure 1.88). Jordan in the Middle East has an average annual rainfall total of less than 250 mm, though slightly more, between 300 and 600 mm, falls in the highland areas. Because of high temperatures and the very high evaporation rates, only 5 per cent of this rainfall infiltrates and recharges the groundwater supplies. The

	1990	1995	2000*	2005*	2010*
Population (millions)	3.7	4.4	5.2	6.1	7.0
Water resources (million m³/yr)	756	832	952	1042	1042
Demand (million m³/yr)					
– domestic	179	216	330	425	497
– irrigation	622	715	800	900	1000
– industrial	20	25	40	50	60
Total (million m³/yr)	821	956	1170	1375	1557
Deficit (million m³/yr)	65	124	218	333	515

* Indicates predicted figures.

Figure 1.89 *Jordan: Present and future water demands, supplies, and deficits.*
Source: *Journal of Water and Environmental Management,* 13, August 1999.

information in Figure 1.89 indicates the present patterns of water demand in Jordan and suggests a future problem.

The Water Authority of Jordan is understandably concerned about the shortfall in water supply predicted for the early part of the 21st century. Various options are being considered. These are shown in Figure 1.90.

In a politically volatile area of the world like the Middle East, politics inevitably play an important part in the decision-making process. The Water Authority of Jordan is most likely to consider the piping of water from Lebanon or possibly Turkey. It is least likely to import water from Iraq.

So far in this section we have considered a range of different ways that human activities, whether intentional or not, can alter drainage basin processes. The way a drainage basin responds to heavy rainfall or even to lack of rainfall will reflect all of these modifications and will not always be predictable.

Details of options	Predicted costs per m³ in pence
Buying water from another country and transporting it to Jordan by sea in container vessels.	80p
Treated wastewater plants: 23 to be built. Capacity 66 million m³/yr by 2000 and 110 million m³/yr by 2010.	50p
Desalinisation: Requires the construction of a desalinisation plant. Could be producing 20 million m³ by 2010.	50–80p
Water harvesting: Already common in rural areas, collecting and storing rainwater from roofs and storing it in reservoirs. Capacity will be 6 million m³/yr by 2000.	not known, likely to be a low-cost option
Importing water in pipelines from other countries: **Iraq:** Up to 160 million m³/yr. Unknown quality. Long pipeline.	80p
Turkey: Up to 10 million m³/yr. Good quality. Long pipeline (nearly 1000 km).	100p
Lebanon: 450 million m³/yr. Another storage dam needs to be built in an earthquake zone. Short pipeline (175 km).	40p

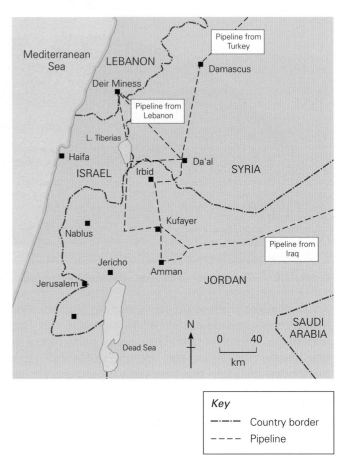

Figure 1.90   *Future options for water supply in Jordan. The map shows where the imported water could be piped from.*
Source: *Journal of Water and Environmental Management,* 13, August 1999.

ACTIVITIES

1 Consider the water resource problem that Jordan is facing. Write a report that:
   • outlines the current situation in terms of water supply in Jordan
   • predicts future problems and outlines the reasons for them
   • suggests a strategy for the short-term and the long-term management of water resources in Jordan.

2 Look at the data shown in Figure 1.91. The phosphate content of the two rivers is very different. The phosphate content is related mainly to differences in agricultural land use in each drainage basin.
   a Find out where these two rivers are located in Britain and mark them on an outline map of the British Isles.
   b Annotate your map to explain the likely source of the phosphates, and the reasons why the two rivers have such different phosphate levels.
   c Explain how the phosphate levels might affect the wildlife in these streams and why humans might be concerned about the phosphate levels in the River Axe.
   d Find out what can be done to reduce the levels of nutrients such as nitrates and phosphates in rivers and lakes.

3 'Those people most affected by dams gain the least.' Do you agree with this statement? Discuss your answer with reference to the Three Gorges Dam project (page 40).

4 Figure 1.92 shows a range of techniques that could be used to reduce the impact of flooding in an urban area.
   a Which of these techniques have been used on the River Trent in Nottingham?
   b Choose one of your local rivers that has been managed, for example to reduce the impact of flooding, or for another purpose such as stabilising the banks or increasing its wildlife habitat value. *The New Rivers and Wildlife Handbook* (1994; RSPB, NRA, and RSNC) contains details and locations of 40 management schemes of various types in England, Wales, and Northern Ireland. Your local Environment Agency office may also be able to provide you with information. Produce annotated diagrams, field sketches, or photographs to show the features of the management scheme in your chosen river. Indicate how the changes that have been made have affected river processes and flow characteristics.
   c Present your work in poster form and add your own assessment of how successful the scheme has been or is likely to be.

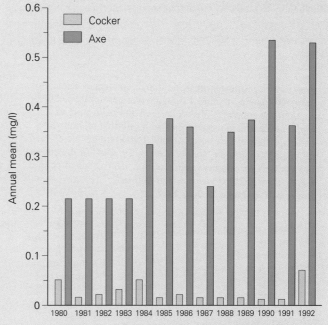

Figure 1.91 *Phosphate levels in different rivers.*
Source: *Wildlife and Fresh Water: an Agenda for sustainable management* English Nature, 1997.

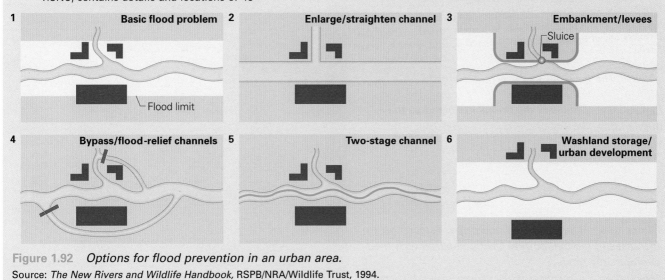

Figure 1.92 *Options for flood prevention in an urban area.*
Source: *The New Rivers and Wildlife Handbook,* RSPB/NRA/Wildlife Trust, 1994.

Flooding in Poland: Not just a case of too much rain!

In July 1997, intense rainfall in central Europe led directly to the worst floods for at least 200 years in western Poland and eastern Czech Republic. The effects were devastating. Towns and cities were inundated, bridges and roads were washed away, agricultural land was rendered useless and many people lost their lives. It is thought that ten per cent of Poland's land area was affected by floodwater, though some estimates suggest that the area was a lot greater.

Certainly the weather conditions were extreme. In the upper reaches of the River Odra (Oder) the river levels were so high that the recurrence interval for another flood of the same magnitude is over 1000 years! Yet the impacts of the high rainfall were undoubtedly affected by the land use within the Odra drainage basin and the ways that the hydrological cycle had been changed both directly and indirectly. Figures 1.93–1.99 reveal some of the effects of the floodwater in Poland.

President Kwasniewski rushed through emergency legislation, designed to help victims of flooding that has devastated the south of the country. Polish television and radio stations replaced scheduled programmes with information bulletins, and flags flew at half mast. Around 16,000 troops were mobilised to reinforce floodbarriers in the south as the country braced itself for another lashing of rain. Thousands of people were put on alert to evacuate their homes.
Source: *The Times*, 19 July 1997.

Thousands of people laid sandbags on the banks of the Oder to stop leaks in provisional dykes. Volunteers, many of whom worked the second day in a row without sleep, complained also of inadequate water and food supplies. The floodwaters rose to first-floor levels in the medieval city of 700,000 people, and residents used motor boats to bring themselves and their belongings to the safety of hilly areas. More than 30 helicopters supplied water, food, and medicine to city residents. Electricity has been cut off since Saturday.
Source: *The Times*, 14 July 1997.

In human lives, homes and factories, grain and livestock, the physical toll exacted by floods is terrible enough. Where the waters are in retreat, the filthy polluted detritus is made more menacing to health by rotting carcasses of drowned beasts and poultry.
Source: *The Times*, 30 July 1997.

Figure 1.93   *Details of the floods in Poland as they appeared in The Times.*

56 people dead
162,000 people evacuated
976 towns and villages flooded
135 bridges damaged
1387 km of roads closed
2000 km of railway lines closed
45,000 Polish troops involved in the rescue operations
Wrocław was without water for two weeks
500 million Złoty ($US160 million) allocated by the Polish government for relief and reconstruction, 60,000 families made homeless given 3000 Złoty each ($US960)
$US560,000 given in humanitarian aid by EC

Figure 1.94   *Some of the consequences of the 1997 floods in Poland.*
Source: *Geography Review* 12, May 1999.

Figure 1.95   *Wrocław, Poland inundated by flood water in July 1997.*

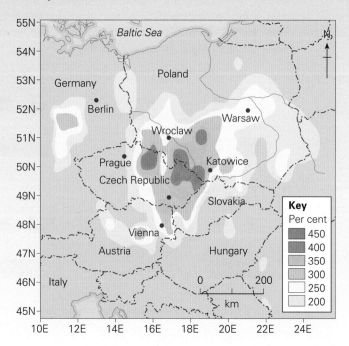

Figure 1.96   *Rainfall in central Europe: Percentage increases in rainfall for July 1997 compared with the average July totals.*
Source: *Climate Assessment of 1997* Climate Prediction Centre.

The main cause of the flooding in this region of Europe was clearly the very high rainfall. As the map in Figure 1.96 indicates, the rainfall that fell in July 1997 over central Europe was in some places more than four times greater than the rainfall expected. The rain was not evenly spread throughout the whole month, but instead concentrated into three short rainfall events of a few days each. The details are described in Figure 1.97.

- Low pressure was centred on central Europe.

- A series of three fronts moved from the south-west to north-east. These fronts met warm tropical air moving from the south-east. This caused intense rainfall on three separate occasions, in the Sudeten and western Carpathian Mountains especially.

- Heavy rain fell between the following dates: 4–9 July, 15–20 July, and 22–26 July. The rain was concentrated especially in southern Poland. The Odra drainage basin suffered the worst. Some areas received three quarters of their annual rainfall in July alone!

Figure 1.97 *A summary of the meteorological conditions that led to the severe flooding in Poland.*

The concentration of heavy rain had a great impact on the rates of infiltration and surface run-off, and as a result, river and stream discharges quickly increased in response to each period of rain. A series of flood waves swept through the Odra drainage basin. In its upper reaches where the Odra crosses the Czech Republic/Poland border the discharge of the Odra was 48 times greater than its normal flow (Figure 1.98).

In upland areas, trees and crops protected the soil, but where tree cover was thin or there were steep mountain tracks, erosion was pronounced. Many footpaths and tracks were completely destroyed, to be replaced by deep gullies. The very high river discharges increased their capacity to transport sediment. Even boulders of over 4m in diameter moved short distances. The sediment carried by rivers increased their ability to cause damage to property. Some rivers even developed braided channels, rather than single channels. Such high discharges and high sediment loads allowed rivers to change the features of their channels dramatically and this had a major impact on human activities taking place close to those channels.

The rising water levels put a great strain on the embankments that, in some areas, protected land and settlements against the risk of flood. Moreover, such was the threat of severe flooding in Wrocław from the approaching flood wave that the authorities considered some extreme measures. Rather than reinforcing the embankments upstream of the city they considered demolishing some of them using explosives! This would have caused the flooding of the Widawa basin, which contained villages and suburban areas. Breaching the flood barriers would have acted like a safety valve, dispersing some of the water away from the river channel and thus reducing the water flow of the Odra as it flowed through Wrocław. The authorities believed this was an acceptable pay-off. The inhabitants living close to the threatened embankments objected strongly, even chasing away the engineers in charge of the project! The embankments remained in place and the flood wave did indeed cause severe flooding in the Wrocław. Though, as Figure 1.99 shows, other factors certainly played a part.

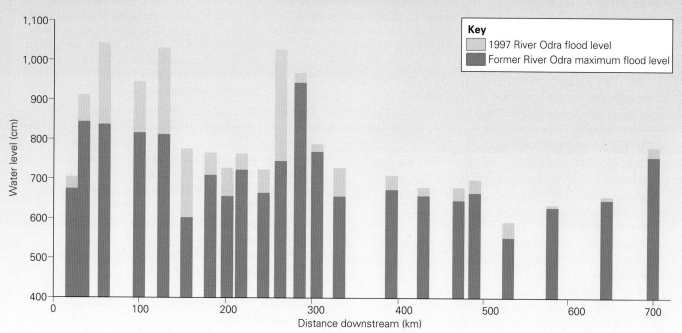

Figure 1.98 *Maximum water levels recorded in selected gauging stations along the Odra during the flood in 1997 (light bars) in relation to former maximum values (dark bars).*

Source: *Geography Review* 12, May 1999.

The Odra has been channelised in many places to improve transport. Its length has been reduced by 16 per cent. This speeds up the flow of the water and it quickly moves downstream.

Emergency reservoirs have not been maintained properly. Many have silted up.

Many trees were chopped down at the beginning of the century (deforestation). Vast numbers have been replanted, but unfortunately air pollution, especially acid rain, means that they are less healthy. As a result, run-off and stream discharges have increased.

Tracks and settlements built in the hills have led to an increase in run-off. Tracks built running straight down the slopes have been found to increase the speed of surface flow and the speed of erosion.

Reservoirs built to defend settlements against flood risk gave people a false sense of security and towns grew on the floodplain.

Weather forecasts and flood predictions were unreliable and warnings were not always given in time.

The state government failed to realise the scale of the problem for at least a week and emergency measures were poorly implemented.

No water was released from the storage reservoirs at Nysa and Otmuchów before the flood arrived. This would have increased their capacity to store flood water. Despite this the reservoirs did help to reduce discharges into the river. Unfortunately, leaking at the base of the Nysa dam required an emergency release of water. This act alone caused flooding of settlements downstream.

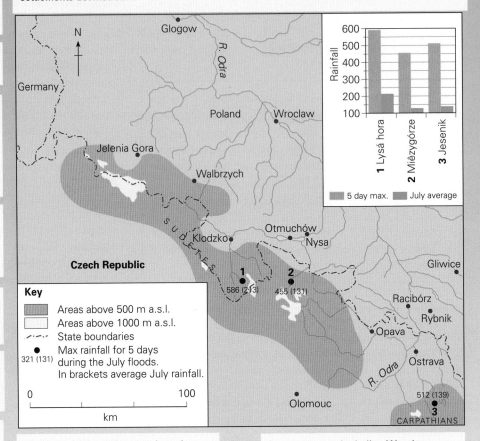

Many mountain settlements have been built on or close to the river banks. Evacuation did not start until the rivers were already flooding.

In some areas, including Wrocław, building over the last 30 years has taken place on areas of the floodplain that at the turn of the century had been left as flood storage zones. Poor flood-bank design or failure also led to widespread flooding.

Fig 1.99   *Factors contributing to the floods in the Odra basin; the floods were not simply the result of high rainfall.*
Source: *Geography Review* 12, May 1999.

ACTIVITIES Planning for the future.

1 Using the knowledge that you have gained about the flooding in Poland in 1997, produce a policy document outlining the advice you would give to the regional authorities to help them prevent future floods, or at least reduce the damage that floods may cause.
This could be presented as a written document or a wall display for public viewing.
In it you should include:
- an introduction to explain the factors that caused the 1997 flood. This should refer to details of weather, land-use change in the Sudeten Mountains, settlement patterns in lowland areas, attempts to modify the river channel, reservoir management, and emergency response by the authorities

- a list of at least five main problems that in your view need to be tackled in the drainage basin
- an action plan to address each of the problems you have identified. To assist the regional authorities in their strategic planning try to suggest the order in which the changes should be implemented
- a sketch map to show the locations where these proposed changes would take place
- a careful explanation of how each of your priorities for action would assist in preventing future floods or reducing the damage caused.

Additional information to support your work can be accessed at the websites listed at the end of this unit.

5 The challenge of managing river systems

Rivers have been managed for thousands of years in many different ways. The purposes of management have included using the river system:

- as a resource, for example, for recreation
- as a transport route
- for hydro-electric power generation
- to reduce the hazard potential of the river, particularly from flooding.

It is these attempts to manage flooding that have been the cause of controversy and alternative methods are being sought. Other issues such as pollution and the overuse of water resources are also management priorities.

Engineering solutions to river management: so what's the problem?

Flood control engineers and local politicians have in the past viewed river management, particularly flooding, as a problem that needs to be addressed along defined stretches (reaches) of a river, rather than a problem that needs to be tackled at the drainage basin level. This is partly for financial reasons as flood prevention is very costly. In many cases, the engineering solutions are short-term solutions and in the past were sometimes made without sufficient consideration of the causes of the problem. Flood risk on the Mississippi in the USA, for example, still exists despite the millions of dollars spent each year to control and manage the river. Building higher and higher levees may reduce small floods, yet the effects of a large flood like that of 1993 were made worse by engineering. In many places levees could not contain the river flow and the sudden breaching of levees caused widespread and more severe flooding.

Studies of the River Tay to the west of Dundee in Scotland have shown that attempts to restrain a river that has a natural tendency in some places to divide into multiple channels, have been largely unsuccessful. Where flood embankments have been built close to the river to protect settlements, roads, railways, and agricultural land, the river has repeatedly broken through them, notably in 1990 and 1993 but also several times in the 18th century.

The 1993 event had a recurrence interval of at least one in 60 years and caused many flood embankments to partly collapse. This allowed the river to burst through and cause subsequent erosion of top-soil by the floodwater. In other areas, the flood caused large-scale bank erosion and

deposition of sediment on farmers' fields. There was also much damage to property. Unfortunately, many of the embankments were breached in 1993 in the same locations as in 1990. Along one particular stretch of the river an embankment that cost £240,000 to repair after it was breached in 1990, was again destroyed in 1993. This pattern of repeated failure of the same flood embankments is very costly and must prompt a review of how the river is managed.

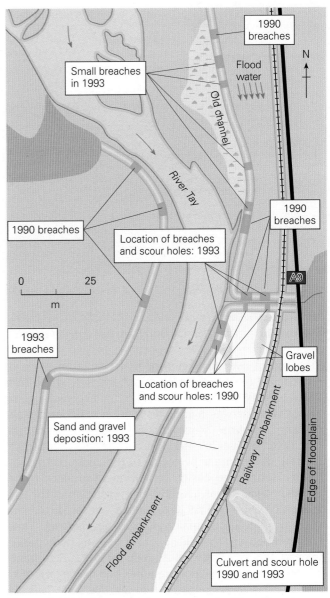

Figure 1.100 *Repeated flooding on the River Tay at Guay, near Dundee.*

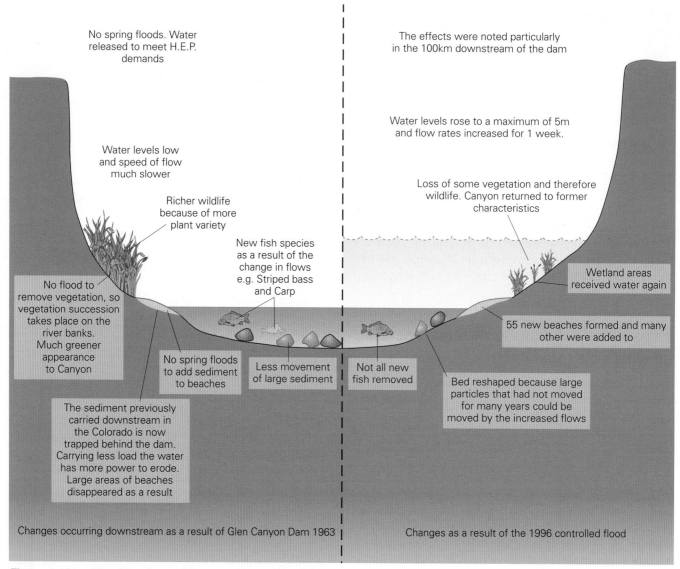

No spring floods. Water released to meet H.E.P. demands

The effects were noted particularly in the 100km downstream of the dam

Water levels low and speed of flow much slower

Water levels rose to a maximum of 5m and flow rates increased for 1 week.

Richer wildlife because of more plant variety

Loss of some vegetation and therefore wildlife. Canyon returned to former characteristics

New fish species as a result of the change in flows e.g. Striped bass and Carp

No flood to remove vegetation, so vegetation succession takes place on the river banks. Much greener appearance to Canyon

Wetland areas received water again

55 new beaches formed and many other were added to

No spring floods to add sediment to beaches

Less movement of large sediment

Not all new fish removed

Bed reshaped because large particles that had not moved for many years could be moved by the increased flows

The sediment previously carried downstream in the Colorado is now trapped behind the dam. Carrying less load the water has more power to erode. Large areas of beaches disappeared as a result

Changes occurring downstream as a result of Glen Canyon Dam 1963

Changes as a result of the 1996 controlled flood

Figure 1.101   *The Glen Canyon Dam has caused downstream changes in the river flow, channel form, and vegetation.*

The type of river management that has taken place on stretches of the Tay, the Mississippi and indeed the Trent (pages 39-40) tends to put hazard management above issues of conservation and preservation of floodplain and wetland habitats. When the Glen Canyon Dam was completed on the Colorado River in 1963, its purpose was to store water for use by people in the upper parts of the Colorado drainage basin, as well as to produce hydro-electric power. It was accepted that upstream of the dam there would be habitat loss, but no one predicted that there would also be major changes downstream. These occurred because there is no longer a spring flood period. Instead, the river flow is much reduced and is determined by the amount of electricity required and hence how much water needs to be released through the dam. This has affected the downstream ecosystem of the river, as shown in Figure 1.101.

In response to these changes, the Glen Canyon Environmental Studies project was set up in 1982 and its research showed that occasional flooding was essential to maintain the Colorado river environment. So in 1996 a spring flood was simulated by releasing 900 million cubic metres of water through special jets in the space of a week. This was more than double the maximum possible through the turbines alone and the river level rose more than 5 m above its normal height. This was the first time such a deliberate release from a dam for environmental reasons had taken place. The flood allowed the return of some of the pre-dam features of the river and was deemed a success (Figure 1.101). Such measures are now being considered for other US rivers, though scientists suggest that controlled floods may need to take place every 7–10 years in order to maintain the downstream river conditions.

Such environmental impacts of large dams and the alteration of river regimes that results from them is one of the reasons why the number of dams under construction is falling, as hydrologists, engineers, and planners develop water management strategies. There is growing awareness, too, that inappropriate management techniques can have serious consequences for people *and* the environment.

As a result of this change in emphasis, the World Commission for Dams was set up in 1997. Its aims are to assess the performance and suitability of large dams, suggest management guidelines, and offer alternatives for water management.

ACTIVITIES

1 Describe and account for the changes seen downstream of the Glen Canyon Dam since its completion in 1963.
2 Explain how the simulated flood in 1996 helped to return to the Colorado River some of its pre-dam features.
3 Research the conclusions reached by the World Commission for Dams in their year 2000 report. Refer to the World Commission for Dams website listed at the end of this unit. Focus your research on:
   • the Commission's main conclusions about building large dams in the future
   • the alternative techniques or management approaches suggested by the Commission.

How does our use of floodplains affect flooding?

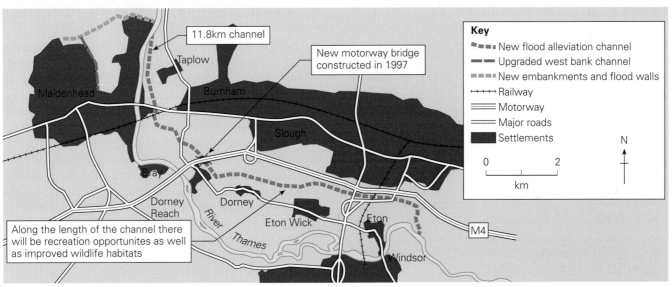

Figure 1.102   *The location of the new flood relief channel and embankments at Maidenhead, Windsor, and Eton.*
Source: *Protecting Your Homes* Environment Agency, 1996.

Undoubtedly the tendency for people to live close to water, particularly on floodplains, means they will be subject to a greater threat from floods. In recent years, riverside properties and marina developments have even gained a certain prestige. The increased development of properties on floodplains adds further to the problem. Not only are more homes and businesses likely to experience flooding, but the increase in impermeable surfaces and the reduction in the storage capacity of the floodplain means that flooding may become more frequent and more widespread.

Maidenhead is situated on the Thames west of London. Here the central business district (CBD) is located on higher land, whilst housing developments have increasingly spread onto the floodplain, especially since the Second World War. In 1947, the area suffered a major flood, with a recurrence interval of 56 years, and over 2000 homes were affected. As a result, a flood alleviation scheme was put in place. However, flood relief schemes or water storage dams tend to give people a false sense of security and the potential hazard tends to be forgotten. As a result, further development has taken place on the floodplain, despite attempts to control it by the local authority and Thames Water. Consequently, in 1990 a small flood with a recurrence interval of only six years flooded 500 homes, whilst a flood the size of the 1947 event would now affect an estimated 5500 properties and more than 12,500 people, at a cost of over £40 million. Consequently, a further flood relief scheme is now necessary. The flood alleviation scheme for Maidenhead, Windsor, and Eton was started in 1996 and is expected to be completed by the end of 2002 at a total cost of over £43 million (see Figure 1.102).

Such large-scale flood defence schemes are very costly and a study of the costs and benefits took place during the planning stage to determine whether the scheme was financially realistic. All figures are based on 1992 prices.

Cost of implementing the scheme and maintaining it for its 65-year life span.

Total costs: £43.783 million

The benefits that can be given a money value (referred to as tangible benefits). These include selling the sand and gravel excavated whilst digging the new channel and savings made because there will no longer be problems caused by flooding, for example damage to property, cost of evacuation, rebuilding costs, traffic disruption.

Total benefits £52.728 million

When the cost–benefit ratio was calculated, it produced a figure of 1:1.21. In other words, for every one pound spent, the benefits brought would be worth one pound and twenty-one pence. The figures were acceptable and were approved by the government in 1995.

Some benefits, however, might be less easy to measure in money terms (referred to as intangible benefits). For example there will be less risk to human life, people will feel less vulnerable, and the amenity value of the area will be enhanced by the new channel. When these factors were included, the cost–benefit ratio rose to 1:1.4 making the scheme even more feasible in economic terms.

ACTIVITIES

Maidenhead, like many urban areas, is surrounded by land that has been declared greenbelt land where no one is allowed to build houses.
1   Where have houses been built as a result?
2   Explain how this has increased the problems caused by flooding in Maidenhead.
3   Why do you think problems like this are likely to be worse in the south of England? Consult an atlas map showing population density if you are not sure.

Alternative methods of river management

In many densely populated areas, river management is essential to prevent wide-scale damage and disruption. This often involves channelisation to some degree. However, there are a number of problems associated with confining the river to an inflexible and unnatural channel. It tends to produce:

- river discharges that are 'flashy' (rising and falling quickly)
- floodwater that moves swiftly downstream and increases the flood risk elsewhere
- channels that are not usually stable (remember straight channels do not often exist in nature)
- changes in the flora and fauna of the river and river corridor, both at the location of the changes and downstream. Wetland areas may no longer receive the water essential for their survival
- rivers that may lack 'character' and amenity value.

During the 20th century views on river management started to change. People realised that an appreciation of the hydrological and geomorphological processes at work within the *whole* drainage basin, of which the river is just one component, allows us to understand the reasons why discharge varies or the channel changes (Figure 1.103). This understanding encourages people to work with the river instead of against it. This holistic or 'whole' approach is similar to a doctor who does not just treat a symptom such as a high temperature in isolation, but looks at the whole person and tries to find out the cause of the illness. In much the same way, river management is likely to be more successful if we understand why a river spreads over the floodplain – rather than just trying to prevent it from doing so.

Whereas people once considered only how they could exploit rivers in the short term, now the long-term preservation of rivers as a resource is being considered far more. The value of natural habitats and the need for conservation is being realised. This idea of **sustainable management** of drainage basins refers to the need for balance between current use of the resource and the need

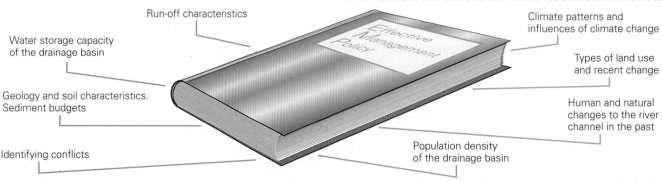

Run-off characteristics

Water storage capacity of the drainage basin

Geology and soil characteristics. Sediment budgets

Identifying conflicts

Climate patterns and influences of climate change

Types of land use and recent change

Human and natural changes to the river channel in the past

Population density of the drainage basin

Effective Management Policy

Figure 1.103   *An understanding of drainage basin processes is essential for river management.*

to preserve it for the future. At the Rio Conference on the Environment held in 1992, water and its sustainable use were a major issue and countries were encouraged to adopt policies to protect and maintain water resources. Emphasis was placed on environmental considerations and management at the catchment level.

Bearing in mind these ideas of sustainability and conservation, one option would be to abandon floodplains and allow rivers to operate naturally. This is not usually an option where the floodplain is used for domestic or industrial development. Figure 1.104 shows a possible compromise between preserving the floodplain as a dry area and allowing it to revert to natural floodplain.

ACTIVITIES

1   Figure 1.104 shows two alternative views of floodplain management. Describe the advantages of retaining some areas of the floodplain as washlands where the river can overflow. Consider especially the benefits for:
   • flood control
   • conservation.
2   Outline any disadvantages of this management approach that you can think of.

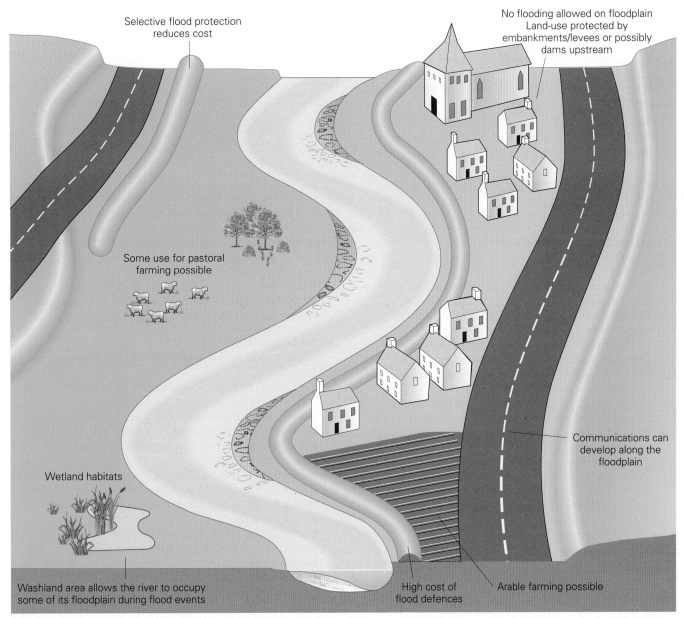

Figure 1.104   *Alternative approaches to floodplain management.*

Bangladesh: River management – a new way forward?

Bangladesh has a history of flooding. It is a very low-lying country with monsoon rainfall occurring over just five or six months of the year. Three major rivers converge in Bangladesh (Ganges, Brahmaputra, and Meghna) though the drainage basins of these rivers include parts of the Himalayas and extend over an area far greater than the size of Bangladesh. Bangladesh is also subject to coastal flooding which can cause the flow of these rivers to back up and increase the area of inland flooding.

After major floods in 1988 that killed almost 2400 people, the Flood Action Plan was set up to investigate the best methods of preventing floods in the future. In the past, the government had always supported large engineering schemes as the best method of flood control. However, a change in political control allowed more say for individual farmers and local people. In some areas building flood banks is the only option, for example close to major cities like Dhaka. In other areas there is scope for river management of a different kind. The options for the Lower Atrai valley (Figure 1.105) in north-west Bangladesh are shown in Figure 1.106.

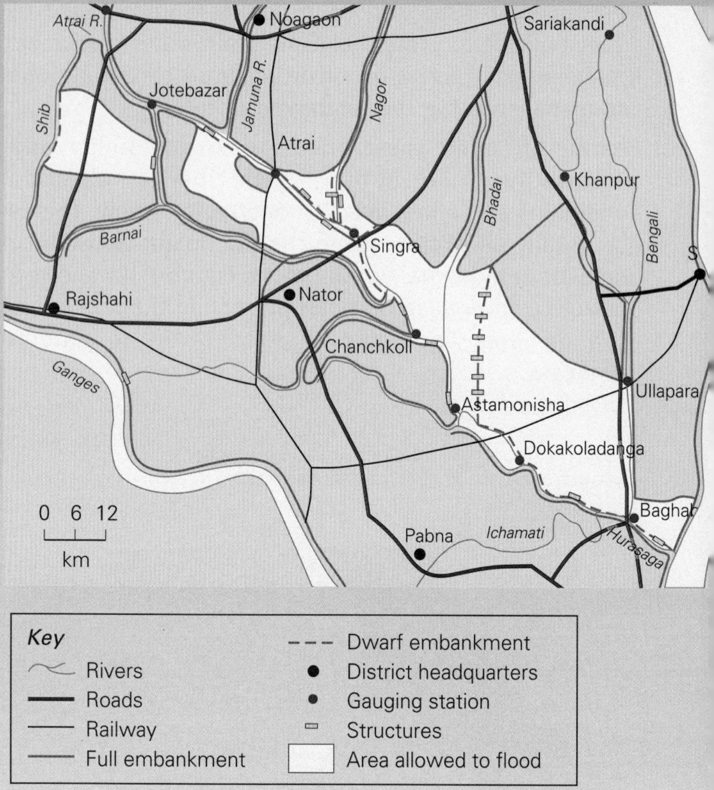

Figure 1.105   *The location of Lower Atrai valley in Bangladesh.*

Source: *Integrated River Basin Development* Wiley, 1994.

ACTIVITIES

1 Which of the two options outlined below do you think is most appropriate for river management in the Lower Atrai valley? Write a report outlining the reasons for your choice. You need to consider the impacts of your chosen scheme on the environment, public safety, agriculture, food supply, navigation, and transport.

Factors for consideration:

- Bangladesh is a poor country with a high population density.
- The area is in a tectonically active zone with a risk of earthquakes.
- Bangladesh is now self-sufficient in rice due to irrigation and the use of high-yielding varieties (HYV). The income for rice farmers is falling and many are looking for alternative crops to grow.
- Fish is becoming an increasingly important part of the diet.
- Groundwater recharge is important to maintain irrigation in the dry season.
- Silt and organic matter brought by floodwater add nutrients to the soil.
- The Lower Atrai valley sometimes floods when the Brahmaputra is full because the Atrai-Hurasagar River water backs up.
- As population increases so does the need for food.
- Floodplain wetlands help to maintain plant and animal diversity.

The flood control options (cost $US500 million at 1991 prices):

- Build drains with a capacity of 1000 m³/sec. to transfer floodwater to the Ganges or the Brahmaputra.
- Artificially regulate the flow of the Atrai-Hurasagar river where it joins the Brahmaputra.

'The Green River' option:

- Allow the Atrai-Hurasagar River to flood during the monsoon.
- Give some protection against the early floods of the year so that one rice crop could be grown.
- During the main flood, farming would probably not be possible in the flooded area, although fishing could take place. At some locations, a second rice crop might be raised.
- Some people will be living in areas at risk of flooding. This might be better than living in an area that is totally protected, but at risk of sudden and major flooding.
- People living in the flood area would need protection. This might take the form of housing built on raised areas or flood warning schemes. Roads and railways also cross the valley, this would need to be taken into consideration.

Figure 1.106   *Options for flood control in the Lower Atrai valley, Bangladesh.*

River restoration: How successful?

In response to the environmental interest shown in river systems, some attempts have been made to restore rivers that have been modified to their more natural state. A number of projects have taken place in Britain, mainly over the last decade, including work on the River Skerne in Darlington, the Whittle Brook in Warrington, the River Cole near Swindon and the Bear Brook at Aylesbury.

The aim of the projects, in common with the 'Green River' option for the Lower Atrai valley, has been to allow rivers to interact once again with the floodplain. In other words, to flood more often and to allow the river system to operate in a more natural way. This has ecological benefits as well as the benefits that replacing the floodplain brings.

The restoration process may involve replacing the meandering river course, changing the shape of the bed and banks, strengthening banks with vegetation, creating conditions suitable for wetland ecosystems, and planting new vegetation. Such restoration is time consuming and the benefits will only gradually become apparent. It is also costly, but these costs have to be set against the advantages, some of which reduce costs elsewhere, for example reduced flood risk and water quality improvements.

Restoration on the Kissimmee

One of the largest river restoration projects in the world has just started on the Kissimmee river in central Florida, USA. The Kissimmee flowed 160 km between Lake Kissimmee and Lake Okeechobee in the south and, before channelisation, meandered often in multiple channels across its floodplain. This floodplain contained large areas of wetland habitat which supported a diverse population of fish, wading birds, and waterfowl.

After severe flooding in the area in the 1940s, the decision was taken to channelise the river to prevent floods and assist navigation. Between 1962 and 1971 the United States Corps of Engineers replaced the Kissimmee River with a 90 km long drainage canal which was renamed rather appropriately C38! Within this canal were storage lakes and various water control features. In addition, the water entering the canal from Kissimmee Lake was limited by controlling many of the lakes in the upper drainage basin in order to store water. Figure 1.107 shows the impact of changing the course of the Kissimmee.

Even before the canal was finished, ecological changes had been observed and only four years after its completion the Kissimmee River Restoration Act was passed with the long-term aim of restoring the river and regaining some of the wetland habitats. In 1999 the work started. The estimated cost is expected to be approximately $US450 million, more than 15 times the original cost of building the canal! The project will not be completed until 2010.

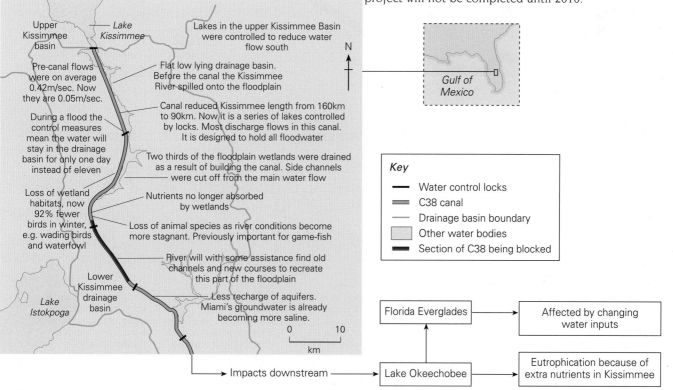

Figure 1.107   *Impact of changing the course of the Kissimmee.*

The restoration plan includes the following changes:

- buying back farmland to replace 104km² of the floodplain
- reinstating 11,000ha of wetlands
- blocking the C38 canal and filling in a 35km stretch of it. The river will then be forced to flow along sections of the original river channel. Some new river channels will be dug to link up some of these sections that are no longer joined.
- restoring ox-bow lakes to create natural habitats
- removing levees in selected areas, to allow flooding of wetland areas
- retaining some of the canal to protect settlements from flooding. Where flooding does occur it will generally be in grazing areas
- allowing the river to return to its seasonal flow.
- encouraging tourism based on hunting and fishing to boost the economy of the area.

Sustainable management

Some flood prevention schemes are also starting to utilise more of the principles of river restoration because of the benefits that they bring. The scheme announced by the Environment Agency in August 1999 for flood prevention on the River Eye, upstream of Melton Mowbray in Leicestershire, includes various techniques of 'green engineering' (Figure 1.108). The use of sediment traps and green dams made from coppice willow will help to reduce discharges, prevent floods, and improve water quality.

The move towards more sustainable management of rivers is not confined solely to those flowing through rural areas. The Environment Agency is working with private developers and local authorities at sites along the Thames to enhance the landscape, improve wildlife habitats, and increase opportunities for recreation (Figure 1.109). The Thames is tidal as far west as Teddington weir and at low tide, beaches and mudflats become visible. In many places these have been lost as new buildings have been developed out onto the shoreline. The typical flood defences of high concrete and steel walls also reduce the habitat value.

Since the completion of the Thames Barrier in 1983 there has no longer been the need for such high flood defences. This, along with the improvements in water quality, has encouraged new practices, including flood protection schemes, to be more environmentally friendly. Practices such as planting reedbeds, replacing beaches and using reclaimed wood from old jetties in flood defence work all help to improve the shoreline habitat. Such work is at a price comparable with traditional methods of flood defence. It is hoped that as flood defences need to be replaced over the next 50 years or so, these new methods being employed will allow great ecological improvements along the whole tidal section of the Thames.

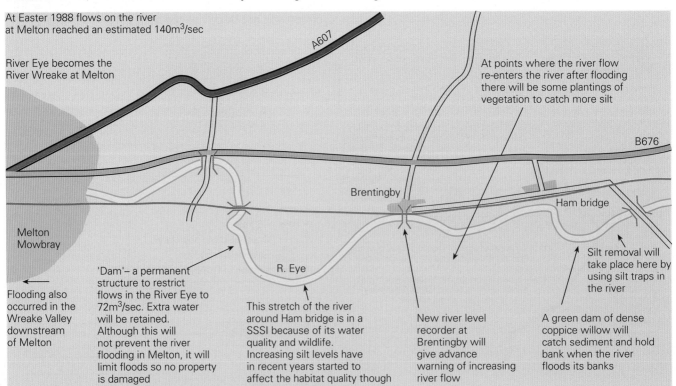

Figure 1.108 *The proposed flood prevention scheme on the River Eye, Leicestershire.*

Source: *Melton Mowbray Flood Alleviation Scheme* Environment Agency, 1999.

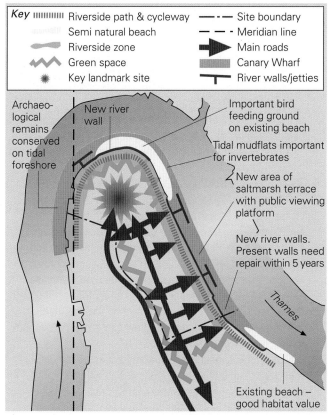

Key ||||||||| Riverside path & cycleway — · — Site boundary
⬛ Semi natural beach — - — Meridian line
⬛ Riverside zone ➡ Main roads
⬛ Green space ⬛ Canary Wharf
✷ Key landmark site ⊤ River walls/jetties

Archaeo-logical remains conserved on tidal foreshore

New river wall

Important bird feeding ground on existing beach

Tidal mudflats important for invertebrates

New area of saltmarsh terrace with public viewing platform

New river walls. Present walls need repair within 5 years

Thames

Existing beach – good habitat value

Figure 1.110 *The Greenwich Peninsula scheme, just part of the planned improvements for the Thames.*
Source: *Millennium Riverbank Experiment* Environment Agency, 1998.

It is important to understand the processes at work within drainage basins if we are going to manage them effectively without causing harm to the environment. Changes in agriculture and increasing urbanisation and industrialisation have meant that management of water has become more concerned with the *conservation* of water resources. As a result, there has been a move towards integrated management at a catchment, or drainage basin, scale. This involves not only managing all aspects of the hydrological cycle but the land and air as well. Such an integrated approach takes account of the fact that the quantity and quality of water sources are related to a host of other processes operating within the drainage basin.

In England and Wales this has been the job of the Environment Agency since 1996. The Environment Agency's approach to integrated environmental management is outlined in Figure 1.110.

The process of environmental management is ongoing and involves developing a policy or overall scheme. Once this has been put in placep, the results will be closely monitored. The results of this monitoring may lead to a change in the action plans or even to the original policy.

In England and Wales, Local Environment Agency Plans (LEAP) are produced by the Environment Agency and

representatives of other interest groups. The plans consider the environmental issues affecting individual catchments and the options available to solve the problems. They are available for public consultation, so that people can express their views. There will always be conflict between different groups and their demands will vary, but before any action is taken the cost of a proposed scheme will be weighed up against the benefits and the environmental impacts. Such cost–benefit analysis may mean, for example, that not all homes alongside a river are protected by a flood prevention scheme, as the very high cost may benefit only a few people. As the costs of such schemes increase, there may need to be an adjustment in people's attitudes to floods and to the way we use our floodplains.

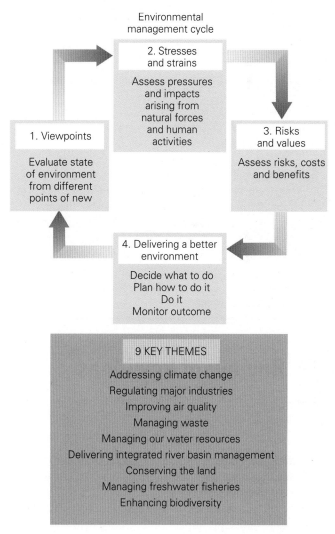

Environmental management cycle

2. Stresses and strains
Assess pressures and impacts arising from natural forces and human activities

1. Viewpoints
Evaluate state of environment from different points of new

3. Risks and values
Assess risks, costs and benefits

4. Delivering a better environment
Decide what to do
Plan how to do it
Do it
Monitor outcome

9 KEY THEMES
Addressing climate change
Regulating major industries
Improving air quality
Managing waste
Managing our water resources
Delivering integrated river basin management
Conserving the land
Managing freshwater fisheries
Enhancing biodiversity

Figure 1.110 *The Environment Agency approach to integrated environmental management in England and Wales.*
Source: *Understanding our Environmental Strategy* Environment Agency, 1998.

ACTIVITIES

1 Consider the Kissimmee River.
   * Following the flooding in the 1940s, what do you think was the overall policy for this river?
   * What plans were made?
   * What action was taken?
   * What did monitoring of the environment show?
   * How was the policy changed as a result?

   Present your findings as a large flow diagram. You could use each of the questions here as headings for a series of boxes. Each box should contain the information that you have discovered. Link the boxes with arrows to show how the original policy was changed as a result of environmental monitoring. Use the structure in Figure 1.110 as a guide.

2 a Using a large sheet of paper draw an annotated diagram to show all of the possible consequences of building a large dam. It is important to consider both the advantages and disadvantages.
   b Add a key or colour code your diagram to distinguish between:
      * social
      * economic
      * ecological
      * hydrological and geomorphic consequences.

3 Find the published catchment plan of a river near your home (contact your Environment Agency office, or Scottish equivalent, or the website listed at the end of this unit). After 1996 these became known as Local Environment Agency Plans (LEAP). They contain a wealth of information about all aspects of the environment, often represented in map form.
   a Read about the environmental issues identified in your particular drainage basin.

   b Choose one or two of the issues that interest you and consider the action that the Environment Agency proposes to take. Locate the areas of concern within the drainage basin; producing a sketch map of your own would help you to do this.
   c Try to predict what improvements you would expect to see as a result of the proposed actions. Describe any other measures that you think could be taken that would help.

4 Try to find out about one of the two river restoration projects that have taken place in England. The schemes on the river Skerne in Darlington and the River Cole near Swindon were part of the EU LIFE projects. There is a third one on the River Brede in Denmark. These projects were set up to restore sections of these rivers to more natural channel and floodplain conditions. An extensive monitoring programme is in place to study the results of the restoration on the characteristics of the river itself, the floodplain, and also on the plant and animal life found in the river environment.

   Alternatively, investigate environmental improvements that have taken place on a river close to where you live. Refer to *The New Rivers and Wildlife Handbook* (1994; RSPB, NRA, and RSNC) and websites listed at the end of this unit for extra information.

5 After the 1997 floods that affected Poland and Germany, Helmut Kohl, the German Chancellor, said it was important that 'the rivers have to be given space to breathe'. Explain what you think he meant by this statement, and with reference to examples that you have studied in this chapter suggest whether or not you think it is a sensible idea.

6 Review of key ideas

In this chapter the following key ideas are important:

* Water flows into, within and out of a drainage basin can vary. These water movements are part of the global hydrological cycle.
* River discharges may fluctuate enormously. This may have a significant impact on both physical and human environments.
* River channels change in time and space as a result of natural processes or human influences. These changes are not always predictable.

* Wetland ecosystems have an important role to play in the drainage basin system.
* Rivers can be managed in different ways. Recently, management strategies have been changing.

Chapter Two Coastal Environments

1 Coasts and people

In this section we consider the following key questions:

* Why are coasts important to people?
* What do we mean by the coastal zone?
* Who manages the UK coast and how?
* What range of coastal types exist?

This section gives you an overview of the key issues concerning coasts and their management. We return to some of them in further detail later in the chapter when we focus on understanding the processes at work in coastal systems and ecosystems, and evaluate how effectively these systems are being managed.

Why are coasts important?

The coast is that unique, valuable, and often threatened area where the sea meets the land. The coastline is an ever-changing boundary zone between the habitable terrestrial environment and the inhospitable (as far as humans are concerned) marine environment. Coasts have long been valued in many ways:

* as premium economic sites for industry and marine trade. They are often used by industries that need much water for their cooling systems or for delivery of bulk material (Figure 2.1)
* as rich and diverse **habitats** and ecosystems such as coral reefs. They are often associated with the combination of fresh and salt water. Coastal estuaries create some of the most productive habitats on Earth, and the marine resources can be of great value to coastal nations (Figures 2.2 and 2.3)
* as highly valued and attractive sites for tourism and recreation (Figures 2.4 and 2.5)
* wide, gently sloping beaches act as natural forms of coastal protection (Figures 2.4 and 2.5)
* historically, as defensive sites for human settlements and more recently, for dense residential development (Figures 2.1, 2.6 and 2.8).

There is considerable competition for land and sea resources by various groups, often resulting in severe conflicts. Coasts form geomorphologically active landscapes, undergoing constant change.

Figure 2.1   *An aerial view of Portsmouth Harbour and Gosport.*

Figure 2.2   *Salmon farming in the Shetland Isles.*

Figure 2.3   *Whaling in Iceland.*

Figure 2.4   *Daytona Beach, Florida.*

Figure 2.5   *Furzy Cliff near Weymouth.*

Figure 2.6   *San Francisco, California.*

Figure 2.7   *The beach at Towyn, North Wales.*

Figure 2.8   *Venice.*

ACTIVITIES

Are coasts important to us? Work through the following six questions. Share your ideas with the rest of class and produce a collective summary.

1   When did you last go to the coast?
    a today **b** this week **c** this month **d** this year **e** other
2   How frequently do you go to the coast?
    a daily **b** weekly **c** monthly **d** annually **e** other
3   Why do you go to the coast?
4   Where did you go?
    a UK **b** Europe **c** elsewhere
5   Who else 'uses' the coast? Make a list of the various ways in which coasts are used.
6   What positive and negative coastal issues make the news?
    a local press   **d** national TV
    b regional TV/radio   **e** others, e.g. documentaries
    c national press

The processes at work in coastal systems must be fully understood if effective and environmentally-sensitive, integrated management is to be achieved. Management programmes are designed to alleviate the erosive effect of the sea and to restrict the depositional problems it may create.

ACTIVITIES

User group	1	2	3	4	5	6
1	✕					
2		✕				
3			✕			
4				✕		
5					✕	
6						✕

Figure 2.9   *A conflict matrix table for the use of the coastal zone.*

1   Make a copy of the conflict matrix table (Figure 2.9).
2   Identify six different groups who use the coastal zone, and write them in the user group boxes. Use the previous activity, and Figures 2.1 to 2.8 to help you.
3   Complete the 15 unshaded boxes in the matrix by considering where there is conflict between two users:
    • if there is a conflict put an X
    • if user groups are compatible put a √
    • if neither put 0.
4   **Optional extension** If there are many conflicts, identify major and minor conflicts using a scoring system:
    • 3 = severe conflict
    • 2 = significant conflict
    • 1 = minor conflict.

Coastal regions cover only 10 per cent of the inhabited land space, yet they are home to more than 60 per cent of the world's population, all concentrated in a narrow ribbon of land around the planet's oceans, seas, and lakes. The World Bank estimates that two thirds of the world's largest cities are situated on coasts, and these are growing faster than inland cities. In Europe, over 200 million people, more than 30 per cent of the European population, live within 50 km of the coast. In the USA, population density is growing faster in coastal states than inland ones.

These large and growing populations increase pressure on valuable and often relatively fragile coastal ecosystems, and can create significant environmental conflicts.

Managing these conflicts successfully depends on achieving an understanding of the natural and human processes at work (Figure 2.10). Figure 2.11 suggests what might happen without effective management.

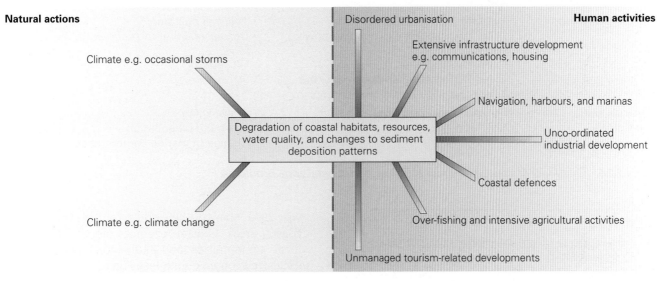

Natural actions

Climate e.g. occasional storms

Climate e.g. climate change

Degradation of coastal habitats, resources, water quality, and changes to sediment deposition patterns

Human activities

Disordered urbanisation

Extensive infrastructure development e.g. communications, housing

Navigation, harbours, and marinas

Unco-ordinated industrial development

Coastal defences

Over-fishing and intensive agricultural activities

Unmanaged tourism-related developments

Figure 2.10   *Natural actions and human activities that cause rapid degradation of coastal habitats and resources, and changes to processes.*

Figure 2.11   *The future of the coastal zone without effective management.*

Human activity	Consequences	Coastal zone degradation problems
Urbanisation and transport	• Land-use changes for ports • Congestion • Dredging and disposal of harbour sediments • Water abstraction • Waste water and waste disposal	• Disruption of coastal ecology and loss of species diversity and habitats • Visual impact • Lowering of groundwater table • Salt water intrusion of aquifers • Water pollution, including eutrophication
Agriculture, fishing and harvesting of marine resources	• Land reclamation • Use of fertilisers and pesticides • Water abstraction • River channelisation • Over-fishing of vulnerable stocks	• Disturbance • Disruption to coastal sedimentation pathways through erosion and accelerated deposition • Increased flood risk • Encouragement of local subsidence
Tourism and recreation	• Land-use changes, e.g. golf courses, marinas	• Traffic pollution • Erosion
Industrial development	• Pollution • Land-use changes, e.g. building power stations • Extraction of natural resources • Effluent processing and cooling water • Tidal barrages, river impoundments	• Thermal pollution • Decreased input of sediment to the coastal zone • Oil spills
Fisheries and aquaculture	• Fish processing facilities • Fish farm effluents	• Over-fishing • Litter and oil pollution • Change in marine communities

Figure 2.12 *Relationship between human activities and coastal zone problems.*

ACTIVITIES

1 Using your work to date and Figures 2.1 to 2.12 summarise the major conflicts that can exist in coastal zones.
2 Produce a map for a varied, extended coastal area of less than 30 km length, based on your own local knowledge, recent fieldwork experience, or research. Annotate with the major coastal conflicts.
   Many UK local authorities produce material that can be helpful for this task as do all the US coastal states and many are available on the Internet. Try key words 'Coastal management' and a specific place.

Defining the coastal zone

There is no easy or commonly agreed definition of what constitutes a 'coastal area or zone', but there are a number of complementary definitions, each serving a different purpose:

The coastal area contains diverse and productive habitats important for human settlements, development, and local subsistence. More than half the world's population lives within 60 km of the shoreline, and this could rise to three quarters by the year 2020. Many of the world's poor are crowded in coastal areas. Coastal resources are vital for many local communities and indigenous people. The exclusive economic zone (see Figure 2.13) is also an important marine area where the states manage the development and conservation of natural resources for the benefit of their people. For small island states or countries, these are the areas most available for development activities.
Source: UNCED (1992) Agenda 21.

At a minimum the designated coastal zone includes all the inter-tidal and supratidal areas of the water's edge (see Figure 2.13); specifically all the coastal floodplains, mangroves, marshes, and tidal flats as well as beaches and dunes and fringing coral reefs. This is the transition zone where government agency authority changes abruptly, and where some of the richest aquatic habitat is found. It is also the place where planning and management programmes are at their weakest.
Source: Clark (1996)

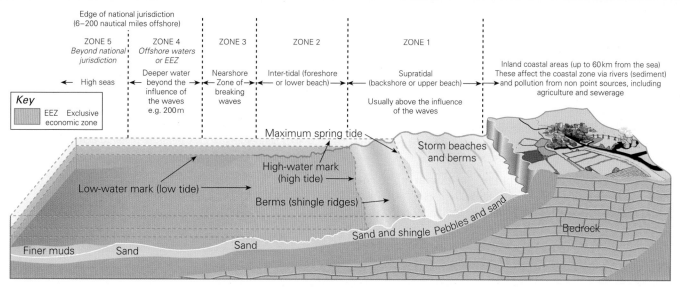

Figure 2.13 *The five subdivisions of the coastal zone. The shoreline (zones 2–4) or coastal waters can also include estuaries and lagoons. Zone 1 can also include coastal wetlands, marshes, sand dunes, cliff faces, and cliff tops.*

Although the term 'coastal zone' is generally understood, it has proved very difficult to put precise landward or seaward boundaries around it. In Europe, for example, some countries extend the term seawards to their territorial limits, others extend it seawards to the 200m depth contour. A general working definition produced by the US Commission on Marine Science, Engineering, and Resources in 1969 is 'the part of the land affected by its proximity to the sea, and that part of the sea affected by its proximity to the land'.

In short, then, the coastal zone is the interface between the land and the sea.

ACTIVITIES

1 Attempt to write your own definition of the coastal zone, and identify subdivisions within this zone using Figure 2.13.

What are coastal management and integrated coastal zone management (ICZM)?

Interest in integrated coastal zone management (ICZM) is high following a number of international meetings including:

- the 1992 Earth Summit and its *Agenda* 21, Chapter 17 on 'Protection of the oceans'
- the continuing work of the Inter-governmental Panel on Climate Change, for example the working group on coastal zones and small islands
- the 1993 World Coast Conference

- the 1995 Washington Conference, sponsored by the United Nations Environment Programme.

All of these meetings have concluded that sustainable ICZM is the appropriate approach with which to manage the diverse problems of coastal areas. These problems range from the pressing issues of coastal pollution and habitat degradation to the long-term implications of changing sea level.

Successful ICZM has three key elements, all of which need to be adequately funded over time if it is to be successful (Figure 2.14).

Policy
Stage 1 The development of an understanding of the coastal zone as a system of interlinked processes and components that leads to the formulation of a clear policy.

Planning
Stage 2 Using this knowledge to create a long-term, sustainable, environmentally acceptable, strategic plan.

Practice
Stage 3 The implementation and enforcement of the plan by regulations and an active and well-informed public.

Figure 2.14 *The three stages of coastal management*

Successful planning requires a single governmental unit, with overall responsibility for integrated planning and development of the coastal zone at all scales. The reason that this presents such a difficult challenge is that ICZM needs to adapt to changes in circumstances, for example public preference, economic conditions, new technology or scientific understanding, and government policies.

Management boundaries rarely coincide with ecosystem boundaries, or other natural processes, for example sediment transport cells (see Figure 2.17). Management boundaries may not even coincide with political boundaries. There is no comprehensive coastal zone management (CZM) scheme for Europe, but there is for the USA. Progress towards such a scheme in the UK and Europe over the last 25 years has been slow, and national legislation tends to focus on coastal protection rather than on producing ICZM.

Humans have tried to control the coast, more often than not unsuccessfully. This is especially the case in the most vulnerable areas, including estuaries, deltas, and low-lying coasts, with high populations such as the Mediterranean Basin and the North Sea. Natural and human processes often combine to create complex environmental problems, for example, coastal pollution can make salt-marsh erosion worse, which might in turn increase flooding.

ACTIVITIES

1 Stresses in one part of the coastal system may affect other parts of the coastal system. Organise the following four actions into a flow diagram to show how they might accelerate coastal erosion:
   - mangrove swamp erosion
   - storm damage of an area once protected by a reef
   - deforestation
   - downdrift degradation of coral reefs as they become choked by sediment.

Who manages the UK coast and how?

The 4800 km coastline of England, Wales, and Northern Ireland includes 1600 km of developed coast and 1600 km of coast which is classified as unimportant scenically or scientifically. The National Trust manages 650 km of the important and interesting coast, and 950 km is either in private ownership or is being managed by other, responsible trusts (Figure 2.16). Much of the coastline is therefore managed in practice by a wide range of designation orders, for example, National Parks, Areas of Outstanding Natural Beauty (AONB), Heritage Coasts, National Nature Reserves (NNR), and Sites of Special Scientific Interest (SSSI), and by a range of non-governmental organisations that concentrate on conservation and amenity.

Unlike the USA, the UK does not yet have a central integrated government body to manage the conflicting demands on our coastline. Even the Ministry of Agriculture, Food, and Fisheries (MAFF), who currently have overall policy responsibility, are campaigning for such an organisation.

There is still confusion over who is responsible for the different aspects of coastal management. The overall responsibility for managing coastal defence (Coastal Protection and Flood Defence) lies with MAFF through their 1993 Strategy for Flood and Coastal Defence. MAFF offers grants for all new defence schemes. Erosion problems are managed by district and unitary councils, flooding is managed by the Environment Agency (Figure 2.16).

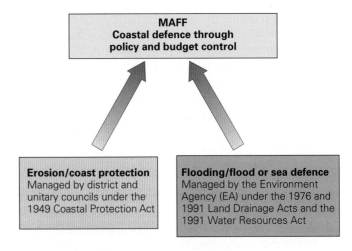

Figure 2.15 *Division of responsibility for the defence of the UK coast.*

The weaknesses of this system include the following:

- Management is fragmented and relatively unco-ordinated, lacking clear guidelines and realistic funding.
- There is a lack of a central government body to manage the conflicting demands in an integrated way.
- Although some recent improvements are noted, generally there is little formal control, even at a local or regional level, leaving some unconfronted conflicts and issues to mature.

Organisation	Status and how funded	Name of management project	Management method and purpose
National Trust	Voluntary charity	Enterprise Neptune 1985	At present manages > 650 km of coastline in England, Wales, and Northern Ireland
Worldwide Fund for Nature	Voluntary charity	Protection of estuaries and wetlands	Conservation of endangered wildlife and habitats
English Nature	Government body that promotes nature conservation in Britain	SSSIs and NNRs Selects, establishes, and manages sites	Protects scientific or ecologically important sites for research, education, wildlife, and recreation
Friends of the Earth	Voluntary charity	Marine dumping of waste	Active pressure group Raises public awareness
Countryside Commission	Advises on conservation and recreation in England and Wales	Heritage Coasts 1972, e.g. Dorset AONBs in England and Wales, e.g. Gower National Parks, e.g. Pembrokeshire Coast	Heritage Coasts attempts to protect 31 scenic areas under heavy visitor pressure. Managed by a consensus of local interested parties
Crown Estate Commissioners		Leases foreshore areas to local authorities, port authorities, harbour commissions	Manages foreshore and inter-tidal areas on behalf of the monarch. The public have common rights of use and access to this land
RSPB (Royal Society for the Protection of Birds)	Voluntary charity		Owns coastal nature reserves for protection and conservation of wild birds and their habitats
Marine Conservation Society	Voluntary charity	*UK Good Beach Guide*. Annually every April, featuring approximately 170 beaches Lundy Island Marine Nature Reserve	Aims to raise public awareness about beach quality as laid down by the EC. Awards are based on sewage, litter, facilities, and access
Greenpeace	Voluntary charity	The Beluga Survey Britain's Threatened Coastline	Active pressure group. Raises public awareness
Nature Conservation Trusts	Voluntary charity	e.g. Hants and Isle of Wight Naturalists Trust	County-level practical conservation projects and public awareness

Figure 2.16 *Coastal management organisations in the UK in the 1990s.*

- Lack of pro-active management. Some local authorities tend to get involved only after a dramatic decline in environmental or landscape quality, or when there is a proven hazard which affects life, livelihood, or property.
- Although the main, developed coastline is primarily controlled by district and unitary authorities, there is no recognised coastal zone in law.
- Current legislation has failed to treat the problems of the coast as an integrated whole. Different authorities have jurisdiction over the seabed, the inter-tidal zone, estuaries, and the beach above the high-water mark. Cliff-top planning, for example, is currently controlled by town and country planning legislation, whereas coastal erosion is controlled by the 1949 Coast Protection Act. Land-use zoning, pollution control, provision of recreational facilities, and wildlife and habitat protection may rest with other authorities. In Norway the problem has been resolved by creating a legally recognised coastal zone, which restricts all

developments within 100 m of the coastal edge, and in Sweden this 'set-back' line is a minimum of 100–300 m inland.
- Local authority administrative boundaries are not geomorphological ones. Engineering structures constructed by one local authority may create major environmental problems in an adjacent planning area. A classic example of this problem is known as Terminal Groyne Syndrome and was widespread along the Hampshire and Sussex coastlines where 'downdrift' local authorities found their sediment

inputs from longshore sources reduced by large groyne structures built by their 'updrift' neighbours. Some encouraging progress has been made here in the late 1990s due to SCOPAC and SMPS.
- Local authority responsibility for the coast is not continuous. Various elements of the developed coast in the UK are managed by independent bodies including British Rail, water authorities, sea defence commissioners, and private landowners. This makes co-ordination virtually impossible.

Standing Conference on Problems Associated with the Coastline (SCOPAC) and Shoreline Management Plans (SMP)

There have been two encouraging developments in the UK:

1 Standing Conference on Problems Associated with the Coastline (SCOPAC). Organisations such as Dorset–Hants–West Sussex Group formed in 1986, promote joint working within natural transport sediment cell management units (Figure 2.17) and encourage joint research on processes and coastal change. They have lobbied central government to adopt a more integrated and holistic approach towards coastal management. The main outcome of this intervention has been the development of Shoreline Management Plans (SMP) in England and Wales (Figure 2.17).

2 An SMP is defined as 'a strategy for coastal defence for a specified length of coast taking account of natural coastal processes and other environmental influences and needs'. It could ensure a strategic approach to coastal defence as it recognises the overall natural processes that operate on the coast. The SMPs:
- acknowledge the dynamic nature of the coast
- require creative engineering solutions that are environmentally sensitive, technically sound, sustainable, and economically viable
- recognise the overall natural processes operating on the coast, and understand that badly planned coastal defences on one part of the coast will affect the coastline elsewhere
- act as the basis for more detailed, long-term strategy plans to ensure greater integration of the UK's CZM.

Although actively encouraged by the government, SMPs are essentially voluntary. They should never-the-less have an increased impact on the future of coastal management.

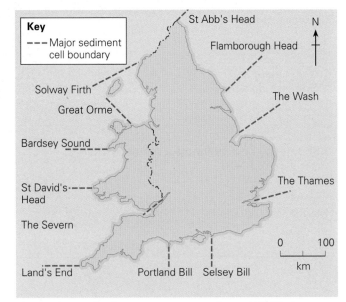

Figure 2.17 *Sediment transport cells and SMPs in England and Wales.* Source: *Managing Environments in Britain and Ireland* Hodder & Stoughton, 1997.

ACTIVITIES
1 Define an SMP.
2 Explain the relationship between SCOPAC and the SMPs.
3 Why are SMPs regarded as an essential early stage in the development of ICZM in the UK?

Recent research suggests that the coastline appears to be divided into 11 regions in England and Wales, called major sediment cells, within which sand and shingle movement is relatively self-contained. Within these larger units are smaller, sub-cells. These sub-cells form natural units for the SMPs. Figure 2.18 shows a section of the Dorset coast with its major sediment cells, its sub-cells, and the SMPs that are being prepared.

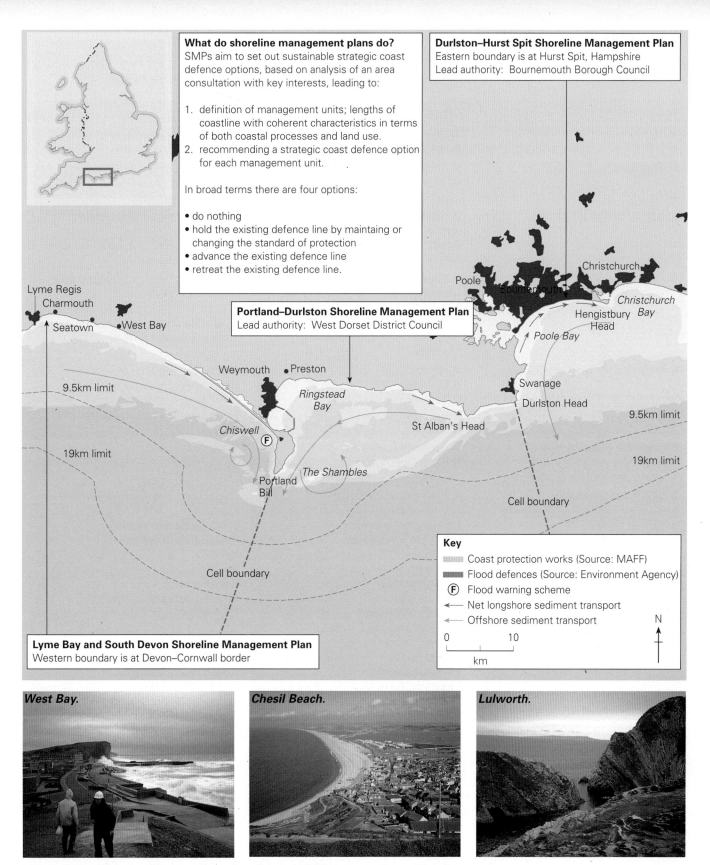

What do shoreline management plans do?
SMPs aim to set out sustainable strategic coast defence options, based on analysis of an area consultation with key interests, leading to:

1. definition of management units; lengths of coastline with coherent characteristics in terms of both coastal processes and land use.
2. recommending a strategic coast defence option for each management unit.

In broad terms there are four options:

- do nothing
- hold the existing defence line by maintaing or changing the standard of protection
- advance the existing defence line
- retreat the existing defence line.

Durlston–Hurst Spit Shoreline Management Plan
Eastern boundary is at Hurst Spit, Hampshire
Lead authority: Bournemouth Borough Council

Portland–Durlston Shoreline Management Plan
Lead authority: West Dorset District Council

Lyme Bay and South Devon Shoreline Management Plan
Western boundary is at Devon–Cornwall border

Lyme Regis
Charmouth
Seatown
West Bay
9.5km limit
19km limit
Weymouth
Preston
Ringstead Bay
Chiswell
F
The Shambles
Portland Bill
Cell boundary
St Alban's Head
Swanage
Durlston Head
Poole
Bournemouth
Christchurch
Christchurch Bay
Hengistbury Head
Poole Bay
9.5km limit
19km limit
Cell boundary

Key
Coast protection works (Source: MAFF)
Flood defences (Source: Environment Agency)
F Flood warning scheme
Net longshore sediment transport
Offshore sediment transport
N
0   10
km

West Bay.

Chesil Beach.

Lulworth.

Figure 2.18 *Major sediment cells, sub-cells, and SMPs on a section of the Dorset coast.*
Source: *Coastal Defence on the Dorset Coast* Dorset Coast Forum, 1999.

What types of coast exist?

Coasts are very diverse, and there have been many attempts to describe the range of coastal types and coastlines. These descriptions are based on a number of factors (including those in Figure 2.19).

Factors	Characteristics	Examples
1 Topography	**A** Bold and high **B** Low	Lulworth Ranges (Dorset) Studland Bay (Dorset)
2 Plan form	**A** Straight **B** Sinous	Atlantic seaboard (USA) Studland Bay and Poole Harbour (Dorset)
3 Rock type/lithology	**A** Hard rock (e.g. chalk, limestone, and igneous rocks) **B** Soft rock (e.g. clays and boulder clays)	Lulworth Ranges (Dorset) and Cornwall Weymouth Bay and Red End Point (Studland, Dorset)
4 Geological structure and the trend of geology	**A** Atlantic (discordant) coastlines (geology is at right angles to the coasts) **B** Pacific (concordant) coastlines (geological trend is parallel to coastline)	south-west Ireland, Studland Bay and Swanage (Dorset) California and south coast of Dorset around Lulworth
5 Degree of human modification	**A** Natural **B** Modified **C** Extensively modified	south-west Ireland, Maldives parts of Weymouth Bay (Dorset) New Jersey (USA) and Portsmouth Harbour (Hants) and Venice
6 (Valentin's classification) Sea-level variations and dominant marine processes	**A** Advancing coasts **B** Retreating coasts	
7 Coastal ecosystems	**A** Predominantly aquatic environments • Sandy foreshores • Shingle foreshores • Lagoons • Muddy foreshores • Salt-marshes • Estuaries • Rocky foreshores **B** Predominantly terrestrial environments • Sand dunes • Shingle formations • Earth (soft rock) cliffs • Rocky cliffs • Reclaimed land • The submarine fringe	 Daytona Beach (Florida) Towyn (North Wales) Venice Poole Harbour Essex coast Thames estuary Cornwall, Gower, Lulworth Cove (Dorset) Studland Bay (Dorset) Chesil Beach (Dorset) Red End Point (Studland Bay, Dorset) Lulworth Cove (Dorset) around Venice and San Francisco Towyn (North Wales)

Figure 2.19   *Table of selected factors used to describe coastal types and coastlines.*

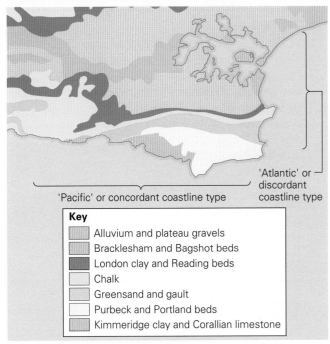

'Pacific' or concordant coastline type

'Atlantic' or discordant coastline type

Key

- Alluvium and plateau gravels
- Bracklesham and Bagshot beds
- London clay and Reading beds
- Chalk
- Greensand and gault
- Purbeck and Portland beds
- Kimmeridge clay and Corallian limestone

Figure 2.20 *The geology of the Dorset coast highlighting 'Pacific' and 'Atlantic' coastline types.*

Erosion = uplift

ADVANCING COAST

Uplift

Erosion — Deposition

Submergence

RETREATING COAST

Deposition = submergence

- **Retreating coasts** include submerged coats and coasts where the rate of erosion is rapid. Submerged coasts often have drowned river valleys (rias) and submerged fjords.
- **Advancing coasts** include emerged coastlines and coasts where there is extensive deposition. Features of emerged coastlines include raised beaches, coastal plains, fossil cliff lines.

Figure 2.21 *Valentin's classification of advancing coasts and retreating coasts.*

(a)

(b)

Figure 2.22 *Two examples of Pacific (concordant) coastlines* (a) *Stairhole, Lulworth, Dorset.* (b) *Sausalito, California.*

(a)

(b)

Figure 2.23 *Two examples of Atlantic (discordant) coastlines* (a) *Red End Point and Old Harry Rocks, Studland Bay, Dorset* (b) *Caherdanil, south-west Ireland.*

Coastlines of erosion and coastlines of accretion

The most widely used way of classifying coastlines is to divide coasts into coastlines of erosion and coastlines of **accretion** (deposition). These have very different processes, conflicts and management methods.

Accretion is a feature of the UK's sheltered coasts and estuaries, where low current speeds allow sediment to be deposited. The Royal Commission on Coastal Erosion estimated that through accretion and subsequent artificial reclamation, Britain may gain up to seven times more land per year than is lost to erosion.

Plants can play a key role in accretionary processes, for example in salt-marshes and sand dunes. The main elements of accretion are wave-built ridges of sand and shingle; sand bars, shingle bars, and beaches. These features may be due to active processes, or they may be 'fossil' features, the results of higher sea levels in Pleistocene times, for example Morecombe Bay and The Wash.

Erosion is a feature of exposed coastlines. It can be very slow, but continuous, for example the great cliffed coastlines of Cornwall and the chalk cliffs of the south and east coasts of England; or very rapid, for example Holderness, where the boulder clay cliffs, which run for 61.5km north of the Humber estuary, have been retreating at an average rate of approximately 1m per year for over 1000 years.

Erosion is caused by ocean currents, tidal movement, wave and wind action. It produces vast amounts of sediments, in the form of muds, silts, and sands that are in constant movement in the marine coastal system.

ACTIVITIES

1 At this stage you should have a sound understanding that coasts are important, varied, and need effective management. A useful summary task is to produce your own glossary of key terms for each section of your work. Be sure you can precisely define:
coastal zone
supratidal (backshore/upper beach)
inter-tidal (foreshore/lower beach)
nearshore/EEZ
offshore
ICZM
coastal defence
coast protection
flood or sea defence
'set-back' line
terminal groyne syndrome
shoreline management plan (SMP)
lithology
hard rock
soft rock
geological structure
Atlantic/discordant coastlines
Pacific/concordant coastlines
advancing coastlines
retreating coastlines
erosion
deposition/accretion

2 Review the photos in this section and try to identify as many coastal landforms as you can.

2 Coastal systems and processes

Coasts are dynamic, they are places of constant change. The changes are the result of four independent controlling influences. Two of these, global tectonics and relative land–sea-level changes, can operate over very long timescales. The third influence is intervention by humans which may have a short-term or rapid impact, for example sea defences, port development, recreation, industrial or residential development. The fourth influence is that of the natural processes of coastal erosion and deposition (accretion). We will focus on these short-term natural processes in this section, and explore how waves, tides, winds, and mass movement processes can change the form of the coast within our lifetimes. The three key questions we will focus on are:

- What are the energy and sediment inputs into the coastal system?
- What are the processes that erode coasts?
- How is sediment transported and deposited?

We will then bring the key ideas together to review the processes and factors that influence the landforms that make up the Dorset coast.

ACTIVITIES

1 Produce your own version of the diagram in Figure 2.24 and annotate it to explain the various sources of coastal sediment.

Sources of coastal sediment

The narrow zone between high and low water (known as the **littoral** zone) is a place where energy and sediment concentrate. The energy sources include wind, waves, and tidal currents. The sediments on the coast include sand, shingle, and clay.

Under natural conditions, there is always a balance between the *energy* levels and the *sediment* movements so that erosion taking place in one location is balanced by deposition taking place somewhere else.

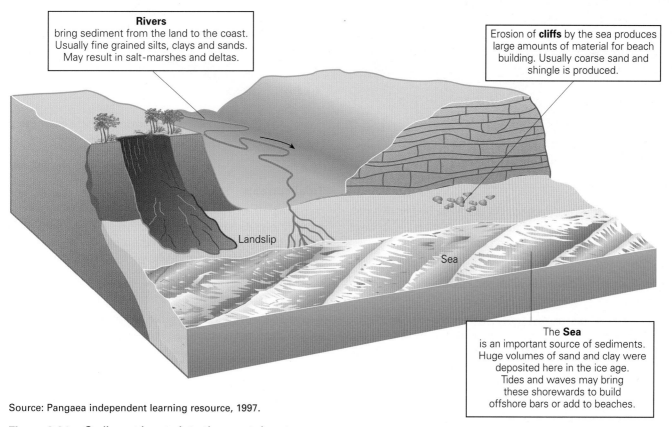

Rivers bring sediment from the land to the coast. Usually fine grained silts, clays and sands. May result in salt-marshes and deltas.

Erosion of **cliffs** by the sea produces large amounts of material for beach building. Usually coarse sand and shingle is produced.

Landslip

Sea

The **Sea** is an important source of sediments. Huge volumes of sand and clay were deposited here in the ice age. Tides and waves may bring these shorewards to build offshore bars or add to beaches.

Source: Pangaea independent learning resource, 1997.

Figure 2.24 *Sediment inputs into the coastal system.*

Sources of coastal energy

There are three main energy sources at work in the coastal zone: the wind, waves, and currents.

The wind

On beaches with shallow, offshore gradients and a large supply of sandy sediment, the wind can be very effective at moving sand inland to produce sand dunes. These often produce important ecosystems that favour specialised plants designed to cope with lack of nutrients, lack of fresh water, and constantly shifting sand.

Examples of important dune fields include the Ainsdale dunes in Lancaster, the Oxwich Bay dunes in South Wales (Figure 2.25) and the Studland dunes of Dorset.

Figure 2.25 *Oxwich Bay dunes, South Wales.*

Figure 2.26 *The fetch power of waves. Burton Bradstock, Dorset. Note the large Atlantic waves.*

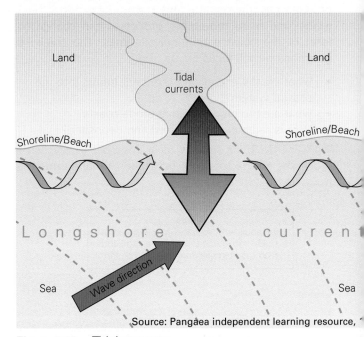

Source: Pangaea independent learning resource,

Figure 2.27 *Tidal currents.*

Waves

The power of waves depends on the wave height. A small increase in wave height produces a large increase in wave energy. The wave height depends largely on:

- the speed of the wind
- the length of time the wind has been blowing over the sea.

This depends on the distance – or **fetch** – over which the wind has been able to blow across water. In Britain, the maximum fetch is west and south-west across the Atlantic. The North Sea coast has a lower fetch. By a happy accident Britain's most resistant rocks (on the west coast) face the highest energy waves from the Atlantic. If the weak boulder clay cliffs of Norfolk and Yorkshire were on the west, little would remain!

Tidal currents

Incoming (flood) and outgoing (ebb) tidal currents can move fine-grained sand and silts. Even coarse sand can be moved if it has been first stirred up by wave action. Tidal currents are most powerful where:

- the tide range is high
- the coastline is a funnel shape.

Where the waves hit the shore at an angle, they set up longshore currents that can move vast quantities of sand and silt.

Erosion at the coast

Erosion can best be seen in action on cliff coastlines. It is most rapid on soft rock coastlines. The processes responsible for cliff erosion can be classified into two types:

- Those that are active at the base of the cliff, known as **cliff-foot** or **marine processes**. These include the three main processes of hydraulic action, **corrasion**, and attrition.
- Those that are active on the cliff face, known as cliff-face or **sub-aerial processes**. These involve the action of weathering and mass movement processes on the face of the cliff.

Although the processes are relatively simple, the patterns of erosion are quite complex, as they are influenced by a wide range of factors including:

- rock type – its resistance to wave action, its resistance to sub-aerial processes (for example landslides and gulleying), and its solubility (for example limestones are one of the more soluble rock types).
- rock **structure** – the way the rock is divided by joints, bedding planes, and faults. Erosion takes place in joints, cracks, and bedding planes. Landward dipping rocks often give steeper cliffs.
- beach character – a wide beach may be protective and halt erosion even on weak cliffs. The size of the beach may vary with the seasons. The beach may shrink if erosion and sediment supply is reduced 'updrift' by sea walls or groynes. Offshore dredging may remove beach material from the coast zone.
- fetch and currents – the fetch of the dominant (biggest) waves, the fetch of the prevailing (most frequent) waves, and the influence of tidal and longshore currents.

Hydraulic action is the action of breaking waves on cliffs. A storm may throw hundreds of tonnes of water against a cliff face with every breaker. The shock of the impact can loosen rocks and air trapped in joints and faults can blast the rock with pressures up to 50 kg/cc.

Corrasion is the process by which pebbles and sand flung against cliffs succeed in wearing away new rock. Corrasion (sometimes referred to as abrasion) produces wave-cut notches under cliffs and – eventually – wave-cut platforms. For corrasion to continue, attrition must be effective.

Attrition is the process by which erosion continues to operate by grinding down cliff fall material.

After hydraulic action and corrasion have eroded cliffs, the eroded material lies at the base of the cliff, forming a protective armour which is often too large for the sea to move. By grinding smaller particles against these large blocks and they are eventually reduced in size until the sea can move them away.

(a) *Hydraulic action.*

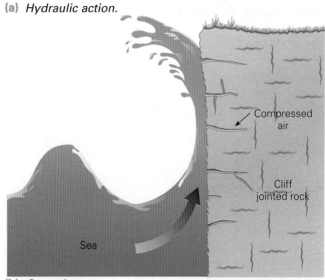

(b) *Corrasion.*

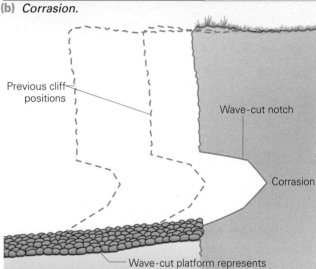

(c) *Attrition.*

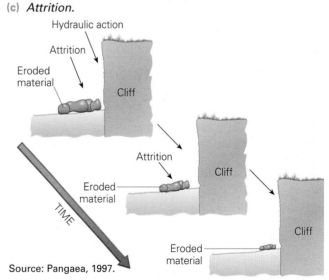

Source: Pangaea, 1997.

Figure 2.28 *Erosional processes at the cliff face.*

Cliff-face processes

(a) *Cliff top, highlighting cliff face processes.*

Figure 2.29   *Cliffs at Barton-on-Sea, Hampshire.*

(b) *Basal section, highlighting cliff foot and marine processes.*

Soft, easily eroded cliffs of clay, boulder clay and poorly cemented sandstone are common around the south and east coasts of England, from Black Ven at Charmouth in Dorset to Holderness on Humberside. Weathering and mass movement processes active at the cliff top and on the cliff face, transport material downslope to the foot of the cliff, thus reducing the upper slope size and angle. These processes reflect the geological character of the cliffs, i.e. rock type and structure, the groundwater conditions, and the degree to which the cliff has been colonised and stabilised by plants.

Weathering is the breakdown of rocks where they are located. There are two types:

- mechanical weathering, which physically splits the rock into small fractions, for example freeze–thaw weathering
- chemical weathering, which dissolves or corrodes rocks, for example weak acids on rocks containing $CaCO_3$ (including chalk and limestones).

Mass movement processes include a variety of types, all of which move material downslope under the influence of gravity. The type of mass movement that takes place depends on how dry or wet the material in motion is, and the speed of the movement. Rock avalanches or cliff collapse, for example, are rapid, dry movements. Landslips and landslides of blocks of land can be slower, and involve water acting as a lubricant on a line of weakness within the cliff. Slumping is similar but is caused by the total disintegration of the structure of the cliff as it falls.

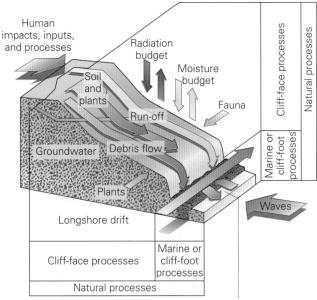

Sand and shingle sediment can migrate into the beach zone from offshore sources, and be returned to the seabed by shore-normal processes. This material input supplements material brought into the area by longshore drift and erosion of the cliff top and face.

Figure 2.30   *Cliff-face and cliff-foot processes within soft-rock cliff systems.*

ACTIVITIES

Study Figures 2.29 and 2.30. Explain how cliff-face and cliff-foot processes interact to produce coastal erosion.

Transport and deposition

Waves approaching at right angles to the coast move material up the beach if the waves are constructive. Constructive waves have a long wavelength but low height. Destructive waves are closer together and higher. As they plunge on the beach they comb down material and flatten the beach gradient.

Waves breaking on a beach at an oblique angle move sand and shingle by the process of longshore drift. The breaking wave (the swash) moves material up the beach at an angle whilst the returning water (backwash) moves the material back at right angles to the beach. The net effect is a longshore movement.

Offshore, the build up of water against the coastline creates a current parallel to the shore. Whilst it can only move sand-sized sediments, it is capable of moving tens of thousands of tonnes of sand per year.

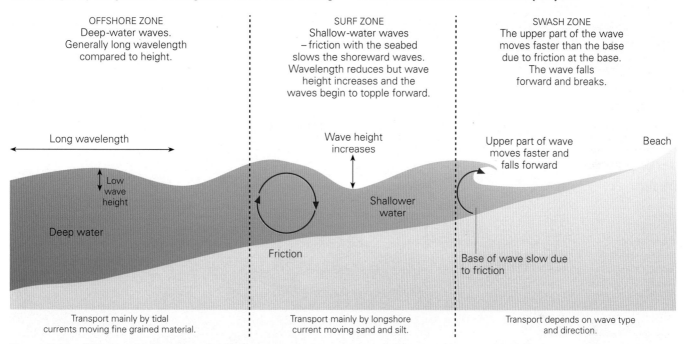

OFFSHORE ZONE
Deep-water waves. Generally long wavelength compared to height.

SURF ZONE
Shallow-water waves – friction with the seabed slows the shoreward waves. Wavelength reduces but wave height increases and the waves begin to topple forward.

SWASH ZONE
The upper part of the wave moves faster than the base due to friction at the base. The wave falls forward and breaks.

Long wavelength

Wave height increases

Upper part of wave moves faster and falls forward

Beach

Low wave height

Shallower water

Deep water

Friction

Base of wave slow due to friction

Transport mainly by tidal currents moving fine grained material.

Transport mainly by longshore current moving sand and silt.

Transport depends on wave type and direction.

Figure 2.31 *Transport takes place in three zones.* Source: Pangaea independent learning resource, 1997

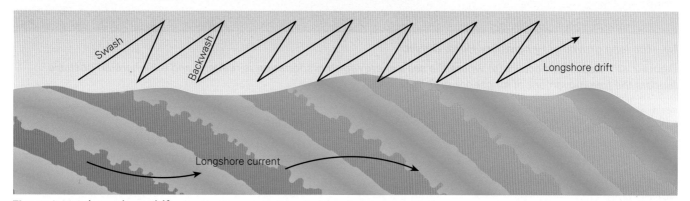

Swash

Backwash

Longshore drift

Longshore current

Figure 2.32 *Longshore drift.* Source: Pangaea independent learning resource, 1997

The sea produces a variety of depositional forms. The most common depositional form is the beach.

Beaches usually align themselves to the dominant (most powerful) waves. This is known as swash alignment and can be seen in the three beaches in Figure 2.34.

Swash alignment is also seen in offshore bars. These form in areas with plentiful offshore sediment (especially glacial sands and gravels left from the ice age), During times of constructive wave activity sediment may sweep inshore to form small bars. If these are colonised by vegetation they may become semi-permanent features.

Spits are more usually aligned with the longshore drift direction and are therefore said to be drift aligned.

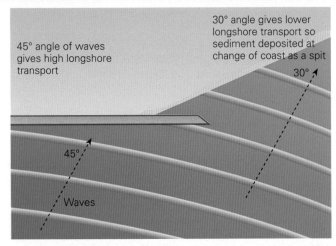

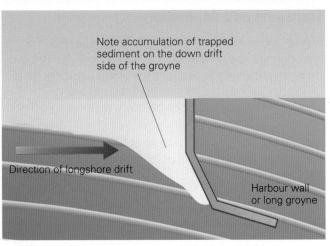

(a) *The smaller the angle of the wave, the lower its ability to carry sediment.*

(b) *An obstacle causes sediment to be deposited.*

(c) *The long groyne at Hengistbury Head, Dorset.*

Figure 2.33   *Deposition occurs* **(a)** *where the sea's energy for transportation is reduced and* **(b)** *where an obstacle hinders the free movement of longshore drift material.*

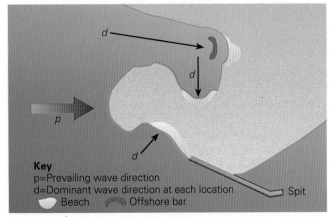

Figure 2.34   *Depositional landforms. Beaches and swash alignment.*   Source: Pangaea independent learning resource, 1997

ACTIVITIES

1 Produce an annotated diagram to explain how a coast can be regarded as a system with energy and material inputs and outputs.

2 Study Figure 2.35 which shows the factors and processes which influence the form of the Dorset coast. Research another area of coastline known to you and try to produce a similar analytic diagram.

3 Scan through the photographs of the Dorset coast in this chapter so far: Figures 2.5, 2.18, 2.22, 2.26, 2.35. Identify the landforms present in these photographs. Select two contrasting images and produce an annotated diagram for each to explain the processes responsible for their formation.

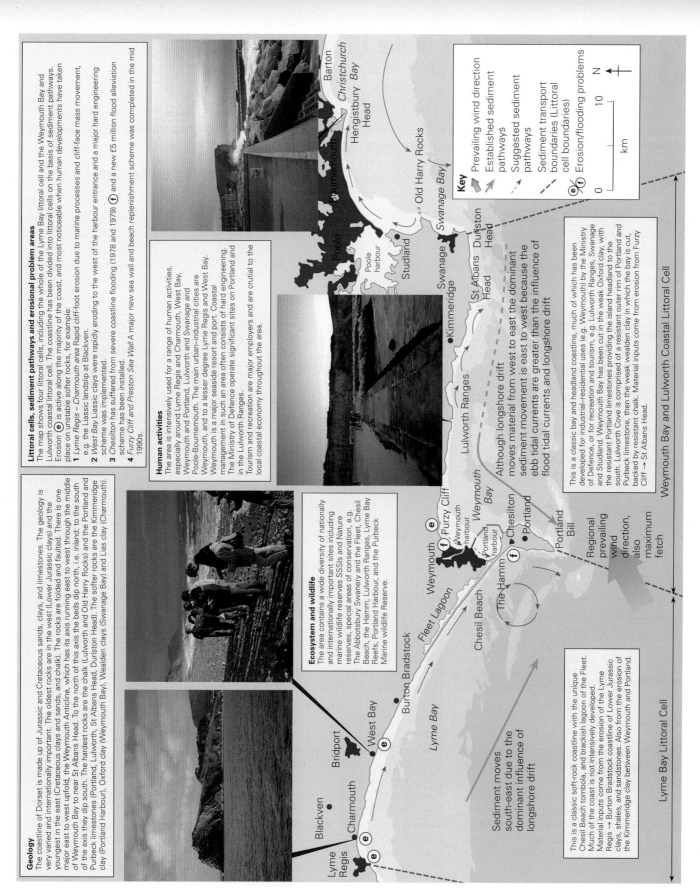

Geology
The coastline of Dorset is made up of Jurassic and Cretaceous sands, clays, and limestones. The geology is very varied and internationally important. The oldest rocks are in the west (Lower Jurassic clays) and the youngest in the east (Cretaceous clays and sands, and chalk). The rocks are folded and faulted. There is one major east to west upfold, the Weymouth Anticline, which has its axis running east to west through the middle of Weymouth Bay to near St Albans Head. To the north of this axis the beds dip north, i.e. inland; to the south of the axis they dip south. The hardest rocks are the chalk (Lulworth and Old Harry Rocks) and the Portland and Purbeck limestones (Portland, Lulworth, St Albans Head, Durlston Head). The softer rocks are the Kimmeridge clay (Portland Harbour), Oxford clay (Weymouth Bay), Wealden clays (Swanage Bay) and Lias clay (Charmouth).

Littoral cells, sediment pathways and erosional problem areas
The map shows four littoral cells, including the whole of the Lyme Bay littoral cell and the Weymouth Bay and Lulworth coastal littoral cell. The coastline has been divided into littoral cells on the basis of sediment pathways. Erosion (e) is active along the majority of the coast, and most noticeable when human developments have taken place on unstable softer rocks, for example:
1 *Lyme Regis – Charmouth area* Rapid cliff-foot erosion due to marine processes and cliff-face mass movement, e.g. the Liassic landslip at Blackven.
2 *West Bay* Liassic clays were rapidly eroding to the west of the harbour entrance and a major hard engineering scheme was implemented.
3 *Chesilton* has suffered from severe coastline flooding (1978 and 1979) (f) and a new £5 million flood alleviation scheme has been installed.
4 *Furzy Cliff and Preston Sea Wall* A major new sea wall and beach replenishment scheme was completed in the mid 1990s.

Human activities
The area is intensively used for a range of human activities, especially around Lyme Regis and Charmouth, West Bay, Weymouth and Portland, Lulworth and Swanage and Poole-Bournemouth. The main urban–industrial cities are Weymouth, and to a lesser degree Lyme Regis and West Bay. Weymouth is a major seaside resort and port. Coastal management in such an area often consists of hard engineering. The Ministry of Defence operate significant sites on Portland and in the Lulworth Ranges.
Tourism and recreation are major employers and are crutial to the local coastal economy throughout the area.

Ecosystem and wildlife
The area contains a wide diversity of nationally and internationally important sites including marine wildlife reserves SSSIs and Nature reserves, special areas of conservation, e.g. The Abbotsbury Swanery and the Fleet, Chesil Beach, the Hamm, Lulworth Ranges, Lyme Bay Reefs, Portland Harbour, and the Purbeck Marine wildlife Reserve.

This is a classic soft-rock coastline with the unique Chesil Beach tombola, and brackish lagoon of the Fleet. Much of the coast is not intensively developed. Material inputs come from the erosion of the Lyme Regis → Burton Bradstock coastline of Lower Jurassic clays, shales, and sandstones. Also from the erosion of the Kimmeridge clay between Weymouth and Portland.

This is a classic bay and headland coastline, much of which has been developed for industrial-residential uses (e.g. Weymouth) by the Ministry of Defence, or for recreation and tourism, e.g. Lulworth Ranges, Swanage and Studland. Weymouth Bay has been cut in the weak Oxford clay, with the resistant Portland limestones providing the island headland to the south. Lulworth Cove is comprised of a resistant outer rim of Portland and Purbeck limestone, then the weak wealden clay in which the bay is cut, backed by resistant chalk. Material inputs come from erosion from Furzy Cliff → St Albans Head.

Sediment moves south-east due to the dominant influence of longshore drift

Although longshore drift moves material from west to east the dominant sediment movement is east to west because the ebb tidal currents are greater than the influence of flood tidal currents and longshore drift

Key
Prevailing wind direction
Established sediment pathways
Suggested sediment pathways
Sediment transport pathways
Littoral cell boundaries (Littoral cell boundaries)
(e) (f) Erosion/flooding problems

N
0   10
km

Lyme Bay Littoral Cell
Weymouth Bay and Lulworth Coastal Littoral Cell

Regional prevailing wind direction, also maximum fetch

Lyme Regis
Blackven
Charmouth
Bridport
West Bay
Burton Bradstock
Lyme Bay
Chesil Beach
The Hamm
Fleet Lagoon
Weymouth
Furzy Cliff
Weymouth harbour
Portland harbour
Weymouth Bay
Chesilton
Portland
Portland Bill
Lulworth Ranges
Kimmeridge
St Albans Head
Swanage
Durlston Head
Swanage Bay
Studland
Old Harry Rocks
Poole harbour
Poole
Bournemouth
Hengistbury Head
Christchurch Bay
Barton

Figure 2.35   *Factors and processes that influence the form of the Dorset coast.*

3 Coastal ecosystems in the UK: A case study of sand dunes

In this section we consider the diversity of coastal ecosystems primarily in the UK, focusing on sand-dune ecosystems in the UK, and undertake a detailed case study of managing coastal dunes at Oxwich on the Gower peninsula south Wales. We consider the following key questions:

- What types of coastal ecosystems occur in the UK?
- Where are the coastal sand-dune systems located, and what types of dune systems and dune habitats can be recognised in the UK and at Oxwich Bay?
- How do these ecosystems form?
- What human activities threaten these ecosystems?
- How is the sand dune environment at Oxwich managed?

Coastal environments and ecosystems

12 different types of coastal ecosystems and environments can be identified in the UK. These include extensive areas of salt-marsh and sand dunes, but, because of the northerly location of the UK, no mangroves or coral reefs. (There is a case study of the Maldive coral reefs in section 4).

Environment	Definition	Named examples and occurrence	Types of pressure	Conservation and management
1 Shingle foreshore	Coarse sediments greater than 2 mm in diameter which occur along 900 km of the UK coast, as spits, bars, cuspate forelands and offshore barrier islands.	Hurst Castle spit The Loe, Cornwall Chesil Beach, Dorset Dungeness, Kent	Human – coastal protection schemes, removal of shingle for building, recreational pressure, grazing. Natural – erosion.	Lack of access and difficulty with walking on shingle is best form of protection. Car park restrictions, reduction of gravel extraction.
2 Lagoons	Shallow bodies of brackish or sea water, partially separated from an adjacent coastal sea by a barrier of sand or shingle.	Found on low-lying coasts, e.g. eastern seaboard of the USA and the Gulf of Mexico: The Fleet, Weymouth, Dorset Zuider Zee, Netherlands	Human – usage as harbours, aqua-culture, recreation and industry. Problems include water quality, reclamation, coastal protection schemes. Natural – siltation.	Reduce dumping of untreated sewage agricultural inputs and industrial pollution. Divert discharges away from sensitive ecological areas.
3 Muddy foreshore	Extensive flat areas of fine-grained sediment in a low energy environment. They are rich in organic debris and are the main feeding medium for migratory wading birds.	Sheltered parts of embayments, estuaries or behind shingle formations or sand dunes: Morecambe Bay Poole Harbour Humberside Solway Firth Portsmouth Harbour (Figure 2.1)	Human – shellfish industries, wildfowling, recreation, birdwatching. Main pressures: 1 land reclamation 2 poor water quality from untreated sewage and industrial effluents. Eutrophication.	Reduce land reclamation. Create more nature reserves. Concentrate access points where they will have least adverse effect on the ecology. Improve treatment of discharges.
4 Salt-marshes	Natural or semi-natural halophytic grassland on alluvial sediments bordering saline water bodies whose water level fluctuates and whose salinity ranges from 5% to 38%.	Sheltered areas of slow sedimentation and low erosion: New England, USA The Fleet, Weymouth, Dorset East Anglian Fens Essex coastline	Natural stress is rare, e.g. increased sedimentation or erosion. Human pressure is extensive: 1 agriculture leads to compaction, turf-layer destruction, application of nitrogen	Manage grazing practised by stocking densities. Reduce spraying and the introduction of foreign species. Reduce land reclamation and marina developments.

[cont]

			and phosphorous fertilisers changes the species composition. 2 land reclamation and drainage. 3 pollution – from agricultural wastes, fertiliser outwash, urban sewage and industrial effluents. 4 recreation.	Purify water before discharge.
5 Rocky foreshores and cliffs	Coastal environment dominated by the outcrop of resistant bare rock as inaccessible cliffs with irregular masses of extensive boulder beaches. Cliffs tend to be high, steep, stable, wave or spray-beaten with little vegetation.	Occur around upland areas, where the harder igneous and metamorphic rocks are found. Also older resistant sedimentary rocks, e.g. Carboniferous limestone Old Red Sandstone. The Lizard and Lands End, Cornwall Gower coast, South Wales Dorset	Pollution, oil spills, outfalls from urban-industrial areas, fishing, nuclear power stations, recreation e.g. long distance coastal footpaths. Limited natural pressures.	Naturally protected by their remoteness. Waste treatment and disposal improvements in coastal townships. Improved oil-spill reatments. Protective ownership and establishment of reserves with reduced access.
6 Sand dunes	Coarse sediments deposited and transported by wind and stabilised by vegetation. Very sensitive to human disruption.	Oxwich Bay, Gower (Figure 2.25) Studland Bay, Dorset Culbin, Moray Firth, Scotland	Limited natural . pressures. Humans can introduce or remove species directly or indirectly by changing environmental factors	Sand stabilisation using dune stabilising grasses and sand fences. Reducing public access to limit trampling. Constructing reinforced artificial walkways.
7 Reclaimed land	An artificially created coastal environment that ranges from partly ditched high level salt marshes, to intensively managed land used for agriculture. Majority consists of an enclosing reclamation bank containing an area with drainage ditches.	Portsmouth Harbour, (Figure 2.1) The Wash Southampton Water Delta Plan and Zuider Zee, Netherlands Land for agriculture, residential development, industry, airports, power stations, ports.	Despite its artificial origins, historical reclaimed land is often ecologically valuable. This is being threatened by recent agricultural improvements, e.g. conversion to arable land, land drainage, use of fertilisers and herbicides. The habitat is also threatened by urban expansion and recreational activities.	Protection by preventing drainage, ploughing, controlled grazing, cutting down invasive scrub, creation of new niche habitats, controlled public access.

Figure 2.36   *Management of selected coastal ecosystems and environments.*

ACTIVITIES

1 Use Figure 2.36 to compare and contrast management of salt-marshes, muddy foreshores, and sand-dune ecosystems.
2 Ecosystems are defined as a biological community of any scale in which organisms interact with their physical environment. To what extent is artificially reclaimed land an ecosystem?
3 What factors might help explain the diversity of coastal ecosystems and environments in the UK?
4 What coastal ecosystems are at greatest risk?
5 Which human activities appear to be threatening most coastal environments?

Distribution of coastal sand dune ecosystems in the British Isles

The 400 km of coastal dunes are an important landform type and habitat of the British Isles and make up 9 per cent of the coastline (Figure 2.37). These 56,000 ha are concentrated in western Ireland, the Western Isles, and the east coast of Scotland, Wales (e.g. Oxwich Bay) and the north coast of south-west England (e.g. Braunton Burrows) and north-east England. They are relatively rare on the south coast, the famous exceptions include Dawlish Warren (Devon), Studland Bay (Dorset), and Sandwich (Kent). Most are calcareous in composition, but some are more acidic e.g. Dawlish Warren and Studland, or of mixed composition e.g. Holy Island, Lindisfarne.

For large sand-dune complexes to form the following conditions are needed:

- a regular and plentiful supply of sediment
- a wide, sandy beach exposed at low tide
- onshore winds strong enough to move some grains
- adequate vegetation to stabilise the dunes
- protection from humans and storms that would erode the dunes.

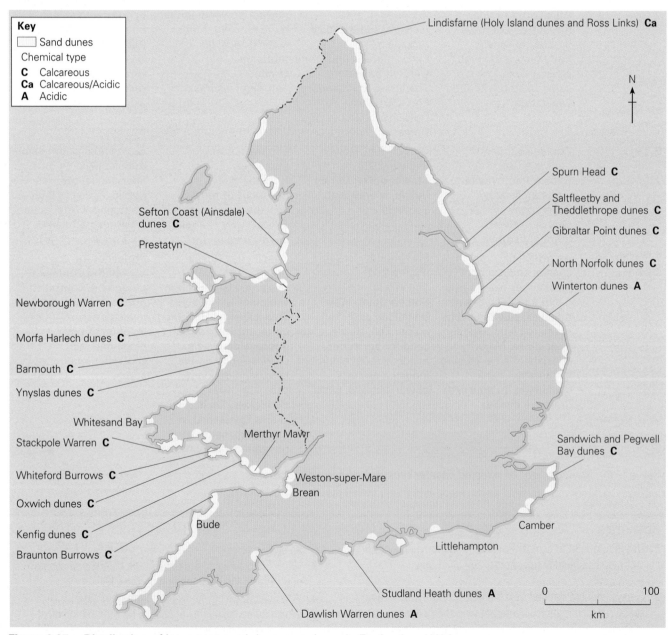

Figure 2.37   *Distribution of important sand-dune complexes in England and Wales.*

The formation of the sand-dune complex at Oxwich Bay National Nature Reserve

Oxwich is one of several sand-dune complexes in south Wales, and lies on the southern side of the Gower peninsula. Oxwich Bay is very shallow, often no more than 10 m deep and has a 3.5 km wide, flat, sandy beach backed by sand dunes (Figure 2.39). These sand dunes, together with the salt-marsh and fresh-water marsh, are of national ecological importance for botanists and birdwatchers, and are under pressure from recreation

Oxwich Bay has been cut into the weaker Carboniferous Millstone Grit, a series of shales and sandstones, and is protected to the south-west by the resistant Carboniferous Limestone of Oxwich Point. These rocks were laid down around 300 million years ago, and have subsequently been folded. The sand-dune complex trends west-south-west to east-north-east, and is much younger, around 2500 years old (Figure 2.40).

The dunes began to form around 500BC when a combination of tides and waves formed an offshore barrier, across the bay. The lagoon trapped behind the sand dunes eventually silted up with sand blown in from the beach and dunes. This led to the creation of the associated fresh-water and salt-marshes, much of which was reclaimed in the 16th century, by ditching and draining, to provide grazing for livestock. In the 18th century a sea wall was constructed to prevent high tides flooding the area; this disrupted the natural drainage so that today the area is again a marsh.

> **ACTIVITIES**
>
> 1 Make your own copy of the three diagrams in Figure 2.40 and annotate them to explain the evolution of Oxwich Bay and the sand-dune complex.

Today the sand-dune complex at Oxwich Bay is in a state of **dynamic equilibrium**; continually responding to the changing interactions between geological, physiological (climate and soil), geomorphological (wind and tidal processes), and human (including recreation and management) factors.

Three distinct constants can be recognised:

1 the amount of sand decreases westwards

2 the height of the sand dunes decreases westwards

3 the maximum recreational use increases westwards

Habitats are continually changing in their composition and structure.

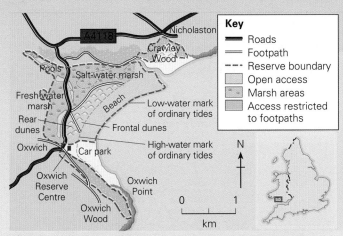

Figure 2.38 *Site map of Oxwich Bay, south Wales.*
Source: Nature Conservancy Council, 1987.

Figure 2.39 *An aerial view of Oxwich Bay, south Wales.*

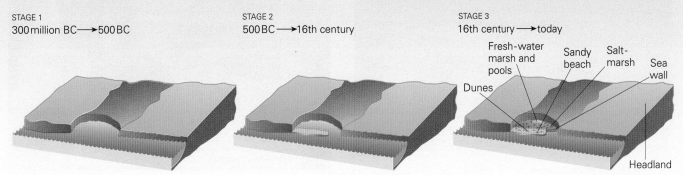

Figure 2.40 *The three stages in the evolution of the Oxwich Bay sand-dune complex.*

Habitats within the Oxwich Bay sand-dune complex

Today, various types of habitat can be recognised within the sand-dune complex at Oxwich Bay:

1 embryonic dunes

2 fore dunes (Figure 2.41a)

3 mobile yellow dunes (Figure 2.41b and c)

4 fixed grey dunes (Figure 2.41d)

5 dune slacks (Figure 2.41e)

6 blow-outs (Figure 2.41f).

1 Embryonic dunes – at every low tide, aeolian (wind) processes rework the exposed sand. Winds can blow the material onshore and it accumulates around small obstacles on the beach. It can pile up around shells or driftwood. These hummocks, above the high, spring tide mark, are consolidated by plants, which can root themselves into the loose sand, for example sand couch grass. This is the first plant to establish and is the main pioneer plant as it can tolerate short immersion in salt water, and can grow up through 1.5m of sand. Other pioneers include saltwort, sea rocket, sandwort, and sea orache.

2 As embryonic dunes grow larger, they become fore dunes and can develop as a small ridge protecting the base of the main dune ridges. Successful plants put out deep taproots to search for what little water is available, or have succulent stems and leaves to conserve it.

The embryonic and fore dunes are often only temporary communities as they are the first to be attacked in severe storms and high tides, or are destroyed quickly by visitors. Bathers and tourists find them very attractive sitting areas, and consequently they are quickly trampled. They can occasionally be seen at the eastern end of the Oxwich Bay site, which is less frequented by visitors. Dominant plant species include seawheat grass and marram grass (Figure 2.41a).

3 Mobile yellow dunes – these are challenging environments for plants and animals. The mobile yellow dunes are located at the seaward side of a dune system, and are the most impressive dunes in the complex, being up to 30 m high (Figure 2.41b). On a hot day, surface sand temperatures can reach 60°C. There is little organic material present in the sub-surface layer, and because sand is a poor heat conductor, temperatures at this depth are much cooler. At night, dew is deposited when moist air comes into contact with the cooler sand grains. Any rain that does occur is not only eagerly absorbed by plants, but it also helps wash salt (NaCl) out of the sand. This community is dominated by marram grass, which has extensive underground stems, enabling the grass to absorb water from deep in the sand. Marram grass grows quickly when covered by new sand, and is well adapted, with shiny rolled leaves, to reduce losses by evapotranspiration (Figure 2.41b and c). Other species present can include sand sedge, sealyme grass, euphorbia, sea holly, red fescue, and sea bindweed (Figure 2.41c).

(a) *Foreshore and foredunes.*

(b) *Mobile yellow dunes.*

Figure 2.41 *Oxwich National Nature Reserve.*

(c) *Marram grass on mobile yellow dunes.*

4 Fixed grey dunes – there is a transition from the mobile yellow dunes to the older and more stable fixed grey dunes which occur further inland, and are too far from the sea and fresh sediment supply to continue growing (Figure 2.41d). The process obviously takes time, and therefore the organic humus content of the sand has built up, and become sufficient to support a greater range of species. The soil is no longer NaCl rich, but may locally be $CaCO_3$ rich, due to numerous concentrations of shell material present in the sand. Marram grass has now disappeared and is replaced by a wide range of species including heather, bracken, bramble, carline thistle, dewberry, evening primrose, wild privet, wild clematis, and even elder in more established areas. Moister areas can contain mosses and lichens. Many of these dunes have taken hundreds of years to mature.

(e)   *Dune slacks.*

6 Blow-outs (Figure 2.41f) – these can occur in the mobile dune belt where strong winds from unusual directions have broken through the dune vegetation cover to scour large, semi-circular hollows (Figure 2.41f). The process starts by the removal of the protective vegetation cover often by trampling. Blow-outs can persist for a long time before eventually being recolonised by sand sedge and marram. Blow-outs, although less common, can even occur in the fixed grey dunes due to disturbance by rabbits, trampling holidaymakers, fire, or even trail bikers.

(d)   *Fixed grey dunes.*

These dunes can eventually be entirely colonised by either heath plants to form a dune heath or scrub plants to form a dune scrub. These in turn will be colonised by woodland species. At this stage a clear soil has developed, and will consist of a black, humus-rich surface layer of about 30 cm, a water-retentive layer overlying a light, grey 10 cm deep layer, above the sand. Animals present will include woodmice, voles, shrews, rabbits and kestrels (Figure 2.44).

5 Dune slacks – depressions between the dune ridges can infill with winter water, in flat-bottomed depressions called dune slacks (Figure 2.41e). These can remain damp even in summer, and consequently support an unusual and rich range of plant and animal species. They are very important sites, containing marsh orchids, hellebores, water mint, wintergreen, rushes, and creeping willow. Spiders and beetles are common. At the Ainsdale-Formby dunes near Merseyside, rare natterjack toads breed in such areas.

(f)   *Blow out.*

Figure 2.41   *Oxwich National Nature Reserve.*

All land-based ecosystems are the result of a process called **primary plant succession**.

Bare earth can be colonised by simple plants that have basic requirements, for example, algae, fungi, or lichens. These colonisers are often adapted to harsh conditions such as excessive heat or cold, and are either adapted to survive waterlogged (hydrophytes) or arid (xerophytes) conditions. These plants help change the land and provide nutrients and the right amount of water for future plant growth.

As plants and animals die, they release nutrients which help build up the organic content of the soil. This increased humus content allows more advanced plants to invade and colonise the area.

Each stage in the process is called a **sere**, for example xeroseres develop in dry conditions and psammoseres in sand dunes.

Eventually a final stage is reached, where the habitat is stable and dominated by advanced plants. This is known as the **climax community**. If this stage is thought to be determined by the climate it is more accurately called the **climate climax community**. In the UK this would be a temperate deciduous woodland.

When humans restrict the development of vegetation, a **plagioclimax** results, for example savannah grasslands. Alternatively succession can be arrested by poor soils, and a **sub-climax** results, for example scrub rather than woodland.

If any type of climax vegetation is dramatically disturbed, for example by a forest fire, flood, or volcanic eruption, a secondary succession follows.

Figure 2.42   *Plant succession.*

ACTIVITIES

1 Identify five factors that explain the distribution of sand-dune ecosystems.

2 a Draw a flow diagram to explain the stages of plant succession in a psammosere (sand-dune ecosystem).

   b Annotate your diagram with evidence from an analysis of the data from Oxwich Bay (see Figure 2.43).

   c How have plants adapted to the challenges of their environment?

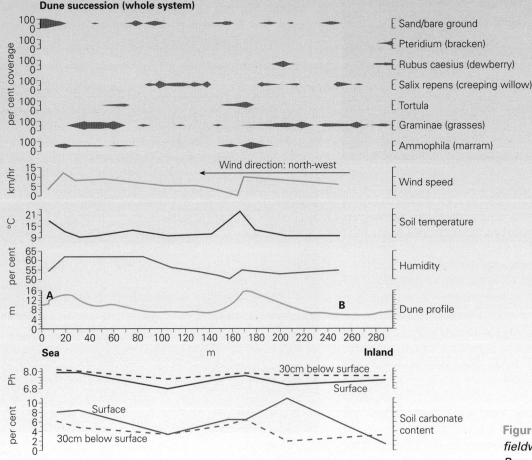

Figure 2.43   *Dune transect fieldwork data from Oxwich Bay.*

Trophic levels in a typical sand-dune ecosystem

The sand-dune ecosystem is made up of living (**biotic**) and non-living (**abiotic**) components. Generally, the level of organic material present, the **biomass**, is low because many of the sand dunes are continually moving and so biomass has little chance to become established. The rate of increase of this biomass, known as **Net Primary Productivity** (NPP) is also low. Both biomass and NPP increase further away from the sea, as conditions become less harsh. Energy and minerals move through the ecosystem and this can be shown in a variety of diagrammatic representations, for example food webs and **food chains**, and in **trophic level** diagrams (Figure 2.44).

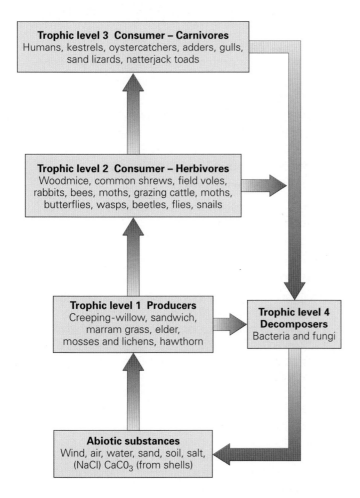

Figure 2.44 *Example of the trophic levels in a typical sand-dune ecosystem.*

Sand-dune ecosystems e.g. Studland, Oxwich are one of the most visited locations for geographical fieldwork because they provide an extensive diversity of potential issues for study, for example:

- What impact do tourists/educational parties have on the site?
- What are the main problems of the site?
- What solutions have been or are being used?
- How effective is the management?
- Has management changed over time?
- Should access and facilities be improved?
- How could increased storminess affect the site?
- Should dune bikes, dogs, and horses be banned?
- Does the impact increase with distance from the car park?
- Why does species diversity increase inland?
- Do blow-outs increase with distance from car park/beach?
- Is there a correlation between species diversity and distance from the sea, carparks, roads?

ACTIVITIES

1 For full details of how to go about investigating coastal sand dunes in the field and undertaking transect surveys, read the *Geography Review*, vol. 4, no. 2 (1990): pp. 30–34.

Human impact on sand-dune ecosystems

Throughout the UK, sand-dune ecosystems are threatened because of their proximity to the seaside and centres of human industrial and residential development. They are delicate ecosystems and can easily be disturbed by humans. At Ainsdale, near Merseyside, the main threat comes from trail biking, which destabilises the dunes, causing blow-outs. Trail biking endangers the rare breeding grounds of the natterjack toads in the wet dune, slacks, and also of the rare orchids and sand lizards. At Oxwich Bay, South Wales, and at Studland Bay in Dorset, the main threat is from the massive numbers of visitors. Oxwich Bay has over 300,000 visitors per year including 10,000 school children or students doing field studies. Yet current pressures on Oxwich Bay are minor compared with those of the 1940s. During the Second World War the RAF successfully decoyed enemy bombers away from a nearby ordnance factory and Swansea by laying out a series of lights on the Oxwich dunes, which mimicked those of the factory. In 1944, a section of the US Allied forces occupied the area to rehearse for the D-Day Normandy landings. Not surprisingly, by the mid 1940s Oxwich was described as 'a sandy waste devoid of vegetation'. However, within 20 years, much of the flora and fauna had recovered, and currently the 262ha that are managed as the Oxwich National Nature Reserve by the Countryside Council for Wales, contain over half the entire list of nature species for Wales, i.e. over 500 flowering plants, 162 birds, 272 beetles, and 530 moths.

1 Erosion	In the past, the main threat has been from recreational use. Trampling, horse riding, lighting of fires, use of vehicles, such as trail bikes, which break up the vegetation and expose the sand to the action of wind which, unchecked, can form blow-outs.
2 Afforestation	Within the last century, afforestation, which was initiated to help prevent major movements of the mobile sand, has destroyed the entire character of the vegetation in the planted areas, e.g. Newborough Warren, Angelsey.
3 Water abstraction	Lowering of the water-table may lead to the drying out of species-rich slacks, which are often breeding grounds for the rare natterjack toad.
4 Over-grazing	Heavy rabbit grazing produces an open, lichen-dominated community. Over-grazing by domestic stock can also be damaging, especially where supplementary feeding is used.
5 Intensive farming	Drainage and fertiliser application reduces plant and animal diversity through soil compaction and nutrient enrichment.
6 Sand extraction	Direct removal of sand from the beach or dunes, or indirect impact of stabilisation works elsewhere along the coast, interrupt the supply of beach material, e.g. Dawlish Warren (Devon).
7 Scrub and bracken invasion	The extensive development of bracken, coarse herbs or scrub will reduce plant diversity. This is now the main problem, e.g. Oxwich Bay.
8 Tipping of domestic waste	Visual impact. Destruction of vegetation cover. Soil compaction.
9 Reclamation for industry and transport	Complete habitat destruction associated with roads, airfields, and pipelines.
10 Development of adjacent areas	Caravan sites. Golf courses – frequent mowing, use of herbicides, manipulation of water supplies can alter the vegetation, e.g. Sandwich Bay, Kent.
11 Military training	Large areas are used for training and exercises.

Figure 2.45   *Threats to sand-dune ecosystems.*

Coastal dune management: An overview

Coastal dunes are important ecosystems containing 50 per cent of the flowering plants of Britain. They also provide an important buffer between the land and the sea, and act as a store for sediment. Because of these wide-ranging assets, and the fragile nature of coastal dunes, considerable time and money has been spent on a range of strategies to conserve and protect these habitats.

- Aiding deposition of sand on beaches by using groynes or beach replenishment.
- Moving sand with bulldozers to shape dunes.
- Replanting and watering dunes.
- Using mulches or biofabrics to help stabilise fragile dune surfaces.
- Fencing to restrict access, and banning trail bikes, horses, and dogs.
- Controlling visitors by walkways.
- Maintaining or promoting species habitat diversity.
- Education using signs, information displays and visitor centres.
- Preserving or increasing rare species.
- Removing scrub and invasive foreign species.
- Land-use zoning – providing car parks, litter bins, cafés, and toilets in less sensitive areas.
- Creating nature reserves.

Figure 2.46   *Management methods used in areas of sand dunes.*

ACTIVITIES

The Ainsdale-Formby dunes (near Merseyside) cover 800 ha, of which 670 ha form a NNR created in 1980. The site is threatened by coastal erosion at the southern end, scrub invasion, and public pressure from recreation including trail bikes, caravan and car parks, road building, and golf course developments.

1 Visit the Sefton Council website (see the reference section at the end of this unit).
2 Summarise:
    a the threats to the ecosystem
    b Sefton Council's management methods.
3 How would you plan a programme of field work (data collection and analysis) to:
    a explore the species diversity of the area
    b report on the pressures on the site, and how successfully these have been resolved.

Management of the dune system at Oxwich National Nature Reserve

At Oxwich there are three elements that need managing:

1 estate management, i.e. the day-to-day work on fences and paths
2 habitat management, i.e. managing the wildlife populations by controlling scrub invasion
3 visitor management by signposts, leaflets, and trails.

The actual methods used have varied over time. In 1978, the focus was on managing the consequences of increased leisure time and car ownership, i.e. trampling from recreation, by using sand traps, fencing, marram grass replanting schemes, patrolling, protecting the mobile dunes from erosion, as well as removing invasive bracken and fern from the fixed dunes. In 1985, a new strategy was tried when restabilisation was complete, which attempted to get a balance between the three objectives of:

- maintaining the *stability* of the dunes
- helping to promote the *diversity* of wildlife
- allowing *access* and improved *education*.

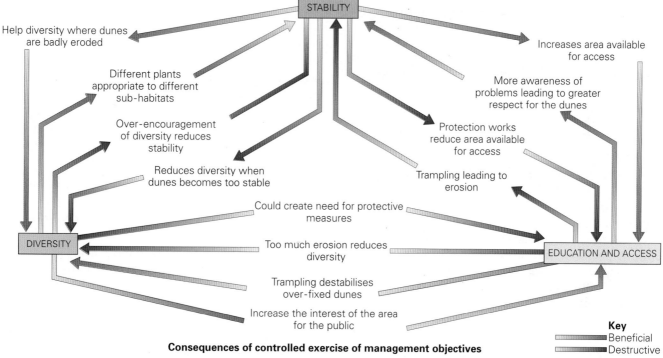

Consequences of controlled exercise of management objectives

Key
Beneficial
Destructive

Figure 2.47 *SEAD (Stability, Education, Access and Diversity) management of sand dunes at Oxwich Bay, south Wales, 1985–95.*

In the late 1990s the frontal dunes began to show signs of losing species diversity by being 'overly fixed', i.e. too stable. In the drier areas, mats of coarse red fescue and bracken became invasive. This was tackled by a range of techniques including:

- using controlled 'disaster' management. Re-establishing the conditions for the early stages in dune community development by taking succession back to square one in controlled scrapes and by re-activating blow-outs
- using feral goats to control invasive birch and alder in the dune slacks, and pony grazing in the winter to restore structural variety to the vegetation
- using selective herbicides, burning, cutting, and rotovating.

ACTIVITIES

1 Compare the management methods used at Oxwich Bay and for the national situation in the UK with those used at the Ainsdale-Formby dunes (see page 88).
2 Research the following case study:
   - 'Plant succession in salt-marshes. How does it compare to sand-dune ecosystems?' Ideas for sources are given in the reference section at the end of this unit.

Structure your notes using the following key questions:
   - What are salt-marshes?
   - How are they formed?
   - How are they threatened?
   - What can be done to manage these problems?

4 Changing coasts

In this section we consider the following key questions:

- What do we understand by sea-level rise?
- What landforms result from sea-level changes?
- How will a rise in the sea level affect the Essex coast?
- Will the impact of a rise in sea level be greater in the Maldives?

Global climate change and sea-level rises

Before we consider the scale and impacts of projected sea-level rises over the 21st century, let us first be clear about what we mean by a 'sea-level rise'. In some respects it is a very misleading term because the relative positions of land and oceans are continually changing. These continuous changes take place at different time scales, from daily tidal cycles, to changes in the ocean volumes due to glacial and interglacial cycles that take place over millions of years. Global sea levels fall in glacial phases and rise in the warmer interglacial periods.

Changes are measured from a mean sea level, a long-term average of high and low tides over a period of 20 years or more. Mean sea level is affected by localised upward and downward movements of the land relative to the sea. These movements are caused by tectonic uplift or subsidence. Another cause is the upward movement of a continental mass when released from the pressure of an ice sheet, (local **isostatic** change). Global changes in the volume of the oceans also cause changes in sea level (global **eustatic** change). Over the past 18,000 years, since the maximum extent of the ice sheets in the last glacial phases, the rising global volume of ocean water as this ice melted, together with complex, localised isostatic changes, has generally produced an increasing mean sea level of about 0.1–0.2 mm per year. This has accelerated to around 0.1–2.5 mm per year in the last 100 years.

Changes in sea level can have both direct and indirect consequences for the human population, especially those living in low-lying coastal areas. Depending on the magnitude of the rise, rising sea level could adversely affect the health and well-being of 16 of the world's largest cities with populations of more than 10 million.

In 1995, the International Panel on Climate Change (IPCC) projected that sea level would rise between 0.3 and 1.0 m by the year 2100, with a best guess of 0.5 m. This increase would be due to the continuation of two effects:

- increased volume of the ocean as the waters warm (steric effect)
- addition of water to the oceans as glaciers and ice sheets melt.

The most immediate threat is to those living in low-lying river deltas, or on small islands such as the Maldives, Kiribati, and Tonga where virtually all land is within a few metres of the current sea level.

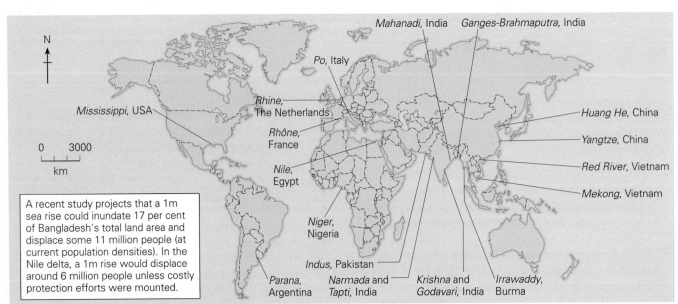

A recent study projects that a 1m sea rise could inundate 17 per cent of Bangladesh's total land area and displace some 11 million people (at current population densities). In the Nile delta, a 1m rise would displace around 6 million people unless costly protection efforts were mounted.

Figure 2.48 *Heavily populated delta regions that are vulnerable to sea-level rise.*

Source: *Climate Change and Human Health,* World Health Organization, 1996.

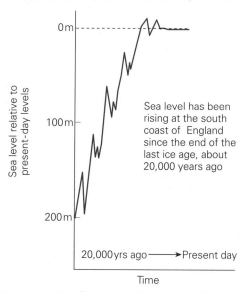

Figure 2.49   *Sea-level changes for the south coast of England.*

Sea level has been rising at the south coast of England since the end of the last ice age, about 20,000 years ago

Changes in sea level can result in distinctive landforms. When land rises relative to the sea, features such as raised beaches may be formed, for example the raised beach at Portland Bill, Dorset (Figure 2.50). Other landform features associated with emerged coastlines include coastal plains and relict cliffs. When the sea rises relative to the land, river valleys may be 'drowned' to form rias, or glaciated valleys drowned to form fjords, for example the Sognefjord in Norway (Figure 2.51).

Submerged forests are sometimes found in areas of submerged coastlines.

ACTIVITIES

1   Distinguish between the terms eustatic and isostatic sea-level changes. Try to explain how the landforms in Figure 2.50 (raised beach) and Figure 2.51 (the fjord) have been produced using annotated diagrams.

Figure 2.50   *The raised beach above the Portland and Purbeck Limestones at Portland Bill, Dorset.*

Figure 2.51   *The Sognefjord in Norway.*

The Essex coast marshes

Background

Much of eastern and southern England has already experienced relative sea-level rises of 4–5 mm per year over recent decades, due to the isostatic adjustment that northern Britain is experiencing after the pressure of the ice cap was removed some 11,000 years ago. As northern Britain rises, southern and eastern England is pulled down. Thus, raised beaches are common in Scotland, and drowned river valleys widespread along the south coast, for example Portsmouth Harbour (Figure 2.1) and the estuaries of Devon and Cornwall.

The impact of further sea-level changes is likely to be greatest on low-lying estuaries and open coast marshes such as the Blackwater Estuary in Essex (Figure 2.52). Currently the marshes act as baffles to wave energy and protect sea walls on the landward side. Rising sea levels will threaten these sites of natural coastal protection. The problem will be further accelerated due to recent land-use changes, because 95 per cent of the estuary is now protected by flood embankments — these limit the ways the marshes can naturally respond to sea-level changes.

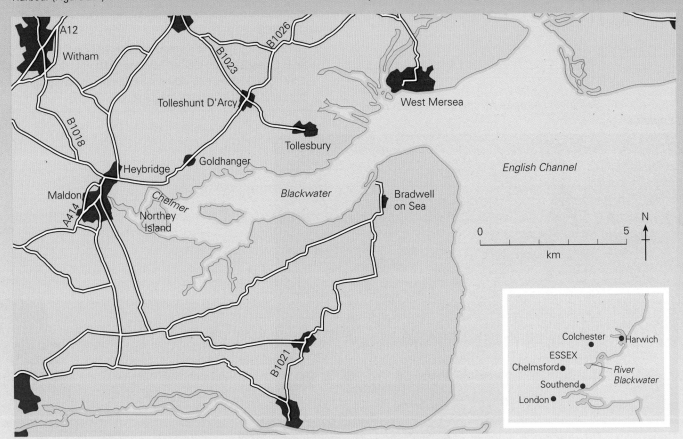

Figure 2.52   *Location of the Blackwater Estuary in Essex.*

Potential threats

The potential threats of further sea rises are:

- accelerated loss of the natural coastal protection (23 per cent total salt-marsh was lost between 1973 and 1988)
- erosion of marshes in the outer estuary, and replacement by sand and gravel habitats
- that inland marshes will become more brackish as salt water penetrates further up the estuary.

Proposed solutions

Some possible solutions are being tried. These include:

- a pilot scheme on Northey Island near Maldon, using 'set-back' techniques involving removing an old, broken-down sea wall and allowing the sea to reclaim the land behind it with new marsh to create a natural protection
- English Nature purchasing 21 acres of arable land at Tollesbury, on the northern shore of the estuary, to be flooded as part of a 'managed retreat' policy
- requiring a more integrated approach for the whole estuary in the long term. A general retreat of all flood embankments will be needed and the outer estuary channel will be allowed to widen.

The threat to the Maldives

Figure 2.53   *Two of the 1200 coral islands.*

Figure 2.54   *The Maldives – low lying settlement at risk from a minor sea-level rise. Most land is within 2 m of sea level.*

Figure 2.55   *The population is scattered and rapidly growing.*

Background

The Republic of Maldives is an archipelago consisting of about 1200 coral islands in the Indian Ocean. Two hundred of the islands are inhabited by a total of about 260,000 people, with the population increasing at a rate of 2.8 per cent a year. Per capita gross national product (GNP) was estimated at $1,200 in 1997.

The Maldives achieved buoyant growth during the 1980s and 1990s. The development of the tourism and fisheries sector, favourable external conditions, large inflows of external aid, and good economic management contributed to steady gross domestic product (GDP), averaging 8.1 per cent between 1990 and 1996. Along with economic growth, social indicators in the Maldives also showed significant improvements as reflected in the falling infant mortality rate, expanding school enrolments, and rising literacy rates.

The Maldives face three key environmental and development challenges as the Republic strives to sustain strong economic growth and improve living standards:

- coping with the challenge of a 0.5 m rise in sea level during the 21st century; protecting the marine environment, which is the most important natural resource in the Maldives; and further successful development of the fishing industry, for example dolphin-friendly tuna fishing. The fishing industry increased production by 300 per cent during the 1980s and 1990s, and is responsible for 10 per cent of GDP and 58 per cent of exports

- sound management of the dynamic tourism sector, which will continue to be the main engine for growth. It is worth 19 per cent of GDP and accounts for one fifth of total employment and more than half of total foreign exchange earnings. Between 1987 and 1997 tourist arrivals increased threefold and resort bed capacity doubled. A major attraction is the coral reefs (Figure 2.54)

- decreasing the 2.8 per cent population growth rate and delivering social services, for example, clean water, primary healthcare, education, to a rapidly growing population scattered over 200 islands.

Threats to the Maldive's coral reefs

Coral reefs consist of billions of coral polyps growing from a calcium carbonate base. The reef is a vast community of varying hard and soft corals, along with numerous other species, that all share the similar requirements of:

- consistent warm temperatures, around 27°C
- relatively shallow, clear, clean, non-polluted and sediment-free water as corals cannot function without sunlight
- constant salinity.

This explains their limited distribution between 30 degrees north and south of the equator in clean seas.

The traditional lifestyles of the people had an almost negligible effect on the environment, but recent socio-economic developments have led to a marked deterioration in the reefs (Figure 2.56).

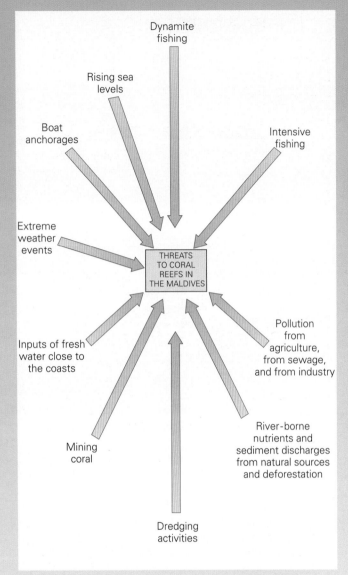

Figure 2.56   *Threats to coral reefs in the Maldives.*

Rising sea levels and other human activities threaten the fragile and complex ecology of coral reefs. Recent human activities that have had the most impact include coral mining, dynamite fishing, and pollution from farm run-off. A proposed expansion of 5000 new hotel rooms during the first decade of the 21st century by the tourist association in the Maldives could create another major threat to reef ecosystems. However, the Maldives do still have some of the least-damaged coral reefs in the Indian Ocean.

The reef system in the Maldives is especially at risk from rising sea levels as a 0.5 m rise in mean sea level could upset the delicate ecological balance of these ecosystems. The low-lying archipelago of 1200 islands could as easily be 'wiped out' and, according to President Maumoon Abdul Gayoom, turn the 225,000 Maldivians into the world's first environmental refugees. President Maumoon Abdul Gayoom stated in 1998 that 'few states stand to lose as much as the Maldives from the adverse effects of global warming and sea-level rise'.

Proposed solutions

The National Environmental Action Plan outlines a programme of environmental management aimed at protecting the Maldivian marine and terrestrial resources from the twin threats of global warming and population pressure.

This plan identifies the following key points:

1 Education, training, and legislation needs, for example banning dynamite fishing and coral mining. Improving public awareness of the problem.
2 Establishing priority areas and a co-ordinated integrated strategy.
3 Emphasising key themes, for example:
   - Protection of coral reefs from coral mining, sewage contamination, waste disposal, and rising sea levels.
   - Managing population growth and migration.
   - Managing broader environmental issues including dredging, fresh-water management, and deforestation.
4 Setting up 19 specific site projects, for example the islands of Gaagandu and Gama.
5 Monitoring, education, land-use zoning, and marine parks.

It is recognised that to be successful, any approach will need to involve the local people and be well co-ordinated. Careful financial planning will be essential and implementation must be effectively carried through.

ACTIVITIES

1 Work in small groups to carry out the following activities:
   a Locate the Maldives, the Marshall Islands, Kiribati, and Tonga on a world map and produce your own location map for these four sites.
   b Research basic details about each country (excluding the Maldives) using sources given in the reference section at the end of this chapter.
   c Produce an annotated map to show details of:
      - how and why these islands are at risk from rising sea levels
      - the possible social, economic, and environmental impact of the sea-level changes, for example a direct impact includes inundation, increased storm damage to the rest of the island; an indirect impact might include contamination of water supplies (aquifers).
   d Write a brief essay to show why there are no easy answers to managing the problem of rising sea levels on the most vulnerable island.
2 Compare the impact of rising sea levels on the coral islands of the Maldives with that on the salt-marshes of the Essex coast, or another low-lying area you are familiar with in the UK or USA.
3 How do the threats of rising sea levels compare with the shorter term impact of rapid erosion and coastal flooding? Write a short report using two case studies.
   You might like to select either Towyn or Chesilton for your case study of flooding. Some ideas for sources are given in the reference section at the end of this unit.

5 Managing the impact of recreation and tourism on the Dorset coast

'Tourism is Dorset's most important industry, and the coast is arguably the county's most important single tourism asset'. This is the view of the Dorset Coast Forum in their briefing paper on a search for an integrated policy for Dorset's coast (July 1998).

Dorset's coastal tourism industry consists of a diverse range of small- and medium-sized businesses supported by a multitude of co-ordinating initiatives. It has a long history: some of the major resorts developed in either the Georgian or Victorian period when sea bathing was in vogue. Railways, increased car ownership, and increases in the number of paid holidays all contributed to the steady growth in the tourism industry between the 1950s and the 1970s. Competition from foreign package holidays and the economic recession of the 1980s affected the seaside holiday industry in Dorset. Trends in the 1990s included the emergence of the Dorset coast as a location for second or third, short, UK-based holidays, increased day tripping, and a growth in niche markets. The family, annual bucket-and-spade holiday, though, is in decline.

In this section we focus on the key questions:

- What is the contribution of tourism to the coastal economy?
- What are the natural and built attractions?
- What are the environmental, economic, and social impacts of recreation and tourism activities?
- What are the issues regarding the sustainable management of tourism?

The contribution of coastal tourism to the economy in the 1990s

Tourism in Dorset provides 38,000 jobs and generates a total annual income of £830 million. The coast is the principal attraction, with over 3.5 million staying visitors per year and 13 million day visitors.

- overnight visitors – 20 per cent of all visitors staying in hotels, cottages, bed and breakfast, or camping
- business trips, largely around Bournemouth
- educational visits – 250,000 per year
- special-interest groups, for example sport, geology, history, literary, wildlife
- day visitors – including those from London, the Midlands, and the West Country
- local resident day visitors.

Of these visitors, 80 per cent are car-based, and there is distinct seasonality, with the majority of visits taking place between June and August.

Coastal resorts and smaller coastal villages are all heavily dependant on tourism both in terms of economic revenue and of employment. 26,000 people are indirectly or directly employed in the tourist sector in coastal areas. These include employees in restaurants, cafes, bars, clubs, hotels, caravan parks, museums, sport and recreation providers, tour operators. Along the Dorset coast, tourism generates £800 million per year.

Natural and built attractions

In the 1997 Dorset Tourism Data Project the prime asset identified was the 'attractive quality of the Dorset coast', for example Portland Bill (Figure 2.50) and Chesil Beach (Figure 2.18). Other key natural attractions identified were:

- beaches, for example Weymouth sands (Figure 2.57) and Hengistbury Head
- high standards of bathing water quality
- urban coastal landscapes, for example the Cobb at Lyme Regis
- country parks, for example Durlston Head near Swanage
- the South-West Coast Path, which attracts 1 million walkers per year
- important geological and geomorphologic sites, for example Lulworth Cove (Figure 2.18), the Fleet, Studland Bay.

The county has over 120 built attractions including historical properties, wildlife attractions, museums, gardens, country parks, and wet weather facilities (retail, leisure, and sports facilities). The five most popular attractions are Poole Pottery, Brewers Quay and Weymouth Timewalk, Weymouth Sea Life Park, Abbotsbury Swannery, and the Bovington Tank Museum.

Special-interest holidays were identified as a key element of any future strategy, especially for out-of-season and higher-income groups, for example geologists and fossil collectors, ornithologists, sub-aqua divers, sailors, wind surfers, climbers, and walkers.

ACTIVITIES

1 Using Figures 2.57–2.60, summarise the current situation regarding coastal tourism in Dorset and the changes that took place during the 1980s and 1990s.

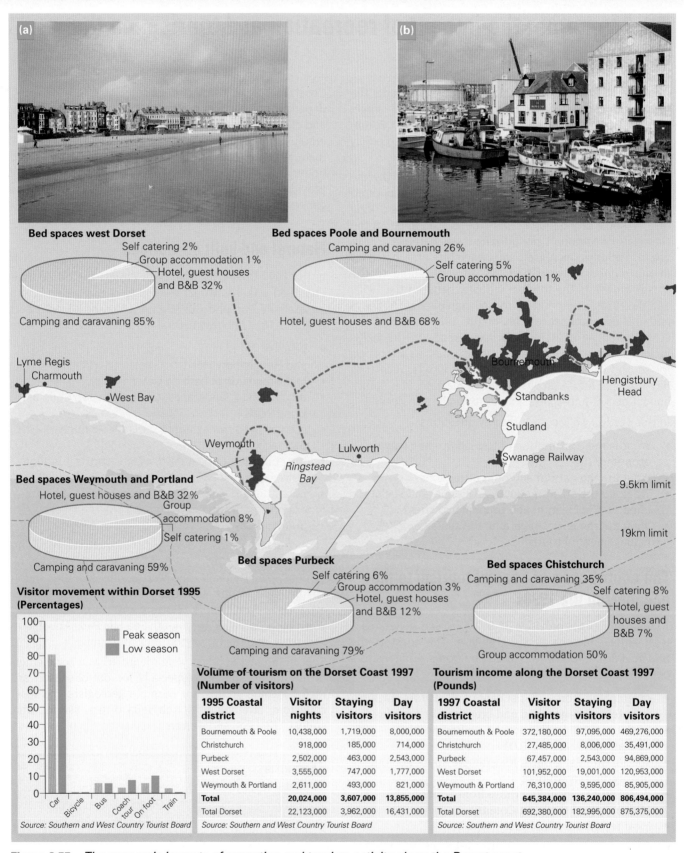

Bed spaces west Dorset

- Self catering 2%
- Group accommodation 1%
- Hotel, guest houses and B&B 32%
- Camping and caravaning 85%

Bed spaces Poole and Bournemouth

- Camping and caravaning 26%
- Self catering 5%
- Group accommodation 1%
- Hotel, guest houses and B&B 68%

Lyme Regis
Charmouth
West Bay
Bournemouth
Standbanks
Hengistbury Head
Studland
Swanage Railway
Weymouth
Ringstead Bay
Lulworth
9.5km limit
19km limit

Bed spaces Weymouth and Portland

- Hotel, guest houses and B&B 32%
- Group accommodation 8%
- Self catering 1%
- Camping and caravaning 59%

Bed spaces Purbeck

- Self catering 6%
- Group accommodation 3%
- Hotel, guest houses and B&B 12%
- Camping and caravaning 79%

Bed spaces Chistchurch

- Camping and caravaning 35%
- Self catering 8%
- Hotel, guest houses and B&B 7%
- Group accommodation 50%

Visitor movement within Dorset 1995 (Percentages)

Peak season / Low season

Car, Bicycle, Bus, Coach tour, On foot, Train

Source: Southern and West Country Tourist Board

Volume of tourism on the Dorset Coast 1997 (Number of visitors)

1995 Coastal district	Visitor nights	Staying visitors	Day visitors
Bournemouth & Poole	10,438,000	1,719,000	8,000,000
Christchurch	918,000	185,000	714,000
Purbeck	2,502,000	463,000	2,543,000
West Dorset	3,555,000	747,000	1,777,000
Weymouth & Portland	2,611,000	493,000	821,000
Total	**20,024,000**	**3,607,000**	**13,855,000**
Total Dorset	22,123,000	3,962,000	16,431,000

Source: Southern and West Country Tourist Board

Tourism income along the Dorset Coast 1997 (Pounds)

1997 Coastal district	Visitor nights	Staying visitors	Day visitors
Bournemouth & Poole	372,180,000	97,095,000	469,276,000
Christchurch	27,485,000	8,006,000	35,491,000
Purbeck	67,457,000	2,543,000	94,869,000
West Dorset	101,952,000	19,001,000	120,953,000
Weymouth & Portland	76,310,000	9,595,000	85,905,000
Total	**645,384,000**	**136,240,000**	**806,494,000**
Total Dorset	692,380,000	182,995,000	875,375,000

Source: Southern and West Country Tourist Board

Figure 2.57 *The economic impacts of recreation and tourism activity along the Dorset coast.*
Views of (a) *Weymouth sands in the autumn and* (b) *the inner harbour at Weymouth, with new large marina.*

Activity	Locations	Level of activity	Scale of importance	Economic and environmental impacts
Walking	South West Coast Path with 1 million visitors per year	Major – most popular activity	National / international	Erosion
Bathing/beach recreation	34 Bathing Beaches, e.g. Weymouth Sands	Major	Regional / national	Vital for economy Congestion/noise
Climbing	Hard limestone cliffs of Purbeck and Portland	Fast growing	Regional / national	Seasonal restrictions to avoid conflicts with nesting birds Vegetation damage, e.g. nationally important Portland sea lavender
Cycling – including BMX and mountain biking	Quiet rural roads, Purbeck Cycle Path	Growing in demand	Regional	Nuisance Damage to coastal paths by mountain bikes
Golf	10 coastal courses	Growing	Local / regional	Controlled by tight planning and environmental impact assessment
Hang gliding and paragliding	Few sites	Localised minority activity	Local / regional	Safety Erosion at landing sitesDisturbance of nesting birds
Jet-skiing	Poole Harbour, Studland and Swanage Bays, Weymouth	Growing – but very controversial	Local / regional	Very controversial Campaign to ban them Disturbance to wildlife Safety concerns Conflict with bathers and other water users – incompatibility is a major concern
Power boating	Royal Motor Yacht Club organise races at Weymouth, Poole and Bournemouth	Popular	Regional / national	Noise Safety
Sailing and marinas	Poole Harbour, 3500 berths, Swanage, Studland, Brownsea Island	Established	Regional / national	Lack of moorings between Poole and Devon creates a safety issue Sewage / pollution
Sea angling – boat and shore-based	Chesil Beach and beaches and piers	Widespread	Regional / (except Chesil Beach national / international)	Concentrated fishing can affect inshore fish population Wildlife disturbance Discarded and lost tackle present health risks
Sub-aqua diving	Wrecks in Lyme Bay, Portland Harbour and Purbeck	Growing in popularity	Regional / national	Pressure on slipways Impacts on wildlife and marine archaeology
Water skiing	3 clubs in Lyme Regis, Weymouth, Poole	Steady	Regional	Noise / safety Incompatibility with other users
Wind surfing	Poole, Christchurch Bay, Portland Harbour and Ferrybridge	Expanding	Regional (except Portland Harbour: international)	Erosion of sensitive shingle vegetation Noise / litter Incompatibility with bathing Car parking

Figure 2.58 *The main recreational activities along the south Dorset coast and their impact.*

Social issues	Environmental issues	Economic issues
• Health concerns – increased concern about the health impact of sunbathing and of poor water quality • School holidays – a review of school holidays and changes away from the six-week summer break could have a huge impact on tourism beyond 2000 • Seasonal closure of recreational facilities • Local resentment due to the sheer numbers of summer visitors and visitor vandalism, anti-social behaviour, and seasonal price increases in resorts	• Caravan parks – visually intrusive • Congestion on narrow country lanes and honeypots, e.g. Lulworth Cove and Studland Bay • Infrastructural overload, e.g. car parks full or visitors using 'locals' shopping car parks • Global warming – warmer weather, higher sea levels, increased storminess • Inappropriate development, out of keeping with the setting, e.g. toilet kiosks, toilets, signs • Wear and tear – footpath erosion in Lulworth Ranges • Traffic congestion in towns, e.g. Weymouth and on major roads, e.g. A351 Corfe–Swanage and A35 Bridport–Lyme Regis	• Second homes – shortages of cheap housing for locals up to 20 per cent in some coastal locations • Second holidays – less stable than traditional, longer family holidays • Seasonality – in the winter a proportion of the visitor infrastructure closes. Many tourism jobs are seasonal • The pound – the strong pound encouraged cheaper foreign holidays in 1999/2000

Figure 2.59   *Tourism issues along the Dorset coast, 1999–2000.*

Figure 2.60   *Litter on the beach at Portland.*

A sustainable strategy for Dorset's coastal tourism

Much of the Dorset coastal tourism industry relies on the quality and good management of the coast. One of the ironies is that there is no direct link between the tourism industry and coastal managers. A co-ordinated and strategic approach to overcome this key structural weakness is now developing. The Dorset Coast Forum Coastal Strategy brings together all the main interest groups. This forum will ensure integration, avoid duplication, and act as a coastal voice for sustainable tourism. Its objectives include:

• attracting more visitors
• improving quality
• making booking easier.

The Dorset Coast Forum Coastal Strategy involves integrating the demands of a range of coastal zone activities including archaeology, coastal defence, education, fishing, geology, landscape and seascapes, marine aggregates, maritime industries, Ministry of Defence, pollution and environmental quality, ports and shipping, wildlife interests, and tourism.

ACTIVITIES

1 You have just been invited for an interview at the Dorset Coast Forum Policy Direction Team as a researcher. They have asked you to prepare a brief five-minute presentation on the future of coastal tourism. The team is especially interested in the quality of your ideas and presentation skills, so include one or two ideas in each section of your presentation. Your presentation should address the following questions:

  a How can Dorset increase out-of-season and/or special-interest holidays?
  b How can the income from visitors be increased without increasing the environmental and social impact?
  c Is Dorset maximising the enjoyment of all visitors along its coast?
  d The coastal environment is likely to continue to attract more visitors – is this sustainable?
  e How should Dorset be looking to enhance its coastal environment?

Chesil Beach and the Fleet – The Ferrybridge management plan

Background

The area of Ferrybridge is the crossing point over the Fleet to Portland, it includes part of Chesil Beach, the Fleet, and Portland Harbour (Figures 2.62 and 2.63). In 1989, Weymouth and Portland Borough Council developed a Management Plan in response to the increasing conflicts and pressures on one of the richest sites of environmental importance on the Dorset coastline.

The area's very high nature conservation interest is reflected by numerous designations including SSSI status, and it is also a Special Protection Area (SPA), a Ramsar Site and candidate for Special Area of Conservation proposed under the EU Habitats Directive 1995.

There were four main targets in the 1989 management plan:

- to manage the conflicts between different recreational uses, and their impact on local ecosystems
- to inform and educate visitors about the high nature conservation value of the landscape
- to reduce erosion and seek other environmental improvements
- to produce an integrated and sustainable plan which involved all interested parties, including landowners and interests, for example: Crown Estates, Ilchester Estate, Harbour master; conservation groups such as the RSPB, Dorset Wildlife Trust, English Nature, and Marine Conservation Society.

Chesil Beach

Chesil Beach is 25 km long. The beach's pebbles are naturally graded, reducing in size from west to east, and are continually moving with the tides and storms. The tides and storms also change the beach's profile (Figures 2.18, 2.61).

Figure 2.61   *Aerial photo of the Hamm and Chesil Beach.*

The beach is essential for coastal protection because it is a natural sea defence, hosting a wide variety of flora and fauna which have adapted to this stony habitat. As well as providing a home for sea campion and carpets of sea pinks, the beach provides a nesting place for Little Tern and Ringed Plovers.

The Fleet

The Fleet is the largest tidal lagoon in Britain, being 13km long and extending from Portland Harbour to Abbotsbury. As well as enjoying SSSI status, the Fleet, together with the adjacent Chesil Beach, is an SPA and Ramsar site in recognition of its value as a bird habitat and wetland.

Although the Fleet provides a habitat for a wide range of marine flora and fauna, some unique to this location, it is also of particular importance for wading and migratory birds. Common species include the turnstone, sanderling, knot, Grey Plover, and flocks of Brent geese; rarities include visiting ospreys, Kentish plovers, and spoonbills.

The Hamm

Running parallel to Chesil Beach and the main A354, which forms Portland's only link to the mainland, is the Hamm, a narrow strip of rough, low-lying grassland and shingle beach. The Hamm has SSSI status and is renowned for its flora and inter-tidal marine species. Being common land, public access is freely available and this has brought with it problems of severe erosion which has resulted in numerous tracks being created by pedestrians who cross from the main car park. Many of these pedestrians are wind surfers, attracted to the comparatively sheltered waters of Portland Harbour and the prevailing south-westerly winds that increase in speed when blowing across Chesil Beach, which effectively acts as an aerofoil (Figure 2.18).

DECISION-MAKING ACTIVITIES

Weymouth and Portland Borough Council needed to develop a plan to manage in a sustainable way, the diverse recreational and leisure uses in an area of very high scenic and nature conservation interest at Ferrybridge.

1   Identify the features of interest and the attractions of the Ferrybridge area on an annotated map of the area.
2   Identify the pressures and conflicts on the Ferrybridge area.
3   Design a programme of fieldwork to evaluate the impact of recreational tourism on the Hamm.

Coastal management issues in the area

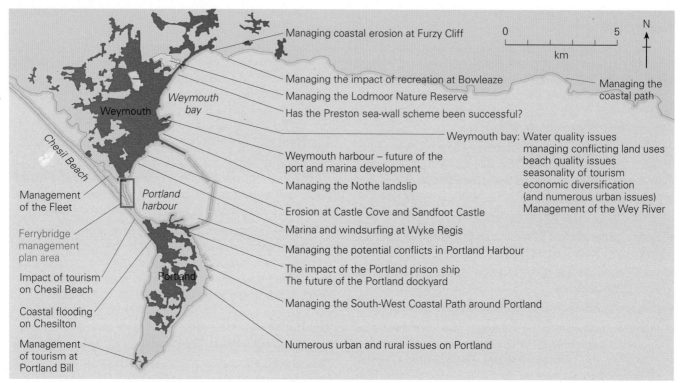

Managing coastal erosion at Furzy Cliff

Managing the impact of recreation at Bowleaze

Managing the Lodmoor Nature Reserve

Has the Preston sea-wall scheme been successful?

Managing the coastal path

Weymouth bay

Weymouth

Chesil Beach

Management of the Fleet

Ferrybridge management plan area

Impact of tourism on Chesil Beach

Coastal flooding on Chesilton

Management of tourism at Portland Bill

Portland harbour

Portland

Weymouth bay: Water quality issues managing conflicting land uses beach quality issues seasonality of tourism economic diversification (and numerous urban issues) Management of the Wey River

Weymouth harbour – future of the port and marina development

Managing the Nothe landslip

Erosion at Castle Cove and Sandfoot Castle

Marina and windsurfing at Wyke Regis

Managing the potential conflicts in Portland Harbour

The impact of the Portland prison ship
The future of the Portland dockyard

Managing the South-West Coastal Path around Portland

Numerous urban and rural issues on Portland

0   5
km

N

Figure 2.62   *Location of the Ferrybridge management plan area and other coastal management issues in the area.*

The diverse pressures on the area

The diverse pressures on the Ferrybridge management plan area are present to varying degrees through much of the year. They include:

- 100,000–150,000 visitors per year, ranging from local people 'walking the dog' to those engaged in specialist sports or activities
- sail boarding/wind surfing with national and international competitions. Portland Harbour is renowned for wind surfing because the prevailing wind is from the south-west and as it comes over Chesil Beach it increases in speed. Chesil Beach also protects the harbour, so that the result is high winds in the harbour but relatively calm water. All wind surfers have to cross the A354 and the grassland on the Hamm, where boardwalks aim to channel the visitor pressure (Figures 2.65, 2.66, 2.67). Wind surfing is not permitted in the Fleet
- boating and canoeing within the Fleet is limited to small craft due to the height of the Ferrybridge which restricts access. Numbers are monitored in order to minimise disturbance to feeding and nesting birds
- bait digging by recreational fishermen on the inter-tidal muds of the Fleet at low tide, if kept to a modest scale, can be accommodated. However, the fishermen's bait is also food to the wading birds. Equally importantly, the waders will not feed if disturbed and the time available is limited to when the sandflats are exposed at low tide
- fishing/angling off Chesil Beach which hosts national competitions. This can lead to problems of litter and the

potential for disturbance to the nesting terns
- diving in Portland harbour and part of Lyme Bay known locally as 'Deadman's Bay', can bring the pressure of trampling on the fragile environment of the beach and the Hamm
- swimming raises safety issues due to the large number of nearshore, fast wind surfers
- educational field study visits; an increasingly significant activity. These are positively encouraged to inform people about the management of the natural environment
- birdwatching, particularly in spring and autumn, around the Fleet
- oyster farming in the high grade waters of the Fleet and Portland Harbour. Some concern about the introduction of non-native, Pacific oysters
- pressure of 'off-road' four-wheel drive vehicles and scrambler bikes on the grassland and Chesil Beach were a major problem causing severe damage to the beach and its flora and fauna. This has been stopped by the provision of large stone blocks which prevent vehicles driving onto the beach
- potential oil spillage from boats in Portland Harbour. The commercialisation of the port could increase the likelihood of spillages
- boat maintenance and repair activities
- Ministry of Defence activity in the Fleet. An accident could affect the Fleet's fragile environment.

Some management solutions

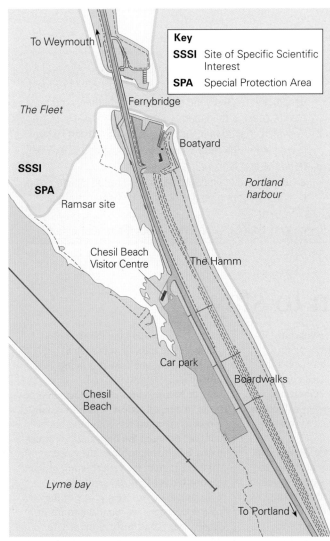

Figure 2.63   *Site map of the Ferrybridge management plan area.*

Figure 2.65   *Three boardwalks now channel people across the Hamm and help reduce erosion.*

Figure 2.66   *The road crossing points link to the boardwalks and help improve road safety by limiting the crossing points over the busy, fast road to Portland.*

Figure 2.67   *An earth bank, wooden railings, and a footway prevent people crossing the road where they like and channel them to crossing points and boardwalks.*

Figure 2.64   *Local materials such as these large blocks of Portland stone now define the edge of the car park.*

Figure 2.68   *A large car park allows wind surfers to park within 50 m of Portland Harbour.*

6 Managing coasts: Organisations and strategies in the UK and the USA

In this final section we focus on five key questions:

- How is coastal management organised in the UK and the USA?
- What engineering and other strategies are used to manage coastal erosion?
- How effective are these strategies?
- What are the specific methods used to manage coastal erosion on the barrier islands of North Carolina?
- How should the Cape Hatteras Lighthouse be protected from erosion?

ACTIVITIES

1 Ensure that you have completed section 1 on coasts and people and remind yourself of basic definitions and how the UK coast is managed.
2 Research coastal management in the USA using sources suggested in the reference section at the end of this unit.
3 Read the article in Figure 2.69.
   a Identify the main issues regarding coastal management.
   b Attempt your own definition of managed strategic retreat.
   c Why do local people not favour the retreat option?

The day the tide came in to stay

Nature chiefs who abandoned flooded land have met a storm of disapproval, *Simon de Bruxelles* reports

The retreat has been sounded over a little bit of England after the forces of authority decided not to fight the force of nature. The decision to allow the sea to invade ancient pastures has outraged a tiny community.

For centuries, the people of Porlock have maintained a long shingle bank which acts as a natural barrier on the north Cornish coast. When a gap formed, they plugged it to prevent the salt water destroying low-lying fields. In 1990, the area was designated as a site of special scientific interest; its unique collection of flora and fauna includes more than 40 species of spider.

Then the village, which featured in *Lorna Doone*, was struck by disaster last year. One of the most violent storms to hit the Bristol Channel this century breached the bank, allowing the sea to inundate fields beyond. A permanent lagoon formed and the rare plants and reed beds died in the saline waters. Local residents expected that approval of works to restore the shingle bank would be a formality.

Instead English Nature and the Environment Agency have said that nature should be allowed to take its course. The coastal path has been diverted inland and an 18th-century system of culverts, which kept out the sea but allowed fresh water to drain away, has been partially demolished. English Nature hopes the sea will create a salt marsh which will attract many species of birds.

Porlock's residents include the novelist Margaret Drabble and her husband, the biographer Michael Holroyd. Opponents of the retreat are being led into battle by a former RAF staff officer. Every day Campbell Voullaire, 76, surveys the shingle bank through his Zeiss field glasses. 'In the past six weeks alone the breach has enlarged considerably,' he said. 'The shingle lies on a layer of clay and each time the tide retreats, the water rushes out like a miniature Niagara, scouring a larger hole.

'We have been pressing for a year to have it restored. Each week that passes means the bill will be bigger and the task more difficult. The trouble is that quangos like English Nature are not democratically accountable. It is very un-British that unelected officials should be allowed to decide what happens to our countryside.'

Joan Loraine, owner of Greencombe, one of Somerset's best-loved gardens, once looked out from her hillside home across the green fields flanking the Bristol Channel. She said, 'It was such a beautiful view, and now it is being destroyed.'

English Nature admitted that the outcome of the 'managed retreat' was impossible to predict. It could leave nothing but mudflats between the high and low water marks, as elsewhere along the coast. Mike Edgington, the conservation officer responsible for Porlock, said: 'In philosophical terms, this is one of the hardest decisions we have had to make. Usually our job is fairly clear: it is to preserve what is already there. But coastal systems are not static and we hope that nature will replace what we have with something better.

'The ridge had been patched up for many years but, from the point of view of coastal management, that was not a sensible course. After a similar breach was repaired in 1990, officers agreed that sooner or later the sea was going to have its way unless a large amount of money was spent, and that no further steps should be taken to stop it. We have made our judgement. We don't know what will happen. Some experts even believe the ridge may well reform a little behind its present position.'

Figure 2.69   *The Times, 27 October 1997.*

Historical background

- Before 1750, very few settlements existed on the coast. The coast was considered a hazardous site.
- By the end of the 19th century coastal populations had grown. Railways encouraged tourism and trade on coastal sites – coastal land use began.
- In 1911 the Royal Commission on Coastal Erosion was set up. The report estimated that 6000 acres were lost to the sea between 1880 and 1905, but 48,000 acres gained by deposition. England was getting bigger!
- In the mid 20th century there were larger populations and more advanced technology. As the value of coastal developments increased, the pressure to defend them with walls and groynes increased.
- By the end of the 20th century coastal protection had become too effective. By reducing erosion, the sea's capacity to form protective beaches (from eroded material) had been reduced. Unprotected areas came under even more wave attack as beach levels fell.
- Newer approaches to managing coasts may rely less on traditional, **hard-engineering** solutions, for example sea walls, and more on beach replenishment and even strategic retreat.

The organisation of coastal management in the USA

Coastal management could be defined as the prudent, sustainable utilisation of coastal environments and resources for maximum benefit with minimum environmental interference. Since the 1972 Coastal Zone Management Act, the coastline of the USA (Figure 2.71) has been managed centrally by the Federal Office of Coastal Zone Management (OCZM). This national organisation provides support services and funds to individual states in order to allow them to implement the four main aims of the multifocus programme:

- to protect fragile coastlines and living marine resources, especially reefs, wetlands, and estuarine sites
- to minimise life and property loss from coastal hazards, including shoreline erosion
- to create better conditions for the use of coastal resources for access and recreation, and to reduce conflicts among competing land and water uses
- to promote inter-departmental co-operation at all levels with minimal bureaucratic hindrance.

The following issues arise from very intensive usage of the coastal zone:

- pressure on fragile and unique habitats and the loss of species diversity
- over-harvesting of biologically productive coastal zones, e.g. over-fishing
- industrial development
- commercial development, which can decrease open space for public usage
- residential development (the population density along the Atlantic seaboard is ten times that of non-coastal states)
- mining resources and fossil fuel extraction
- transport and navigation. There are 189 ports handling 1.3 billion tonnes of cargo per year. Dredging can have major impacts on habitats and wildlife
- waste disposal pollution
- the impact of recreation, especially inappropriately located seasonal homes, on high-risk barrier island sites (Figure 2.76)
- erosion and flooding due to Atlantic storms and hurricanes. Most vulnerable is Florida which contains over 80 of the 300 low-lying barrier islands that occur in the 18 states of the Atlantic seaboard.

Figure 2.70 *The top ten coastal conflicts in the USA.*

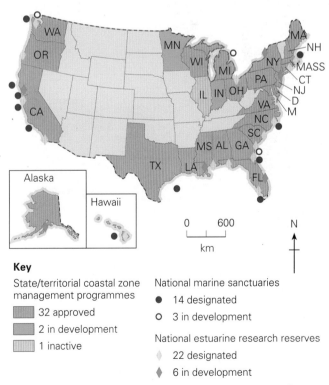

Key

State/territorial coastal zone management programmes
- 32 approved
- 2 in development
- 1 inactive

National marine sanctuaries
- ● 14 designated
- ○ 3 in development

National estuarine research reserves
- ◊ 22 designated
- ◆ 6 in development

Figure 2.71 *Map of the states participating in the Coastal Zone Management Act of 1972.*

1 *Global seal-level changes*
Global sea level has risen approximately 12 cm in the last 100 years. The increase in ocean volume is due to global temperature changes melting the polar ice caps and causing thermal expansion of the surface waters of the oceans. The greenhouse effect may cause even more dramatic increases in the future.

2 *Subsidence of the coast*
Much of the US coastline is sinking relative to the ocean, so local sea levels are rising faster than global averages. UK coasts are far less vulnerable. Scotland is rising in slow rebound after the melting of the Pleistocene glaciers. Southern England, which was never covered by ice, is sinking very slowly at approximately 1 mm each year.

3 *Nature of the topography*
Much of the coastline south of New Jersey consists of flat coastal plains, some with offshore or nearshore barrier islands. Miami is the lowest-lying city in the USA with very few areas 3 m above sea level. Many of the barrier islands from New York to the Mexican border are being driven onshore.

4 *Weather conditions*
Coastal storms and hurricanes are not uncommon along the US coastline. Wind-driven waves can create storm surges, which, if combined with high tides, flood low-lying areas.

5 *Extensive human coastal development*
It is estimated that 75 per cent of all Americans live within 100 km of a coast or the Great Lakes. (Britain and Europe have a much lower coastal population.) These urban centres are billion-dollar investments and many are located on the barrier islands. Miami Beach, Atlantic City, and Longport on New Jersey and Galveston, Texas, are all built on barrier islands. Elsewhere, settlements are threatened by the accelerated erosion of their beaches, often related to the construction of coastal protection structures on shoreline communities updrift e.g. Florida.

Figure 2.72   *Causes of coastal erosion in the USA.*

1 Boundaries of the coastal zone and critical areas are defined.
2 Inter-government co-ordination.
3 Areas of special concern for economic, social, historical, and environmental reasons.
4 Public participation is encouraged.
5 Public beach access is improving.
6 Beach erosion control is effective.
7 Management of major land and water uses, including those of regional and national interest.
8 Monitoring nearshore waters for pollution.
9 Environmental impact statement co-ordination and funding.

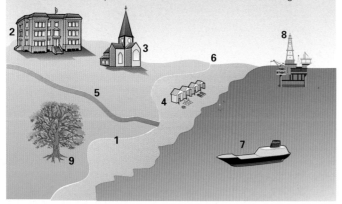

Figure 2.73   *Major components of a successful state coastal management programme in the USA.*

ACTIVITIES

1   How is the coast managed in the USA? Be sure to identify the key organisations and legislation.
2   Are there similar coastal conflicts in the USA and UK?
3   How does USA management compare with management in the UK?
4   What are the features of successful coastal management at national, state, and local level?

North Carolina: Managing the barrier islands

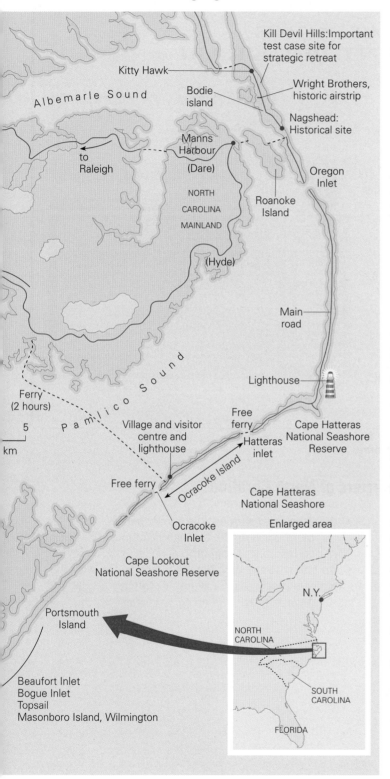

Figure 2.74 *The outer barrier banks from Kitty Hawk to Portsmouth Island.*

Figure 2.75 *Satellite image of the North Carolina coast.*

COASTAL ZONE MANAGEMENT PROGRAM

Program description

North Carolina Coastal Management Program

Wetlands loss, coastal hazards, and the impacts of population growth and development are among the pressures confronted by the North Carolina coastal management program. The State ensures responsible development and the use of the coast by overseeing coastal activities. Set-back laws keep property out of harm's way during storms, and a prohibition on erosion structures keeps the beaches, vital for tourism, from starving.

Tourism, shipping, agriculture, forestry, and fishing are the State's dominant coastal industries.

Administration and support

The Division of Coastal Management, within the Department of Environment, Health, and Natural Resources, is responsible for coastal program funding and administration. The governor-appointed Coastal Resources Commission adopts rules and policies for the program, and coastal counties develop local land-use plans.

· The state uses beach clean-ups, Coastweeks celebrations, boat tours, and nature walks on Rachel Carson Island to involve and educate the public in the coastal area.

Figure 2.76   *North Carolina coastal management programme.*

Coastal erosion on the developed coastal barriers of North Carolina

It is estimated that at least 80 per cent of the world's shorelines are eroding, and this is especially noticeable on the coastal barrier islands of the Atlantic seaboard of the USA, including North Carolina (Figure 2.75). Under the 1987 Coastal Area Management Act, the Department of Environment, Health, and Natural Resources is responsible for trying to manage coastal erosion (Figure 2.76). It is obliged to consider three strategies:

- to attempt to control the erosion by hard engineering, for example sea walls, or softer engineering, for example groynes and beach replenishment

- to attempt to alleviate the consequences of the problem, for example through insurance (the National Flood Insurance Program)

- to adjust to the problem, and learn to live with the coastal processes, for example strategic retreat and land-use zoning.

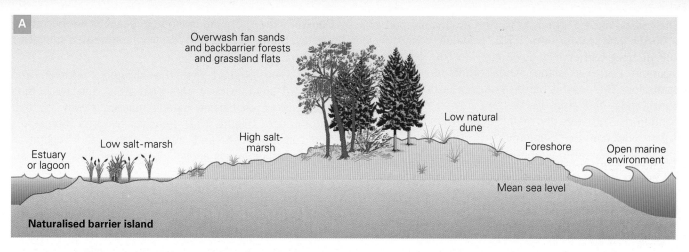

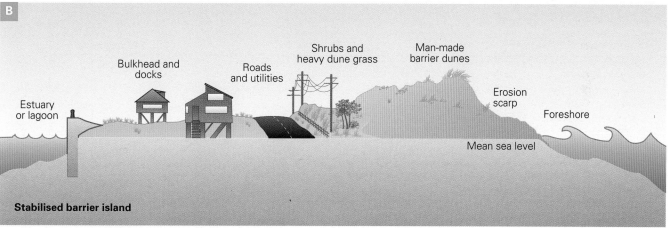

Figure 2.77 *Cross-sections contrasting* (a) *natural and* (b) *developed coastal barriers.*

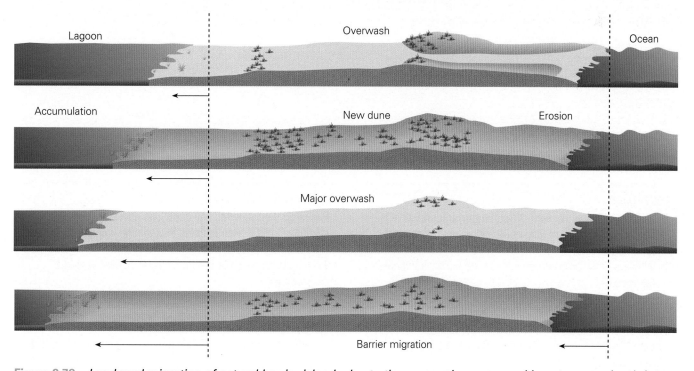

Figure 2.78 *Landward migration of natural barrier islands due to the overwash process and long-term sea-level rise.*

The coastal barrier islands of North Carolina are part of a 2700 km long feature from Texas to Maine, consisting of 400 distinct barrier islands. Some are true islands, for example Hatteras Island, while others are spits and tombolos. The coastal barrier complex is not static but continually changing in response to environmental conditions. This state of dynamic equilibrium represents a balance between four elements:

- beach sand
- energy inputs from waves, winds, tidal currents, and hurricanes
- sea-level changes
- the width gradient of the beach.

Generally the shoreline is eroding, beaches are becoming narrower and steeper, and the whole system is migrating landward (Figure 2.79).

It has been argued that the shoreline erosion and landward migration of the system is due to human intervention, as barrier islands migrate slowly in their natural state (Figure 2.78). Beaches restored themselves from offshore bars and dune systems and vegetation recolonised overwash areas.

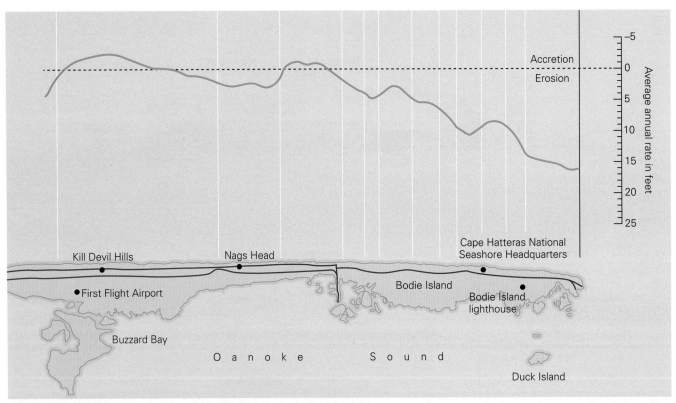

Figure 2.79 *Erosion–accretion rates from Cape Hatteras to the Kill Devil Hills.*

ACTIVITIES

1 What are coastal barriers? Why are they important?
2 Produce an annotated diagram to show what controls the form of a coastal barrier.
3 Why are these areas potentially hazardous environments for people?
4 Explain how the human occupation of the coastal barrier system creates management problems.
5 Are erosion rates even along the barrier islands? Comment on the stretch between Cape Hatteras and the Kill Devil Hills.

ACTIVITIES

Research the following key questions using the North Carolina Coastal Management Programme website listed in the reference section at the end of this unit.

1 Who is responsible for managing the coast in North Carolina?
2 What are the main issues?
3 How is the responsible agency managing the coast, and how is it trying to involve local people?
4 Why are the barrier islands regarded as being at high risk from coastal erosion?

The Kill Devil Hills debate

Kill Devil Hills is a coastal resort located on North Carolina's outer banks. Each summer the town's resident population of 2500 swells to around 35,000, indicating the importance of tourism to the local economy. Known as the 'birthplace of aviation', the town takes its name from the famous sand dune, Kill Devil Hill, where the Wright Brothers first piloted their Wright Flyer into history in 1903. Kill Devil Hill is named from historical accounts of the rum that used to wash ashore from shipwrecks laid to rest in the nearby 'grave of the Atlantic', Cape Hatteras, North Carolina. That rum, it has been said, was so potent, it would '... kill the devil'.

The extracts in Figure 2.80–2.82 illustrate the problems of managing coastal erosion.

In the Kill Devil Hills land-use plan, hard engineering was banned in an early attempt to implement a policy of retreat in the mid 1980s. During the winter of 1982 the policy of retreat met its first real test. During that winter, five subtropical storms battered the coast of north-eastern North Carolina with hurricane-force winds and record rainfall. The north-east orientation of the northern beaches of Dale County combined with three-foot storm tides and 18- to 24-foot waves resulted in the loss of hundreds of feet of shoreline from Kitty Hawk to Oregon Inlet. Dozens of cottages were washed out to sea, septic tanks were crushed and broken, and four ocean-front motels in Kill Devil Hills were endangered by shoreline erosion. In the spring of 1983, the property owners sought to implement erosion mitigation techniques, but of course they were refused planning permits to construct such structures, because of the State of North Carolina's policy of strategic retreat.

Predictably, faced with the loss of their property and/or livelihood, owners responded by erecting their own, unsightly erosion control structures. Their plight soon became national news headlines on TV, and made the cover of Newsweek and Time magazines. Public views on both sides became very aroused, and became more polarised in the election year of 1983, when winter storms did further damage. Vandals turned vacant motels into eyesores, and vagrants inhabited the buildings. The policy of 'retreat' had become 'abandonment', and the pressure to 'do something' mounted steadily. The newly elected Kill Devils Board of Commissioners voted to instruct the planning department to allow the use of sandbags to protect endangered ocean front property and asked them to recommend a management strategy for dealing with the erosion on the outer banks. The planners identified five options:

1   Allow the current situation to continue, i.e. no intervention.

2   Use sandbags to protect endangered structures.

3   Allow short-term, privately funded engineering structures including groynes, artificial seaweed, rip-rap, offshore breakwaters, or other similar measures permitted under the 1972 Coastal Zone Management Act.

4   Undertake large-scale nourishment projects to maintain the beaches.

5   Undertake long-term efforts to protect the public beach through the funding of a beach nourishment project using state, local, and federal funds and the use of offshore breakwaters, artificial seaweed, sandbags, relocation, acquisition, and other similar measures as may be necessary as interim, temporary, remedial action to protect private or public property owners, provided such measures meet the specifications of and secure permits as required by the North Carolina Coastal Area Management Act of 1974.

The planning department staff's recommendation was in favour of alternative number 5, a compromise policy that approached shoreline management from both the long-term and short-term perspectives. Beach nourishment was the preferred long-term response, but funding to implement a nourishment project could not be expected for at least seven years. A number of short-term responses were also recommended to cover the interim period. These measures, in order of preference, included relocation, acquisition, sandbags, offshore breakwaters, and wooden bulkheads.

The retreat alternative has major pitfalls in the 'real world'.

Figure 2.80   *'The retreat alternative in the real world: The Kill Devil Hills land-use plan' by Raymond Sturza II, town planner at Kill Devil Hills, North Carolina.*

Our view – Beach programs let tax dollars wash out to sea

Why spend millions on sand that Hurricane Felix is washing away even as you read this?

Fickle Hurricane Felix may or may not finally come ashore this weekend, but its waves already are causing damage that should put taxpayers in a stormy mood.

Foot by foot, the sea is washing away millions of dollars worth of sand brought in at federal expense to protect beachfront property. And added millions will be spent to put more sand right back.

At Virginia Beach, VA, with Felix still more than 100 miles away on Wednesday, seaside residences were threatened in spite of millions spent on beach protection and replenishment. And Virginia's powerful members of Congress have already pushed through amendments grabbing another $1.1 million in scarce federal funds for

next year, shovelling more sand against the tide. At Monmouth Beach, NJ, the nation's largest beach-replacement project is expected to cost $1 billion – some say $3 billion – over 50 years but will never be done. Even before the first wave from Felix, more than half of a 350-foot beach completed last November had already washed away.

Picking the pockets of the nation's taxpayers to finance beach projects of primary benefit to a handful of landowners and nearby businesses has cost at least $500 million – more likely $2 billion or more, according to experts.

Canute the great King of Denmark, England, and Norway nearly 1000 years ago, once had to show his sycophantic nobles that even he couldn't order back the tide. When are we taxpayers going to wise up and stop paying for the futile effort?

Opposing view – Joint effort saves beaches

Local jobs depend on these beaches, and local governments pick up a chunk of the tab.
By a senior member of the Senate Environmental and Public Works Committee

Criticizing the Corps of Engineers' hurricane-protection programs is a surprisingly shortsighted position which overlooks some basic facts.

Our beaches, our coastal zone, are national resources. Clearly, it is in the best interest of the federal government to participate in their preservation.

Our nation's beaches contribute greatly to the national economy. The 'multiplier' effect of the coastal economy is significant.

In 1985, 31.7 per cent of the GNP – almost $1.3 trillion – originated in the 413 counties that constitute the nation's coastal zone. They also provided 28.3 million jobs, with almost $480 billion in payroll.

Hurricanes such as Felix make it grimly clear that hurricane-protection plans must be in place for vulnerable communities such as Virginia Beach. The Water Resources Development Act (WRDA), which authorizes the corps' civil works programs,

has worked extremely well, providing permanent, structural long-term protection, flood control and storm damage reduction, and inland flood and coastal storm protection – not just sand shovelling.

Perhaps more importantly, by requiring local cost sharing, WRDA has ensured that the most worthy projects with strong local support receive scarce federal funding.

For every federal dollar invested in a project, the taxpayer must receive more than a dollar of benefits.

In my role as a US senator, I have been and will continue to be supportive of federal water resources projects partially financed by local governments because a favourable benefit-to-cost ratio is demanded and because localities like Virginia Beach have given them a high priority, assuming 35 per cent of the cost burden.

No, we must not trivialize the corps' central mission – protecting lives, resources and property – as little more than shovelling sand against the tide.

Figure 2.81 *Two views on protecting beaches.*

I would like to present a scientist's view of the coastal crisis, particularly the crisis on our recreational beaches.

- Can we afford to carry on with hard engineering? In 1984 the coastal village of Sea Bright in New Jersey was hit by a 1:10 year storm. None of the village buildings (valued at $US65 million) was destroyed or even damaged to any significant degree, yet the total damages are estimated at $US82 million. Surely we cannot continue to afford such repair bills to the beaches and sea walls of such communities?

- We now understand the processes of barrier island migration and sea-level rise caused by the greenhouse effect, and know we need to rethink our attitudes to coastal management. However, as our understanding of coastal processes has increased over the last ten years, ironically so has the incredible amount of development along the highest-risk part of coastal barriers – the oceanwards shoreline – as has the value of this land. This has been accompanied by a change in attitudes towards managing erosion. In the 1930s engineers and geologists wrongly agreed the answer was artificial dune construction on outer banks; by the 1950s sea walls were the most popular solution; by the 1980s hard engineering was much less favoured as it destroyed recreational beaches, and beach replenishment is now more publicly acceptable. However, the costs of trying to replenish the entire Atlantic seaboard are not sustainable in the medium and long term.

- Taking into account sea-level rises, high costs of beach replenishment, the fact that erosion is very widespread, and the fact that hard engineering has massive environmental impacts including the loss of the beach (for example Sea Bright, New Jersey), it boils down to the situation where we can have shoreline buildings or beaches, but we cannot have both. This is why we must be courageous in North Carolina and support the law banning sea walls on a sandy beach, and retreat from the oceanward shoreline. Not so much abandonment, but learning to live with the shoreline!

- What we now need to do is research how we retreat, for example halting all new construction, a rolling programme where repairs are not allowed beyond a critical point, and it could be partly paid for from the National Flood Insurance Program or by newly created 'local set-back taxes'. It is an economic and environmental necessity and there are no other national-scale alternatives.

Figure 2.82 *'A time for retreat' by Professor Orrin H Pilkey, in Cities on the Beach Conference, 16 January 1985.*

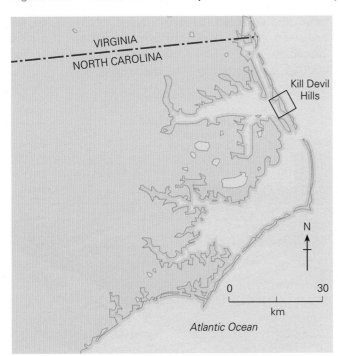

Figure 2.83 *Location map of Kill Devil Hills, North Carolina.*

ACTIVITIES

1 Draw up a table which summarises the arguments for and against protecting beaches.
2 Identify the major factors that might influence people's opinions on the debate.
3 Why does Professor Pilkey (Figure 2.82) argue that retreat is essential in the medium to long term, to manage coastal erosion and protect beaches?
4 Why do the town planners favour 'alternative 5' for the Kill Devil Hills area?
5 Which of the five recommendations put forward by the Kill Devil Hills planning department do you think that the Kill Devil Board of Commissioners decided to implement? Why?
6 What pitfalls does the situation at Kill Devil Hills expose regarding strategic retreat? Why is strategic retreat more likely to be effective if implemented from the outset on an undeveloped coastal barrier?

Human responses to coastal erosion in the USA

As early as 1970 it was noted that 25 per cent of the shoreline of the USA was suffering from severe erosion at a real cost of over $US200 million per year. In response, five main approaches to the problem of coastal erosion were developed, including strategic or managed retreat.

1 *Hard engineering* Immovable structures designed to absorb the wave energy – these include sea walls and groynes (see Figure 2.84), rip-rap, gabions, and revetments (see Figure 2.86).
2 *Soft engineering* This approach involves working with the natural processes in more flexible ways – it includes beach nourishment, cliff drainage, and cliff regrading (Figure 2.88).
3 *Land-use zoning* This is often the least popular but most sustainable long-term approach and involves implementing planning controls that prevent immovable structures (roads and buildings) from being built in hazardous places. If the buildings already exist they may be compulsorily purchased and allowed to fall into the sea – often a cheaper option than building sea defences. Strategic or managed retreat is an extreme version of land-use planning as we saw in the previous Kill Devil Hills case study.
4 *The National Flood Insurance Program* This scheme is available to all pre-1982 properties and new buildings that are not in high-risk areas, i.e. on the landward side of barrier islands. Owners who construct on the oceanward side of barrier islands now do so at their own risk. However, this has not acted as a deterrent to development in these high-risk oceanward zones.
5 *Public preservation* Public acquisition and management have preserved nine undeveloped barrier beaches and their associated ecosystems as National Seashores, including Cape Cod, Cape Canaveral, and Cape Hatteras. In addition, there are numerous smaller parcels managed by the state, local governments, and trusts. The Department of the Interior estimates that about 356 million hectares, about 50 per cent of the barriers are protected by public preservation of various kinds.

1 Hard engineering

Traditionally, before the 1980s, the coastline was fortified to cope with a storm event with an intensity likely to occur every 50 to 100 years. Hard engineering is costly, has major environmental impacts, and does not tackle either the physical or human causes of an event, but attempts to control it. At best it alleviates the problem, at worst it transfers the problem elsewhere (Figure 2.85). Hard engineering solutions are likely to be increasingly ineffective as sea levels rise and maintenance becomes expensive. Yet sea walls are common from New Jersey to Texas. Between 1936 and 1975 over 75 coastal schemes were implemented by the United States Corps of Engineers at a cost of over $US100 million. The most 'protected' state is New Jersey, where most of the ocean frontage is protected by hard engineering.

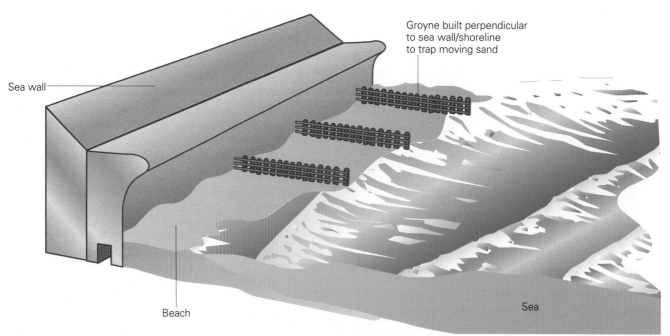

Groyne built perpendicular to sea wall/shoreline to trap moving sand

Sea wall

Beach

Sea

Figure 2.84   *Base diagram showing hard-engineering solutions: Sea walls and groynes.*
Source: ABM Pangaea.

	Advantages	**Disadvantages**
Sea walls	Offer highest protection to property in the short term. Lifespan up to 50 years. Effectively halt erosion locally.	Waves reflecting off the wall scour the beach (basal scour). The beach level drops and may undermine the wall. The beach becomes less accessible for recreation. Lack of beach material (due to reflection scour and zero cliff erosion) causes greater erosion problems 'downdrift'. Erosion often continues where the scheme ends on unprotected areas (terminal scour), e.g. Cape May, New Jersey. Here scour has removed over 1 km to the west of the sea wall. Expensive and not permanent, and so need careful maintenance to prevent concrete shrinkage, debonding, and micro-fracturing.
Groynes	Cheaper than sea walls. By reducing longshore drift they build up beach locally.	Shorter lifespan than sea walls. Reduce the recreational value of the beach. Reduction of longshore drift causes higher erosion rates 'downdrift', known as Terminal Groyne Syndrome.
Revetments	Reduce the power of the waves without causing reflection scour. Longshore drift not hindered. Cheap.	Limited lifespan. Limited effectiveness in storm conditions. Reduce recreational value of beach. Unsightly.
Rip-rap	Cheaper than sea walls. Absorbs wave energy without causing reflection scour. Long lasting.	Reduces recreational value of beach. Unsightly. Acts as groyne to reduce downdrift sediment movement.
Gabions	Use of smaller rocks gives more flexibility in design. Less easy to erode (depending on quality of mesh). Can use local beach material to reduce visual impact.	Unnatural appearance. Unpleasant if mesh breaks (risk of injury).

Figure 2.85   *Advantages and disadvantages of hard-engineering solutions.*

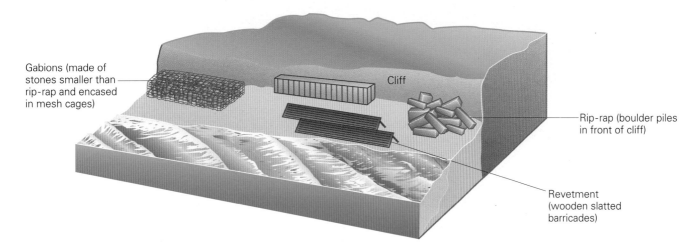

Gabions (made of stones smaller than rip-rap and encased in mesh cages)

Cliff

Rip-rap (boulder piles in front of cliff)

Revetment (wooden slatted barricades)

Figure 2.86   *Base diagram showing hard-engineering solutions: Revetment, rip-rap, and gabions.*

Source: Pangaea Independent learning resource, 1997.

Soft engineering

Beach nourishment/replenishment was developed in the 1950s. Imported coarser sediment is dumped on or near the beach face, or gradually fed in to nourish a beach over time. It is often used as a technique in conjunction with groynes, for example Miami Beach, Florida. The beach nourishment programme at Miami Beach is the largest such scheme yet undertaken where 17.7 million m^3 of sediment were moved to create a 200 m wide x 18 km long beach by dredging sand from offshore and pumping it onshore. The scheme was installed between 1976 and 1982 and cost $US67 million. However, this was a small outlay to protect a resort worth $US5000 million from hurricane force surges, and to provide unimpeded public access to 18 km of recreation beach.

Solution	Advantages	Disadvantages
Beach nourishment/ replenishment	Low environmental impact, if local material is used, maintains the 'natural' appearance and recreational value of the beach. Locally used, it can be economically attractive as construction cost can be minimal.	Potentially short lifespan due to the fact that one severe storm can move vast quantities of expensive sand fill sediment. Physical and ecological impacts of acquiring the sand fill, especially if it involves marine dredging. Expensive, e.g. Miami Beach, the largest such scheme yet undertaken where 17.7 million m^3 of sediment were moved to create a 200 m wide x 18 km beach by dredging sand from offshore. The scheme US$ installed between 1997 and 1982, cost, 67 million. This was a small out lay to protect a resort worth 5000 million dollars from hurricane force surges, and to provide unimpeded puplic access to 18 km of recreation beach.
Cliff regrading and drainage	Cliff becomes more stable and less prone to unexpected movement.	May be impractical if valuable land use exists on cliff top.

Figure 2.87 *Advantages and disadvantages of soft-engineering solutions.*

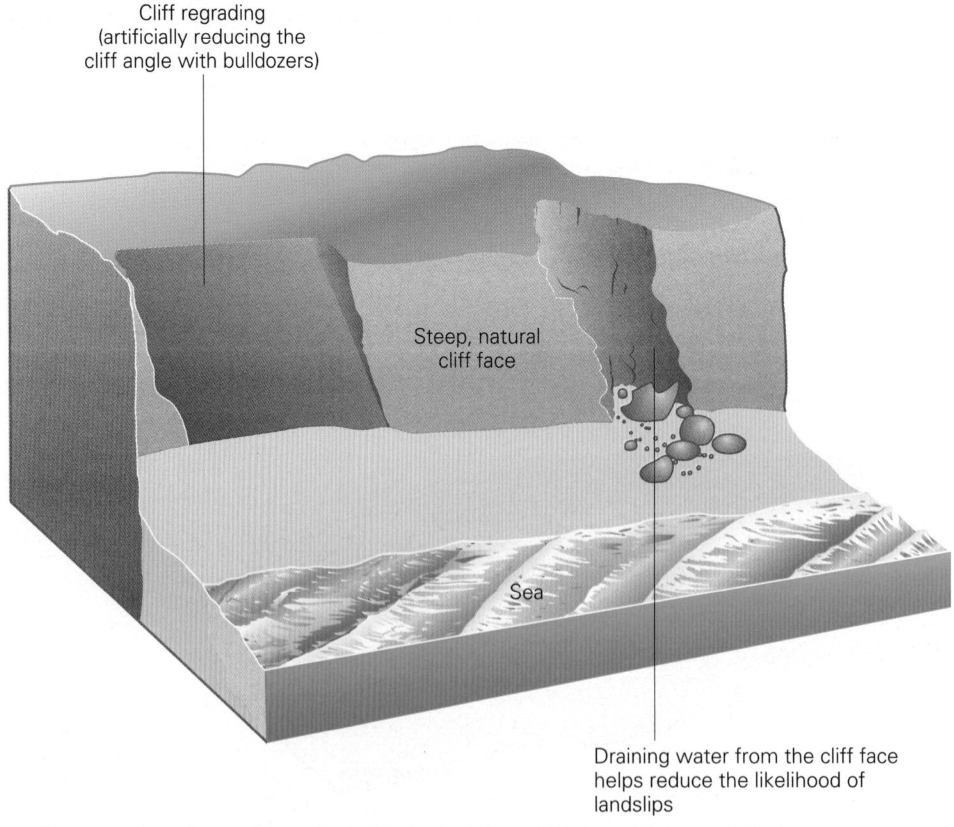

Figure 2.88 *Base diagram showing soft-engineering solutions: Cliff regrading and drainage*
Source: Pangaea Independent learning resource, 1997.

Cost–benefit analysis of coastal defence

Any coastal defence scheme has its costs and benefits. A cost–benefit analysis is an evaluation of a scheme usually carried out before it is given the go-ahead, but not all the costs or benefits are easy to measure (Figure 2.89).

Costs	Benefits
• cost of building defences • cost of maintaining/repairing defences • cost of dealing with accelerated erosion downdrift from beach starvation or reduced LSD	Value of protected buildings, roads, and infrastructure (gas, water, sewage, electricity services) is preserved Land prices may rise once a commitment to protection is in force
Reduced access to beach during works Reduced recreational value of beach Reduced accessibility • sea walls need steps or ramps for beach access • groynes are difficult to climb over Reduced width of beach due to scour	Reduced stress levels on residents Local employment generated by coastal defence works
Disruption of shoreline and cliff line ecosystems and habitats Visually unattractive coastline	Coastal engineering works are rarely beneficial because the works disrupt natural processes and responses Natural balances that have existed for hundreds of years or more are threatened.

Key Economic ▉   Social ▒   Environmental ░

Figure 2.89 *Examples of the types of cost (disadvantage) and benefit (advantage) to be considered when evaluating a proposed coastal defence scheme.*

If a cost–benefit analysis is completed (and values are given for social and environmental costs as well as for economic costs) the cost–benefit ratio is often rather poor, making it perhaps cheaper to purchase threatened properties than to defend them. Choosing not to defend land is the concept of strategic retreat. This is not always popular with local residents (see the previous case study on the Kill Devil Hills). Strategic retreat is sustainable and very cost effective. It saves lives and preserves the natural coastline and beaches for recreation and wildlife. The greatest problem lies in changing public attitudes, especially home owners'.

Defending properties threatened by the sea encourages development to continue in potentially hazardous areas. By strategically abandoning threatened properties the natural balances can be maintained; erosion of the cliff builds up the beach – and a wide gently shelving beach offers the best form of natural cliff defence.

ACTIVITIES

1 Annotate a copy of Figure 2.84 to show how sea walls and groynes modify the natural processes at work along the coast.
2 Complete the table below to summarise the impact of coastal management strategies.

Method	Position	Form	Purpose	Potential problems
Sea walls	Parallel to the shore	Static. Rigid. Massive. Non-porous. Normally stone or concrete		
Groynes				
Rip-rap				
Revetments				
Gabions				
Beach nourishment				
Cliff regrading				

Saving the Cape Hatteras Lighthouse from the sea

Background: The lighthouse and erosion

Cape Hatteras Lighthouse, the tallest brick lighthouse in the USA, faces eventual destruction due to coastal erosion. The lighthouse was built in 1870, 1500 feet [460 m] from the shoreline, replacing a lighthouse built near the present site in 1803. It is 200 feet [61 m] tall and weighs approximately 2800 tons [2450 tonnes]. Protective measures to reduce the rate of beach erosion in front of the lighthouse have provided a temporary respite, but by late 1987, the lighthouse stood only 160 feet [49 m] from the sea. The motivation for protecting the lighthouse and its associated structures is to preserve a famous and historic landmark; modern navigational aids have made its original function of protecting shipping in the stormy waters off the outer banks redundant.

Cape Hatteras Lighthouse is on one of the barrier islands that constitute North Carolina's outer banks. These islands are subject to powerful currents and storms that, in general, cause erosion of east-facing shorelines and accretion of south-facing shorelines. Thus, the east-facing shoreline in front of the lighthouse is expected to continue to recede until storm-driven waves undermine the tower's foundation and topple the lighthouse. The lighthouse now stands close enough to the water's edge to be vulnerable to damage by a severe hurricane.

At the request of the National Park Service, the government formed the Committee on Options for Preserving Cape Hatteras Lighthouse in July 1987. The committee's task was to evaluate and develop several options for preserving the Cape Hatteras Lighthouse from the encroaching Atlantic Ocean. It is important to note that the committee's charge was *how* best to preserve the lighthouse, not *whether* to preserve it. Political feasibility of the various options or the nature and extent of public sentiment associated with them were not within the scope of the committee.

Rate of shoreline retreat at Cape Hatteras

The rate of beach erosion (and hence shoreline retreat) is affected by changes in sea level, among other factors. Sea level has been rising for at least the past 10,000 years, during which the barrier islands of the outer banks have been migrating westward.

The committee concludes that a conservative estimate of sea-level rise for the next few decades would be a continuation of the rate of the past century – a relative rise of about .08 inch [2 mm] yearly at Cape Hatteras. Recently, another National Research Council committee also considered three possible scenarios of sea-level rise, accelerating at different rates from the present to the year 2100.

If present trends continued, sea-level rise would be 2.4 inches [60 mm] by the year 2018; the highest National Research Council scenario would yield 6.1 inches [155 mm] by 2018. Based on this range of values, the committee estimates that the shoreline in front of the lighthouse would retreat 157–407 feet [48–124 m] by the year 2018. By the year 2088, the retreat might reach 525–3280 feet [160–1000 m].

Management and protection of the coast: The national picture

The USA has 80,560 miles [129,621 km] of coast (excluding the Great Lakes), of which 19,240 miles [30,957 km] is erosional. Marine shorelines generally are retreating in response to sea-level rise. This natural process of shoreline migration clashes with demographic growth and development pressure in the coastal zone. Coastal development has increased dramatically in recent decades. Population pressure on the coast is a severe test of environmental and land-use planning capacities.

An array of federal statutes and regulations govern development and protection of the coast as well as contiguous marine areas. North Carolina's Coastal Area Management Act (1974) discourages efforts to harden or artificially stabilize retreating shorelines. Notwithstanding these measures and historic concern for the American coast, the nation and its coastal states have yet to formulate an adequate response to the increasing problems of a shoreline moving landward and a population moving seaward.

Resolving the conflicts between historic preservation and conservation of natural areas

In selecting an option or combination of options to preserve the lighthouse, the National Park Service will need to comply with public policies concerning historic preservation as well as those concerning coastal management and protection. The main conflict in the present case – between policies that would preserve the historic lighthouse and policies that would allow natural processes to occur unimpeded – is representative of a large class of conflicts between historic preservation and natural conservation. With its dual mandates of historic preservation and conservation of natural areas, the National Park Service must deal with such conflicts frequently.

The preservation options and evaluations identified by the National Park Service

The committee evaluated ten options for preserving the lighthouse and associated buildings, three of which were considered in depth.

1 Incremental relocation of the lighthouse intact

This option involves moving the lighthouse complex 400–600 feet [122–183 m] south-west of its present position to a new site near the far side of the existing parking lot and landscaped area. The committee estimates that this relocation would cost approximately US\$4.6 million and take approximately one year, including planning and site preparation. The committee estimates that a future move of an additional 500 feet [152 m] in the same direction as the first would cost approximately US\$1,600,000 in 1988 dollars. Despite the apparent difficulty of moving a large brick structure, the operation entails minimal risk. Many structures larger and older than Cape Hatteras Lighthouse have been moved successfully, and the technology for such operations is well established.

The committee envisions that subsequent moves eventually will be required and, therefore, suggests that the steel lifting beams that would be inserted through the lighthouse foundation be left in place for use in future moves. Incremental relocation would provide a reliable, cost-effective, and long-term protection for the lighthouse by allowing it to be moved away from the approaching sea as the need arises. This option best satisfies public policies regarding historic preservation, conservation, and coastal management, minimizes ecological damage; and involves little risk to the lighthouse. The committee also believes that moving the lighthouse would attract much attention and, therefore, would provide an opportunity to educate the general public concerning problems of coastal erosion and the value of historic preservation.

2   Sea wall revetment

The design for a sea wall and revetment was prepared for the National Park Service by the United States Corps of Engineers in 1985. The proposed design involves four elements: a concrete sea wall encircling the lighthouse, a cut-off wall below the sea wall, an underground stone revetment fronting the sea wall, and a compacted earth-fill behind the sea wall. The crest of the wall would be 23 feet [7 m] above mean sea level and 15 feet [4.6 m] above grade at the base of the lighthouse. The underground revetment would reach 208.5 feet [63.6 m] seaward of the lighthouse.

The United States Corps of Engineers estimated a construction time of 20 months from award of the contract at a total cost of $US5,575,000 in 1985 dollars.

The committee judges that the sea wall/revetment probably would protect the lighthouse for 20–30 years or more. The sea wall would obstruct the view of the lower portion of the lighthouse, and this would change the appearance of the historic landmark. The associated lighthouse keepers' dwellings and other structures would be separated from the lighthouse, which would degrade the historical integrity of the site. Constructing a large, hard, defensive structure around the lighthouse would conflict with several national, state, and National Park Service policies. In addition, the beach in front of the sea wall would be lost when the shoreline eroded to the sea wall, impeding movement along the beach. Eventually, the encircled lighthouse would become a tombolo or an island, which would further degrade the historic integrity of the site and make it difficult for the public to visit the lighthouse. During construction, the lighthouse's vulnerability to storms would be increased. Finally, the sea wall/revetment would effectively foreclose future relocation of the lighthouse.

3   Rehabilitation of groynefield with revetment

This option involves repairing and shortening the existing three groynes, constructing one or two new groynes south of the lighthouse, and building a below-grade, reinforced concrete revetment around the lighthouse. The revetment would protect the lighthouse from the undermining effects of storms, but not from the battering of waves. The rehabilitated groynefield would stabilize the beach in front of the lighthouse, and the beach would prevent storm waves from directly battering the lighthouse, except during the most severe storms.

The estimated cost would be $US4.7–6.7 million and would require less than one year to construct. This option would protect the lighthouse for 20–30 years, barring a disastrous storm. Eventually, as the shoreline outside the groynefield continued to retreat, it would become increasingly expensive, and perhaps impossible, to maintain a beach in front of the lighthouse, which would become increasingly vulnerable to wave damage in severe storms. The groynefield/revetment option would make future relocation of the lighthouse more difficult and expensive. In addition, placing hardened defensive structures on the beach, even below ground, is not in accord with state and national coastal policies.

Of the options that would preserve the lighthouse in situ by defensive means, this offers some protection to the lighthouse at relatively low cost.

Other options

Other options considered by the committee were rejected for a variety of reasons. The primary reasons included excessive cost (continue beach nourishment), uncertain effectiveness and cost (artificial reefs), failure to protect the lighthouse for any period (artificial seagrass and no action), failure to provide either long-term protection or reliable short-term protection (rehabilitation of the groynefield without a revetment), violation of various coastal policies (offshore breakwaters and rehabilitation of the groynefield), and failure to preserve the historic lighthouse (new lighthouse).

A brief historical synopsis

In 1797, Congress recognized the need for a navigational aid in the vicinity of Diamond Shoals at Cape Hatteras, North Carolina, and authorized the erection of a lighthouse. The first lighthouse was completed in 1803 and stood about one mile [1.6k m] inland from the ocean beach. It was considered less than satisfactory from the time it first came into service, as it was only 90 feet [27 m] high, and the light was inadequate. In 1854, its height was increased to 1590 feet [46 m], and the best available lens was installed. However, problems with the structure persisted. Inspections in the late 1860s showed growing cracks in the sandstone structure, and construction of a new lighthouse was recommended.

The second (and existing) Hatteras Lighthouse was activated in December 1870, and the original structure was razed. The new light towered 208 feet [63 m] in height and was located 1500 feet [457 m] from the water's edge. With its distinctive black and white candy-cane design, it soon became a landmark of the Carolina coastline. It is the tallest lighthouse in the USA, and has served as a primary navigational aid for mariners rounding the treacherous Diamond Shoals. Because of its historical importance to the region and the nation, the lighthouse and its associated station buildings have been placed on the National Register of Historic Places.

The history of the erosion problems

Responding to the gradually rising sea level of the past several thousand years, barrier island systems have migrated westward. Hatteras Island is no exception. This migration occurs as storm-driven ocean tides wash completely over the islands, moving sand sediments towards the sound shoreline. Because of this migration, barrier islands are among the most unstable landmasses on the face of the earth. Under these conditions, stationary structures built on them, such as the Cape Hatteras Lighthouse, are inevitably threatened.

In 1870, the lighthouse was situated 1500 feet [457 m] from the ocean. By 1919, the ocean had advanced to within 300 feet [91 m] of the tower and to within 100 feet [91 m] by 1935. A combination of natural changes and a number of protective measures postponed the threat for a number of years.

1930s	274 m of interlocking steel sheetpile groynes were installed along the beach shoreline, and a barrier sand-dune system was constructed along the entire length of Hatteras Island. In 1936, the coastguards abandoned the lighthouse, and transferred ownership to the National Park Scheme.
1966	A beach nourishment scheme using fine sediment from Pamlico Sound failed.
1967	Large, nylon, sand-filled bags were placed in front of the lighthouse to slow erosion.
1969	Three reinforced concrete groynes were installed.
1970–73	Further beach nourishment using coarser sand from Cape Hatteras Point.
1980	A severe storm required emergency rip-rap to be placed at the base of the lighthouse, and a groyne extended.
1981	250 units of 'seascape' (artificial seaweed) were dropped in 3 m of water to trap sediment and create an underwater sand bar, thus helping to build up the beach. Further rip-rap and groyne extensions, and the statewide appeal 'Save Cape Hatteras Lighthouse Committee' established.
1982	Environmental impact assessments carried out for a range of options by the United States Corps of Engineers; this identified a sea wall encircling the lighthouse as the preferred option. In the interim, 5000 units of seascape and 700 large sandbags placed in a protective dyke around the lighthouse were installed. Groynes were also extended.
1983–86	Tank modelling of the 'sea wall' allowed specifications to be completed. More rip-rap, and a further 2700 units of artificial seaweed was installed.
1987	Funding secured for a sea wall. A private organisation, 'Move the Lighthouse Committee', presented new evidence about relocation option. The National Park Service asked for a full cost–benefit analysis and environmental impact assessment of all the options (groynes/sea wall/relocation, etc.) to be done by the National Academy of Sciences. Their report 'Saving Cape Hatteras Lighthouse from the sea' was published in 1988.
1990s	Further strengthening of the sandbag revetment, and groynefield repairs. Halloween storm of 1991, Hurricane Emily 1993, Hurricane Gordon 1994, all damage the temporary repairs.
1996	United States Corps of Engineers issue proposals for the 'fourth groyne alternative'. State government asks North Carolina University to re-assess the findings of the National Academy of Sciences 1988 report. A best-value (cost–benefit analysis) survey was made to identify their preferred option.
1997	A public forum is held to allow all interested groups to explain their views.

The Save Cape Hatteras Lighthouse Committee's view

When Cape Hatteras Lighthouse was seriously threatened by erosion in 1981–82, the Save Cape Hatteras Lighthouse Committee was formed to raise money to aid the National Park Service in protecting the historic beacon. North Carolina counties bordering Tennessee were as enthusiastic in supporting the fund drive as were counties near the lighthouse, and the committee was able to purchase sandbags, sand fences, and seascape synthetic seaweed, which helped the National Park Service protect the lighthouse for 15 years. In 1998, when the lighthouse was again threatened by the sea, the Save Cape Hatteras Lighthouse Committee continued to strongly advocate protection of the lighthouse at its present location. The committee, however, is absolutely opposed to a high risk proposal to try to move the 208-foot [63 m] structure, the tallest brick lighthouse in the world, 2900 feet [884 m] from its current location.

Alternative solutions to protect Cape Hatteras Lighthouse

Several options are available that might be implemented separately or in combination to reverse beach erosion activity which threatens Cape Hatteras Lighthouse. These include:

1 construction of a fourth groyne on the beachfront at the Lighthouse. The fourth groyne, estimated to cost $US1.7 million, is the most popular option, and the best understood by residents in the area. The United States Corps of Engineers has drawn up plans for it, as originally requested by the National Park Service, but those plans were later cancelled. As a supplement for building up the beach in conjunction with the fourth groyne, the Save Cape Hatteras Lighthouse Committee offered in its July 1997 report to pay for an installation of seascape synthetic seaweed comparable in size to that used successfully in 1982.

In 1970 the United States Navy built three groynes for protection of its installation just to the north of Cape Hatteras Lighthouse, with the third groyne located a few feet south of the lighthouse. A southward moving current swirling around the end of the three groynes is believed to be a leading contributor to erosion dynamics that formed the lagoon and which now leave the lighthouse vulnerable to storms. The best understood and most popular solution for protecting the lighthouse is to construct a fourth groyne that would be located south of the lighthouse. By altering ocean current patterns along the shoreline, a fourth groyne would help protect the south flank of the lighthouse.

2 installation of Holmberg erosion control stabilisers along the Hatteras shoreline to build up the beach. These stabilisers are underwater groynes or jetties made of elongated bags of durable cloth filled with concrete and positioned on heavy mats. They function like speed bumps, slowing the movement of the water currents causing the deposition of sand. They have been very effective in Florida and Michigan

3 supplemental instalment of seascape synthetic seaweed to accelerate beach replenishment, which was used to successfully build up the beach in 1982–83.

DECISION-MAKING ACTIVITIES

Prepare a report on the management of erosion problems at the Cape Hatteras Lighthouse. Use the materials presented in the case study and additional sources provided in the reference section at the end of this unit. Before you start, be sure you have also studied:

- the map of North Carolina locating Cape Hatteras (Figure 2.74)
- the graph of erosion–accretion rates from Cape Hatteras to the Kill Devil Hills (Figure 2.79).

1 Prepare a report which:
  - clearly identifies the threats to the Cape Hatteras Lighthouse
  - briefly explains what solutions have already been tried
  - states the options to tackle the erosion threat:
  - identified by the National Park Service
  - identified by the Save Cape Hatteras Lighthouse Committee
  - evaluates the strengths and weaknesses of these solutions (use a large A3 table to present your findings)
  - recommends and justifies a scheme to preserve the Cape Hatteras Lighthouse
  - is illustrated with key diagrams, for example for each of the options.

7 Review of key ideas

This section reviews the key ideas presented in this chapter and suggests summary activities.

- The world's coastal environments are varied and are under severe pressure from people. These stresses are likely to increase due to rising sea levels, and human occupation of the coastal zone.
- Many coastal environments, including dunes, beaches, reefs, and marshes, are dynamic and fragile, and require sensitive management based on a sound understanding of coastal processes.
- There is no universal approach to managing coastal environments. In the past there were two distinct models, the 'American' and 'British' models. Both had their political, economic, and environmental strengths and weaknesses.
- The American model was based on specific national legislation, with well-defined strategies, and a national co-ordinating agency, which delegated authority at state level. It was comprehensive and well funded, but fraught with difficulties in attaining its targets. Budget cuts at national level threatened the effectiveness of this integrated model.
- The British model was unco-ordinated at national level, fragmented, and driven by events. Significant progress was made in the 1990s towards co-ordinating management, but further improvements and funding changes were needed.
- Both the American model and the British model shared similar problems: inadequate finance, bureaucratic inflexibility, and an absence of co-operation and consistency between agencies and projects; a lack of priority in terms of government spending compared to military security, and economic and social well-being programmes.

ACTIVITIES

1 **Vision 2020 – A future for coastal management**
Prepare a short article for inclusion on the Vision 2020 website entitled 'The challenges for coastal managers over the next 20 years'. Use your knowledge of coastal processes and case studies on coastal management to consider what the main issues will be over the next two decades, and how they might be resolved.

2 **Checklist of technical terms** Using key geographical terms accurately is an essential examination skill. The best way of ensuring you understand and can use these terms is to build up your own list of key definitions and terms.
Refer to the glossary provided at the end of this unit to check your own definitions.

3 A helpful way of revising is to write a summary essay. You may find it helpful to answer any one of these three summary essays:
a 'Strategic retreat is the only sustainable way to manage coastal erosion.' Discuss.
b 'The world's coastal environments are under severe pressure from people, and these stresses are likely to increase in the future.' Discuss.
c 'People, not natural processes, create coastal management problems.' Discuss.

Unit 1 Reference materials

Chapter 1

Websites

- *Environment Agency*: Lots of up-to-date information including an online version of the Environment Action Newspaper:
www.environment-agency.gov.uk
- *Fraser River Action Plan*:
www.pyr.ec/frap/index.html
- *Institute of Hydrology* and *British Geological Survey Hydrological* data: Information about river flows and groundwater stores:
www.nwl.ac.uk/ih/.
In the current yearbook there is a gauging station location map showing the rivers for which there is flow data available.
- *International Rivers Network*: A group supporting sustainable river use:
www.irn.org/
- *Kissimmee river restoration*:
www.sfwmd.gov/orb/erd/krr/index.html
- *Mississippi river*: Environmental engineering:
www.mvs.usace.army.mil/engr/river/en01.htm
- *Poland flooding*: Donosy archives (electronic news bulletin from Warszawa):
http://info.fuw.edu.pl/donosy-english/
Also information at:
www.rec.org/REC/Bulletin/Bull83/flood.html
and
gemini.most.org.pl/ZB/GB/24/
- *Rivernet*: Regularly updated information about all aspects of rivers and their management:
www.rivernet.org
- *The impacts of the controlled flood on the river Colorado*:
wwwdaztcn.wr.usgs.gov/flood.html
- *The River Restoration Project*: Information about river restoration, including projects on the rivers Skerne and Cole in England:
www.qest.demon.co.uk/rrc/rrphp.htm
- *World Commission on Dams*:
www.dams.org

Articles

- *Environment Action*: A free magazine from the Environment Agency which includes current news items about the environment, including various water issues such as flooding, water quality, river restoration, drought, pollution, etc.
- The October 1998 Shrewsbury floods part 1: causes and impacts *Geography Review* 13,11-15 (1999).
- Flooding in Shrewsbury part 2: management *Geography Review* 13, 17-21 (2000).
- The imperilled Nile delta *National Geographic* 191, 2-35 (1997).
- Troubled waters: the problems of large dams *Geographical* 71,18-24 (1999).

Chapter 2

Websites

- **Coastal management:**
  http://www.nos.noaa.gov/icm
- *Ainsdale-Formby dunes*:
  http://www.merseyworld.com
- *Cape Hatteras Lighthouse*
  http://www.nps.gov/caha/lighthousereports.ttm
  http://www.savehatteraslight.org
- *Coastal resource management in the* USA:
  http://www.nos.noaa.gov/ocrm/czm/welcome
- *Coral reefs*:
  http://www.nos.nooa.gov/icm/links/reefs.html
  http://www.panda.org/livingplanet/spaces/global/1200/caribbean-reef/summary
- *Maldives*:
  The Third World Guide 1999/2000 March 1999 ISBN 1-869847.687 or CD ROM 1-869847.695
  Internet World Bank or World Resources Institute
- *North Carolina*:
  http://www.ocrm.nos.noaa.gov/czm/czmnorthcarolina.html

Articles

- Towards an integrated approach
  Coastal Systems and processes 10, 31-33 (1996).
- Chesil sea defence scheme
  Coastal Systems and processes 10, 8-10 (1996).
- Studland Bay and the South Haven Peninsula, Dorset
  Coastal Systems and processes 10, 33-35 (1996).
- The impact of mass movement on Furzy Cliff, Weymouth, Dorset *Coastal Systems and processes* 10, 33-35 (1996).

Texts

For general use:

16–19 *Core Geography* Longman 1994 , – Chapter 1 'Landforms and environmental management' is very good on coastal management.

The Earth Transformed, Blackwell 1997 – Good on a range of environmental issues for AS and A level.

Managing Environments in Britain and Ireland, Hodder & Stoughton 1997 – Especially Section 1.4 'Managing the north-east coast of Ireland'.

Integrated Geography Nelson 1996 – Good on landforms and their origins.

Europe in Transition: The Yorkshire Region, Hodder & Stoughton 1998 – Chapter 7 'Saving the Yorkshire Coast' provides a most useful additional case study of an extended coastline, using Holderness as an example.

Teacher's Guide to Portland: Island of Discovery, Weymouth and Portland Borough Council 1996 – Excellent resource for coastal case studies and fieldwork ideas.

Preston Beach Sea Defences Scheme, Environment Agency 1995 – Best resource on an individual scheme.

Coasts 1 & 2 'Slideshows', Pangaea, Independent Learning Resource 1997 – Best resource/software on coasts, especially Coasts 2 which is an excellent case study of Christchurch Bay and Barton.

Unit 1 Glossary

abiotic   The non-living components in an ecosystem.

abrasion   See corrasion

abstraction   The removal of water from above ground sources, e.g. rivers, lakes, or from groundwater. Abstraction is needed to meet the demands of agriculture, industry, and domestic users.

accretion   The build up of coastal sediment. When accumulation of sand and shingle exceed depletion (deposition).

aggradation   The buildup of the land surface or river bed by deposition of sediment.

alluvium   Particles of silt, sand and gravel that are usually found on floodplains.

aquifer   A rock that can store water because it has tiny holes or cracks in it, e.g. chalk, limestone.

attrition   The process by which erosion grinds down cliff-fall material.

base flow   The water that flows into a river from groundwater stores. On a storm hydrograph this usually appears as an estimated amount.

biological oxygen demand (BOD)   This indicates the amount of organic pollution present in the water. It is mainly bacteria that decompose the organic matter. As they do so they absorb oxygen. The amount of oxygen required by the bacteria can be measured to give an indication of the amount of pollution present.

biomass   The amount of organic material present in a given area of an ecosystem measured in dry weight per unit area.

biotic   The living components of an ecosystem.

bluffs   The line of cliffs marking the edge of the floodplain caused by lateral (sideways) erosion of a meandering river. These bluffs would have originally extended out into the valley as spurs.

braided channel   A river channel which divides and rejoins around piles of large sediment.

capacity   The total amount of sediment that a river can carry. This will vary according to the amount of water present and in different places along the river's course.

channelisation   Human alterations to a river channel for a specific purpose such as flood prevention. It may involve changing the course of the river or making the river channel wider or deeper.

cliff-face processes   Mass movement processes active on and in the cliff face.

cliff-foot processes   Marine processes active at the cliff foot.

competence   The largest size of particle that can be carried by a river as part of its load.

concordant   Coasts where the rock structure is parallel to the coast, e.g. Lulworth Cove, Dorset (also Pacific coastlines).

consumers (or heterotrophs)   Consumers rely on other animals or plants (or both) for their supply of food. All animals are consumers.

corrasion (abrasion)   Process by which sand and pebbles are flung against a cliff, wearing away the rock.

corrosion   A type of chemical weathering where minerals are broken down, often by weak acids.

decomposers   These are animals that live off dead and decaying matter. Especially important are bacteria and fungi that cause the breakdown of organic matter and the release of nutrients.

deposition (by a river)   When there is insufficient energy for the river to carry the material in its load this material is dropped. Larger particles require most energy to transport them and are deposited first.

diffuse source (of pollution)   Pollution coming from an area of land rather than a specific location. For example, nitrogen fertilisers or pesticides applied by a farmer may enter a river in a number of ways i.e. overland flow, throughflow, or even in groundwater flow along a large length of the river channel.

discharge   The amount of water flowing in the river channel at a particular point. It might be measured at the mouth of the river or anywhere along its length. Discharge is usually measured in m3/sec.

discordant   Coasts which cut across the rock structure, e.g. Swanage Bay, Dorset (also Atlantic coastlines).

drainage basin   The area of land from which a river receives water. The edge of it is marked by the watershed.

dynamic equilibrium   A steady state or state of balance maintained despite continuous change e.g. in the case of coasts, balance is maintained despite impacts of plate tectonics, human activity, relative sea level change and erosion/desposition.

ecosystem   A set of plants and animals along with their physical (non-living) environment.

erosion   The wearing away and removal of rocks and sediments by a moving force. Rivers, ice, wind, and waves can all cause erosion. Rivers may erode laterally (sideways), vertically (downcutting), or back into the upland area (headward).

eustasy   A global sea-level change (eustatic change) brought about by changes in the volume of the oceans.

eutrophication   This occurs when too many nutrients are added to water bodies, especially ponds and lakes. The nutrients cause the plants and algae to grow rapidly. Much of the algae is short lived and when it dies it is decomposed by bacteria that use up the oxygen in the water.

evaporation   Water changing from its liquid form into a gas (water vapour).

evapotranspiration   The loss of water from plants either as evaporation from the leaf surface or as transpiration through tiny holes in the leaf surface.

fetch   The distance the wind blows over the sea. Longer fetch can generate higher-energy waves.

floodplain   The area of land over which a river periodically floods. The river deposits alluvium each time it floods.

food chain   The transfer of energy through a sequence of organisms in which each eats the one below in the chain, and is eaten by the one above it.

gauging station   A measuring centre where equipment is used to monitor changes in the height of the river and the speed of the flow over time. It is then possible to calculate the discharge at any point in time and make predictions which may assist in flood warning.

geomorphology   The study of land forms on the Earth's surface.

groundwater   The water stored in aquifers. Groundwater flows are the movements of water within and between aquifers.

habitat   The environment in which an organism lives.

hard engineering   Conventional fixed structural solutions to coastal erosion, e.g. sea walls.

heterotrophs   See consumers

hydraulic action   The action of breaking waves on a cliff.

hydraulic radius   A measure of the efficiency of the river channel that takes into account its shape and the roughness of the bed.

hydrograph   A graph that shows the changes in river discharge or river height over time. An annual hydrograph shows the pattern of flow over a whole year, whilst a storm hydrograph shows the response of the river to a single rainfall event.

hydrological cycle   The continuous movements of water between the atmosphere, the Earth's surface, and the rocks just below it.

hydrosere   The pattern of vegetation that develops in wet conditions, e.g. in an ox-bow lake.

infiltration   Water soaking into the soil from the surface.

interception   Plants trap and hold some precipitation. This water may be evaporated, or reach the ground eventually by flowing down plant stems (stemflow) or by dripping through the leaves (throughfall).

isohyets   A series of lines on a map that join up places receiving the same amount of rainfall, in the same way that contours join places of the same height.

isostatic   A localised change in the relative land–sea levels.

lag time   The period between the time of peak rainfall and the time the river reaches its maximum flow (peak discharge) .

levees   Raised banks at the edge of a river channel caused by repeated flooding and deposition of sediments.

lithology   Geological rock type, e.g. hard rock – chalk, granite; soft rock – clay, till.

littoral   A physical unit with clearly identified sediment pathways, e.g. Lyme Bay.

load   The sediments carried by a river.

marine processes   Sea-based processes associated with waves and tidal currents.

mass movement   Extreme movement of loose material down a slope under the influence of gravity, for example a landslide.

meander   A large bend in the river. Meanders usually occur in areas where the river is flowing across a gently sloping valley floor.

Net Primary Production (NPP)   The rate of the accumulation of the biomass.

nutrient cycling   The movement of minerals through food chains in an ecosystem.

overland or surface flow   Water moving across the surface of rock or soil.

ox-bow lake   A lake formed when a river cuts off a meander, usually in times of flood.

percolation   Water moving from the surface layers of soil into deeper layers of soil or rock.

photosynthesis   This process only takes place in plants. They use light energy and carbon dioxide to produce sugar (glucose) and oxygen.

phytoplankton   Tiny floating plants that make up part of the plankton. They are important producers in aquatic ecosystems, especially ocean ecosystems where rooted plants do not exist.

point bar   An area of deposition that occurs on the inside of a meander bend where the water flow is slower.

point source (pollution)   Pollution that enters a river from a specific location. For example, water pumped into the river from a factory , quarry, mine, sewage works, etc.

precipitation   Any form of water deposited on the Earth's surface, e.g. rain, sleet, snow.

producers (or autotrophs)   The first stage in a food chain. Plants can produce their own food by photosynthesis.

recharge   Water added to groundwater or soil water stores to replace water lost or used up. Recharge can take place naturally or be assisted by human activities, e.g. recharge lakes.

recurrence interval   The expected time between floods (or droughts) of a certain size.

regolith   The layer of weathered material at the upper surface of a rock. This is the starting point for soil development.

rip-rap   Large fragments of broken rock dumped along a shoreline to protect it against wave attack.

river profile   The changing height of a river channel as it passes from source to mouth.

river regime   The usual pattern of water flow in a river over a year.

slope wash   Movements of water at or close to the surface of a slope, that result in the removal of material.

soft engineering   Non-structural responses to managing coasts, e.g. beach replenishment.

strategic retreat   The managed withdrawal of human occupation of areas with high risks of severe flooding and erosion.

structure (rock)   The arrangement of the beds of rock.

sub-aerial processes   The action of weathering and mass movement on the cliff face.

succession (plant)   The evolutionary process of change in ecosystems.

sustainable management   Managing the environment using techniques and approaches that will preserve the environment for the future.

throughflow   Water moving slowly down hill in the soil layers. If the water follows plant roots or weaknesses in the soil the process may be a lot quicker.

trophic level   The position an organism occupies in the food chain.

water budget   The annual balance between water losses from an ecosystem or soil system, and the input from precipitation.

water-table   This marks the level in the bedrock (or soil) below which the rock is saturated with water. The water-table will vary seasonally.

watershed   A watershed marks the boundary between drainage basins. It usually follows the line of higher ground.

weathering   The breakdown of rock at the surface or close to it. It may involve the physical break up of the rock particles or chemical changes to its structure. Only after weathering is the material removed.

wetted perimeter   The line of contact between the water and the river channel.

xerosere   The pattern of vegetation that develops in dry conditions, e.g. sand dunes.

Chapter One Rural Environments

1 What are rural environments?

Defining rural and urban environments

The word urban refers to towns and cities. The United Nations (UN) defines these as settlements with over 20,000 inhabitants. Most of us live in these urban environments: in built-up areas with many other people. Cities usually have a broad mix of inhabitants, each with different types of job, and each demanding a wide range of services. In contrast, rural environments are those in the countryside, where the densities of population and buildings are generally much lower. The Countryside Agency refers to rural settlements as those containing less than 10,000 people. Fewer people usually means fewer services. Rural employment has traditionally been in agriculture and other primary activities, but in many parts of the world this is now changing rapidly.

In more economically developed countries (MEDCs), people who live and work in rural areas use nearby towns and cities for services which they do not have locally: the large supermarket, the night life, or the wide range of shops. City dwellers, on the other hand, use the countryside for recreation, at weekends or when on holiday. For many people, living near the edge of a city or just beyond it allows them to enjoy the benefits of both the urban and the rural environment: hence the great popularity of **rural-urban fringe** areas.

In less economically developed countries (LEDCs) most people still live in rural areas where there are fewer life choices. The need to survive and the chance to find employment have led to increasing migration to the cities. Rural-urban migrations on a large scale are no longer seen in MEDCs.

Perceptions of the rural environment

The rural environment is made up of a variety of places, people, and activities. Your view of rural environments depends greatly upon your own experience: who you are, where you live, and what picture the media gives you.

ACTIVITIES

1 Look at the resources on pages 126 and 127: they all show rural environments. For each resource decide what it shows and why it may have been chosen as a rural image.
2 Prepare a list of 12 words which you think describe rural environments. Use the resources on pages 126 and 127 to give you ideas. Compare your list with the lists of other members of the class. Do you agree?

Figure 1.1 *'Chocolate box rural'.*

Figure 1.2 *'Poverty stricken rural'.*

Figure 1.3   *'Adventurous rural'.*

Figure 1.4   *'Awesome rural'.*

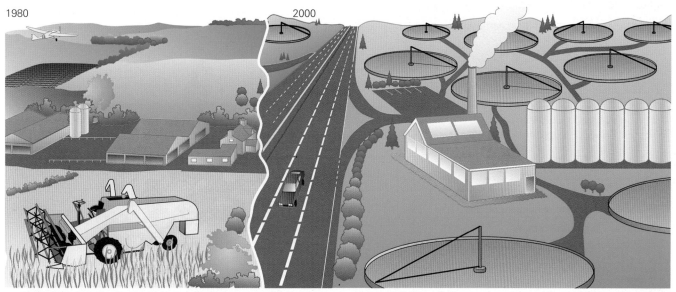

1980   2000

Figure 1.5   *'Farming rural'.*

Viewed from outside:

- 1980 prediction was that all rainforest in Rondonia, Brazil would be gone by 2000
- 1990 only one billion of Brazil's 1.6 billion hectares of rainforest now remain
- 2000 WWF estimate that over 20 hectares of rainforest are destroyed every minute

Viewed from Brazil:

- current losses in most Amazon states are about 12%, with much Hylaea (virgin) forest still untouched

- satellite evidence about fires includes all land not just forest

- current logging rates in Brazil are one third of those in the USA

Figure 1.6   *'Conflicting rural'.*

Figure 1.7   *'Threatened rural'.*

A definition of rurality

Clearly some places are best described as urban, whilst others have recognisable rural characteristics. However, just as the busy central business district (CBD) of a city is very different from a leafy suburb, so the rural-urban fringe differs considerably from, for example, a remote moorland. The transition from one to the other is often gradual and is therefore referred to as the **rural-urban continuum**. The characteristics used to measure **rurality** may include data about people: their number, density, age, type of employment, and income. Other criteria might be the level of services provided, the land use (including open space), and the accessibility of nearby towns and cities for commuters.

ACTIVITIES

1 a Using Cloke's map of rurality (Figure 1.8) try to explain the patterns of rurality in north Wales, Norfolk, Hampshire, and Berkshire.

b Are there any places on the map where the pattern is not what you expected?

2 As a group, devise your own index of rurality.

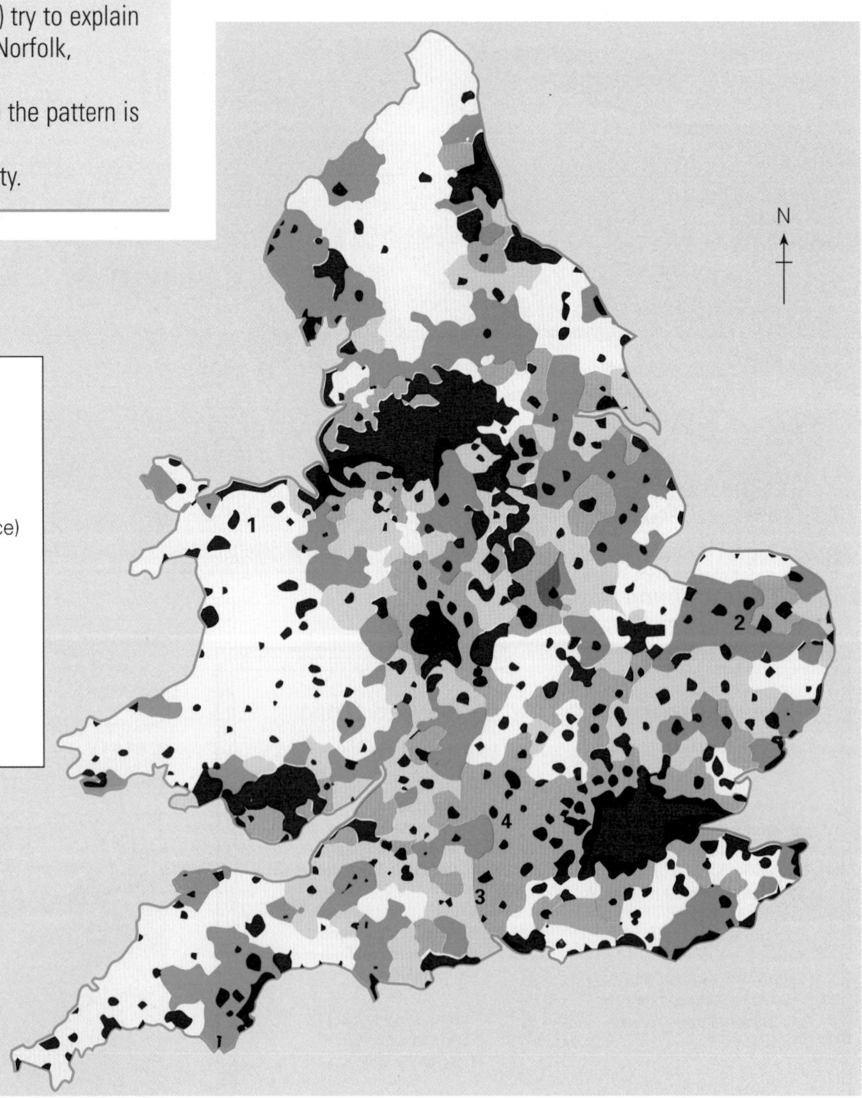

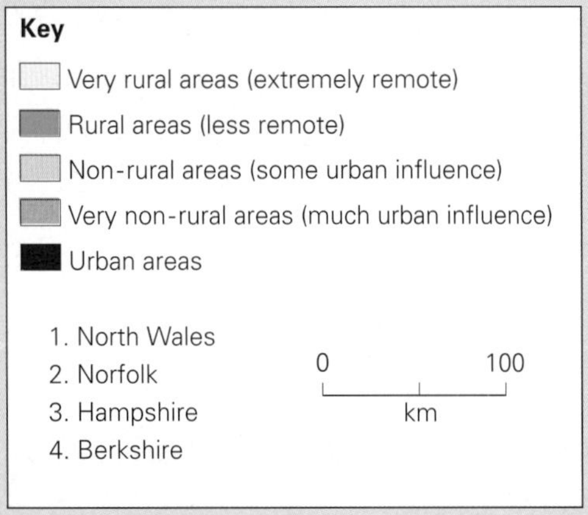

An index of rurality

One such index was suggested by P J Cloke in 1977, who was able to draw a map of England and Wales using the sort of criteria already mentioned (Figure 1.8). His conclusion was that beyond the urban area proper there were four levels of rurality, which he called:

- extreme rural: remote areas, like the Lake District or the northern Pennines
- intermediate rural: still very rural, like south Devon
- intermediate non-rural: with growing urban influence as in Northamptonshire or Bedfordshire
- extreme non-rural: rural-urban fringe areas around London, for example in Hertfordshire or Berkshire.

Key

- Very rural areas (extremely remote)
- Rural areas (less remote)
- Non-rural areas (some urban influence)
- Very non-rural areas (much urban influence)
- Urban areas

1. North Wales
2. Norfolk
3. Hampshire
4. Berkshire

0 — 100 km

Figure 1.8 *Cloke's map of rurality (using census data from 1971).*
Source: *Regional Studies*, 11, 1977.

Cloke's map (Figure 1.8) used 16 different criteria to identify the pattern of rurality in England and Wales, and it is now over 20 years old. Figures 1.9–1.11 show the distribution of population in the UK, the rail network in the UK, and mobile phone coverage in the UK.

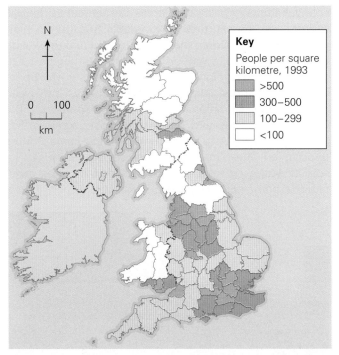

Figure 1.9 *Map of population distribution and density in the UK.*

Source: *OS Statlas*, HMSO, 1993.

Figure 1.10 *Map of rail networks in the UK.*

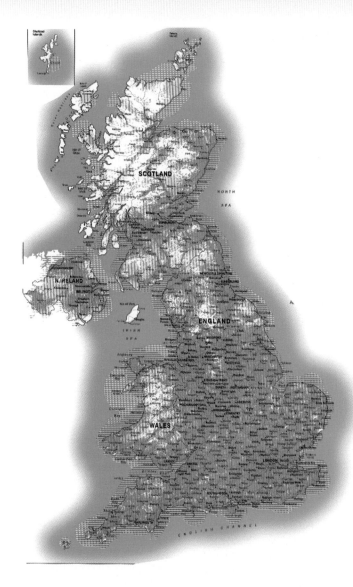

Figure 1.11 *Map of mobile phone coverage in the UK. (The darker the orange colour, the better the quality of coverage)*

Source: *Orange Personal Communications Services Ltd*, 1998.

ACTIVITIES

1 Using all of the maps, write an explanation of how the population density and communications are linked to rurality.

2 Suggest why Cloke's map and its criteria may be less valid now than they once were. Give examples from Figures 1.9–1.11.

3 Which areas of Scotland or Northern Ireland do you think might still be considered remote?

Changes in the rural environment

In the UK, those rural places closest to a growing city are most likely to change in response to urban pressures. This brings changes in land use, buildings, population patterns, and employment. Some villages are absorbed by the expanding city, whilst others are linked by **linear developments** along the main roads. Away from these roads, smaller settlements may be less altered or even protected by planning controls. Where there are large cities nearby, **greenbelts** have been established to restrict further building on farmland or areas of recreation.

Further out from the city, housing has been added to existing villages or built in new or expanded towns. Many people use these as <u>dormitory</u> or <u>commuter</u> settlements, because they live in the 'country' but still work in the city. In a recent survey across the European Union (EU), British workers, on average, travelled some of the largest commuting distances in both actual distance and journey time.

In the more remote areas, the size and appearance of villages may not seem to have changed: it is too far to travel to work in the city. This lack of external change may hide important social changes that are taking place. Many younger adults have left rural areas, pushed out by the lack of jobs and the shortage of affordable housing. In their place have come people seeking retirement and those with the money to buy <u>second</u> or <u>holiday homes</u> (Figure 1.12). <u>Honeypot</u> villages for tourists may have grown up at attractive locations. Many distant rural areas have seen <u>depopulation</u>. A combination of poor transport links, the decline of farming, and the loss of basic services, has encouraged people to move away, leaving some houses unoccupied. These more remote places are returning to a sort of <u>wildscape</u>, and may be included in areas given national park or other conservation status.

Craven Herald & Pioneer
The Voice of the Dales

Gloomy picture of rural living

It took the Women's Institute to draw national attention to a fact of modern life which seems glaringly obvious – that rural life is in a bit of a crisis.

In one of the largest studies of rural life ever commissioned, the WI highlighted the alarming decline of services in rural villages, a decline which has been documented piece by piece in this newspaper over many years.

One in three villages now lacks a shop and almost 500 rural post offices have closed in the last 10 years.

Villages are changing. They are less and less a social and economic unit and increasingly a mere dormitory for commuters who want a rural idyll to escape to. As the demand for a country retreat grows, so house prices spiral upwards and those born and bred in the village but living on a low income are squeezed out.

It is difficult to see how the trend can be reversed.

Source: *Craven Herald* June, 1997

Halfway down, I had my wife stop the car by a field gate. My favourite view in the world is there, and I got out to have a look. You can see almost the whole of Malhamdale; sheltered and snug beneath steep, imposing hills, with its arrow-straight drystone walls climbing impossibly ambitious slopes, its clustered hamlets, its wonderful little two-room schoolhouse, the old church with its sycamores and tumbling tombstones, the roof of my local pub, and in the centre of it all, obscured by trees, our old stone house, which itself is far older than my native land.

Source: Bill Bryson (1995) *Notes from a Small Island*, Black Swan, London: p. 351.

Figure 1.12   *Two views on rural living.*

Changing population in Malham

Figure 1.13   *Malham village, Yorkshire Dales.*

The area shown in Figure 1.14 stretches north-west from the large metropolitan areas of Bradford and Leeds, through former textile towns, into the rural-urban fringe beyond. Further on, the open farmland gives way to the upland scenery of the Yorkshire Dales National Park. These changes occur over a distance of under 50km, and cover most of the features of the rural environment described previously.

ACTIVITIES

1   Using Figure 1.14, identify the changes in settlement, roads, and land use you might see as you travel into the countryside, away from the city. Design a model which shows how features change across the rural-urban continuum.

2   How and why does the A65 road alter this pattern?

3   Draw up a table to show some of the advantages and disadvantages of rural living from the viewpoint of a person who has lived all his/her life in the Yorkshire Dales, and from the viewpoint of a new arrival who commutes to Leeds to work.

4   Identify four planning issues for a village such as Malham.

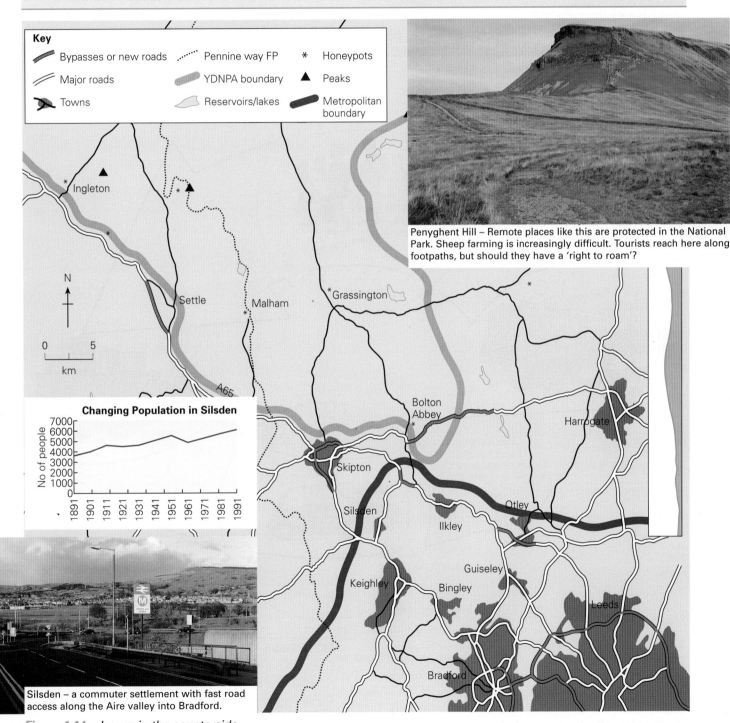

Key

⟋	Bypasses or new roads
⟋⟋	Major roads
✈	Towns
⋯⋯	Pennine way FP
▬	YDNPA boundary
◇	Reservoirs/lakes
✳	Honeypots
▲	Peaks
▬	Metropolitan boundary

Penyghent Hill – Remote places like this are protected in the National Park. Sheep farming is increasingly difficult. Tourists reach here along footpaths, but should they have a 'right to roam'?

Changing Population in Silsden

Silsden – a commuter settlement with fast road access along the Aire valley into Bradford.

Figure 1.14   *Issues in the countryside.*

The changing relationship between rural and urban environments

Population movements can lead to a change in the balance between rural and urban environments.

Urbanisation is the process by which increasing numbers of people become city dwellers. This growth may be partly due to natural increase, but more often it is because people move from the countryside into the towns. The process of rural-urban migration is found in all parts of the world, but its current impacts are strongest in LEDCs.

Counter-urbanisation is the process in which people begin to question the value of living in the city and look increasingly to the rural areas as a better environment in which to live. This is only possible if people have sufficient income, transportation, and freedom of choice, and therefore this process is a feature of MEDCs. **Pull factors** of the rural areas are physical (the scenery), economic (lower business costs), and social (supposedly less stressful). There may be strong **push factors** too. Some people move out to the suburbs, others to the rural-urban fringe, but most retain daily links with the city for work and services. Older people may retire much further into the countryside and, increasingly, communication technology allows more people to work 'remotely', from their homes and away from the office (teleworking).

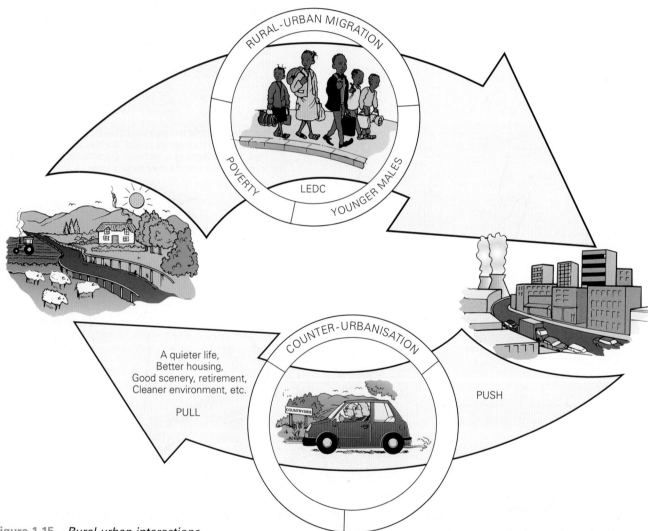

Figure 1.15 *Rural-urban interactions.*

Factors which push people from rural areas may be physical (natural disasters), economic (no paid jobs), or social (wars). The pull of the cities is that they are seen as able to provide the chance of a better way of life. This migration is often forced on people, and ultimately, for many, is not what they had hoped for.

ACTIVITIES

1 Read the text and suggest what additional information you might put into Figure 1.15.
2 Are there any weaknesses in this model?

Changes in rural areas globally

1 Spatial patterns

Maps of the pattern of global urbanisation are a common feature in atlases but looking at the equivalent rural map (Figure 1.16), you will notice that many parts of the world still have a large rural population. There is often a strong link globally between a country's rurality and its level of economic development, as illustrated by the data about gross national product (GNP) (Figure 1.17).

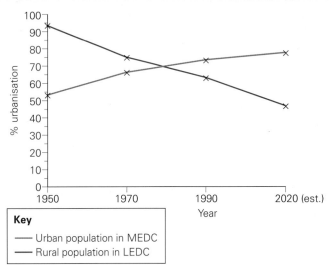

Figure 1.18   *Changing rates of urbanisation.*

Key
— Urban population in MEDC
— Rural population in LEDC

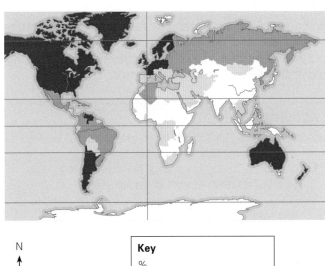

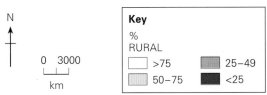

Key
%
RURAL
☐ >75   ▨ 25–49
▧ 50–75   ■ <25

Figure 1.16   *World rural population by country.*

% rural population		GNP per capita (US$)	% rural population		GNP per capita (US$)
15.3	Australia	17 510	46,3	Malaysia	3 160
21.8	Brazil	3 020	24,7	Mexico	3 750
72.8	Burkino Faso	300	60,7	Nigeria	310
68.7	China	490	19,8	Saudi Arabia	8 000
55,2	Egypt	660	0	Singapore	14 598
27.2	France	22 360	74,3	Somalia	500
13.5	Germany	23 560	49,2	South Africa	2 900
73.2	India	290	75.6	Tanzania	140
33.4	Italy	19 620	10.5	United Kingdom	18 340
22.4	Japan	31 450	23.8	USA	24 750

Figure 1.17   *Data on the rurality and gross national product of selected countries.*

2 Patterns over time

The change in the number and proportion of people living in rural or urban areas varies over time, as well as with levels of economic development. Urbanisation occurred in most MEDCs throughout the 19th century, but in LEDCs it has happened very rapidly in the second half of the 20th century alone (Figure 1.18).

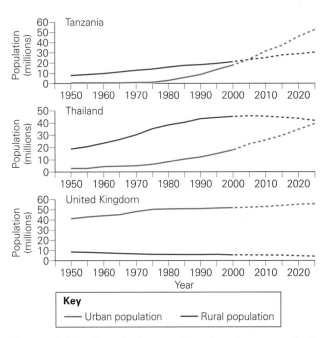

Figure 1.19   *Trends in rural and urban population.*
Source: *Edexcel Foundation*, Paper 6213,1999.

ACTIVITIES

1   Identify places on Figure 1.16 which still seem to have a high percentage of people living in rural areas.
2   Use the table on the left to draw a scattergraph to show the links between rurality and level of development. Summarise the result. (You could use a statistical technique such as Spearman's Rank Correlation Co-efficient to assess the strength of the correlation.)
3   Compare the trends in rural and urban population shown in Figure 1.19. Describe the differing implications for rural planners in the three countries.

2 How and why do rural environments vary in landscape and character?

Why do rural environments differ?

Rural environments can vary considerably. They may simply look different, especially when the location of the area and its physical geography combine to create a distinctive landscape. A desert oasis, a coral island, an alpine village, and a river delta each show the impact of climate, vegetation, geology, or soils. These environmental factors have a big influence on people's activities in the rural landscape, particularly upon the type of farming practised.

Economic factors are also important. The landscapes of traditional subsistence and modern commercial farming look very different, reflecting both the level of technology available and the scale of operation. Water storage, forestry, mineral excavation, and tourism are other important rural activities whose economic development relies not just on natural resources but also on access to their various markets.

Social and cultural influences, too, may play a key role, but their effects are often more subtle. In LEDCs, religion and customs may determine the type of livestock that is reared or dictate the pattern of fields, whilst traditions of ownership and the inheritance of land may limit economic development. Where there is a large rural population, farming is likely to be the predominant occupation and these activities will be labour intensive.

When analysing a photograph of a rural area, the pattern of land use and the character of the settlements often provide as much evidence about the environment as the physical landscape in which they are set.

ACTIVITIES

Three contrasting rural areas are shown on pages 140 and 141 and each is represented in a different way.
1 For Figure 1.20, identify and list the physical, economic, and cultural factors at work in the landscape.
2 For Figure 1.21, annotate a sketch of the photograph to bring out its distinctive characteristics.
3 For Figure 1.22, explain how economic factors have played an important part in shaping the environment.

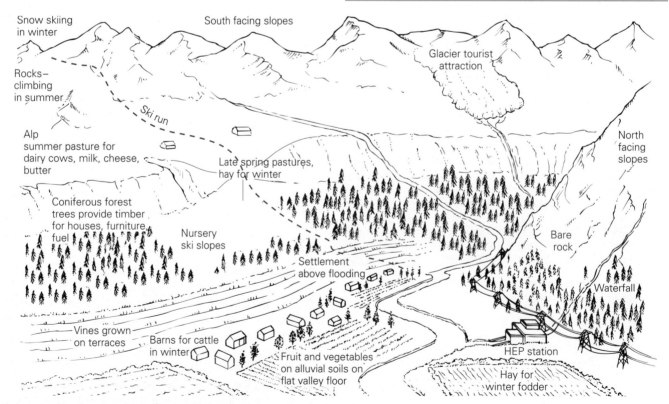

Figure 1.20 *An annotated field sketch of an area in the Swiss Alps.*
Source: David Waugh, *Europe*, Thomas Nelson, 1983.

Figure 1.21 *A photograph of a landscape in Bali.*

Lynford House Farm

FACT FILE

This 504 hectares farm in the Cambridgeshire Fens, near Ely, is almost entirely arable. The land was reclaimed by draining the land 200 years ago. It is owned and run by Robert Sears and family, though part of it was purchased from Scottish Life Assurance Society in 1998. The farm is on flat land just above sea level. Its fertile silt and peat soils receive an average annual rainfall of 559 mm. In March 2000 the labour force was 2 family members and 3 full time workers. Some work is done by contractors. Over the last ten years the farmer has bought almost £300,000 worth of machinery, which has included items like a combine harvester, tractors and a JCB. In 1999 the farm used £7671 worth of tractor diesel. There are many specialist buildings including a cold store for potatoes and another to dry grain. Nitrogen fertiliser costs £15,285 annually, and pesticides (including fungicides and insecticides) a further £43,538. Overall less chemicals are now being used. Recent additions to the farm include a 12 million gallon reservoir and irrigation system. There are 12 bungalows on the farm which have been freed up as farm labour has gradually reduced. The lettings contribute 2% of the farm's income but most are to be sold off.

Output (tonnes) in recent years has changed:

crop	1995	1999	marketing
Feed Wheat	1207	2252	co-operative (subsidy)
Seed Wheat	465	0	seed merchant
Sugar beet	3453	4900	British Sugar (quota)
Potatoes	2166	0	(let to specialist contractor)
Peas	400	0	canning & freezing

Future plans for the farm include:

- wind turbines to provide local electricity (sustainable)

- new systems for accounts, records and finance (computerised)

- if wheat prices fall move back into vegetables like lettuces and onions

- with beet production growing, harvest it himself and not use a contractor

Figure 1.22 *A factfile for a modern farm in Cambridgeshire, UK.*

Source: www.nfu.org.uk

Contrasts between rural areas in MEDCs and LEDCs

One way to explore the differences between rural areas in MEDCs and LEDCs is to look at people's lifestyles and how they have begun to change, contrasting their traditional images with the changing reality of the present, and the likely trends for their futures. The highlands of Kenya in east Africa and the Craven district of North Yorkshire are two very different rural areas, which show their changing patterns of population, settlement, and economic activities.

1 The Kenyan highlands

In the highland areas of Kenya, the Maasai people were traditionally **nomadic**, their wealth, lifestyle, and status being dependent upon their herds of cattle or goats. However, overgrazing, increasingly frequent droughts, and political pressures have forced many nomadic groups to settle and become **sedentary** farmers. Although this is still farming, it is for nomads a totally new way of life.

Further east, between Mount Kenya and Nairobi, the fertile volcanic soils and higher rainfall enabled Kikuyu farmers to practise a traditional form of cultivation known as 'bush fallowing'. Here too there have been changes. In the 19th and 20th centuries many Kikuyu became estate workers in the tea and coffee plantations set up by British firms, such as Brooke Bond. These plantations have now largely been broken up and Kenyan farmers work their own small plots of land. Large-scale production is in the hands of **transnational** food companies, and flowers and peas are just two of a growing list of new exports that leave Nairobi airport each day destined for European supermarket shelves. However, cash crops for export do not provide food for local people.

As population pressure in the highland area increases (Kenya has a very high rate of population increase: over 3.0 per cent per year), both the Maasai and the Kikuyu tribal groups are finding that many of them will inevitably move away: the Mathare valley is only one of the many shanty town areas in Nairobi which has resulted from this trend. The problem for the Kenyan authorities is how to reduce overgrazing and soil erosion and provide basic services in the rural areas, and so prevent further rural-urban migration.

Kenya's tourist industry is now its major source of overseas income. Whilst the 50 game parks in Kenya do provide jobs and conserve the landscape, they also bring problems. The Maasai and their cattle are not allowed to live or hunt in what was traditionally their homeland, and having to 'dress up for the tourists' to make a living by providing tribal dancing displays is perhaps not a change for the better.

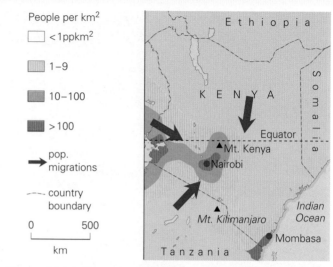

People per km²
- ☐ <1ppkm²
- ▨ 1–9
- ▨ 10–100
- ▨ >100
- → pop. migrations
- ---- country boundary
- 0 ___ 500 km

Figure 1.23   *Changing lifestyles in the Kenyan highlands.*

Poverty in Kenya is not measured by relative 'indicators' like car ownership but by absolute measures like infant mortality (which actually rose during the 1990s to 62 deaths per thousand born) and access to clean water (only 47 per cent of the population).

Figure 1.24   *Time is running out for Kenyan farmers.*

ACTIVITIES

1 Why is time running out for Kenyan farmers?
2 **a** Summarise the changes in population density and settlement revealed in the text and Figures 1.23 and 1.24.
   b The changes have been described as a 'mixed blessing' for the Maasai and the Kikuyu. Assess the evidence for this statement.

You can do further research on a range of websites (see the reference materials at the end of this unit).

2 The Craven district of North Yorkshire

The Craven district, shown in Figure 1.25, is part of the area introduced in Figure 1.14. Traditionally, the hill farmers reared sheep which they marketed locally, and farmers in the dales kept dairy cows, sending milk to the creameries. Quarrying for limestone and other minerals was also locally important. The railway network in the area once served many of the towns and villages. In the south of the district, textile manufacturing produced both cotton and wool. By the 1990s most of these activities had fallen on hard times.

Quarries, now reached by road, still produce large quantities of crushed stone, though using a much reduced workforce. Tourism is proving to be a lifeline in an area where employment opportunities are decreasing, and farming is declining. A number of honeypot sites exist, both within and beyond the Yorkshire Dales National Park boundary. Another, more recent, change has been the rapid growth in the number of new residents, some coming to retire, but many others choosing to live in suburbanised villages along the main roads, and to commute daily into nearby towns and cities (Figure 1.25). Increasing salaries, rising car ownership, some improved transport routes, and new housing developments have all encouraged this 'dormitory' trend.

However, for some people the daily commute, which uses up valuable disposable income and time, is too wasteful (Figure 1.26). The arrival and rapid growth of information technology has given them the opportunity to telecommute. Teleworkers are already a noticeable feature of many villages (Figure 1.27). Telecottaging, in which people telework in local centres, is increasing, and is supported by rural councils and EU funding.

In this section we have looked at two very contrasting areas – the common thread is the amount of change and the fact that changes can bring both benefits and costs.

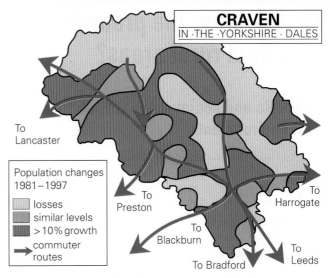

Figure 1.25 *Population changes and commuter patterns in Craven.*

Source: Craven District Council.

Figure 1.26 *The new car park at Silsden station. Commuters take advantage of cheap rail fares into Bradford.*

ACTIVITIES

1 Why have economic activities changed in the Craven district?
2 What impact (physical, social, and economic) does increasing commuter travel have on the rural environment?
3 What are the advantages and disadvantages of teleworking for both people and the environment?
4 Investigate teleworking in your own area using the Internet.

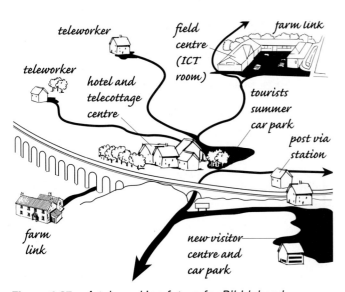

Figure 1.27 *A teleworking future for Ribblehead.*

3 What are the processes of change which affect rural areas?

Economic and social processes change rural environments

Rural environments are modified by changes in economic activity. Land use is often closely linked to land value. Land value in turn is related to location, the resources found there, and the demand for those resources.

Farming is the predominant rural land use in most parts of the world, especially in LEDCs where it is still the main occupation. Land in rural areas can be exploited in many other ways. Mining, quarrying, water supply, and forestry are other activities which exploit valuable natural resources in rural areas. Remote areas, too inhospitable for permanent settlement, may be useful for military activity and for some types of wilderness tourism. In contrast, accessible countryside attracts developments for recreation and leisure, and both greenfield and rural brownfield sites close to urban areas have potential for a wide variety of developments. Transport and other utilities are growing consumers of land, whilst new settlements can appear in both suburban and pioneer locations. The arrival of large numbers of new rural dwellers, with their commuter lifestyle, higher disposable incomes, and demand for permanent and holiday property is causing rapid changes in the countryside in MEDCs.

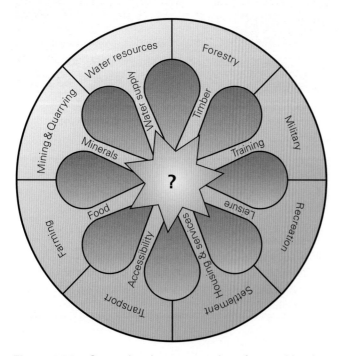

Figure 1.28 *Some development options for rural land.*

How changes in farming have affected rural environments

Inevitably, changes in farming have had a great influence on rural environments. In particular they have altered what the landscape looks like. These changes occur in a variety of locations and can be studied using photographs, maps, and statistics.

The landscape of the Yorkshire Dales, with its patterns of dry stone walls, traditional farm houses and field barns, results from a farming lifestyle that has developed over many centuries. If landowners choose to adopt a more intensive style of farming this landscape will change. However, if farming becomes uneconomic, land and buildings may then be neglected and abandoned and the landscape will also change. If this happens, as is the case in the Lake District and the highlands of Scotland, other activities such as forestry or recreation may take over and alter the landscape.

'Farming ain't what it used to be'

Farming in the Lakes is in decline. The land has always been poor and it still rains most days. The difference is you can't make a living anymore. With market prices for beef and lamb at rock bottom, and financial support being reduced, many farmers are leaving the land or turning to other things.

Much of the land in the Lake District is grade 3 or worse and rainfall reaches up to 3552 mm/yr, so sheep, currently 730,000 of them, and cattle have been the only options. Much of the area is still in private hands (58.7 per cent) making most farmers only tenants. The number of people in farming continues to fall (by 15 per cent between 1981 and 1991) and there has been a shift to part-time and seasonal work. In recent years some farmers have received as much as 80 per cent of their income through subsidies and support payments for farming these uplands. Others (58 per cent at present) are helped by grants for conservation as virtually all of the National Park is designated as an environmentally sensitive area (ESA). These conservation grants relate to woodland or wetlands, or to farmers delaying hay cutting until birds have fledged or wildflowers seeded, for example.

In future, more farmers will supplement their income by **diversifying** into tourism or other money-earning activities, usually by providing accommodation. Without sheep grazing and wall maintenance, the landscape will look very different, and without farming families, the way of life in local communities will have changed for ever.

Figure 1.29 *Extract from the Lake District Gazette, Oct. 1999.*

ACTIVITIES

1   Look at figure 1.29. What makes hill farming economically difficult?
2   Explain how its decline would affect the landscape and local communities.

Some of the more striking changes in rural landscapes have resulted from the introduction of modern farming technology and intensive production methods, particularly in the lowlands. This 'hi-tech' farming has become very sophisticated (Figure 1.30). Farmers have taken advantage of developments in the selective breeding of cattle (hybridisation), in the use of high-yielding variety (**HYV**) seeds, fertilisers, chemicals, and biocides. Modern machinery has allowed a bigger scale of operation and the use of irrigation and glasshouses can provide year-round operation.

Lowland farming has more options than hill farming. Arable farmers in Cambridgeshire (see also Figure 1.23) concentrate on cereal production or on oil seed rape. Further west in Bedfordshire, mixed farms rear poultry and pigs (these are capital intensive), whilst eastwards into the Fens, there is an increase in market gardening (technology intensive). Some market gardening enterprises in the Fens are also relatively labour intensive, for example in vegetable processing operations.

The increasing mechanisation of farming in areas like Cambridgeshire has meant that the average field size (13ha) more than doubled between 1945 and the early 1970s. Over one third of the hedgerows which existed in 1945 were also removed during this period. Many farms have been amalgamated and family-run farms are giving way to large '**agribusinesses**' run by farm managers for their companies. Although these trends have slowed down considerably in the 1990s, they have both influenced the landscape and affected levels of employment in agriculture. Many of the changes seen in Cambridgeshire are reflected in the national picture, but to a lesser extent (Figure 1.31).

Economic Reform of the Common Agricultural Policy (CAP) commodity support payments (premiums) for UK farmers, worth £1.38 billion in 1999, will in future have an environmental emphasis. The £2.173 billion farm income of 2000 is only one third of the equivalent figure of 25 years ago.

Social Jobs in farming will decrease (14 per cent in the 1990s). Many farmers and farm workers have become part time (29 per cent) or work seasonally (13 per cent). Farming in 2000 involves only 1.7 per cent of the UK workforce, just 4.4 per cent of the rural population.

Landscape Hedgerows were removed at a rate of 8000 km/yr between 1945 and 1993.

Figure 1.31   *Changes in UK farming 1945-2000.*

ACTIVITIES

1   Hi-tech farming develops higher yields at lower costs using less land'. Using your research, assess this statement.
2   Evaluate the positive and negative effects of hi-tech farming in the UK. Think about environmental costs versus economic gains.

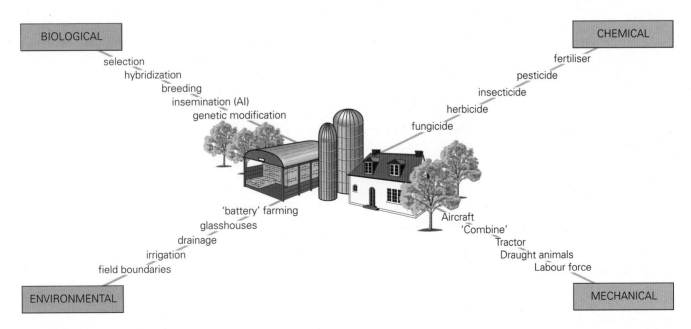

Figure 1.30   *Technological change.*

The Lake District 'on the edge'

The Lake District is a potential 'wildscape' designated as a national park at the outer edge the rural-urban continuum.

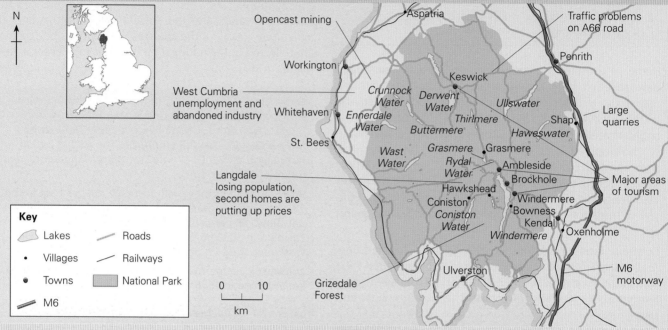

Figure 1.32   *Some impacts of rural development in the Lake District.*

The impact of social and economic developments in South Lakeland

With farming in decline, it is not surprising to discover that nearly one third of Lakeland jobs are linked to tourism. Many services (29.8 per cent) are also directed mainly at tourists, and developments in retailing, transport, and catering make up 37.5 per cent of regional employment. Most of this is concentrated in the three largest settlements – Ambleside, Keswick, and Windermere – and in a number of rural honeypots like Grasmere. The increasing demand for tourist accommodation, visitor services, and retailing has led to changes in the employment structure and land use (Figure 1.33).

However, there are drawbacks (Figure 1.32). Employment in the tourist industry is largely seasonal, part time, and poorly paid, and there is also an impact on existing activities like farming due to litter, trespassing, and footpath erosion. The traditionally quiet village life is affected by noise and traffic, and by an increase in house prices. Many 'local' shops and services (schools and buses) have gone, and young people have left: the resident population continues to decline. In Langdale, at Elterwater, a brownfield site became the Lake District's first timeshare complex in 1985. This £5 million investment provides both full-time and part-time jobs, and is open all year round. In contrast, the decline in traditional employment has led to rural depopulation from the nearby hamlet of Chapel Stile, which has been labelled a 'ghost village'. In the Langdale valley as a whole, almost 40 per cent of houses are not permanently occupied and are now holiday cottages or second homes.

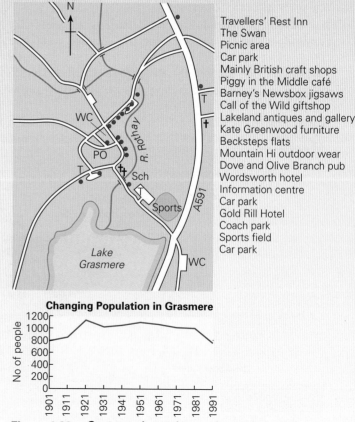

Travellers' Rest Inn
The Swan
Picnic area
Car park
Mainly British craft shops
Piggy in the Middle café
Barney's Newsbox jigsaws
Call of the Wild giftshop
Lakeland antiques and gallery
Kate Greenwood furniture
Becksteps flats
Mountain Hi outdoor wear
Dove and Olive Branch pub
Wordsworth hotel
Information centre
Car park
Gold Rill Hotel
Coach park
Sports field
Car park

Figure 1.33   *Grasmere's tourist services, 2000, and changing population.*

The shutters are down in the village at the heart of Lakeland. The streets are deserted, the houses – resplendent in the local green slate – largely empty. And the few locals remaining at Chapel Stile, in the shadow of the Langdale Pikes, are restless.

'This used to be a thriving community, but we never thought it would end up as a ghost town,' laments Nellie Mallett, born in the village 76 years ago. 'Now look at it. Most of the houses don't seem to be occupied and locals can't afford to live here any longer.'

Like many communities in England's most famous national park, Chapel Stile has been overrun by outsiders – richer folk from the cities who buy houses at inflated prices, rent them out for part of the year and often pay only token visits.

Half the houses in Chapel Stile are now second homes.

Figure 1.34   *Impacts on Langdale.*
Source: *The Guardian*, 19 May, 1998.

ACTIVITIES

Look at the Figures 1.34 and 1.35.
1   What are the impacts of tourist growth in Langdale?
2   **a**   Using the data provided about second homes, copy and complete the map in Figure 1.36.
    b   Do you see any pattern? Suggest possible reasons for this.
3   What issues result from the growth in the number of second homes in areas such as the Lake District?

Figure 1.35   *Weekend arrivals in the Lakes.*   Source: NEAB.

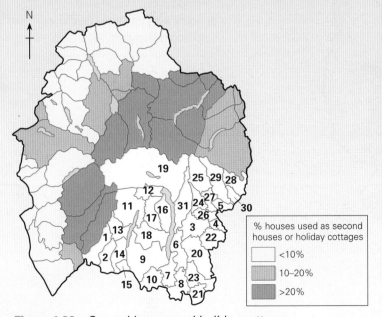

Figure 1.36   *Second homes and holiday cottages.*
Source: Lake District National Park, 1991.

% houses used as second homes or holiday cottages
<10%
10–20%
>20%

South Lakeland Parish					
Map Ref.		%not occupied permanently	Map Ref.		%not occupied permanently
1	Broughton West	11.5	17	Hawkshead	23.2
2	Kirkby Ireleth	17.6	18	Satterthwaite	13.6
3	Crook	12.5	19	Lakes	21.3
4	Strickland Ketel	6.0	20	Crosthwaite and Lyth	16.9
5	Strickland Roger	14.8	21	Meathop	
6	Cartmel Fell	30.5		and Ulpha	10.3
7	Staveley-in-		22	Underbarrow	4.3
	Cartmel	35.1	23	Witherslack	4.6
8	Upper Allithwaite	7.3	24	Hugill	9.8
9	Colton	11.8	25	Kentmere	12.7
10	Haverthwaite	14.0	26	Nether Staveley	5.2
11	Coniston	20.7	27	Over Staveley	11.0
12	Skelwith	13.8	28	Fawcett Forest	11.1
13	Torver	13.4	29	Longsleddale	0
14	Blawith	15.6	30	Witwell and	
15	Lowick	29.4		Selside	23.5
16	Claife	13.8	31	Windermere	13.7
				and Bowness	
				Mean = 15.9%	

Changes in population are linked closely to employment, which in turn affects services. Influences from outside can be irresistible and a cycle of decline can result. Some of the factors involved are set out in Figure 1.37.

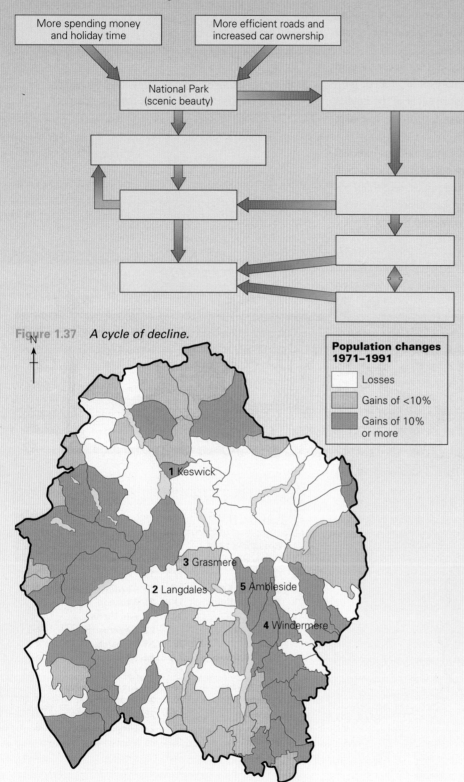

More spending money and holiday time	More efficient roads and increased car ownership

National Park (scenic beauty)

Local services reduced

Planning control of building

Locals move away

Demand for second homes

Increased house prices

Lack of permanent employment

Building of new houses

Figure 1.37 *A cycle of decline.*

Population changes 1971–1991

Losses

Gains of <10%

Gains of 10% or more

N

1 Keswick

3 Grasmere

2 Langdales

5 Ambleside

4 Windermere

Figure 1.38 *Map of population trends in Lakeland.*
Source: Lake District National Park, 1991.

ACTIVITIES

1 Using the words listed in Figure 1.37 complete the flow chart showing how a cycle of decline can develope in a national park.

2 Why is it difficult to plan for the future of rural villages in areas like this?

3 Try to account for the population changes shown in Figure 1.38.

Cambridgeshire 'beyond the fringe'

Cambridgeshire is at the inner edge of the rural-urban continuum where the rural-urban fringe is under very great pressure from development (Figure 1.39).

'The Cambridge Phenomenon'

With a long history as a centre of education behind it, Cambridge has become a magnet for high technology and research and development companies. Computer firms like Acorn and IBM arrived in the Science Park (christened 'Silicon Fen') in 1973, with Microsoft and Sony the most recent investors in the city's highly skilled workforce. The M11 motorway corridor and the triangle of major roads that surround the city have ensured good access to the city and the greenbelt has remained relatively secure. One result of this is that as an established regional centre, Cambridge generates considerable amounts of commuting throughout its rural-urban fringe. Other centres, especially those further south in north Hertfordshire, are also part of London's bigger commuter belt and **sphere of influence**.

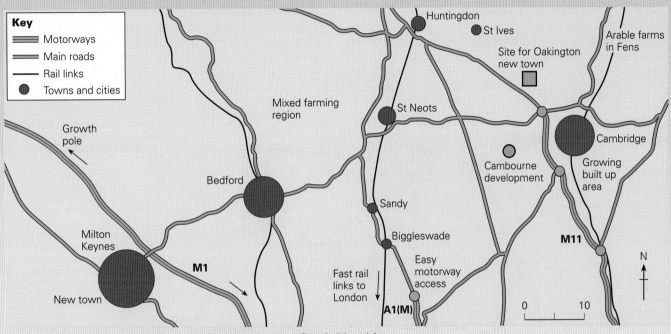

Figure 1.39   *Some impacts of development in rural Cambridgeshire.*

ACTIVITIES

1   How well does the Cambridge area fit in with the generic view of the rural-urban fringe?

The rural-urban fringe

The inner margin of the rural-urban continuum is called the rural-urban fringe. The rural-urban fringe is not a boundary line at the edge of a city, but a zone that has both rural and urban characteristics: a zone of growth where land use and population density can change rapidly. As the urban area expands, so the position of the rural-urban zone moves outwards. The rural-urban fringe is therefore more dynamic than its remote counterpart, and the demographic and economic trends are typically upward. The impact on the rural environment of suburbanisation and **urban sprawl** also has implications for conservation at least as important as the development issues facing the national parks. In the UK, the growth of public transport between the First and the Second World War led to large-scale residential expansion on the rural-urban fringe, especially around London. Increased car ownership since the 1960s accelerated this, and industrial estates and new road networks were developed. New towns were built to house overspill from the larger conurbations. These were (it was hoped) to be self-contained, providing jobs and services as well as housing. **Science parks** have developed since the 1970s, with large, out-of-town shopping centres and numerous leisure developments, such as golf courses, following in the 1990s. In the late 1990s came a growing resistance to such development from rural and environmental groups, and the advent of much tougher planning laws.

Changes in population and services

In Cambridgeshire, rapid demographic and economic processes are at work. In villages like Cambourne, beyond the greenbelt and seven miles to the west of Cambridge, new job opportunities in the city are increasing demands for housing and local services. This has led to changes in land use. Those who move in are younger, more skilled, and better paid (than the local people) allowing them to commute to work and to pay higher prices for property. This situation may seem to be similar to that in remote areas like the Lake District national parks, but it is not. The population numbers and density in Cambridgeshire are increasing, and the age structure is younger overall with a much larger, economically active group. The number one issue for farmers in Cambridgeshire is the way in which their land is ripe for development. If planning permission exists the land is worth a great deal.

Cambourne was until recently three small villages, but that is changing (Figure 1.40). It has been chosen by planners to become one of a series of locations beyond the greenbelt that are being carefully expanded to house Cambridge's growing army of commuter families. The planned 3300 new houses will be divided amongst the three villages. The traditional features of village green, pub, and shop are being retained but new leisure facilities, a business park, and improved transport links are being added. The varied housing types include 900 affordable homes beginning at £56,212 (1999): The top-of-the-range executive house is currently advertised at £229,950. The nearby secondary school at Comberton is building new facilities ready for the growing number of children who will need to be educated. With its attractive surroundings and good access to Cambridge, Cambourne is clearly going to grow rapidly, and house sales are booming.

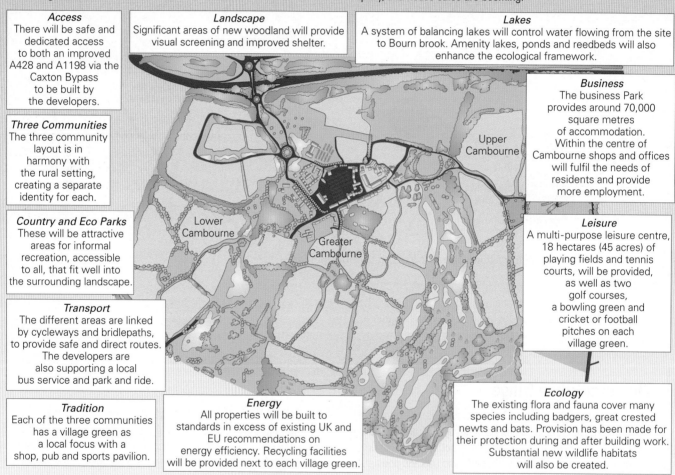

Access
There will be safe and dedicated access to both an improved A428 and A1198 via the Caxton Bypass to be built by the developers.

Three Communities
The three community layout is in harmony with the rural setting, creating a separate identity for each.

Country and Eco Parks
These will be attractive areas for informal recreation, accessible to all, that fit well into the surrounding landscape.

Transport
The different areas are linked by cycleways and bridlepaths, to provide safe and direct routes. The developers are also supporting a local bus service and park and ride.

Tradition
Each of the three communities has a village green as a local focus with a shop, pub and sports pavilion.

Landscape
Significant areas of new woodland will provide visual screening and improved shelter.

Energy
All properties will be built to standards in excess of existing UK and EU recommendations on energy efficiency. Recycling facilities will be provided next to each village green.

Lakes
A system of balancing lakes will control water flowing from the site to Bourn brook. Amenity lakes, ponds and reedbeds will also enhance the ecological framework.

Business
The business Park provides around 70,000 square metres of accommodation. Within the centre of Cambourne shops and offices will fulfil the needs of residents and provide more employment.

Leisure
A multi-purpose leisure centre, 18 hectares (45 acres) of playing fields and tennis courts, will be provided, as well as two golf courses, a bowling green and cricket or football pitches on each village green.

Ecology
The existing flora and fauna cover many species including badgers, great crested newts and bats. Provision has been made for their protection during and after building work. Substantial new wildlife habitats will also be created.

Upper Cambourne

Lower Cambourne

Greater Cambourne

Figure 1.40 *The growth of Cambourne, Cambridgeshire.*   Source: The Cambourne Centre, 1998.

ACTIVITIES

1   Identify the changes Cambourne and other villages in the rural-urban fringe may be experiencing.
2   What impact will the changes have on village shops and services?
3   Look again at Figure 1.35 and suggest 'speech bubbles' for a cartoon about possible conflicts in a place like Cambourne.

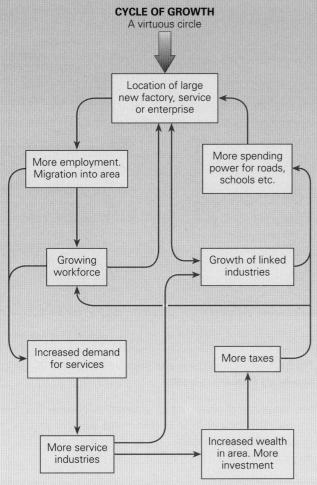

CYCLE OF GROWTH
A virtuous circle

Location of large new factory, service or enterprise

More employment. Migration into area

More spending power for roads, schools etc.

Growing workforce

Growth of linked industries

Increased demand for services

More taxes

More service industries

Increased wealth in area. More investment

Figure 1.41 *The cycle of growth (multiplier effect).*

'Cambridge futures'

Faced with rapid and continuing development (a predicted 44 per cent increase in population by 2050, with 47 per cent more jobs and 40,000 new homes), Cambridge in 1999 launched a strategy document for its future. Within this strategy document were seven proposals for managing the city's growth (Figure 1.42). People were asked their views about the proposals. At least four of the proposals will greatly affect the rural-urban fringe.

Working in a group or as a class, ask each individual to score each option. Think about the environmental impact and the economic costs of each option. Pool your results and work out your preferred plan. An alternative exercise might be to divide the options between members of your group/class, with individuals preparing reasons for supporting each scheme. Write a summary of your discussion.

Whichever option is chosen is no doubt that the Cambridge area, along with Ashford in Kent, Micheldever in Hampshire, or the Horsham area in Sussex, will be the growth hot spots in south-east England. The changes caused by this are inevitable, the issue is how to manage them.

ACTIVITIES

1 Imagine you are a resident of Cambridge. Using Figure 1.42 decide which option you would prefer using a scale of 1 to 5 (1 = strongly dislike; 3 = indifferent; 5 = strongly like).
2 What has brought such sustained development to Cambridgeshire?
3 How has the cycle of growth worked?

Option	Title	Description	Impact on rural-urban fringe	Score
Option 1	Minimum growth	Preserve the city as it is with no transport developments	Increase in commuting but preserves greenbelt	
Option 2	Densification	Redevelop land and transport inside city only	Increase in jobs but also in pollution and traffic congestion	
Option 3	Necklace	Concentrate development in a 'necklace' of villages beyond the greenbelt but no transport development, e.g. Cambourne	Increase in commuting but preserves greenbelt	
Option 4	Green Swap	Develop poorer areas of the greenbelt e.g. airport site. And replace these with new green amenities further out	More jobs, less commuting and new facilities	
Option 5	Transport links	Upgrade rail services to London, Huntingdon and Ely and build new stations	Expensive but environmentally sound	
Option 6	Virtual highway	Large-scale teleworking provision – Cambridge has expertise in this field	Reduces commuting and environmentally sound	
Option 7	New town	Build a single new town beyond the greenbelt,	Expensive but environmentally sound	

Figure 1.42 *Cambridge futures.* Source: Cambridge futures, Cambridge County Council, 1998.

The effects of changes in rural environments and populations

As we have seen in the two preceding case studies, changes in rural areas can cause population to decline or expand (Figure 1.43). The contrast in the futures of rural areas results from their locations and their potential for development. The Lake District illustrates an area of overall decline, albeit rescued by tourism, where problems are related to seasonal unemployment, housing costs, isolation, and the loss of public services like schools, buses, and local shops. The Cambridge region highlights the impact on the rural-urban fringe of rapid developments in housing, transport, and industry.

The Countryside Alliance rallies, in March 1998 and September 1999, put many rural matters firmly on the British political agenda, by publicising a range of rural concerns. Issues such as rural deprivation and exclusion, 'right to roam' proposals, rising house prices, and congested roads.

It is important to examine these changes and their effects at a variety of scales and the remainder of this section will deal with larger-scale trends in MEDC and LEDC areas.

Population changes in the 1990s in the UK reveal three clear trends. Firstly, there is a north to south drift fuelled by the loss of employment in traditional mining and manufacturing areas and the employment potential of the south-east. Secondly, those who can afford to have moved from the inner cities to the suburbs. Lastly,

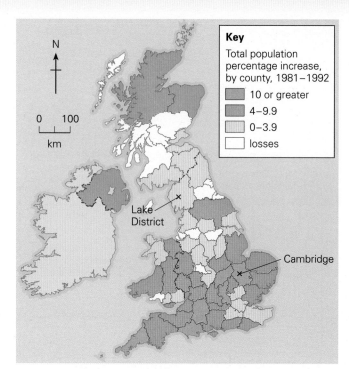

Figure 1.43   *Changes in the population of the UK.*
Source: *OS Statlas* HMSO, 1993.

the largest and most rapid internal migration has been counter-urbanisation: it is this trend which has affected rural (and coastal) areas. It is estimated that this has moved one million people out of London.

Core and periphery

Core regions are essentially prosperous, urbanised, and economically strong. They attract skilled workers, services, and investment. Such areas have a multiplier effect economically.

Peripheral regions are usually rural, often economically weak, and fail to attract investment or services. Here unemployment and low wages can create a cycle of decline.

Industries and businesses in the core use resources from the periphery, both human and material. This sustains the core region but there is of course always a danger that the core region will exhaust the periphery and cause further decline (divergence).

Ideally the core might, through investment, be able to spread its prosperity outwards (spread effect) and help the periphery to catch up (convergence).

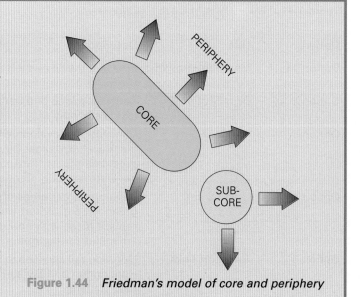

Figure 1.44   *Friedman's model of core and periphery*

ACTIVITIES

1 **a** Identify, using an atlas, those areas of the UK with the greatest population growth and decline.
   b Suggest reasons for the location of these areas.

Contrasts in the EU

The 'banana' shape marked on Figure 1.45 is seen by economic planners as the central area of Europe, to which people and industries are attracted. Away from this core, the outer areas are tending to lose population. Clearly, Cambridgeshire is within the EU core region, whilst the Yorkshire Dales and the Lake District lie outside it. Places in the rural periphery, with poor transport facilities and failing agriculture, may experience deprivation and poverty, In mainland Europe these areas include the Mezzogiorno of southern Italy and areas such as northern Portugal. The continuing development of the Mediterranean coasts of France and Spain suggests that these areas are part of a growing core region.

ACTIVITIES

1 Does the pattern of agricultural employment shown in Figure 1.45 support the idea of a 'hot banana'? Give examples. Are there exceptions?

Northern Portugal: the outer limits

The most northerly region of Portugal is one of the poorest areas in Europe. Sixty per cent of jobs in Portugal are dependent upon agriculture. This is the highest in the EU and ten times higher than in the UK. Farming in northern Portugal is in decline for three basic reasons. Firstly, the region is on Portugal's Atlantic fringe, with all of the major development taking place in the Algarve at the opposite end of the country. Secondly, farming is being slowly strangled by the traditional system of land inheritance. Thirdly, it is a very remote area with poor services and communications.

Agriculture in northern Portugal is labour intensive and based around maize, vines and vegetables. Traditionally, land passes from a father to his children in equal shares and farms become progressively more fragmented, and reduced to smallholdings.

This area has a high density of population (162/km²) but it is increasingly ageing due to the continuing loss of young people to opportunities in Lisbon. There is much emigration too: traditionally to Brazil, with many sending part of their income home. Ironically, empty properties in northern Portugal are being sold to foreigners for summer homes.

Despite attempts by the Portuguese government and the EU to promote the area's Costa Verde as a tourist package, the economic profile of northern Portugal remains poor. Improving transport links in particular would be too expensive an undertaking.

ACTIVITIES

1 What tells you that northern Portugal is on the periphery economically as well as geographically?
2 Why is this area so poor by EU standards?

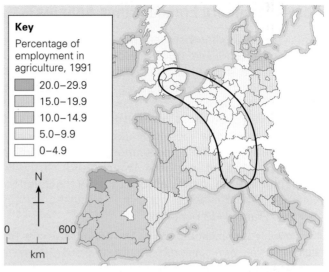

Figure 1.45   *The rural regions of the EU (map based on percentage in agriculture).*   Source: *OS Statlas* HMSO, 1995.

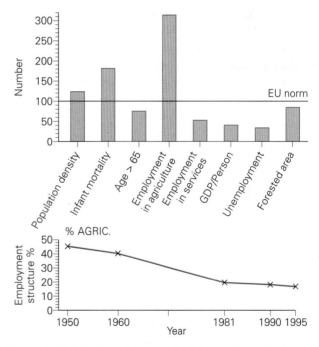

Figure 1.46   *Decline in agriculture in northern Portugal.*
Source: *Brian Dicks,* EIT, Hodder, 1999.

Figure 1.47   *Peasant farming in northern Portugal.*

Central southern France: fringe benefits?

Languedoc-Roussillon between the Rhône delta and the Pyrenées had until the 1970s one of the lowest rates of GDP in France, in spite of considerable economic growth along the coast. Major international firms like IBM and Nestlé set up in Montpellier for example. Unemployment has been very high at 14 per cent but this is changing rapidly as most new jobs in France are in the south, fuelled partly by a drift in population from the declining industrial areas of northern France, and partly by immigration from north Africa. In 1999 Languedoc-Roussillon had the largest net gain in population of any region in France (+13 per cent).

The French government through its **DATAR** initiative sees the area as its very own 'California'. Tourist developments along the Mediterranean coast, which match those in Spain, investment in water supply, and new road links from the Rhône corridor, are all designed to bring long-term prosperity to the region. Already the departement of Hérault in this region boasts some of the highest incomes outside Paris.

However, inland to the north-west in the Cévennes and Les Causses there is little new employment. Even tourist developments near to the national park cannot seem to prevent rural deprivation. Traditionally the people here worked as subsistence farmers, in mining and crafts, with seasonal work in the vineyards of Languedoc. By the end of the 20th century this economy, based on small farms, had collapsed. Rural depopulation is occurring and there is a growing legacy of deserted farmhouses and an ageing population: not unlike northern Portugal. What is its future? Will the area become like the Lake District: an area of forestry, conservation, and second homes (for people in Marseilles), or will the spread of the adjacent 'sun belt' provide the economic incentive for the area to grow (Figure 1.48). Will it be the natural environment that pays the price?

ACTIVITIES

1 What suggests that Languedoc-Roussillon is now part of Europe's 'hot banana'?
2 What strategies should planners adopt to help reduce the 'gradient' for people on the periphery of the region?

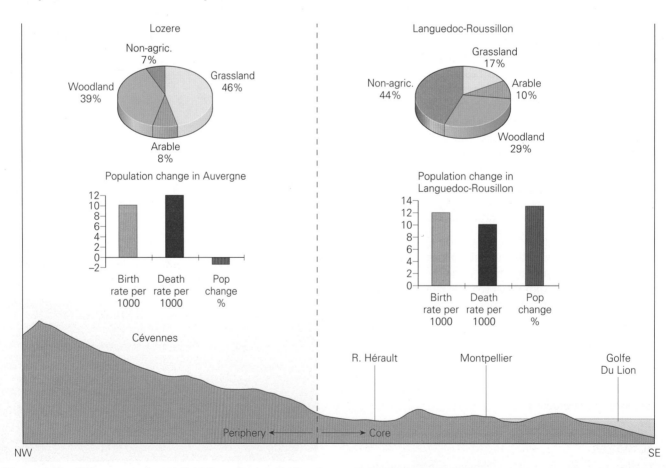

Figure 1.48 *The economic gradient from the sun belt.* Source: Eagle's Nest CD Rom, Discover Ltd, 1999.

Contrasts in central and east Africa

Population patterns in central and east Africa show areas of both high and low density (Figure 1.49). The highlands of Kenya have become a focus for in-migration. Population has increased as people live longer and infant mortality lessens. Kenya's population doubled between 1970 and 1990. This pressure is taking its toll: with widespread deforestation, overgrazing, and soil erosion. As population has grown, services have developed and links with market towns improved. Land reform has taken place and this has consolidated the small plots of land (shamba), enabling production to increase, despite rural-urban migration.

In Tanzania, the pattern of population density has been affected by government policy. Some farms were collectivised. This moved people (sometimes forcibly) into larger villages called *'ujaama'* and allowed schools and shops to be built. Levels of education and health improved dramatically, though food production did not.

In Uganda, population densities in rural areas have been affected by war and disease. Throughout much of the 1970s and 1980s there was genocide on a massive scale, matched by destruction and poverty. At the start of the millennium half of the population was under 15 and the rate of growth is 5 per cent per year. The incidence of HIV in rural areas is over 10 per cent (25 per cent in cities), the second highest in Africa. Unlike other diseases, AIDS infects the higher socio-economic groups most.

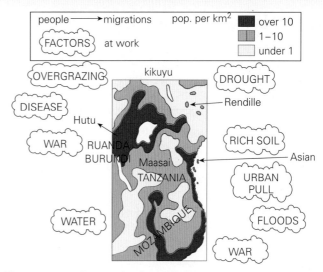

Figure 1.49   *Population patterns in central and east Africa.*

ACTIVITIES

1 What changes have occurred in the Kenyan village (see Figure 1.50) and the people's activities between 1950 and 1990?
2 What political factors have influenced population and development in east Africa?
3 Explain how AIDS might affect the progress and the economy of LEDC countries such as Uganda.

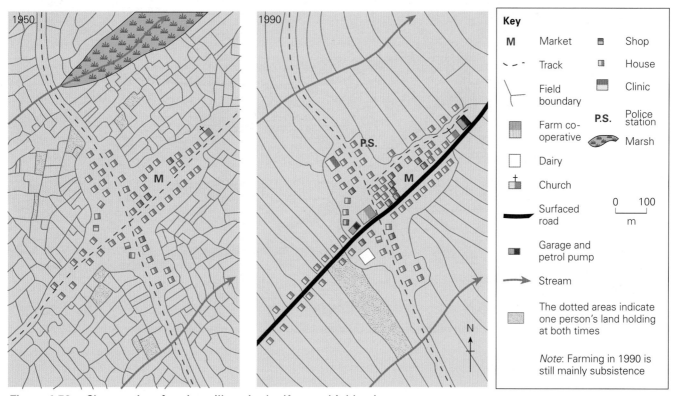

Figure 1.50   *Changes in a farming village in the Kenyan highlands.*   Source: Adapted from Hornby and Jones, *A Geography of Settlement*, CUP, 1986.

The UK: A tale of two villages

This is a planning enquiry concerning two small villages, Clapham and Austwick, on the edge of the Yorkshire Dales National Park (Figure 1.51). The enquiry looks at the issues raised when development occurs.

> Basic ideas about rural settlements
> SITE = places where villages are built
> FORM = their shape on the ground
> FUNCTION = what the settlement does (e.g. a bridging point) or what people do who live there (e.g. farming village or market town)
> HIERARCY = the way in which settlements of different sizes have different levels of service provision, and form a pattern across the countryside e.g.
> Hamlet 100 people, telephone
> Village 1,000 people, church, shop, PO, pub, primary school
> Small town 5,000 people, banks, offices, shops, secondary school

ACTIVITIES

Before beginning this enquiry, you are asked to complete a mapwork exercise to help you get to know the area better.

1 Clapham and Austwick are sited along the Craven Fault, a geological line running across the map, with limestone hills to the north and a broad valley to the south. Use the map in Figure 1.51 to suggest why the site of each village may have been chosen by early settlers: consider water supply for humans and livestock, defence, fuel, building materials, shelter, varied farmland, and accessibility.

2 Using the map, identify the shape or form of each village. Choose from nucleated, linear, or dispersed. In each case, what may have caused this pattern?

3 How many types of rural land use and activity can you identify on the map? Give examples (remember this is a quite a small area).

Figure 1.51 *An Ordnance Survey map of the area (OS Outdoor Leisure 2, Yorkshire Dales Western Area, 1:25000).*

YORKSHIRE DALES
National Park Authority

Dear Jim

Welcome to the Ranger service. I hope that the other National Park staff are helping you settle in. As you'll have seen, this part of the Dales has some really special places: I suppose that's why it gets so many visitors. The easy access from nearby cities is of course another reason for its popularity.

I'd like you to do some basic research and report back to me, so that I can get some idea of what you feel the challenges are. I know the places are unfamiliar to you but I'd be glad to have a fresh view of things.

I've sent you some Yorkshire Dales National Park information about the villages. It seems that the views and concerns of people in Clapham and Austwick are different, and we must be prepared to help if any conflicts arise.

Good luck, and I'll expect your report soon.

Heather

Figure 1.52   *A letter from the head of the Yorkshire Dales National Park to a university student on work experience.*

The Yorkshire Dales National Park Authority's purpose is set out in the 1995 Environment Act as:

'Conserving and enhancing the natural beauty, wildlife and cultural heritage of the area …

Promoting opportunities for the understanding and enjoyment of the special qualities of the area by the public.'

In pursuing these purposes … 'to foster the economic and social well-being of local communities …'

Any changes in building or land use must be approved by us. This is probably our most difficult job of all.

All new developments must respect their surroundings; be of an appropriate form or scale; be of a high standard of design; use suitable materials.

You should also be aware that outside the Yorkshire Dales National Park Authority boundary the rules are not as tough and here my colleagues at Craven District Council look after the planning applications.

Figure 1.53   *Advice from the planning officer.*
Source: Yorkshire Dales National Park Authority, 1995.

DECISION-MAKING ACTIVITIES

Use the resources on page 150–153.

1   How do the villages of Craven and Austwick differ from each other?
2   How and why do the two villages have different concerns?
3   What sort of conflict do you feel is likely to emerge locally?
4   For each village decide whether the following should be permitted and, if so, where:
   a   Only very minimal development (conservation).
   b   Housing development.
   c   Tourist development (car park, services).
   d   Any increase in other rural land uses.

Figure 1.54   *General view of Austwick.*

Figure 1.55   *General view of Clapham.*

Clapham

CLAPHAM

Clapham has plenty to interest visitors. A beck flows down its centre, and several attractive bridges cross the tree-lined water course. There is a splendid array of stone cottages on one side, while on the other, there is an inn, national park centre and the Cave Rescue Organisation. Near the church is Ingleborough Hall, now an outdoor centre, but once the home of the Farrer family.

FOR SALE £66,500

FOOTPATHS run from Clapham to Ingleborough Cave and Gaping Gill

May 1996 – Residents awoke to find the new tourist signs on the approach to Clapham, daubed in paint-stripper. Obviously some villagers did not feel happy about the £4,000 signs being put up.

Hall is now an outdoor centre

New family houses inside N.P. boundry.

The POST OFFICE is now at the village store, as the old P.O was sold in 1999 for housing.

POST OFFICE – with CAVE RESCUE HQ.

Key
- ● Cafés
- ○ Shops
- ■ N. Park Inf. Centre
- ▬ N. Park boundary

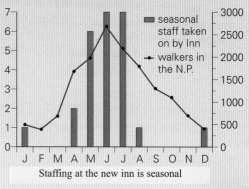
Staffing at the new inn is seasonal

NP centre, café and shops

Tourist dependant businesses **85%**

Pop age profile %
- 22 — over 65
- 18 — 51–65
- 43 — 31–50
- 7 — 21–30
- 10 — 0–20

%

SCHOOL ROLL
- **1996 – 47**
- **1997 – 50**
- **1988 – 39**
- **1999 – 38**
- **2000 – 46**

Biggest Problems in village? – traffic, parking and litter.

Timeline of firms starting up

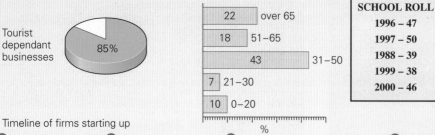

Figure 1.56   *Clapham, Yorkshire Dales.*   Source: G. Robinson, Settle High, 1999.

Austwick

AUSTWICK

A SECRET gem removed from the bustling highway that skirts the western edge of the Yorkshire Dales. Austwick remains a backwater that most travellers only see on a signpost.

Being such a sleepy hollow used to conducting its own affairs within the confines of the village, locals are less than keen on outsiders attempting to change their cherished way of life.

FOR SALE

Austwick Hall. Grade II listed manor house. 6 bedrooms Executive owner wants family buyer not retirement home. 1999 value £410,000

HALL CLOSE - (retirement) bungalow built in 1995

Typical dales cottages, asking price £95,000

BUS ROUTE to nearest town at Settle (4 miles)

Austwick Wood

Austwick Hall

Farm

Hall

Close

School

Inn

Guest House

Smithy
Chapel
Village Hall

P.O.

Church
Farm

Farm

Hotel
Farm

Builder

Austwick Beck

'Dalesbred'

Traditional furniture and upholstery made in former smithy premises

POST OFFICE – GENERAL STORE open 7 days per week in the summer. "Use it or lose it." Last remaining shop in village.

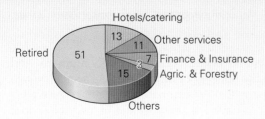
VILLAGE GREEN – Idylic scene but parking problem in summer.

SCHOOL ROLL	
1996 – 47	
1997 – 50	
1988 – 39	
1999 – 38	
2000 – 46	

HOUSING OCCUPANCY
Residential 84%
2nd or Holiday homes 10%
Vacant property 6%

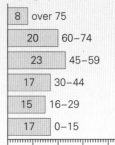
BRIDGE END FARM – Owner is seeking planning permission to convert barns into house as farming declines.

Employment (1996)

Hotels/catering 13
Other services 11
Finance & Insurance 7
Agric. & Forestry 3
Others 15
Retired 51

Pop age profile %

8	over 75
20	60–74
23	45–59
17	30–44
15	16–29
17	0–15

%

Biggest Problem in village? – cost of rural travel to work and services. Now 87% of households rely on a car.

Figure 1.57   *Austwick, Yorkshire Dales.*   Source: C. Hordern, 1996.

4 Rural planning issues

Managing the countryside for recreation and tourism

Recreation and tourism have arguably become the fastest growing industries in the world. They are a large part of the economy of most MEDCs, whilst in LEDCs tourism is often perceived as a way out of poverty. Greater affluence, increased mobility, and more leisure time are all factors in tourism's global growth. Rural tourism in the UK really began with the post-war formation of the national parks. Increasingly affordable cars and the building of the motorway network has meant that all areas are more accessible. Modern marketing now promotes 'Brontë Country' and 'Emmerdale' and purpose-built **enclaves** like Center Parcs in Sherwood Forest. Other developments include the safari park at Longleat, theme parks such as Alton Towers, and heritage sites like Blists Hill industrial museum at Ironbridge: all in rural locations. Some rural tourism is trying to become more **sustainable** and to present itself as 'ecotourism'. In many cases it is the sheer volume of visitors that has a major impact on the countryside.

> Nationally we make 1.3 billion day-visits to the countryside each year and 41 per cent of our nights away from home, are spent in rural areas. Travel to the country is usually by car (55 per cent) though most journeys appear to be of five miles or less. Once there, walking is still the top activity (33 per cent). Economically, we spend £9 million, which creates around 350,000 jobs.

Figure 1.58 *'The Country File'*
Source: *State of the countryside,* The Countryside Agency, 1999.

National parks

When first set up after the Second World War, the national parks had a duty to promote both conservation and recreation. This was very much a balancing act, and local people often felt that the visitors got the best of this bargain. To redress this, the 1995 Environment Act requires the national parks to 'foster the economic and social well-being of communities within the parks'. This should help residents, but could make the National Park Authority's job harder. The challenge it faces is to manage over 12,000 km² of rural England and Wales, which receive 100 million visitors a year and are home to over 300,000 people. The ease with which visitors reach the national parks is obvious – you only have to look at honeypot sites on Bank Holiday weekends. Since 1999 three new national parks have been added to the original ten (Figure 1.59).

Wider issues of land use also occur in national park areas. These are looked at in section 5 on developing resources in the countryside.

> **ACTIVITIES**
> 1 a What challenges face the National Park Authority?
>   b Why is its job such a balancing act?
> 2 Use the website listed in the reference materials section at the end of this unit to choose one national park to research these issues.

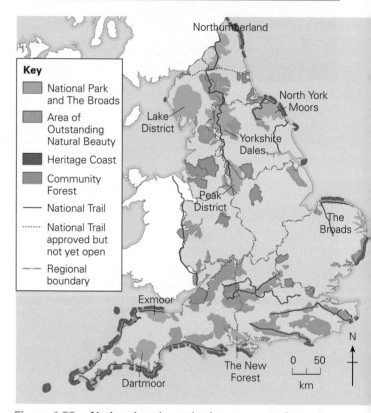

Figure 1.59 *National parks and other conservation areas.*

In the Yorkshire Dales National Park, Malham and Aysgarth top the honeypot visitor tables. As a small village of only 150 people (1997 estimate), Malham (Figure 1.13) would expect to have few services, and indeed the school and chapel (now the National Park Visitor Centre) have gone. However, there is an extensive range of tourist facilities:

- 256 bed spaces
- 6 cafes and restaurants
- 5 shops (including a post office)
- 2 pubs
- 2 campsites.

These facilities generate jobs in the community and visitor spending helps keep local businesses afloat, when many rural areas are struggling to retain basic services.

Recreation presents Malham with a number of challenges. Different members of the community see different sides of the problem (Figures 1.60 and 1.61).

- 90 per cent of the 10 million visitors come by car, weekend holiday traffic prevents some local activities, parking demand exceeds supply (168 cars and 8 coaches), erosion on footpaths is a continuing problem [*National Park Visitor Centre*]
- Litter can choke animals, walls are damaged, and people park across field gates [*Local farmer*]
- Limestone pavements are worn down or even taken away, animal and plant diversity suffers [*National Park education officer*]
- The number of holiday homes is growing, house prices are now beyond the reach of locals, there is a loss of privacy and considerable extra noise, constant questions from fieldwork groups [*Resident*]

Figure 1.60 *Challenges facing Malham.*

ACTIVITIES

1 How successful do you feel that Malham's management has been so far?
2 Which of the following more radical solutions listed below might work in Malham? Explain why or why not.
   - park and ride only areas
   - visitor taxes/fees
   - closing areas once full
   - reducing car park spaces
   - having car-free zones

THREE TOURIST ISSUES IN NATIONAL PARKS

1 Public access

Public access issues include the so called 'right to roam' legislation which will allow people access to open land in the parks. Members of the Country Landowners' Association object to this legislation. Pressure groups like the Ramblers' Association want commonsense agreements. Some National Park authorities are currently establishing voluntary agreements to avoid problems between farmers and visitors. Legal issues are also involved when vehicles use bridleways and green lanes. Rights of way on many upland tracks are not properly established in law, and the big increase in recreational use of off-road vehicles and motor cycles is worrying farmers and landowners. The National Park Authority, and most countryside organisations would like to ban this traffic.

Some efforts being made to manage these challenges. The National Park Visitor Centre and Education Service try to educate people about conservation. Litter bins have been removed and visitors seem to be learning to take their litter home.

National Park staff have built steps near to Malham Cove, diverted footpaths or surfaced them with crushed limestone.

Malham woodland has been preserved and enhanced (Woodland Forum). Local children have planted trees.

An Open Access Agreement was made by local farmers in the Countryside Stewardship Scheme. Landowners have entered into wall maintenance agreements with English Nature.

The Malham Postbus combines mail delivery with passenger travel (help from Rural Development Commission), but the experimental traffic management scheme had to be abandoned.

Figure 1.61 *Attempted solutions to the challenges facing Malham.*

Figure 1.62 *An off-road vehicle tackles a green lane.*

Recreational **carrying capacity** is a measure of the level of activity which a location or a feature (a footpath, a road, or open ground) can sustain. Can it physically stand up to the number of people using it? Is the ecosystem able to survive? Will the site deteriorate so much that it becomes unattractive?

Footpath erosion is another access issue in national parks. To monitor this, stiles on key footpaths in the honeypot areas of the Yorkshire Dales National Park have counters placed under their treads to record the number of visitors passing. New versions will be photo-sensitive and be recorded using Geographical Information Systems (**GIS**). The pedestrian flow data for the Three Peaks area is shown in Figure 1.63. Paths are also being surveyed for physical damage on a scale of 1 to 13. The critical score beyond which the path will not recover without help is 9 (meaning extensive vegetation loss or a, worn width of 2–5m).

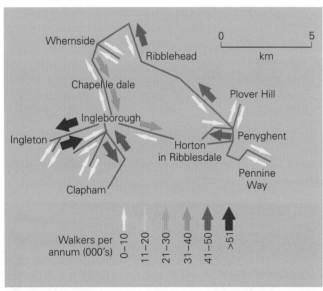

Figure 1.63   *Footpath usage in the Three Peaks.*
Source: Yorkshire Region, Hodder & Stoughton, 1998.

Having established the location of a problem, diversions, alternative paths, and even seasonal closures are set up. Experiments in the past have involved various restoration techniques, but with growing expertise, the Yorkshire Dales National Park Authority relies upon three methods which do appear to resist erosion:

- Stone pitching is used on drier, steeper slopes, but it is expensive (Figure 1.64).
- Aggregate paths (crushed rock) are laid on a geotextile mat on gentler slopes (Figure 1.64).
- Sub-soil paths (the ground is turned upside down) are used on moderate slopes and is relatively cheap.

The park now boasts effective management costing less than £100,000 each year, and boardwalk is now used on only very wet ground.

a   *Stone pitching.*   b   *Aggregate paths.*
Figure 1.64   *Path repairs at Malham Cove.*

2 Farm diversification

With livestock farming in decline, it is not surprising that farmers are looking for other ways to make a living. The choices are varied, but most are connected to tourism. The national park planning committee tries to be sympathetic to farmers where appropriate. Diversification can involve a variety of schemes:

- accommodation – bed and breakfast, farm cottages, holiday homes, bunk barns, camping and caravan sites
- sporting – riding, fishing, shooting, falconry, ballooning, paint balling and hang gliding
- natural features – caving, climbing and bird watching
- catering – teas and meals
- farm-based activities – farm visits, farm shop, open days and heritage
- public events – shows and competitions
- changes in land use – golf courses.

All of these activities bring in supplementary income for the farmer from outside agriculture. Grants for capital, feasibility studies, and marketing are available. In 2000, subsidies will be diverted to protect moorland and woodlands. They will be paid to farmers wishing to diversify into tourism, as part of the changing emphasis of the CAP.

ACTIVITIES

You are a member of a local council or national park planning committee.

1   What are your views on managing access?
2   Explain which of the diversification schemes suggested above would best:
   a   create more jobs
   b   allow farming to continue
   c   conserve the environment.
3   Are there any activities you would not support? Explain why.

3 Second homes and holiday cottages

The high percentage of houses that are second homes, an issue which has been looked at earlier (see page 141), is a serious problem. (Figures 1.65–1.67).

see page 141

ACTIVITIES

1   Explain why you might agree with the proposals to discourage second-home ownership in the Lake District.

New homes in Lake District to be sold solely to locals

by Mark Rowe

The Lake District is pulling up the drawbridge around its picturesque scenery.

A major source of disquiet is second-home syndrome, where city dwellers purchase houses in the Lake District. In some areas, such as Skelwith Bridge, near Ambleside and Patterdale, near Ullswater, as many as 40 per cent of houses are second homes. The average across the Lake District National Park is 15 per cent.

Last week the Lake District National Park Authority approved its local plan, under which virtually all newly-built housing in the region must be sold to people who live or work in Cumbria.

In a further attack in the south Lakes region, there are plans to raise the council tax on such properties to bring in £1.7m a year.

The plan was proposed by Stan Collins, a Liberal Democrat councillor in South Lakeland.

Prices in the heart of the lakes are higher than the national average, with a three-bedroom cottage in Ambleside fetching up to £85,000, while bungalows overlooking Lake Windermere start at £500,000.

However, many of the houses sold as second homes are at the bottom end of the market, leading to what Mr Collins described as 'the forced migration of the younger generation'. There is also a culture clash, according to Mr Collins. 'Second home owners don't mix with local people. They don't go to things like the local dances. In many cases they don't even go to the pub.

'They turn up with bags of stuff from supermarkets and don't shop locally. They even fill up with petrol elsewhere.'

The plan is being promoted as a Private Bill – and would only apply to the Lakes. It could, however, prompt similar actions by councils in other tourist areas.

The plan is 'whole-heartedly' endorsed by the National Park Authority. 'We hope it will help free up some of the existing housing for local people,' said Chief Planning Officer John Pattison.

Figure 1.65   *The problems brought by the high percentage of second homes – and a proposal to discourage second-home ownership.*   Source: *Independent on Sunday,* May 1998.

Sir, I have read with interest the debate regarding the 50 per cent discount in council tax applicable to second homes. This is only a fraction of the taxation benefits that can be gained.

I am legally entitled to make my property available for holiday letting for 139 days each year. In addition to all this, there are tax-saving benefits in buying a second home.

Therefore, it is little wonder that people like myself are queuing up to purchase property in the Lake District.

Figure 1.66   *Reasons to buy a second home.*
Source: *Westmoreland Gazette,* 1998.

Top Award for Rosthwaite Housing

Providing new housing to satisfy both local needs and strict development policies is not easy. A recent development of five houses at Kiln Orchard, Rosthwaite, in Borrowdale achieved this successfully and received the top national award for the best housing development in a rural settlement, in 1998.

Figure 1.65   *Homes for locals.*
Source: *Westmoreland Gazette,* 1998.

Rural resorts

Rural resorts are specialist resorts in accessible rural locations. Their closeness to large numbers of people is a vital ingredient. Some are theme parks like Alton Towers, with 20 million potential customers within two hours' drive, others like the Center Parcs are holiday villages. Alton Towers is a 200 ha estate in Staffordshire. Visitor numbers reached 3 million in 1994 and, with new 'white-knuckle' rides and hotel accommodation, will continue to increase.

ACTIVITIES

1   What social, economic, and environmental impacts does Alton Towers have on the local area?
2   Why do local people increasingly support developments.

'Towers win British Tourism "oscar" – July 1985'

'Such intrusion into quiet and beautiful countryside is sheer sacrilege' [Phil Drabble, naturalist]

'The Towers are breaking "change of use" planning rules in setting up a Disney-type operation' [Parish council]

'Our dream home is ruined with 8,500 cars a day converging on the complex' [Retired couple living nearby]

'A great help to the community providing jobs and road improvements' [Alton Residents' Association]

'It is a damn shame to have to put a strip of tarmac through this area – but it will benefit the economy of Staffordshire' [County council leader on new access road]

Figure 1.68   *'Views from the Towers' – local paper reports.*
Source: *Geography Special , Stoke Sentinel,* 1998.

Rural tourism in LEDCs

As the **pleasure periphery** of tourism increases, so do the flows of MEDC tourists to long-haul LEDC destinations.

Tourism in many LEDCs tries to provide valuable income from abroad and create jobs.

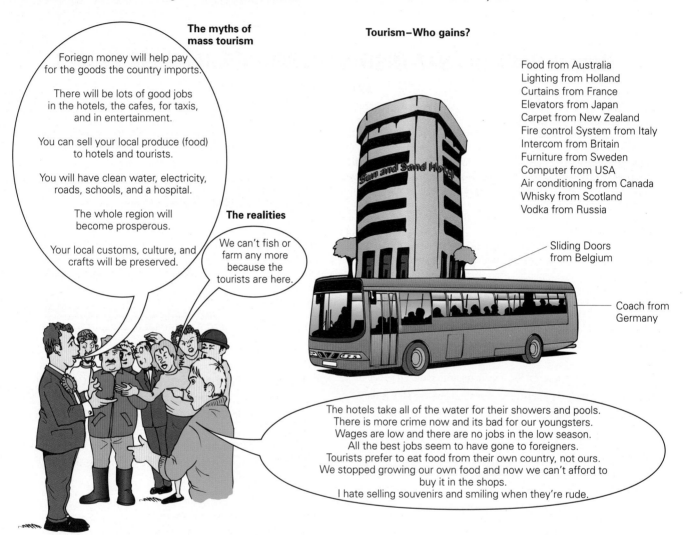

The myths of mass tourism

Foriegn money will help pay for the goods the country imports.

There will be lots of good jobs in the hotels, the cafes, for taxis, and in entertainment.

You can sell your local produce (food) to hotels and tourists.

You will have clean water, electricity, roads, schools, and a hospital.

The whole region will become prosperous.

Your local customs, culture, and crafts will be preserved.

The realities

We can't fish or farm any more because the tourists are here.

Tourism – Who gains?

Food from Australia
Lighting from Holland
Curtains from France
Elevators from Japan
Carpet from New Zealand
Fire control System from Italy
Intercom from Britain
Furniture from Sweden
Computer from USA
Air conditioning from Canada
Whisky from Scotland
Vodka from Russia

Sliding Doors from Belgium

Coach from Germany

The hotels take all of the water for their showers and pools.
There is more crime now and its bad for our youngsters.
Wages are low and there are no jobs in the low season.
All the best jobs seem to have gone to foreigners.
Tourists prefer to eat food from their own country, not ours.
We stopped growing our own food and now we can't afford to buy it in the shops.
I hate selling souvenirs and smiling when they're rude.

Figure 1.69   *The myths and harsh realities of foreign tourism.*

ECOTOURISM

Encouraged by holiday programmes and the desire for an alternative to package deals, today's travellers have increasingly opted for ecotourism. Unlike mass tourism, this type of tourism is frequently small scale. Rainforests, tropical islands, and mountain locations dominate the market. For example, 100 km south of Manaus, Brazil, offers customers the chance to see the real rainforest. Visitors can experience nature safaris in this remote area using local guides. It is advertised as one of the few ways in which income can be generated from undisturbed rainforest. Parties are limited to 25 people, travel is largely by boat, and food is locally produced. It is sustainable.

Some holiday destinations, once seen as 'green' and exclusive, have begun to drift towards mass tourism. More tourists means more money and so carrying capacities are exceeded. The Kenyan Game Parks like Amboseli and Reserves like Maasai Mara are fragile environments and honeypot pressures can damage tracks, habitats, and the local culture.

ACTIVITIES

1 Can rural tourism in LEDCs be sustainable? Discuss under the following headings:
   a conserving the environment, ecology, and culture for future generations
   b supporting the local community and culture,
   c providing the tourist/traveller with a worthwhile experience.

Managing rural deprivation and rural poverty

Deprivation means having to do without. Poverty is closely linked to employment, as jobs earn money which can buy food, and tends to affect groups such as the elderly, the disabled, those with large families, and those in rural areas. **Relative poverty** may be experienced in MEDCs by those who earn less than average wages, have no access to a car, or are isolated from key services. (**Absolute poverty** affects life itself, rather than standards of living; it is more common in LEDCs.)

Planning agencies refer to this situation as **rural exclusion**. Census data for many rural areas in the UK also shows significant levels of deprivation, using four indicators. The Townshend **Material Deprivation Score** is based upon levels of car and home ownership, unemployment, and overcrowding.

In 1999, a survey by the Women's Institute in England and Wales revealed that life in villages is changing, and for those who grew up in the country, standards of living are falling. The biggest challenge was seen as having to cope with an increase in population against a background of declining levels of services (Figure 1.70). The survey revealed an increase in housing development and traffic, whilst shops and post offices were closing and local health and bus services were being reduced.

Figure 1.70   *An expedition to the shops. "When is the next bus, Granny?"*

Another report launched by the government in June 1999, 'The Rural Audit – A Health Check on Rural Britain', also attempted to assess the needs of rural communities (Figure 1.71).

In the Craven district of North Yorkshire the changes to rural life are regularly commented upon in the news articles and readers' letters of the local weekly paper (Figure 1.72).

It should not be forgotten that this poverty is relative, and whilst semi-rural areas like west Cumbria and east Kent may have the fastest-worsening deprivation figures in the UK, inner boroughs of London, Liverpool, and Manchester do still have the worst poverty levels.

But [...] it shines a light on the hidden poor and the inadequately housed, those who have never had the ready access to the National Health Service (NHS) or the social services which many of us take for granted. It highlights the fragility of social infrastructure and the consequences for it when people lose the shops, schools, and bus services which had been their community's landmarks. It charts what happens to those left behind when the young have migrated to the towns for homes and jobs because commuters and the retired have colonised, gentrified, and geriatrified their villages.

Figure 1.71   From The Rural Audit – a Health Check on Rural Britain, *June 1999.*

Tosside – Save our school campaign launched

Stainforth – Post office seeks lifeline

Langcliffe – Mobile Library visits cut to every three weeks

Austwick – Village chapel sold

Kildwick – Local community group buys village store and post office

Horton – Bus service now Tuesdays only

Figure 1.72   *The* Craven Herald *keeps track.*

ACTIVITIES

1   What do you think are the key features of rural deprivation?

2   Which of the following measures do you think would have the greatest impact on rural deprivation?
  - A government decision to insist benefits are paid direct into individual bank accounts.
  - The withdrawal of local transport subsidies on marginal bus routes.
  - The increase of duty on petrol by 10p per litre.
  - The decision to shut all schools that have less than 50 children.
  - Closure of local cottage hospital.

How can relative poverty in MEDCs be managed?

Although local councils have some freedom to make funds for transport, health, education, police, and other rural services a high priority, local initiatives to combat rural deprivation and exclusion vary considerably.

Health

Some health services have joined with social services to cut transport costs. Voluntary services like Meals on Wheels are filling gaps in official provision. Day care has been offered in sheltered housing schemes. The Swaffham Project in Norfolk, funded by lottery money, offers primary healthcare from the local community hospital.

Education

The village school is often very important in a small community as a focus for activity. On purely economic grounds many rural schools are not viable, but there are good reasons, related to travel and safety, as well as education, for keeping them open. Cumbria and other rural Local Education Authorities have a Rural Schools Initiative which supports smaller village schools.

Transport

Transport can be subsidised in remote areas using funding from EU sources, supporting minibus services and postbuses on rural routes. Grizedale in South Lakeland and Malham in North Yorkshire both have this type of service. Shared taxi services are available by phone in suburban villages in Suffolk. Many rural bus grants have become available, especially for Sunday services such as the 'Round the Long Mynd' bus or the STARS scheme in Shropshire.

Housing

It is not easy to provide housing for village people against a background of rising property values. However, the 1998 Lake District National Park Plan (Shaping the Future) deliberately discriminates in favour of local people. '... no other new housing development will be allowed unless it is to fulfil a local housing need. Similarly the conversion of barns [...] to permanent residential use will only be allowed [...] to local people. The Plan also makes provision for low-cost rented housing available to local people on sites [...] where planning permission would not normally be given, for example on greenfield sites adjoining the boundaries of settlements.'

Shops

Sub-post offices and general stores are another part of this 'bottom line' of survival. The Countryside Agency offers advice and grants of up to £5,000 to help village shops develop their business. Some supermarkets, seen as the 'villains' by some village communities, are offering support of a different kind (see Figure 1.85).

Cash points

Co-op rural stores are to provide 2000 cashpoints, available free of charge.

Figure 1.73   *Local communities first.*

Stainforth Post Office is the first in Craven to become an outlet for the supermarket giant Sainsbury's.

Postmistress Debbie Prior told the Herald she would be selling the supermarket's products from Saturday onwards as part of the Sainsbury's Assisting Village Enterprises Scheme (SAVES).

Mrs Prior said: 'Not many people can get to a supermarket and have to go to either Skipton or Settle from here. The idea behind the scheme is to assist villages and it's another way of reaching people who could not otherwise go to the supermarket on a regular basis.

'The closest Sainsbury's in this area are in Lancaster, Clitheroe and Keighley.'

She added: 'We took over the business after it was under threat of closure when the former owner retired and without this kind of scheme, other post offices would face certain closure.'

The scheme was set up by Sainsbury's as a way to assist small rural businesses under constant threat from closure.

Shops suitable for the scheme are ones which act as a focus for the village and provide 'essential services that residents would otherwise have to travel a distance to obtain.'

Figure 1.74   *Scheme to save village shops.* Source: *The Craven Herald*, Sept.1999.

ACTIVITIES

1 Explain to which of the schemes described in Figure 1.73 you would give a high priority. How would you prioritise?
2 What else might be done?

Funding from government and EU sources has helped to sustain rural areas through rural development agencies (Flgure 1.75).

In the Lake District and much of Wales, funding has traditionally been given to rural development areas and places with Objective 5b (upland) status. This was 'to promote development in rural areas which suffer sparse populations and declining services'. Future funding will be part of Objective 2, which is targeted at areas seriously affected by industrial decline, although it does include Cornwall as one of the most deprived rural areas.

A further type of funding, Objective 1, has been given to areas 'lagging behind'. In the Irish Republic this initiative, which is community based, has done much to promote rural tourism and Irish food industries.

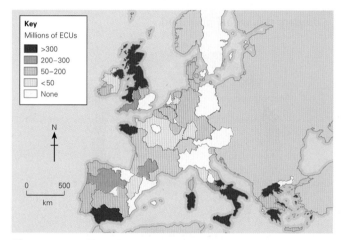

Figure 1.75   *European Development Fund (EDF) spending in the EU.*

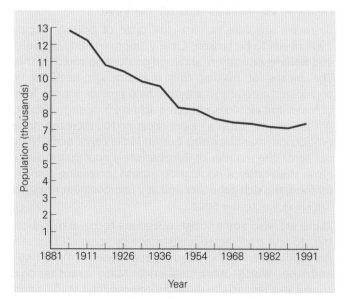

Figure 1.76   *Chanaging population in the Lozère (a 'département' within central southern France).*

Source: Eagle's Nest CD Rom, Discover Ltd, 1999

In central southern France the pattern of deprivation is a familiar one: poor infrastructure (roads, electricity, and services), declining farming, and continued migration out of the region (Figure 1.76).

In 1970, the French government set up the Parc National des Cévennes, and with EU help attempted to reverse the trend of migration out of the region. Whilst much of the Parc National des Cévennes agenda was concerned with conservation, it also promoted schemes to raise prosperity levels. Between 1994 and 1999 a total of FF168 million was spent on six types of scheme, very similar to those in the rural areas of the UK:

- wildlife conservation
- rural development projects (e.g. forestry and crafts)
- diversifying farming with tourism
- upgrading roads and tracks (except where in a sensitive area)
- improving education (for visitors)
- housing improvements.

In Lozère specifically a lot of financial help was offered to modernise equipment and site services. Grants and low-cost loans were also available to help businesses which would create jobs. Investment in these schemes is set out in Figure 1.77.

Green shoots appear in France's desert

Rural depopulation has been a fact of life in France for more than a centruy. Schools, shops and cafes have closed, and villages have been dying away as young people decide that the city lights are brighter than the prospect of eking out an existence in the countryside which the French have come to term 'the green desert'.

In 1929 France had 4m farms; it now has fewer than 750,000. More than 1m agricultural jobs have gone since 1970 alone, and over the same period 50,000 small rural businesses have disappeared. Rural departments such as Lozere have seen their populations more than halve.

Lozere is saddled, too, with an unfortunate reputation as the most backward of all France's departments. In its pretty county town, those extra 684 inhabitants are a reason for solid satisfaction.

Some of the reasons for this windfall are, of course, part of a bigger story. There is the gradual recent drift away from the vast urban sprawl of Paris.

But Lozere has worked hard to bring in newcomers. Nearly 500 jobs were created here last year, a 16% increase that was the highest in France.

In one Lozere village, the council ploughed 450,000 into a small business complex. Le Collet-de-Deze, population 718, boasts 21 new jobs, 60 new inhabitants, a garage and a cafe.

Several newcomers have invested in green tourism, opening self-catering *gites* and small wilderness hotels. The sector now provides jobs for some 3,000 people. 'Tourists need village shopkeepers, and village shopkeepers need tourists, and villages need shops.'

Figure 1.77   *Green shoots appear in France's desert.*

Source: *The Guardian*, Feb 19, 2000.

Absolute poverty in LEDCs

Absolute poverty is a more urgent state of affairs. Absolute poverty implies that levels of, for example, food or health, are inadequate. Absolute poverty is more likely to occur in LEDCs. Access to food, clean water, and shelter are the criteria here, rather than wage levels or lack of services. Fatal diseases, malnutrition and famine, clean water, and having nowhere to live, are problems which face many rural communities in LEDCs.

Since 1990 the UN has used the human development index (HDI) as a measure of quality of life. This index represents an absolute figure based upon adult literacy rates, life expectancy, and purchasing power (Figure 1.78).

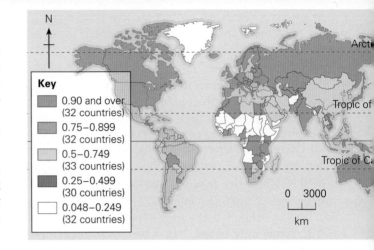

Key
- 0.90 and over (32 countries)
- 0.75–0.899 (32 countries)
- 0.5–0.749 (33 countries)
- 0.25–0.499 (30 countries)
- 0.048–0.249 (32 countries)

0   3000
km

Figure 1.78   *World pattern of poverty using the HDI. Compare this with Figure 1.16.*

Illness → Less work → Low productivity → Poverty → Poor food and water → Malnutrition → Illness

Figure 1.81   *The cycle of poverty.*

If we use health and life expectancy as indicators of poverty, people in sub-Saharan Africa are amongst the poorest in the world.

- Many countries in the Sahel and elsewhere have experienced droughts recently.
- Average life expectancy here is 52 years (UK average life expectancy is 78 years).
- In Kenya and Uganda life expectancy has fallen (by five and four years respectively) in the last decade.
- Infant mortality has gone up in Kenya and Mozambique to a level ten times that in the UK.
- Only half of sub-Saharan people have access to clean water.
- AIDS/HIV affects 67 per cent of the population in sub-Saharan African countries (in south-east Asia the figure is 20 per cent, and in the rest of the world the percentage is in single figures).
- Long-term International Monetary Fund debts in Kenya are US$5.6 billion (a typical example).
- Half of Kenya's population lives on less than 35p per day.
- Most African countries have experienced warfare recently.

Figure 1.79   *A profile of poverty in sub-Saharan Africa.*

Despite putting poverty eradication on the agenda in all five-year plans since independence, the number of poor people in Kenya is still growing. In a country which has the potential to feed itself, a combination of incompetence and corruption has made matters worse. Plans seem to do little more than drive more people from their tiny plots of land into inhospitable cities, and allow roads, factories, and other infrastructure to decay.

Figure 1.80   *Kenya's plans to end poverty.*

How can absolute poverty be managed?

To tackle absolute poverty, the cycle of poverty (Figure 1.81) needs to be broken. Clearly, improvements in health and welfare, education, and food production could do this. The means of making this breakthrough need to be considered carefully as external help provided in the form of loans and aid does not often achieve long-term change. Whilst many LEDCs have begun to increase food production, manufacturing output (8 per cent), and GNP (6 per cent), the number of the absolutely poor continues to grow. High rates of population growth increasing demand for food; the rich get richer and any improvement does not 'trickle down' to the poor.

There are also some tough questions to be asked about the aid and trade agreements made by some MEDCs. Are decisions taken by the International Monetary Fund (IMF) and the World Bank realistic? Many transnational companies (especially those processing food stuffs) seem to exploit LEDCs and their workers. Too many LEDCs put their faith in a one-crop, export-led economy based on cocoa or palm oil, for example.

Percentage of people without
access to health services

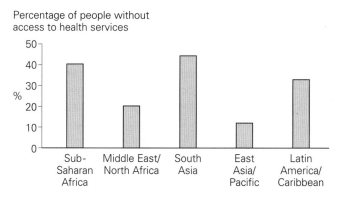

a *Percentage of people without access to healthcare.*

Percentage of people
who are illiterate

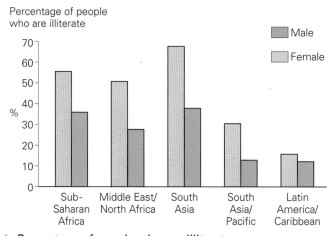

b *Percentage of people who are illiterate.*

Percentage of people without
access to safe water

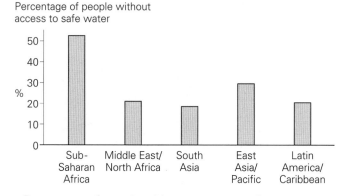

c *Percentage of people without access to safe water.*

Figure 1.82 *Poverty levels in LEDCs.*
Source: *NEAB Syllabus C Geography GCSE paper 2,* 1999.

Kitenga in Uganda is not far from Lake Victoria. After recent history of genocide the people here are, with the help of non-government organisations (NGOs) like Action Aid or Farm Africa, trying to rebuild their lives and escape the grip of poverty.

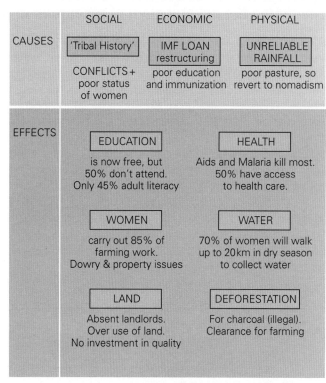

	SOCIAL	ECONOMIC	PHYSICAL
CAUSES	'Tribal History'	IMF LOAN restructuring	UNRELIABLE RAINFALL
	CONFLICTS+ poor status of women	poor education and immunization	poor pasture, so revert to nomadism

EFFECTS	EDUCATION is now free, but 50% don't attend. Only 45% adult literacy	HEALTH Aids and Malaria kill most. 50% have access to health care.
	WOMEN carry out 85% of farming work. Dowry & property issues	WATER 70% of women will walk up to 20km in dry season to collect water
	LAND Absent landlords. Over use of land. No investment in quality	DEFORESTATION For charcoal (illegal). Clearance for farming

Figure 1.83 *The causes and effects of poverty in Kitenga, Uganda.*

In Uganda community schemes are tackling problems from the 'bottom up'. One project to build a water tank and well (Figure 1.84) demonstrates how local women, with help from Action Aid, have solved one of the problems particular to their community. The water tank and well has helped meet the pressing need for local, clean water.

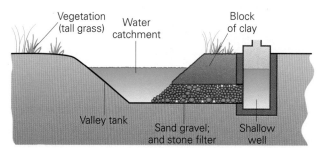

Figure 1.84 *'Kirinda Women's Group builds a water tank and well'.*

ACTIVITIES

1 Why is the water tank and well scheme particularly suitable and valuable for rural Uganda?
2 Does it classify as an example of:
    a a bottom-up scheme or
    b intermediate or appropriate technology?
Give evidence in your answer.

Managing the development of resources in the countryside

After agriculture, three of the main uses for rural areas are forestry, reservoirs, and mineral extraction. Wood, water, and minerals are basic resources and have been for people since earliest times. As the Industrial Revolution dawned, ponds, charcoal, and iron ore became an important combination. The 20th century equivalent is destroying Brazilian rainforests to provide hydro-electric power from reservoirs like Tucuri, timber from Rondonia, and iron ore from Carajas. Agriculture suffers too, when plans for coal mining threaten rural land. More positively, trees are used to screen the scars of quarrying and lakes are created in abandoned gravel workings. On a larger scale, the catchments of many reservoirs are planted with trees to prevent siltation, and local materials are used to build dams. People want the benefit that these rural resources bring, but not the costs that acquiring them incurs. The challenge is to use the resources responsibly and sustainably. As Agenda 21 suggests, people must 'act locally and think globally', even though sometimes the benefits of a resource are not always evident locally.

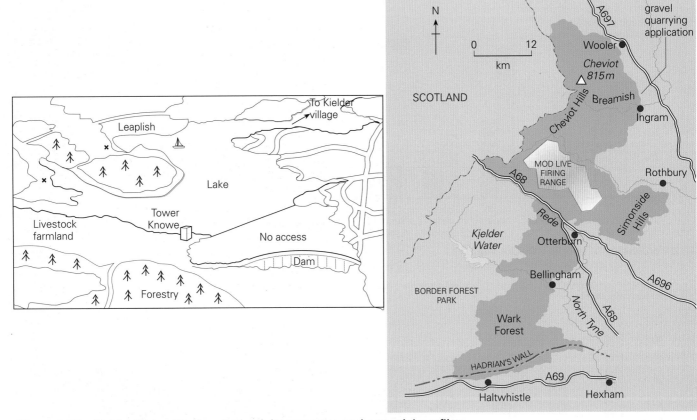

Figure 1.85 *Kielder Water, Northumberland: Its resources and potential conflicts.*

Kielder Water

Kielder Water in Northumberland demonstrates many of the challenges and management issues which relate to the development of more remote rural land. It is one of the largest artificial lakes in Europe (over 1000ha) and is surrounded by over 100,000 ha of planted coniferous forest (Figure 1.85). Like other remote upland reservoirs, it regulates the flow of rivers and gathers water which can be transferred to urban areas. As a multipurpose scheme, it was planned to generate hydro-electric power. Recreational facilities developed jointly by the Northumbrian Water Authority and the Forestry Commission have created honeypots at Leaplish and Tower Knowe. Quarrying for felsite takes place at Harden Quarry in the nearby Northumberland National Park. The felsite is used for road chippings.

ACTIVITIES

1 Identify the various land users and organisations at work in upland Northumberland.
2 Construct a matrix to show how their activities and interests may conflict.

Reservoirs

Surface reservoirs are built for a variety of reasons: to provide water for domestic or industrial use, to generate electricity, or to irrigate farmland. Recreation and transport may be secondary benefits. Kielder Water seems to be a model scheme in an ideal location. The charge that it was too big and 'a white elephant' has been withdrawn now that its extra capacity can provide water for West Yorkshire. Since the drought in 1995, Kielder Water has been connected beyond the Tees and on into the Swale.

In the UK, reservoirs are either natural lakes that have been converted, for example Lake Windermere, Cumbria, or lakes built in confined valleys. The local impact is therefore limited, although abandoned villages do lie beneath lakes like Ladybower in the Peak District. Private water companies control most of the water supply in the UK but the Environment Agency looks after the natural lakes and rivers.

The two obvious drawbacks for reservoirs, apart from the financial costs, are the effects of the loss of land, and any downstream impact on the river system which may result, for example the Three Gorges dam in China.

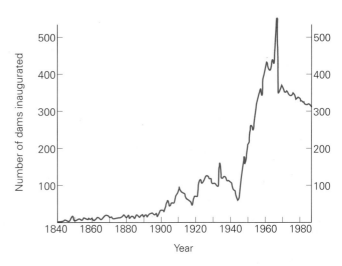

Figure 1.87   *That dam business.*
Source: *The State of the World* Earthscan, 1993.

Between 1960 and 2000 there have been many large reservoirs built, such as Lake Nasser in Egypt. Globally there are over 40,000 large dams which collectively have flooded 400,000 km² of land. However, the days of the mega-dams may be drawing to a close, not least because of their immense costs. The cost of Brazil's Carajas development scheme, which includes large dams, could eventually reach US$62 billion. International agreement is really needed for many of today's large undertakings, for example in the Indian subcontinent, where Bangladesh receives virtually all of its water via India. Schemes like those on the Volta, the Colorado, and the Nile have ultimately caused considerable environmental impacts downstream and along the coast. The risks of debt and future impacts are likely to be even greater for LEDCs than for MEDCs, and many of the proposals are extremely controversial.

Even the World Bank, itself no stranger to lending money for such projects, in 1998 helped set up a World Commission on Dams to 'rigorously investigate the benefits and costs to society of dam projects'.

Dammed to destruction

The Aswan Dam, hailed in the 1960's as a triumph of engineering and water management, is now seen as a major cause of the Nile Delta's impending devastation.

Denied the fertile silt that has sustained farms, Egypt already uses more fertiliser per hectare than any other nation.

Modern irrigation canals bring natural salts, eroded upstream and dissolved in the water.

The country is spending tens of millions of dollars each year, laying the largest drainage network in the world in an attempt to flush out the salt. Even so, salt is already reducing crop yields on more than a third of the fields.

Once, much of the delta was composed of marshes and brackish lagoons, protected from the sea by sand bars.

But soon the lagoons may disappear altogether. Deprived of silt, the sand bars are fast eroding and will collapse. They and the lagoons form the main defence against the sea for the entire delta.

Another factor is the greenhouse effect. A rise of one metre over the next century could inundate the northern third of the delta.

Figure 1.86   *Impact on the Nile Delta of the Aswan Dam.*
Source: Edexcel, June 1998.

ACTIVITIES

1   Using Figure 1.86, summarise the long term impacts of the Aswan dam on the Nile delta.
2   Using Figure 1.87, describe and explain the trends in world dam building.
3   What do you see as being the most important 'benefits and costs to society of dam projects'? Use the resources provided at the end of this unit in your research.

Should the Upper Ribblesdale reservoir be built?

Whenever there is a proposal to build a reservoir there are always going to be winners and losers. The valley shown on the map in Figure 1.88 is on the edge of the Yorkshire Dales, south of Settle. In the UK, the decision whether or not to go ahead with a project ultimately rests with a government minister, but if a public inquiry were set up, the inspector appointed would have to consider evidence from all interested parties and make a recommendation.

North West Water PLC needs another 500 million litres of water per day. The Ribble valley is hydrologically suitable (impermeable), has the right morphology (site of old glacial lake), and is in a strategic location (for water distribution). At the southern end of the proposed reservoir there is a narrow gorge.

Northern Leisure Ltd wishes to develop recreational facilities around the lake, ranging from hotels to caravans and camping. It has a good reputation in educational and outdoor activities.

Local residents are divided. Those in Settle seem supportive, particularly the younger ones. In Giggleswick there are worries about sewerage, algae, midges, and flooding. Long Preston, already troubled by holiday traffic, HGVs, and a deferred bypass scheme, is against it. Villagers in Rathmell worry about the closure of the road to Settle.

Local business interests on the whole are for the scheme, and would take on more staff. This might stop young people leaving. The Settle Chamber of Trade has worries about outside competition.

Other groups are Manchester Anglers, a local historian, a gamekeeper, and a local vicar.

Environmental groups include English Nature and the Council for the Protection of Rural England who oppose the plans totally. They have information about likely biodiversity losses. Some buildings near Wigglesworth Hall are grade 2 listed.

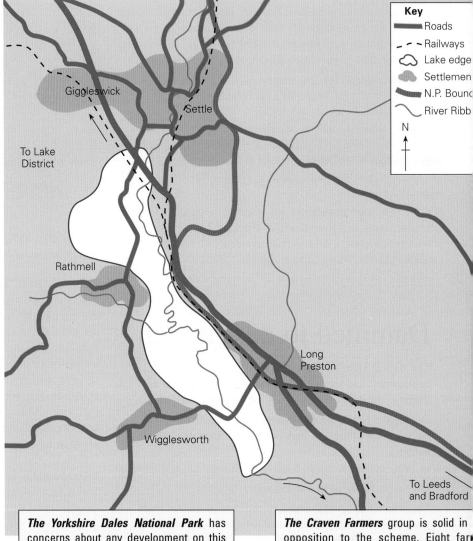

The Yorkshire Dales National Park has concerns about any development on this scale, but as the area is outside the park it can only advise Craven District Council.

The Ramblers' Association argues that local as well as long-distance footpaths like the Ribble Way will be lost.

The Environment Agency will monitor developments to safeguard water quality.

The Craven Farmers group is solid in opposition to the scheme. Eight far[m]s would be ruined and others would have [to] change from dairy to sheep. For som[e] farmers it is more than their farm, it is th[eir] heritage: they can trace ownership back [to] Domesday. The valley is used for fatteni[ng] stock from a wide area and this cou[ld] affect 200 jobs as well as land, proper[ty] and equipment.

Economic Forestry Group (EFG) ha[s] already surveyed surrounding land [for] planting Lodgepole Pine.

Figure 1.88   *The Upper Ribblesdale reservoir project.*

Forestry

Afforestation of uplands seems to be a sound strategy economically. Since the Second World War, the planting of coniferous trees has increased rapidly in the UK, especially in Scotland. Part of this was due to grants and tax incentives (even tax loopholes) which encouraged private companies to grow mainly Lodgepole Pine or Sitka Spruce. Grizedale in Cumbria and the Kielder Forest Park in Northumberland are high-profile forest areas planted and looked after by the Forestry Commission. The arguments for and against 'blanket' planting are championed on the one hand by groups like the Forestry Commission and the Timber Growers Organisation, and on the other by the Council for the Protection of Rural England (CPRE) and the Royal Society for the Protection of Birds (RSPB). A summary of these views is set out in Figures 1.90 and 1.91.

	Conifers	Broadleaved	Other	Total
Forestry Commission	1670	340	180	2190
Private woodland	2160	4490	1060	7710
Totals	3830	4830	1240	9900

Figure 1.89   *Woodland cover in England in 1998 (km²).*
Source: Countryside Agency, 1999.

For	Against
Saves on imports of wood and paper	Not a natural landscape
Protects land from erosion	Jobs are costly at £50,000 each*
Helps control flooding	Slower returns than farming
Promotes tourism (five jobs versus one in farming)	Lowers the biodiversity
Economic use of marginal land	Contributes to water pollution

*via tax concessions and grants

Figure 1.90   *The blanket afforestation debate.*

1 Impact on the Landscape

The problems are the use of straight planting boundary lines, monoculture of pine and spruce, planting (and therefore felling) all at the same time, and the use of land at increasingly higher altitudes. The solution is to carry out more appropriate planting, but the general appearance is still one of regimental lines of similar trees.

(Creeping coniferisation is a controversial issue at high-value sites such as along Hadrian's Wall.)

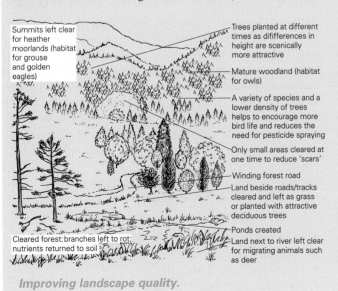

Improving landscape quality.

2 Impact on the Environment

The problems here are potentially worse. The most noticeable changes which result from afforestation are the loss of ground cover, as reduced light and water levels wipe out many plants, and birds. Water courses, and water supplies, are affected by the acidity of the needles and soils, and the aerial application of chemical pesticides. The Flow country in the north of Scotland was planted with conifers by private companies in the 1980s. As the RSPB warned, rare birds and a unique habitat of blanket-bog were all but lost.

Before you buy (RSPB).

Figure 1.91   *The two biggest impacts which afforestation has are visually (on the landscape) and ecologically (on the environment).*   Source: Forestry Commission on New Planting Policy and Procedure, Paper 3.

Most of the UK's broadleaved woodland has been removed. What remains suffers from neglect and grazing by sheep and rabbits. The traditional practice of coppicing (thinning and cutting in rotation) is no longer economic, and some woodlands are dying of old age.

Private owners have received help through the Woodland Grant Scheme and Woodland Premium Scheme. Various other groups offer advice. Organisations like the CPRE welcome the target of doubling the UK's woodland by 2025, but only if this woodland is broadleaved. Biodiversity would improve dramatically in British mixed woodland if walls and fences were made stockproof. Because broadleaved trees take longer to mature than conifers, there is no early profit, and groups like English Nature are pressing for grants to be based on management rather than planting. Education and publicity about woodland is important. 'Wilderness' schemes in the north of the Northumberland National Park were awarded the 'top tree trophies' for replacing unsightly plantations with native woodland.

Softwood production is greatest in the Boreal forests of northern Eurasia and Canada. Logging in these countries provides a major source of income (from woodpulp and paper). The shorter lifecycle of conifers, and the practice of leaving branches and needles on site means that the forest can regenerate itself. However, there is increasing concern from environmental groups like Friends of the Earth, that this practice is in fact only creating secondary forest, which will become progressively poorer.

In the tropical forests, whilst the rate of deforestation is slowing, losses are still estimated at over 7 million hectares per year (20 football pitches per minute!). Large-scale clearance causes soil erosion, floods, and desertification. In these conditions, regeneration is impossible, and the impact on biodiversity and climate is immeasurable.

There are many ways in which losses from logging and clearing might be prevented or reduced, but implementing them will be difficult. The economic investment by transnational companies, and the demands of MEDC customers, are not easily countered. In south Asia the monsoon forests are also under threat, with less than 7 per cent of India now forested. Here the pressure for more farmland and fuel supplies is the main cause of deforestation, together with the grazing of livestock in forests. Soil erosion in Nepal and floods in Bangladesh have been linked to this Asian deforestation by some researchers.

- Press for agroforestry which retains 'layer' structure
- Promote selective logging and replanting
- Set up reserves for the native Americans to allow them to return to shifting cultivation
- Establish wilderness areas linked to ecotourism (biosphere reserves)
- Debt for nature agreements (World Bank) and Jubilee 2000
- Promote production of non-timber forest products (fruit, rubber)
- Police illegal activities better (logging in Philippines/imports in Japan)
- Store tree ashes and top soil to allow replanting after mining
- Make 'green' agreements with big companies (B&Q)
- Reward eco-friendly production (Worldwide Fund for Nature and Forest Stewardship Council)
- Carry out media campaigns (Friends of the Earth 'Mahogany is Murder' campaign)

Figure 1.92   *Management options for more sustainable tropical rainforest.*

ACTIVITIES

1 How does coniferous planting affect the environment?
2 Which of the schemes referred to in Figure 1.92 have you heard of?
3 Which options do you feel are most likely to work?
4 How would you investigate the differences between coniferous and broadleafed ecosystems?

Mining and quarrying: The shape of things to come

Perhaps the most important development in the quarry business is the move by transnational companies to create vast superquarries, often in coastal locations. Material from these superquarries has been used in motorway construction and for projects such as the channel tunnel. Sales of aggregates were worth £2 billion in the UK in 1999. Sites have been identified on Harris and Shetland, as well as on the mainland. One estimate is that 18 billion tonnes of rock may be removed. This will have a major visual impact as 'half the hillside' is removed. One site at Glensanda will excavate 1 km³ over the next 150 years. Crushed granite will be sent out in 75 000 tonne ships.

The advantages of coastal superquarries are:

- removal by sea avoids road traffic
- creates jobs in rural areas
- saves the cost of imports
- deep quarries take less land
- sparse population is less affected.

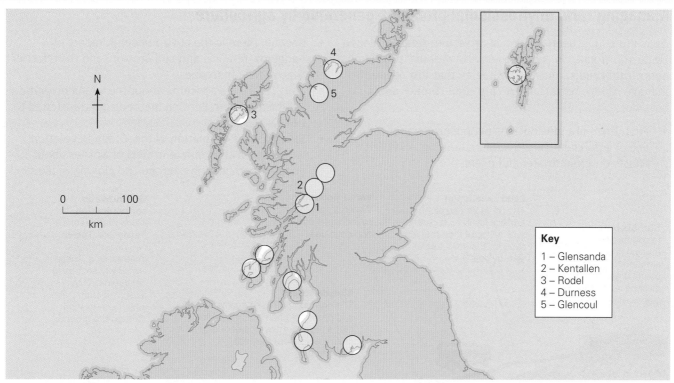

Figure 1.93   *The location of future superquarries.*

Source: Ecology and environmental science factsheet, Sept. 1995

Key

1 – Glensanda
2 – Kentallen
3 – Rodel
4 – Durness
5 – Glencoul

The Rough Guide to Quarrying in the Dales

The good, the bad, and the ugly!

Good – because people can use the minerals for industry, roads, and building (4.6 million tonnes per year)

Bad – because the resources are non-renewable and provide few jobs in modern quarries

Ugly – because of the visual and environmental pollution The quarries create dust, noise and traffic in rural areas

Let's face it! Mining and quarrying have a bit of an image problem

So what are 'they' doing about it?

Well, the Yorkshire Dales National Park has set up the Yorkshire Dales Minerals and Waste Local Plan, and at Ingleton, the new £7 million plant includes environmental improvements e.g. landscaping, dust control and tree planting.

Sorted!

Figure 1.94   *Quarries in the Yorkshire Dales National Park.*

All mining operations have the potential to damage the environment, but in LEDCs there is an extra degree of sensitivity as the companies involved are often based in MEDCs. At Fort Dauphin in Malagasy, Friends of the Earth are calling for the mining of local sands to be halted. The biodiversity of the rainforest there is exceptional, and the effects would be irreversible.

ACTIVITIES?

1 Study all the resources on quarries. Do you consider the issue to be 'sorted'?

Managing rural environmental problems generated by agriculture

Agriculture has been looked at in some detail already. Here the focus is on the environmental problems agriculture brings, and the strategies that are needed to manage them better. There are four broad areas to consider:

- First, there are the concerns people have about the use of agro-chemicals in modern farming, and their effects on groundwater and rivers.

- Second, there is the environmental impact of hedgerow removal and soil erosion, and the effect of this on the landscape.
- Third, there are concerns about the 'green revolution' in which modern farming methods are transferred to LEDCs.
- Finally, some evaluation of the 'Green Revolution' would seem appropriate in view of worries about genetic modification of crops and cloning of livestock.

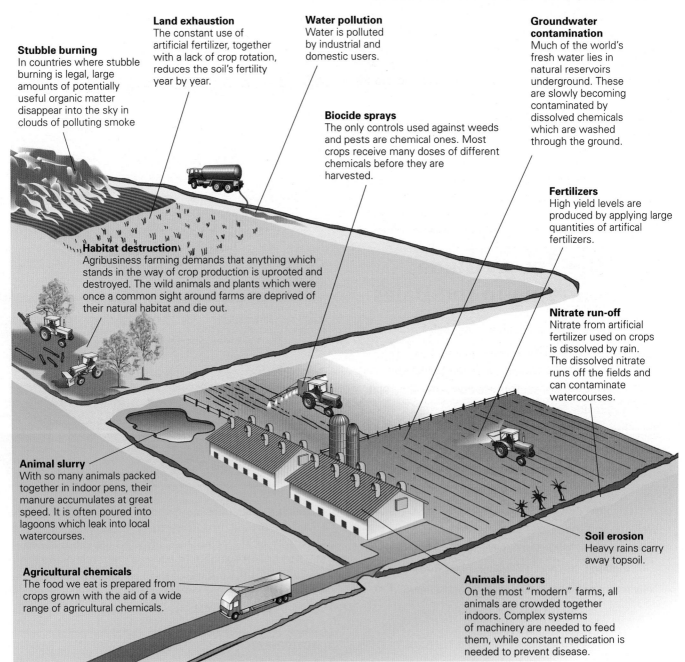

Land exhaustion
The constant use of artificial fertilizer, together with a lack of crop rotation, reduces the soil's fertility year by year.

Water pollution
Water is polluted by industrial and domestic users.

Groundwater contamination
Much of the world's fresh water lies in natural reservoirs underground. These are slowly becoming contaminated by dissolved chemicals which are washed through the ground.

Stubble burning
In countries where stubble burning is legal, large amounts of potentially useful organic matter disappear into the sky in clouds of polluting smoke

Biocide sprays
The only controls used against weeds and pests are chemical ones. Most crops receive many doses of different chemicals before they are harvested.

Fertilizers
High yield levels are produced by applying large quantities of artifical fertilizers.

Habitat destruction
Agribusiness farming demands that anything which stands in the way of crop production is uprooted and destroyed. The wild animals and plants which were once a common sight around farms are deprived of their natural habitat and die out.

Nitrate run-off
Nitrate from artificial fertilizer used on crops is dissolved by rain. The dissolved nitrate runs off the fields and can contaminate watercourses.

Animal slurry
With so many animals packed together in indoor pens, their manure accumulates at great speed. It is often poured into lagoons which leak into local watercourses.

Soil erosion
Heavy rains carry away topsoil.

Agricultural chemicals
The food we eat is prepared from crops grown with the aid of a wide range of agricultural chemicals.

Animals indoors
On the most "modern" farms, all animals are crowded together indoors. Complex systems of machinery are needed to feed them, while constant medication is needed to prevent disease.

Figure 1.95   *The downside of modern hi-tech farming.*
Source: Adapted from: NEAB GCSE June 1998.

Inorganic fertilisers and chemical biocides play an important part in modern agriculture. Fertilisers based mainly on nitrogen are used to increase arable crop yields (average 127.5 tonnes per hectare in the UK, Nitrate is a vert effective fertiliser but there are always some losses from the system. The excess nitrate leaches into groundwater supplies or runs off into rivers. Over-use is both wasteful and can lead to **eutrophication**. The nitrate in the water creates a nutrient-rich environment which causes aquatic plants and algae to multiply rapidly. With little oxygen available, fish and fresh-water animals die. If the nitrate contaminates human water supplies, it is a health hazard, and the Ministry of Agriculture, Fisheries and Food (MAFF) has accepted the link between nitrates and cancer. Phosphates from farm slurry and sewage, have also contributed to pollution in areas like the Norfolk Broads.

Biocides and related chemicals are used to prevent damage to crops by various organisms: effectively to poison them. The most common methods of application are to spray by vehicle or air. Organo-phosphates used in insecticides and sheep dips are also a health risk. The history of some now-banned pesticides (DDT and Aldrin) and their effect on the food chain make gruesome reading, although their use is still necessary to control malaria in LEDCs. Pesticide residues in herons of 3 parts per million, and 12 parts per million in their eggs may not seem much, but they are significant. The decline in farmland birds is related to rapid, large-scale agro-chemical use from the 1970s onwards. (In many LEDCs accidental poisoning of people is common and there is widespread misuse of some chemicals because of language difficulties.) The Ministry of Agriculture, Fisheries and Food approves all new products in the UK and groups like Friends of the Earth regularly target major food retailers to check residue levels in vegetables or fruit. Nitrate levels in rivers are monitored by the Environment Agency, and the British Trust for Ornithology surveys bird populations.

Given all these problems, what are the options available to farmers and consumers?

- use mulching and crop rotation (traditional approaches)
- return to mixed rather than specialised farming
- use organic farming methods (currently less than 1 per cent of UK farmland) (Figure 1.97)
- introduce insect predators (biological pest control)
- cultivate less intensively (losses below 10 per cent)
- reward nitrate-free farming (extend the nitrogen sensitive areas scheme)
- fine polluters or tax pesticide users
- limit biotechnology (introduce sterile insects)
- use genetically modified (GM) crops, such as a soya bean that requires no pesticides.

Bird	1972	1996	% losses
Skylark	7720	3090	60
Willow warbler	6060	4670	23
Linnet	1560	925	41
Thrush	3620	1740	52
Lapwing	588	341	42
Yellow-hammer	4400	1760	60
Blackbird	1254	8400	33
Tree sparrow	650	84.5	87
Corn bunting	114	30	74

Figure 1.96   *Bird losses (in thousands)*
Source: *The Sunday Times*, 25 July, 1999.

UK organic farming target should be 25 per cent by 2010:

- increases in farm jobs (10–19 per cent in Germany)
- widens the biodiversity
- means healthier food with no chemical residues
- organic food suppliers currently import two thirds of goods
- sustainable food production is six times more energy efficient
- it takes 300ha of land to raise 100 tonnes of beef, but only 20ha to produce the same weight of grains or vegetables
- the UK imports very large quantities of animal feed
- most agricultural grant schemes favour quantity over quality.

Figure 1.97   *Friends of the Earth's organic factfile 1999.*

ACTIVITIES

'Can we afford to use less chemicals?'
'Can we afford not to?'
1   Write a critique of the development of organic farming in MEDCs, emphasising the arguments for and against it.

Hedges, soil, and the landscape

Figure 1.98 *Hedgerows under threat.*

Hedges contain:
15% of native broadleaved trees
65 species of birds
25 species of hedgerow plant
600 species of wildflower
1,500 species of insect
20 species of mammal

Figure 1.99 *The value of hedgerows.*
Source: CPRE Hedge facts, 1997.

In large-scale arable farming, hedges, planted mostly between 1750 and 1850, cause problems for the farmer. They use up valuable soil moisture and nutrients, protect insects which will damage crops, and allow pests like rabbits to hide. Herbicide sprays cannot reach the weeds. Small fields with hedges make some mechanical operations uneconomic, and land along field boundaries and in corners is wasted. As a result, hedges tend to be neglected or 'grubbed out' to create bigger fields. Between 1984 and 1993 the length of hedgerows in England fell by one third to 329,000 km, most being replaced by fencing. In 1994, there were 112,600 km of dry-stone walls, of which only one third was stockproof. Walls also have important landscape and habitat functions, shelter for example.

To help, the government paid out over £54 million on agri-environment schemes in 1998, mostly in ESAs or as part of the Countryside Stewardship Scheme (Figure 1.100). There were, however, twice as many applications for grants as funds available.

ACTIVITIES

1 Assess the economic advantages and disadvantages of hedgerow removal. Should they be replanted in areas such as Cambridgeshire and East Anglia?
2 Outline the direct and indirect environmental impacts of hedge removal.

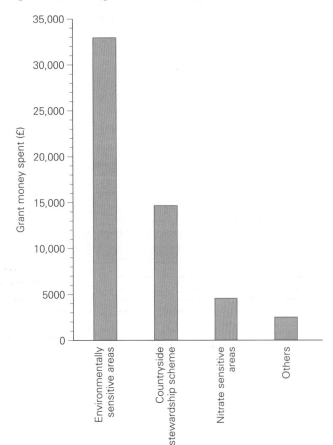

Figure 1.100 *Spending on agri-environment schemes.*
Source: *The State of the Countryside*, Countryside Agency, 1999.

Soil erosion

Soil erosion is a natural process, and in some parts of the world it happens easily. The yellow loess deposits in the Loess Plateau in China are easily eroded by water, and in dry areas like the Sahel belt in Africa top soil is blown away. In the extremes of drought and heavy rainfall, this erosion is considerable.

The misuse or over-use of land invariably makes matters far worse. If the protective cover provided by vegetation is removed, soils are prone to attack. The larger field units preferred by modern farming techniques offer little shelter from the wind. Ploughing for arable crops and keeping too many animals per hectare (exceeding the **carrying capacity)** can further damage soil structure. In dry years, soil losses of 200 tonnes/ha have been recorded in Norfolk.

In the Sahel of Africa or the drought polygon of north-east Brazil, similar combinations of factors have occurred, though it is often over-grazing rather than over-cultivation which is to blame. In Burkina Faso on the southern edge of the Sahara and in the drier areas of northern Kenya, soils are degrading rapidly.

The removal of forest cover in many parts of the world is also to blame for soil erosion. With no trees to intercept rainfall or to hold the soil together, erosion is increasing. One estimate prompted by figures from India, China, Brazil, and the Sahel suggests that one third of the world's soils could be lost by 2030.

The root of the reasons for managing soil badly is population pressure; misuse of land in the search for fuel, for food, and for living space. Putting the soil back is unfortunately not an option and so effort has to be concentrated on preventing further losses.

There have been considerable developments in soil science and in the technology of dry farming (Figure 1.101). Large-scale irrigation is not always the answer and in many cases low-level technology is more appropriate. The 'lines of stones' much publicised in Burkina Faso and the terracing in Kenya are examples of successful conservation schemes. These schemes can be considered sustainable solutions.

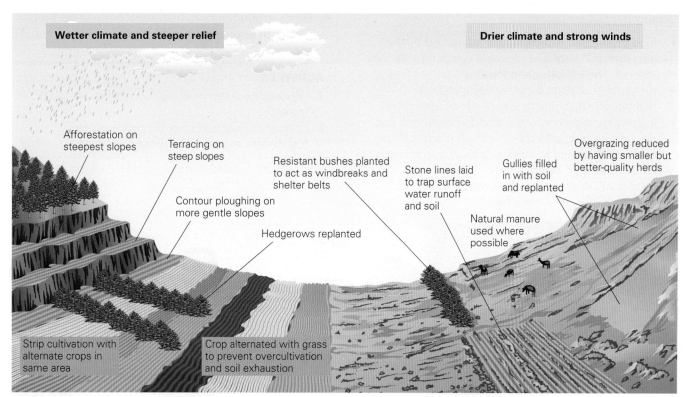

Figure 1.101   *Soil management options.*
Source: Waugh, *Wide World*, Nelson, 1998.

ACTIVITIES

1   Draw a flow diagram to show how soil erosion can occur.
2   Put the management strategies shown in Figure 1.101 into groups and explain how they might work.

The Green Revolution

The Green Revolution is a term used to describe the application, beginning in the 1960s, of MEDC farming techniques to developing countries. It was an attempt to feed the world. Horticulturalists and vegetable growers had for many years been able to cross-breed varieties to produce better seeds, or to introduce exotic plants. In the 1960s, however, these laboratory techniques produced HYV food crops which were seen as the answer to the food problems of the growing populations in LEDCs. Two plants in particular, the so-called 'miracle wheat' (CIMMYT) in Mexico and 'miracle rice' (IRRI) (Figure 1.102) in the Philippines, are examples. Maize, sorghum, and potatoes followed. The success of these crops has been judged by the fact that Pakistan no longer imports wheat nor the Philippines rice, and India is self-sufficient in both. This fact does imply that the success was all due to the Green Revolution. It disregards the developments in appropriate technology and good husbandry which took place at the same time.

The Green Revolution brought four, basic changes to farming in LEDCs:

- food production is increasingly influenced by the multinational seed and chemical companies such as Pioneer, Shell, Sandoz and Pfizer
- the number of plant varieties being sown is dramatically reducing (a loss of agri-biodiversity)
- a growing proportion of the world's population does not own its own land, a figure which reaches 85 per cent in Bolivia and Indonesia, both of whom have crippling foreign debts
- All the MEDC environmental problems such as eutrophication were imported.

For many, the Green Revolution did not bring the success it promised, in fact quite the reverse. High-yielding variety seeds need high levels of water (even irrigation) and fertiliser, and so those with little land and money were not able to grow two crops per year or treble their output. The use of agri-chemicals also had an impact on the environment, causing river eutrophication, and health problems. Poorer farmers or those on less fertile land were unable to compete and soon lost their land to moneylenders or other landowners. With subsistence farming no longer an option, the Green Revolution increased rural-urban migration because fewer farm workers were needed.

Better managing or reversing the negative effects of the Green Revolution is not easy and will require major decisions on a national scale.

- How do you give land back to landless farmers?
- How do you persuade migrants to return to the countryside?
- How can you reverse the impact of pollution and salinisation?
- How can you return to traditional farming yet keep pace with population growth and consumer demand?

ACTIVITIES

1 Why was the Green Revolution not good for many LEDC farmers?
2 Using all the information on this page, carry out a cost–benefit analysis of the Green Revolution.

Figure 1.102 *'Miracle rice'?*   Source: NEAB Syllabus D paper 1, 1993

The 'Gene' revolution: The way ahead

Genetic engineering is a comparatively new technology. It allows scientists to create products that have valuable food properties. By the end of the 20th century it had become possible to transfer genes between very different species. A number of high-profile actions by environmental groups opposed to government trials of genetically modified (GM) crops raised public awareness of this technology. New legislation in the UK is forcing food outlets and manufacturers to declare which of their products have GM ingredients. Many environmental groups have pressed for a 'five-year-freeze' on genetic engineering in food and farming.

ACTIVITIES

1   Do you agree with Prince Charles (Figure 1.103)? Should the genetic engineering of crops be the way ahead?
2   What are the environmental effects of GM crops?

GM food – the Prince's 10 key questions

Prince Charles asked 10 questions about GM food – and partly answered them with his own views

1) Do we need GM food in this country? On the basis of what we have seen so far, we don't appear to need it at all. The benefits seem to be limited to the people who own the technology and the people who farm on an industrial scale.

2) Is GM food safe for us to eat? There is certainly no evidence to the contrary. But how much evidence do we have? Only independent research, over a long period, can provide the final answer.

3) Why are the rules for approving GM foods so much less stringent than those for new medicines produced using the same technology? Before drugs are released into the marketplace they have to undergo the most rigorous testing – and quite right too.

4) How much do we really know about the environmental consequences of GM crops? If the pollen of GM maize, already grown commercially in large areas of the United States, can be shown to damage Monarch butterflies, what damage might it cause other species? Surely this effect should have been discovered at a much earlier stage?

5) Is it sensible to plant test crops without strict regulations in place? Will it really be possible to prevent contamination of nearby wildlife or crops, whether organic or not?
Since bees and the wind don't obey rules – voluntary or statutory – we shall soon have an unprecedented and unethical situation in which one farmer's crops will contaminate another's against his will.

6) How will consumers be able to exercise genuine choice? If crops can be contaminated by GM crops grown nearby, people who wish to be sure they are eating or growing absolutely natural, non-industrialised real food will be denied that choice. That seems to me to be wrong.

7) If something goes wrong with a GM crop, who will be held responsible? Will it be the company who grows the seed or the farmer who grows it? Or will it, as was the case with BSE, be all of us?

8) Are GM crops really the only way to feed the world's growing population? This argument sounds suspiciously like emotional blackmail to me. Is there really any serious academic research to substantiate such a sweeping statement? African countries which might be expected to benefit take a different view. They think "it will destroy the diversity, the local knowledge, and the sustainable agricultural systems – and undermine our capacity to feed ourselves".

9) What effect will GM crops have on the people of the world's poorest countries? Will they do anything to help? Or will they make the problems worse, leading to increasingly industrialised forms of agriculture, with larger farms, crops grown for export while indigenous populations starve, and more displaced farm workers heading for a miserable displaced existence in yet more shanty towns?

10) What sort of world do we want to live in? We are at a crossroads of fundamental importance. Are we going to allow the industrialisation of Life itself, redesigning the natural world for the sake of convenience and embarking on an Orwellian future?

Or should we be adopting a gentler, more considered approach, seeking always to work with the grain of Nature in making better, more sustainable use of what we have, for the long-term benefit of mankind as a whole?

Figure 1.103   *Prince Charles's '10 questions' – and his own views.*
Source: *The Daily Telegraph*, 2nd June 1999.

5 What is the future for rural areas?

Sustainable development is needed to improve rural environments and people's lives

LEDCs make arrangements with richer countries or organisations like the World Bank, to fund development. These may be 'trade and aid' agreements or large loans to allow important projects to take place. However, there is a growing realisation that to solve the problems of the world's poorest people, help has to be given at community level, through 'bottom-up' projects like a water tank or a well rather than through hugely expensive 'top-down' projects such as a mega-dam. Growing world poverty and debt have led to an international target to cut poverty by half by 2015.

Non-governmental organisations like Action Aid working alongside farmers and villages can make a real difference. The use of appropriate schemes, with the help of groups like the Intermediate Technology Development Group means that improvements made can be sustained. Whilst

Figure 1.104 *Aid, not always what it seems.*

organisations like Oxfam and CAFOD have a high profile when disasters strike, they and other NGOs are at work continuously around the world. Many of these organisations, like Save the Children are charities but others, for example Traidcraft, are businesses which promote fair trade.

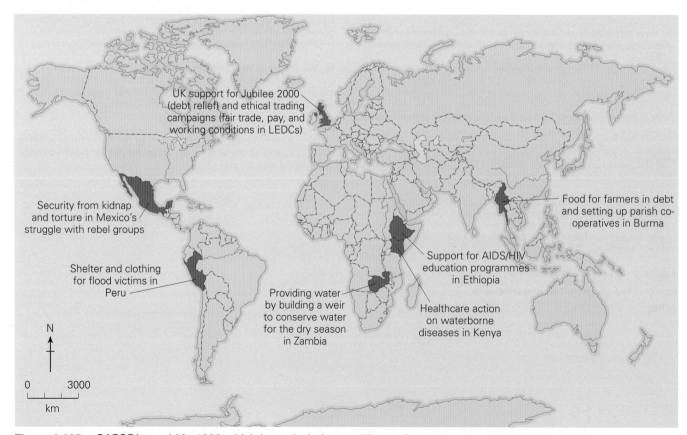

Figure 1.105   *CAFOD's world in 1998 which brought help to millions of people.*   Source: CAFOD Annual Report, 1998.

Women are helping Mozambique's rural population to break the cycle of poverty. Two hundred co-operatives are already producing eggs, poultry, and maize for the workers and to be sold in nearby towns. In one example near Maputo, money has been reinvested in the business and a new water tank has allowed it to expand into pottery. Some groups have begun making buckets and furniture, and have opened bakeries. Others have been given farm training, tools, and seeds. The number of flour mills and craft workshops is also growing. This type of development is based on teaching the skills to use basic or intermediate technology and not on buying-in higher level technology from MEDCs.

Healthcare in the rural areas is improving slowly. In the north of the country in Nampula there are now 16 rural clinics. Malnutrition and disease are commonplace and one in three children do not reach their sixth birthday. Among adults, tuberculosis and malaria are widespread. The 70-bed hospital at Netia has in- and out-patients, and an ante-natal clinic. It is funded by CAFOD and staffed by the Comboni order of nuns. This will help greatly, as the government cannot afford hospitals beyond the towns.

Figure 1.106 *CAFOD 'working in partnership', Mozambique 1995-98.*
Source: Adapted from CAFOD project reports 1995–1998.

A little further up the development ladder, in Bangladesh, the NGO 'Forum for Drinking Water Supply' is helping villagers get clean water and basic sanitation. Working with local groups, the Forum has installed 22,050 tube-wells and 576 village sanitation centres where latrines are made by local people. Women no longer have to carry water over long distances or use pond water. This has dramatically reduced child deaths and illness from water-borne diseases.

In Indonesia, the United Nations Children's Fund (UNICEF) provided the design and materials for wells, water tanks, and latrines (Figure 1.107). Because water is often near the surface, wells can be dug by hand. Women are often involved in this, as hygiene, cooking, and water collecting are traditionally seen as their roles. What is different however is that because the women run these schemes they have more opportunity and time to become educated in basic literacy.

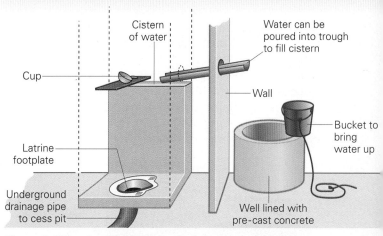

Figure 1.107 *A well and latrine built by local women in Indonesia using the design and materials provided by UNICEF.*

Indonesia's Family Welfare Movement (PKK) has set up a ten-point programme for villagers. These include ideas about self-help, nutrition, and co-operatives. Primary healthcare is also provided in community health centres. They look after maternal and child health, immunisation, first aid, and family planning. Each is staffed voluntarily by women, who are backed up by doctors and nurses in the 5,500 state medical centres.

In the Indian state of Kerala, the Intermediate Technology Development Group (ITDG) has helped local fishermen to cope with competition from commercial trawlers, and problems with logging companies who cut down the giant mango trees from which the fishermen traditionally made their boats. With funds from CAFOD, local people were able to buy land to set up a boatyard near Trivandrum. ITDG then helped them to design and build new plywood and fibreglass boats that allow the fisherman to go further out to sea and reach new fishing grounds (Figure 1.108). They have also persuaded the local government to try to control over-fishing.

Figure 1.108 *New fishing boat in Kerala, India, made with help from the Intermediate Technology Development Group.*

Other work by the Intermediate Technology Development Group involves their large list of practical guides and manuals, designed for workers to use in the field, *Appropriate Technology* and *Waterlines* being the most respected (Figure 1.109). In these manuals, for example, there are details of energy-saving stoves and low-tech ways of developing cool storage, all illustrated by pictures, diagrams, and simple cartoons.

Figure 1.109   *Publications from the Intermediate Technology Development Group.*

Traidcraft plc is a fair-trade organisation helping to fight poverty in a number of LEDCs. For many people selling basic commodities like coffee and tea, this is their only livelihood. Selling them through Traidcraft is one way to avoid the ups and downs in world markets. *Café Direct* is a famous example. Traidcraft deals with smallholders, co-operatives, and village workshops all over the developing world.

Three schemes in Nepal (Figure 1.111) illustrate how Traidcraft works:

- In the village of Banepa near Kathmandu, a rural centre produces knitting and tailoring to pay for children to go to school.
- Elsewhere, the bark of a shrub called 'lokta' is harvested by upland villagers and then made into paper by others in the lowlands of Kathmandu valley. This gives seasonal work to 1000 subsistence farming families. 170 craft workers now have full-time jobs printing cards for Traidcraft. Part of the profit goes to safeguard sustainable supplies of 'lokta'.
- At Kumbeshwar, women handknitting at home have funded a primary school, paid for vocational training, and set up an orphanage.

Other examples of sustainable development are being run by The Nepal Trust. In the remote Humla area near Tibet, subsistence farmers struggle in a harsh and fragile environment. There are no roads here and the nearest hospital is 14 days walk away. Ill health is the most pressing problem, and local people are being trained in basic healthcare. Women work to educate themselves, sell handicrafts, and operate a lodge for the trekking co-operative. The lodge has bought solar panels for its roof.

ACTIVITIES

1   In what ways are all the schemes mentioned above 'sustainable'?
2   Why are women key players in such developments?

Nepal, amidst one of the most spectacular landscapes on earth, also illustrates how tourism needs to be made more sustainable. Worries in recent years have included 'leakage' of profits overseas, and an over-concentration of tourism in the Kathmandu valley (which has been classed as a world heritage site) (Figure 1.110). Environmental damage has been high for the relatively small number of jobs created. Particular environmental concerns include disposal of trekkers' waste (the Kleenex trail), over-use of footpaths leading to erosion from hillsides, and the cutting down of trees to fuel trekkers' cooking stoves.

Figure 1.110 *Kathmandu valley, Nepal.*

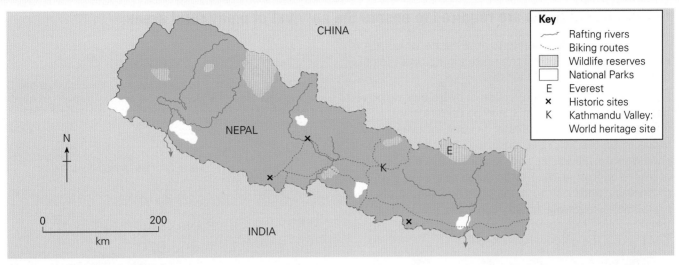

Figure 1.111   *Map of Nepal.*

Mountain tourism

Trekking developed as a separate activity in the 1960s and was based on the approach walks of the climbing parties which had conquered the great Himalayan peaks such as Annapurna (1950) and Mt Everest (1953). Trekking permits are needed beyond the Kathmandu valley and the number issued has increased very rapidly from 13,891 in 1976 to 61,273 in 1988. As trekking becomes more popular, the government has become concerned to identify the costs and benefits of an activity conducted in environmentally marginal, easily damaged environments occupied by hill people living at a subsistence level.

Some of the advantages – and the disadvantages – of mountain tourism are illustrated in the Khumba district surrounding Mt Everest.

Within 15 years the area has been changed from a subsistence to a cash economy. A large number of the 15,000 indigenous Sherpas are guides and porters, for at least part of the year, or work in tea-houses, stores, medical posts, and lodges. New facilities have been provided, particularly with assistance from the New Zealand Himalayan Trust founded by Sir Edmund Hillary. Previous high rates of outmigration have been reduced, local cultural monuments preserved, and cash employment created at a slack time in the agricultural calendar.

Against these advantages a series of problems must be weighed. There is evidence that traditional social structures are breaking down with an increasing differentiation of earnings; traditional hospitality is abused by some trekkers; begging has increased; food prices have increased locally; porters and cooks who are cheap to hire may be badly treated, some have even died of cold outside the warm tents of their employers.

In terms of environmental stress, large quantities of litter detract from the visual quality of the landscape, and there is an increasing problem of the contamination of springs. Trekking puts a strain on wood supplies for construction and fuel purposes especially at altitudes where tree growth is slow (60 years to reach maturity). The area under woodland has decreased rapidly in Khumba, despite attempts by the government to ensure that trekkers bring their own kerosene.

Ecotourism is a response to the costs of conventional mass tourism and green tourism is now the fastest growing sector in global tourism. The best models of ecotourism try to be a positive force for change rather than create cultural and environmental exploitation. They attempt to let foreign money benefit the local economy directly and to sustain natural resources. Ecotourism is defined as 'an economic process by which rare and beautiful ecosystems and cultural attractions are marketed internationally to attract tourists'. In a country such as Nepal, which is visited by over 300,000 tourists annually, 30 per cent on a trekking holiday, ecotourism may not always be sustainable tourism.

In Nepal ecotourism has become ecotrekking. One example is Getaway Eco-Treks, a specialist company which operates in Nepal, Tibet, and Bhutan. Their 'classic offer' is the Khumbu Everest Lodge Trek which takes place over 20 days with group sizes of between four and twelve people.

The company claims to:

- camp ecofriendly using paraffin stoves
- take back all non-degradable waste
- dispose of biodegradable waste carefully
- use local guides and lodges wherever possible
- be sensitive to local culture, customs, and beliefs
- use staff sensitive to the natural environment.

ACTIVITIES

1 Do you consider ecotrekking, as stated in the Getaway Eco-Treks brochure, to be sustainable? Give evidence to support your answer.

Figure 1.112   *The past costs of long-haul tourism.*

Innovative solutions are required to ensure the survival of many rural areas

A final area of sustainability to investigate in LEDCs is energy production. Too often in developing countries like Nepal this has led to deforestation.

Mini-hydro is a small scale version of hydro-electric power based on a weir in a stream. It may be used to power a corn mill, work a loom, run lights or heating, or even allow a fridge to be used to store medicines at a health post. It should make life easier and 'lengthen' the day to allow access to education. Mini-hydro schemes are low cost, low technology, and easy to maintain. They should also be sustainable, following initial help from groups like the Intermediate Technology Development Group. Figure 1.113 shows the mini-hydro in Nepal.

A related problem in many LEDCs is that there is no longer a large supply of wood to use as fuel. This lack of wood for fuel creates an energy crisis in the countries affected. One solution is to use animal waste (Figure 1.114). This means that there is then no manure to put on the land.

Why is not more sustainable development in place? Large, expensive schemes such as dams and irrigation systems are usually relatively easy to monitor. Sustainable developments, however, are almost always small and evaluation in the field is complicated by their remoteness. Figure 1.115 shows some of the differences between sustainable projects and large-scale super projects.

Since the 1970s it has become apparent that MEDCs solutions do not work well in LEDCs. The success of the transfer of technology (TOT) is better being replaced by farmer-friendly (FF) solutions'.

The 'super project' approach does not work for some rural dwellers in MEDCs either. Marginal farming, poor woodland management, soil erosion, resource depletion, poverty, and environmental damage affect them as well. People are choosing organic food, alternative energy sources and low-tech transport. These are sustainable choices, that are meeting today's needs without threatening those of future generations.

ACTIVITIES

1 What are the benefits of the two schemes shown in Figures 1.113 and 1.114?

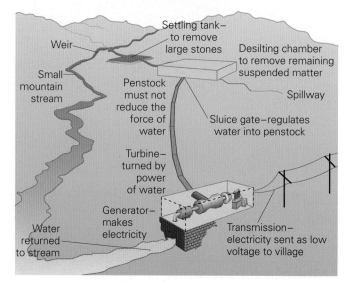

Figure 1.113 *Mini-hydro in Nepal.*

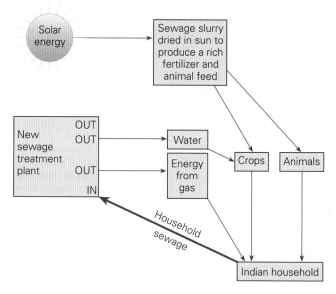

Figure 1.114 *Sustainable waste.*
Source: NEAB Paper 1 June 1998.

Super projects	Sustainable projects
Large scale	Small scale
Capital intensive	Labour intensive
Inorganic	Organic
Commercial	Subsistence
Mechanical	Human or animal
Hi-tech	Low tech
Begun in core	Begun in periphery

Figure 1.115 *Technological differences between super projects and sustainable projects.*

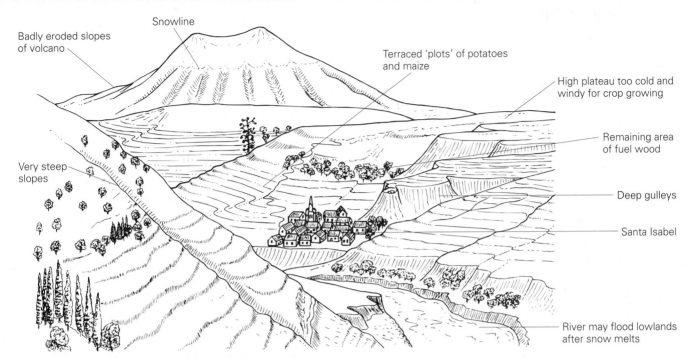

Figure 1.116   *A field sketch of Santa Isabel, Bolivia.*

The area varies in height from 800 m above sea level to over 6000 m. The valley is very isolated as it can only be reached by a winding dirt road (15 hours from La Paz, the capital of Bolivia).

Only about 10 per cent of the people speak Spanish (the national language) and there is only a 25 per cent literacy rate in the local Indian language.

About 2500 people live in the district (80 per cent of them in Santa Isabel itself). 65 per cent of the people are aged under 20 and the population growth rate is 3 per cent per year. Health standards have improved since the arrival of the 'barefoot doctor' (nurse) sponsored by our charity.

Agriculture, the main means of support, is largely subsistence. The crops are wheat, maize, and potatoes with some rearing of goats, sheep, and llamas on the plateau.

At present, agriculture takes all the available labour, but there is great concern about unemployment in the future. Throughout the year the whole village works as a team when carrying out the various tasks.

Figure 1.117   *Notes by a charity aid worker about Santa Isabel.*
Source: C.R. Warn.

DECISION MAKING ACTIVITIES

1   Consider the following development schemes:
   Scheme 1   Tourist village with facilities for winter ski tourism and foreign visitors.
   Scheme 2   A series of mini-hydro stations.
   Scheme 3   Llama and cattle ranches on the high plains.
   Scheme 4   A village co-operative to sell pesticides and fertilisers and to arrange marketing.
   Scheme 5   Women's knitting co-operative to weave and knit llama and alpaca jumpers.
   Scheme 6   Sugar-cane mill in Santa Isabel for processing local sugar grown in newly irrigated areas on the valley floor.
   Scheme 7   'All-weather' surfaced road out of the valley to link with the national road system.

Prepare a development plan for Santa Isabel.
   • From the list of seven schemes, choose the *four* schemes which you think would be the best for your overall plan.
   • Use the information provided in Figures 1.116 and 1.117 and your own knowledge of similar development schemes to explain why you have chosen each one.
   • Explain why you rejected the other three schemes.

Source: NEAB Syllabus D Geography, 1995.

The future in MEDCs

Integrated development in rural Wales

The rural areas of Wales exhibit many of the characteristics which have been shown elsewhere in this book. Mid Wales and Snowdonia in particular have much in common with the Lake District and the Yorkshire Dales. The challenges these areas face are the decline of traditional economic activities such as hill sheep farming, a dispersed and ageing population, and the loss of local services and community facilities.

Gwynedd	Cardiff
Little growth	Population losses
Lower birth rate	Higher birth rate
Higher death rate	Lower death rate
Retired > 30%	Retired < 20%
Low GDP	High GDP
Higher unemployment	Lower unemployment

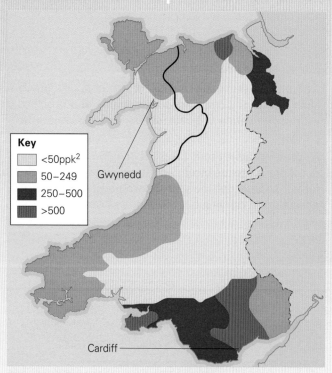

Key
- <50ppk^2
- 50–249
- 250–500
- >500

Gwynedd

Cardiff

Figure 1.118   *Wales and its population.*

The Welsh Development Agency

The aim of the Welsh Development Agency (WDA) is to develop an integrated plan that 'promotes sustainable economic, social, cultural, and environmental development in rural Wales'. Its new Rural Policy Unit in Aberystwyth will work closely with the Rural Partnership for Wales. The areas to be tackled will be agriculture and food production, forestry, business enterprise, and community regeneration.

Support for agriculture and food production will involve a budget of £5.5 million, and will include help and advice on livestock quality, machinery rings (co-operatives), and technical support for farmers and food processors. The Forestry Commission and Coed Cymru have a pilot programme (TIMBER) aimed at small companies. £13 million (44 per cent) of the WDA's business development budget will go to rural areas, both for existing firms and to attract new ones. This money will be used to find development sites, build advance factory units and, in a new scheme, refurbish disused rural properties (CADEG).

Spending on capital projects in rural areas in Wales was over £28 million between 1998 and 1999. Community regeneration has been funded by eight LEADER (EU Objective 5b) groups, which support local business networks, tourism initiatives, ICT projects, and environmental improvements. EU Objective 1 funds have also been used in the valleys and in west Wales.

Three of the many innovative schemes in rural Wales are Menter Mon (Anglesey Enterprise), the Slate Valleys Initiative in Gwynedd, and the planned Small Towns and Villages initiative in north Wales.

1 *Menter Mon* is a Leader II group supporting community-level projects. Since 1995 it has attracted £2.8 million of WDA money. The four strands in this programme are food and agriculture (which includes farm enterprise grants), rural tourism, language and culture, and rural environment. Rural environment includes village enhancement, rural skills centres and community enterprise, as well as wildlife projects.

2 *The Slate Valleys Initiative* is a priority for WDA investment. The magnificent scenery in the Slate Valleys hides the long-term unemployment, poor health, and difficult housing conditions of people in these areas. Schemes include a centre for teaching traditional building skills near Bangor, and workshop premises set up in old slate mills near Bethesda. The 'slate trails' set up near footpaths and cycle trails are to increase tourism in remote villages. The development by private companies of former slate quarries as tourist attractions has shown the way.

3 *The Small Towns and Villages initiative* has enabled local groups to develop their own proposals for their own towns and villages. Dolgellau is using Snowdonia as its visitor magnet. Ffestiniog has its railway and mines – both huge tourist attractions. The first ten proposals all focused on either tourism developments or community projects.

The WDA is an example of the new ways in which groups are working in partnership to promote the sustainable development of rural areas. Although these approaches involve higher unit costs and lower returns from resources, early evaluations suggest a lower rate of failure. This is the so-called rural premium.

ACTIVITIES

1 How does the approach being developed by the WDA differ from traditional schemes of regeneration?

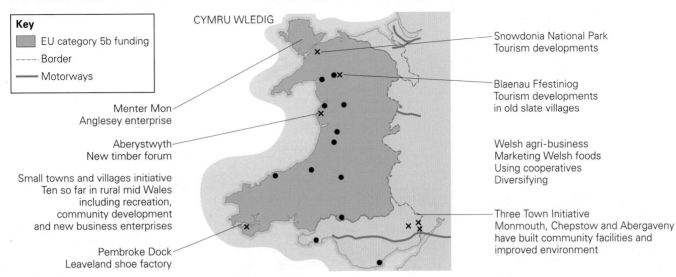

Figure 1.119   *New rural developments in Wales, 1998.*

Whilst some people have argued that there can be no blueprint for development in the LEDCs, those who advocate sustainable living in rural areas do at least have a guide. Whether through a local community, the country at large, or at an international level there is much that can be done (Figure 1.120).

ACTIVITIES

1   To what extent do you agree with the following statement:
'We must provide jobs and homes, conserve resources, and retain traditions and landscapes, if we are to have rural areas worth handing down to future generations.'

2   Study the six possible visions for a remote rural upland landscape (Figure 1.121) such as that found in the Scottish borders, central Wales, or the Lake District. Briefly explain how the vision may become reality. Rank the visions in terms of how suitable they would be as a way ahead. You should consider landscape quality, ecological factors, impact on rural communities, likely provision of rural employment, and potential sustainability. Justify your choice.

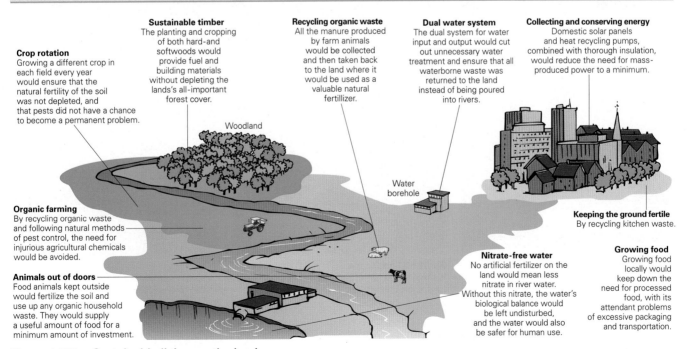

Figure 1.120   *Sustainable living on the land.*

Landscapes of tomorrow

The Present Landscape
A scene created by landowners and farmers.

Abandoned Landscape
Subsidies withdrawn, walls not repaired, forestry and tourism.

Subsidised Landscape
Financial support leads to intensive farming, fewer walls, overstocking.

Agribusiness Landscape
Subsidies, livestock ranches, bigger fields, conifer plantations, GM crops and stock.

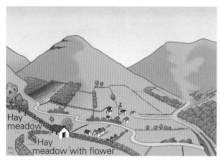

Conserved Landscape
Landscape maintained, farm-based tourism, broadleaved woods and meadows planted.

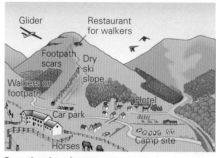

Sporting Landscape
Large estates with hunting and field sports, local jobs, exclusive.

Wildscape
Nature reserves, little grazing return to woodland.

Figure 1.121 *Landscapes of tomorrow.*

Source: *Core Themes in Physical Geography*, Oliver & Boyd, 1991.

Chapter Two Urban Environments

1 What are urban environments?

Most people in the UK live in towns and cities. Throughout the world, increasing numbers of people are also living in urban areas. In 2000, over 5700 million people were living in towns and cities (Figure 2.1). So towns and cities seem to be a big success. But are they?

Figures 2.2-2.5 show conditions in a range of cities around the world. They show that urban landscapes can vary greatly. They also show that the world's cities have some of the best and some of the worst conditions in which people live.

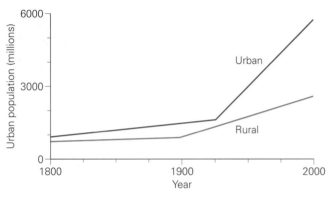

Figure 2.1 *World population living in urban and rural areas.*

Source: *Urbanisation* Collins, 1998.

ACTIVITIES

1 Study Figures 2.2, 2.3, 2.4 and 2.5.
   a Briefly describe each picture and your first reaction to it.
   b Working in a group, compare your results with those of others in your group. On which pictures do you agree? On which do you disagree?
   c Work in pairs to produce a list, ranking the four places as towns which you would like to live in. Give reasons for your ranking.
   d What other pictures could be included to give a more complete picture of urban environments?

Figure 2.2 *A cul-de-sac in Milton Keynes, UK.*

Figure 2.3 *High-rise tenements in New York, USA.*

Figure 2.4   *Shanty settlements in Nairobi, Africa.*

Figure 2.5   *Homes near factories in Merseyside, UK.*

What is urban?

Geography dictionaries often define urban as 'a city or town' and rural as 'the countryside'. This is a simple definition of what is meant by 'urban' settlements, but the reality is more complex than this. Urban settlements are defined in a variety of ways:

- by population size: for example, in Norway 'urban' settlements are those with over 200 people in them. Different countries have different minimum sizes of an 'urban' settlement (Figure 2.6). There is little agreement over how big a settlement has to be before it can be called urban, although Figure 2.7 shows one attempt to do this. Sometimes, urban areas are defined by the high density of housing as well as by population size. For example, in Sweden urban areas

are defined as having a population of 200 and not more than 200m between the houses.
- by employment: in some countries villages are differentiated from towns by the number of people in different types of job. For example, in the Netherlands towns are settlements that have less than 20 per cent of their economically active male population working in farming. Generally, urban areas have a large percentage of their population working in manufacturing (secondary) or office (tertiary) activities.
- by facilities and functions: urban settlements can be defined by the high level of services they offer, such as piped water, sewerage, and medical services, and the functions they perform, such as centres for shopping.
- by government legislation: governments in places such as Iraq designate some administrative areas as being 'urban'.

Norway	200	Belgium	5,000
Sweden	200	Greece	10,000
Ireland	1,500	Spain	10,000
Germany	2,000	Netherlands	20,000
France	2,000		

Figure 2.6   *Different definitions of 'urban' based on population size.*

Settlements	Population
Small town	2,001–10,000
Large town	10,001–100,000
City	100,001–1,000,000
Millionaire city	1,000,001–5,000,000
Supercity	500,000,001 or more
Megacity	800,000,000 or more

Figure 2.7   *Classifying settlements on population size.*

ACTIVITIES

1 Study Figure 2.7.
   a What is the population of the settlement you live in? Is this a small town, large town, city, millionaire city or supercity according to Figure 2.7?
   b For each of the different types of settlement listed in Figure 2.7 find two examples:
   i in Europe   ii in the rest of the world.
2 Study a range of towns near you that vary in size. Which of the different definitions (by population size, employment, facilities and functions, or government legislation) seem to be the most useful in terms of defining what is urban and what is rural? Give reasons for your answer.
3 Summarise the main features of urban areas from the information given on pages 185-6.

How and why do urban environments develop?

Urbanisation

The process by which more and more people live in towns and cities is called **urbanisation**. This is an important part of life for most people in the world. Urbanisation is also the process of change from a rural society in which people lived in scattered villages to an urban society in which people live in densely populated centres. Urban areas have a concentration of buildings, people, infrastructure (roads, railways, power lines), and economic activities.

The growth of cities

Cities are not something new in the world, nor are they confined to the richer, more economically developed countries (MEDCs). For example, there were cities in the Middle East and Asia over 4000 years ago. In Turkey, archaeologists have found nine cities buried one below the other dating back to 3800BC. Similarly, in the valley of Mexico, the Mayan city of Teotihuacan dominated the area from AD250 to AD750.

Why do cities grow?

There are two main reasons for the growth in the population of cities:

- migration from the countryside
- natural population increase.

Migration from the countryside

In the UK in 1801, 17 per cent of the 10 million people lived in towns of over 20,000. By the census of 1891, 54 per cent of a population of 33 million lived in these towns. There had been a massive increase in the country's total population, plus a movement of population from rural areas to towns. Many people in 19th-century Britain migrated from the countryside into the growing towns, in search of better-paid jobs and with the hope of better housing and living conditions.

More recently, cities in less economically developed countries (LEDCs) have grown even faster than those in MEDCs. Within LEDCs in 1995, 63 per cent of the increase in city size was due to natural population growth and 37 per cent was due to in-migration. For example, every week some 4000 people arrive in Mexico City from the rural areas. Most come in search of a better job, but there are other reasons for the move as Figure 2.8 shows.

Natural population increase

Cities, especially those in LEDCs, grow as a result of natural population increase. This increase is related to a declining death-rate, which itself is the result of improved medical care and better hygiene. The urban population increase is also related to the birth-rate which, although it declines in cities, is still high enough to be responsible for nearly two thirds of the urban population increase.

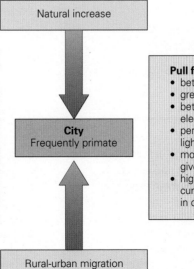

Increasing population accounts for approximately 60 per cent of the rise in urban population, caused by high birth-rate but a decrease in death-rate (medical technology)

Natural increase

Push factors:
- lack of job opportunities in countryside
- lack of investment by government in rural areas
- monotomy and harshness of rural life
- increased commercialism and mechanisation of agriculture cause lower demands for agricultural labour
- problems of crop failure, etc. result in rural famine
- insufficient land reforms and over-population cause lack of suitable land in rural areas

City
Frequently primate

Pull factors:
- better health care in cities
- greater educational opportunities
- better provided services, e.g. piped water/electricity in cities
- perception of excitement, pace, and bright lights of city life
- more public and private investment in cities gives greater job opportunities
- higher wages/greater job availability in cities cumulative influence of success of relatives in cities

Rural-urban migration

Rapid migration accounts for approximately 40 per cent of the rise in urban population

Figure 2.8 *The main causes of urban growth in LEDCs.*

The pattern of urbanisation

Figure 2.9 shows how the world's urban and rural population has changed since 1900. However, this figure is only an average figure and it conceals big differences between parts of the world. These differences are highlighted in Figure 2.10, whilst Figure 2.11 shows the world pattern of urbanisation.

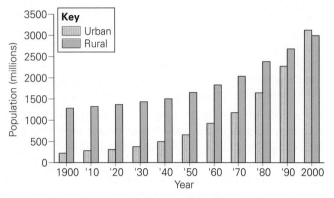

Figure 2.9 *Changes in the world's urban and rural population between 1900 and 2000.*

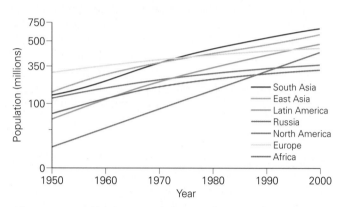

Figure 2.10 *Urban growth by continent.*

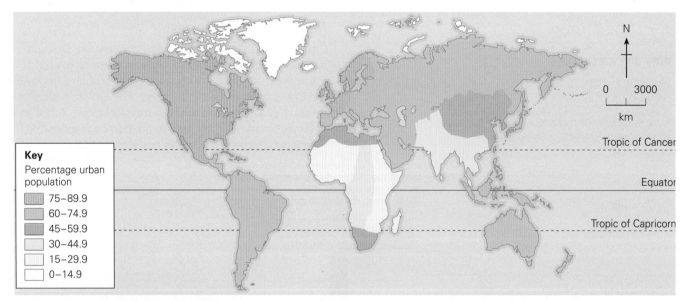

Figure 2.11 *Map of world urbanisation.*

ACTIVITIES

1 a Study Figure 2.8 then write a paragraph explaining the attractions of cities to people living in rural areas.

   b Explain the 'push' factors which encourage people to leave rural areas and migrate to cities.

   c Are 'push' factors more important than 'pull' factors in causing people to move to cities?

2 a Study Figure 2.9. Describe the general trends in the world's total population between 1900 and 2000.

   b How many people lived in cities in:
   i 1900   ii 1950   iii 2000?

   c How have the urban and rural percentages of the total world population changed between 1900 and 2000?

3 a Study Figure 2.10. By how many million did the population of: i Africa   ii Europe   iii south Asia increase between 1950 and 2000?

   b In which three parts of the world is urbanisation taking place at the fastest rate (the steepest graphs)?

4 a Describe the general world pattern of urbanisation shown in Figure 2.11.

Urbanisation in MEDCs

In general, the rich MEDCs have over 70 per cent of the people living in towns and cities. In the UK, for example, the percentage of people living in urban areas grew from 33.8 per cent in 1801 to 78 per cent in 1901 and 92 per cent by 2000.

What was urbanisation in MEDCs like?

Urbanisation in most MEDCs like the UK or Germany was closely linked to industrialisation in the 19th and 20th centuries. The Industrial Revolution began in the UK about 1750, and later spread to most of Europe, as well as the USA and Japan. The Industrial Revolution was based on the use of steam power and coal, together with mechanisation and mass production. New production techniques needed big new factories, which were mostly built on coalfields to be close to their power source. The new factories were also built close together and in towns because it was important to have a large local labour force. As the factories grew and developed, long rows of terraced houses were built nearby to house the workers who flooded in from the countryside. In the UK thousands of people migrated to the new industrial towns. For example, Manchester in 1801 had a population of 70,000. By 1901 this had grown to 544,000 (Figure 2.12). As a result, the towns sprawled outwards and were soon dotted with factories, mines, mills, railways, and terraced houses.

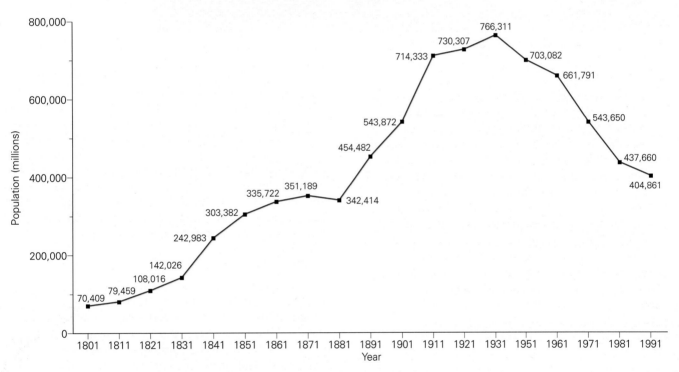

Figure 2.12 *Population change in Manchester, UK, between 1801 and 1991.*

Industry not only attracted workers to the new towns, it also attracted services such as railways, roads, and a safe water supply. In turn these improvements attracted even more factories, so the whole process snowballed. The improvements also created jobs in tertiary occupations, such as transport, as well as in banking, finance, and commerce. So towns had even more job opportunities.

However, the very speed of urban growth created problems. Huge areas of back-to-back terraced houses were built quickly and cheaply for factory workers. Despite the speed of building, there was great overcrowding in the houses, which often had no proper water supply or sanitation system (Figures 2.13 and 2.14). It was therefore no surprise that diseases like cholera and typhoid were widespread in UK cities throughout the 19th century. In the 1840s, the death-rate was 36 per 1000 and people could only expect to have a lifespan of about 30 years. Only with the passing of Public Health Acts after 1848 and the first Dwellings Act of 1875 did conditions start to improve. A few employers, such as Titus Salt at Saltaire near Bradford and the Lever Brothers at Port Sunlight near Liverpool did build better homes for their workers, but these were the exception.

Figure 2.13 *Manchester in the 1800s.*

Earth and air seem impregnated with fog and soot. The factories extend their flanks of fouler brick one after another, bare, with shutterless windows, like colossal prisons... and inside, lit by gas-jets and deafened by the uproar of their own labour, toil thousands of workmen, penned in, regimented, hands active, feet motionless, all day and every day, mechanically serving their machines... What dreary streets! Through half-open windows we could see wretched rooms at ground level, or often below the damp earth's surface. Masses of wild children, dirty and flabby of flesh, crowd each threshold and breathe the wild air of the street... Even to walk in the rich quarter of the town is depressing...

Figure 2.14 *Extract from* Manchester in 1859 *by Frederick Engels,* Panther, 1969.

ACTIVITIES

1 a Study Figure 2.12. By how much did Manchester's population grow between:
  i 1801 and 1851
  ii 1851 and 1901?
  b Can you suggest reasons for the differences?
2 a Study Figures 2.13 and 2.14. What were the main problems facing poorer people in Manchester in the 1850s?
  b Imagine you are a factory worker in Manchester in 1859 who has recently migrated to the city. Write a letter to relatives at home in a village. Describe the conditions you found on arriving in Manchester.

Suburbanisation

Urban growth in MEDCs was also linked to the development of suburbs. City centres soon became busy, noisy, and polluted places crammed with factories, so those people who could afford to moved, away from the city centre to live on the edge of the city. This process of suburbanisation was made possible by the development of transport systems such as trains and railways. These allowed people to live some distance from their place of work. Towns and cities spread outwards and there were constant extensions to boundaries to take in the new settlements, and the income from rates that they would bring.

Counter-urbanisation

Following industrialisation and suburbanisation, the third process operating in cities in MEDCs has been **counter-urbanisation**. In the 1970s and 1980s people in cities in the UK, Europe, the USA, and Japan began to leave cities in order to live in the countryside. This created a pattern of population decline in inner-city and suburban areas, and population growth in small towns and villages. Counter-urbanisation is made easier by:

- rising car ownership and motorway construction which allow people to work in cities but to live in villages
- progress in telecommunications and information technology which allows people to communicate over long distances.

Re-urbanisation

In the 1980s cities in MEDCs began a process of **re-urbanisation**. Here cities redevelop their inner-city areas. The aim is to attract companies and people back into city centres by improving the environment. New shopping centres, flats, housing schemes, and leisure facilities are all designed to give city centres a facelift and to make them more attractive to people and to firms thinking of locating in the area.

Birkenhead, UK

Birkenhead on the south bank of the Mersey estuary grew rapidly during the 19th century. In 1821, there were only 200 people living in 60 houses in what was a relatively remote settlement. However, a regular steam-powered ferry service began to operate between Liverpool and Birkenhead, and William Laird began a shipbuilding and repair industry in the Wallasey Pool. Soon Birkenhead began to grow as people arrived in search of jobs in the shipyards. The 1830s and 1840s were decades of rapid growth and by 1851 Birkenhead had a population of 24,000. Figures 2.15 and 2.16 show the changes to the town between 1824 and 1844.

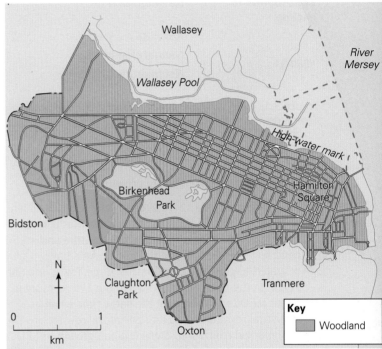

Figure 2.15 *Birkenhead in 1824.*

Figure 2.16 *Birkenhead in 1844.*

ACTIVITIES

1 Study Figures 2.15 and 2.16. Describe the main changes in land use that took place in Birkenhead between 1824 and 1844.

Urbanisation in LEDCs

Whilst urban growth seemed quite fast in MEDCs during the 19th century, the growth of cities in LEDCs in the 20th century has been even faster. For example, São Paulo in Brazil was founded in 1554 but remained a small town of 25,000 until the 1870s. Then the boom in coffee growing began. São Paulo became the centre for this growth. By 1890 São Paulo had a population of 65,000 and by 1920 this had mushroomed to 579,000. By 1960 São Paulo had a population of 6 million, by 1985 12 million, and by 1991 15 million (Figure 2.18).

Figure 2.17 *Skyscrapers in São Paulo, Brazil.*

		Greater São Paulo	City of São Paulo	State of São Paulo
Population	1970	8,139,730	5,924,615	17,771,948
	1980	12,588,725	8,493,226	25,040,712
	1991	15,416,416	9,626,894	31,546,473
1970-80 Contribution to change	Absolute increase	4,448,995	2,568,611	7,2268,764
	Natural change (%)	26.45	24.05	6.28
	Net migration (%)	28.20	19.31	17.35
1980-91	Absolute increase	2,827,691	1,133,668	6,505,761
	Natural change (%)	24.64	22.25	23.64
	Net migration (%)	–2.18	–8.90	2.34

Figure 2.18   *Population growth, natural change, and migration in São Paulo, 1970–91.*
Source: *Brazil*, Hodder and Stoughton, 1998

Why have towns and cities in LEDCs grown so rapidly?

The reasons for the rapid urban growth in LEDCs are:

- the modernisation of agriculture. Many countries such as Chile, South Africa, Brazil, and Kenya now use more machinery and chemicals in their agriculture and so need fewer workers. Many of these workers have migrated to cities such as Caracas, Cape Town, and São Paulo. In the past, urban growth in the 19th century in richer MEDCs took place at the same time as an industrial revolution and an agricultural revolution. This is in marked contrast to present urban growth in LEDCs where agricultural change pushes people away from the land but where there is little industrial growth to provide alternative jobs in towns

- rapid population growth resulting from a high birth-rate and a low death-rate. So cities grow in two ways:
  - from the natural increase of the existing population
  - from people forced to leave the countryside because local resources cannot support the pressure of the population. Figure 2.18 shows the changing importance of natural increase and migration in São Paulo's growth

- the decline of traditional industries such as textiles and metal working. This decline has been caused by competition from cheap imported goods from MEDCs. The people who lost their jobs in traditional craft industries in LEDCs are often forced to move to cities to find other work

- the attraction of 'better' housing, employment, and services in cities. The media, especially television and radio, have made people in the countryside aware of the possibility of a better life in cities. This encourages people to migrate.

ACTIVITIES

1 a Use the data in Figure 2.18 to draw graphs of population change in São Paulo between 1970 and 1991 (include Greater São Paulo, the City of São Paulo, and the State of São Paulo).

b Describe the changes shown on your graphs.

c Outline the changing relative importance of natural increase and migration in the growth of São Paulo.

What have been the effects of the rapid growth of cities in LEDCs?

1 Housing issues

One of the problems facing planners in cities like São Paulo is how to provide enough basic housing for the 2000 people who continue to arrive each week in the city. During the 1970s São Paulo built hundreds of low-grade apartment blocks for the new arrivals. These still did not provide enough housing to meet demand, so migrating families had to live in shanty towns called favelas in Brazil, where people built their own basic shelters from scrap materials. These settlements usually have no water or electricity supply or sewage disposal system. They occupy the least desirable parts of the city (Figure 2.19)

2 Employment issues

So many people have moved to cities that there are often not enough jobs, especially in manufacturing industries, to support them. Urbanisation in LEDC cities has not gone hand-in-hand with industrial growth, so many migrants cannot find work and are unemployed. National and local governments provide many jobs in cities such as collecting taxes or administering public works. Even this sector cannot provide enough jobs so people move to the informal sector becoming fruit- or water-sellers, or

4 Transport

Transport is a fourth issue in fast-growing cities. It is hard for planners to keep pace with the spread of cities. Underground systems are expensive to build, but are efficient ways of moving people. In 1991, 75 per cent of São Paulo's 3.4 million public transport users depended on 10,000 buses, 16 per cent used the subway and 8.7 per cent the suburban trains. In 2000, more buses have been ordered to improve the system and to provide jobs in local engineering factories. There are two main subway lines – a north–south one and an east–west one. There are plans for new lines and new stations to connect the centre with richer areas to the west. However, in the short term, the growth in bus and car traffic is only likely to lead to increased traffic congestion and growing air pollution.

> **ACTIVITIES**
> 1 How far are the problems created by urban growth in cities like São Paulo:
>   **a** similar to
>   **b** different from
>   those faced by 19th-century cities such as Manchester?

Megacities

A megacity is defined as a city with a population exceeding 8 million. In 1950, only London and New York City satisfied this definition. In 2000 there were about 28, of which 22 were in LEDCs. Since the idea of 'megacities' was conceived, only London (which was on the original list) has lost this status. There are two reasons for this. Firstly, there has been a tremendous flight of people from the inner areas of London to the suburbs, many of which have sprawled beyond the greater London boundary. Secondly, there has been strong counter-urbanisation to market towns and rural areas all over south-eastern England. By 2000, central London had experienced re-urbanisation and its population was growing again, so London may yet be reinstated in the megacity league.

Why have megacities developed?

A number of factors are important here, all of which fuel the growth or enhance the status of already large, millionaire cities:

* many megacities have developed from historically important sites such as former colonial trading ports (e.g. Shanghai, China) and were then re-assigned capital city status post-independence (e.g. Dhaka, Bangladesh)

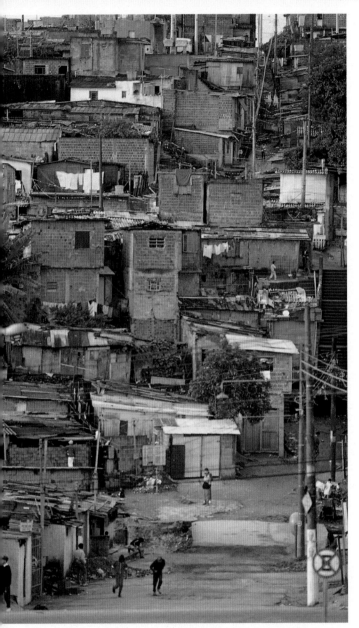

Figure 2.19   *A favela in São Paulo.*

barbers, or even prostitutes. Much of this informal work is seasonal (for example based on tourism) and so many people are underemployed and can only work for part of the year.

3 Pollution

Planners in cities like São Paulo also face problems of waste disposal. In 1995, only 10 per cent of São Paulo's solid waste was collected and treated. The city grew so fast that services like waste disposal did not keep pace. Yet São Paulo spends $US1 million a day on rubbish collection, and these costs are rising due to population growth. In 1999, the city had only two landfill sites for rubbish, so much remained decaying in streets, or was burnt in two waste incinerators opened in 1999. However, these incinerators add to air pollution.

1950	1970	1900	2000
More developed regions			
New York London	New York London Tokyo Paris	Tokyo New York Los Angeles Osaka Paris	Tokyo New York Los Angeles Osaka Paris
Less developed regions			
None	Shanghai Mexico City Buenos Aires Beijing São Paulo	Mexico City São Paulo Shanghai Calcutta Buenos Aires Bombay Seoul Beijing Rio de Janeiro Tianjin Jakarta Cairo Delhi Manila	Mexico City São Paulo Shanghai Calcutta Bombay Beijing Jakarta Delhi Buenos Aires Lagos Tianjin Seoul Rio de Janeiro Dhaka Cairo Manila Karachi Bangkok Istanbul Teheran Bangalore Lima

Figure 2.20   *Urban agglomerations with 8 million or more people, 1950–2000.*

Source: *World Urbanization Prospects* United Nations, 1991.

- some megacities spearheaded industrialisation (e.g. São Paulo) as LEDCs developed into NICs
- with very favourable factors of site and situation, many cities became **primate** cities, by far the most important city in a country, for example Bangkok or Mexico City. Thus megacities have cultural, political, and economic importance
- megacities have developed because of a rapid net growth in their population. This particularly applies to LEDCs which have declining death-rates for both infants and adults, as a result of basic health and sanitation provision and imported medicines such as vaccines. This is combined with rapid rural-urban migration, resulting from a combination of push and pull factors. Whereas megacities are not growing very quickly in MEDCs, the combination of a youthful, fertile population and rapid rural-urban migration can lead to growth rates of over 5 per cent in LEDC cities (as in Lagos, Delhi, Dhaka, and Bangalore) and for a megacity of 10 million that means half a million more people each year! Many millionaire cities (i.e. those with a population of between 1 and 8 million) are growing even more rapidly and will soon develop into megacities. Populous countries such as China and India are likely to generate many megacities over the 21st century
- a final reason for the development of megacities is that large cities often become hosts to international investment. They are often in the economic core areas and so are most advanced (in terms of education and technology and service provision).

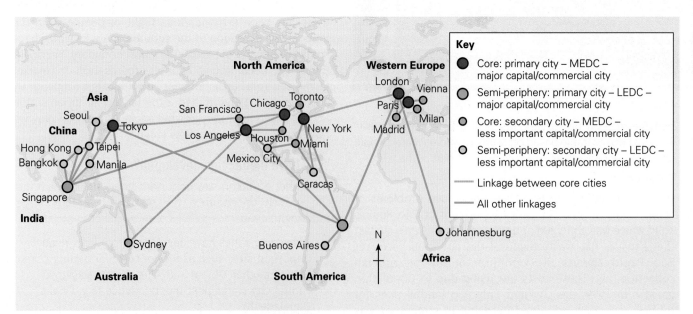

Figure 2.21   *Friedman's hierarchy of world cities, 1986.*

Some megacities develop into **world cities**. World cities can be defined as the command and control points for global capitalism (the dominant force in the world economy). World cities are not distinguished only by their size, but by the range and extent of their economic power. This power is demonstrated by the number of multinational enterprises which have headquarters in these cities, and by the range of the financial and business services available.

Megacities have a number of advantages and disadvantages, which it could be argued are applicable to all cities. However many of the disadvantages get worse as the size of the city increases. Size can be measured in terms of real extent as well as sheer population. It follows that most megacities do sprawl over a very large area, but some of the less compact ones such as Los Angeles or Mexico City are more unsustainable because of their enormous demands for energy.

Advantages	Disadvantages
Allows for advantages of agglomeration for concentration of industry and finance. The megacity provides both a ready market and access to a pool of labour.	The wide range of economic opportunities acts as a magnet for the migrant populations. Inward movement outstrips the pace of economic and social development. Rapid economic development leads to enormous industrial pollution.
Provision of education and services and basic infrastructure (roads, piped water, and electricity) is often better in urban areas (compactness).	The provision of services is numerically misleading as services are often concentrated in richer areas, leaving poor slum areas inadequately served. There are enormous inequalities.
The concentration of health and educational services produces a better educated, more healthy population. Basic literacy, family planning services, self-help schemes, etc. can be more easily delivered.	Many megacities face enormous environmental problems (in LEDC cities the Brown Agenda is a serious problem). The sheer scale of the poverty combines with the problems of rapid development: waste, sewage, water shortage, and air pollution.
The emergence of the informal employment sector provides scope for local entrepreneurial talent and helps urban unemployment problems.	Many migrants remain homeless and jobless. Lack of business support and credit are a problem. A large, informal sector and a large population of beggars can lead to harassment (street children).
Provision and organisation of self-help housing facilities helps to provide viable housing opportunities for growing populations.	Land occupied by shanty towns is often unsuitable for dense urban settlement. It may be subject to landslides and flash floods, e.g. Caracas, 1999.
Potential for effective community development can be used by national governments to spearhead improvements, e.g. in the slums of Bangkok.	Public administration of megacities, encompassing many different municipalities is extremely difficult. There is rarely one unitary authority. Large size can equal mega-problems and complexity.
Megacities provide a wide variety of environments for development and investment, both in the centre and on the periphery.	**Dual cities** develop, often with a poor inner area, and filtering leads to rich suburbia (edge cities, etc.). Social segregation and urban sprawl accentuate transport problems.

Figure 2.22   *The advantages and disadvantages of megacities.*

2 Urban functions and urban land use

Towns and cities in MEDCs

The centre of most towns and cities in MEDCs is the **CBD**. This is the social, cultural, and commercial heart of a town or city. It is also traditionally the most accessible part of the town or city where transport routes start and finish. The CBD is dominated by department stores, specialist and variety goods shops, offices and theatres. These are the land uses which can best afford the high rents of city-centre sites (Figures 2.23, 2.24 and 2.25).

Figure 2.23   *The city centre of Birmingham, UK.*

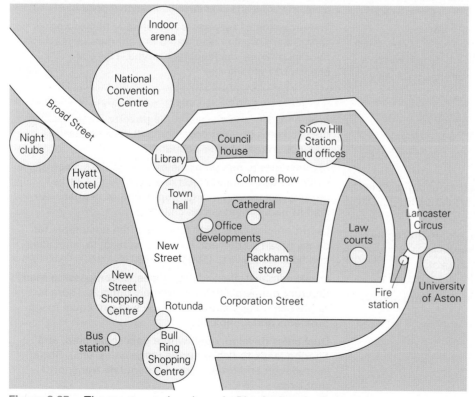

Figure 2.25   *The most popular places in Birmingham's city centre.*

Main Features of Central Business Districts

Concentration of Shops
Large department stores, such as Marks and Spencer, C&A and British Home Stores, are found at the heart of the CBD. They attract large numbers of people from a wide area. Other specialist shops, such as book shops and jewellers, are also concentrated in the CBD.

Concentration of Offices
Regional head offices of large companies concentrate in the CBD. They are attracted by the accessibility of the city centre. Well-known companies like a well-known location for their head office.

Little Manufacturing Industry
The CBD is not a suitable location for most manufacturing industries. However, a few specialised industries, such as newspaper and magazine publishers, do locate in the CBD. They need to be near to other CBD services and to have access to road and rail transport for distribution.

Growth of Functional Zones
Similar activities tend to concentrate in certain parts of the CBD. It is usually possible to find areas given over almost entirely to entertainment, banks and financial services, educational facilities and shops.

Multi-storey Development
The CBD has to grow upwards as well as outwards because of high land values. The most expensive sites have the tallest buildings. In a multi-storey block different activities may often occupy different floors.

Low Residential Population
There is little housing in the CBD because of the high level of land values. However, a few people live in luxury flats and apartments.

Figure 2.24   *The main features of a central business district.*

Beyond the CBD is the **inner-city area**. This varies from city to city, but its main features are:

- old, often terraced housing
- some vacant or derelict buildings
- car parks, often on sites where slums or factories have been demolished
- older factories
- tall blocks of flats, built in the 1960s and 1970s to replace slums (Figure 2.26).

Figure 2.26   *Inner-city flats in Birmingham.*

Beyond the inner-city areas are the **suburbs**. The outward sprawl of the suburbs began in the UK in the 19th century when improved public transport and better facilities to borrow money for house purchase allowed more people to live some distance from their place of work. Later, the spread of bus services and private car ownership, especially after 1945, led to the construction of large housing estates along and between the main roads linking major UK towns and cities.

There were two main periods of suburban growth in UK towns and cities:

- 1920–35, when many three-bedroom, semi-detached houses were built, with small front gardens and long back gardens, in crescents and cul-de-sacs. These estates had a small parade of shops but few other services. Some estates were built by local councils, others by private developers.
- 1960–78, when a wider range of houses was built, from large detached to terraced. Some maisonettes and small blocks of flats were also built, but public transport provision was often poor. Local authorities built schools, and health and library facilities to service these new housing areas.

These suburbs often have more open space in the form of parks and green areas than inner-city areas, whilst factories tend to be grouped along main roads. Housing, however, remains the dominant land use. This pattern of urban growth is clearly shown in Birmingham (Figures 2.27, 2.28).

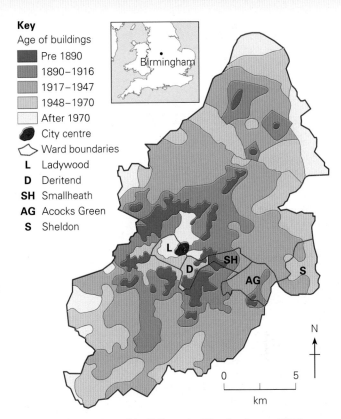

Key

Age of buildings

- Pre 1890
- 1890–1916
- 1917–1947
- 1948–1970
- After 1970
- City centre
- Ward boundaries
- **L**   Ladywood
- **D**   Deritend
- **SH** Smallheath
- **AG** Acocks Green
- **S**   Sheldon

Figure 2.27   *Age of buildings in Birmingham, 1997.*
Source: *Urbanisation* Collins, 1998.

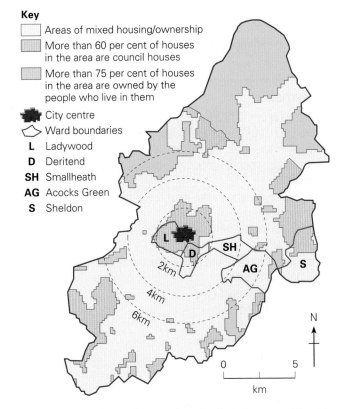

Key

- Areas of mixed housing/ownership
- More than 60 per cent of houses in the area are council houses
- More than 75 per cent of houses in the area are owned by the people who live in them
- City centre
- Ward boundaries
- **L**   Ladywood
- **D**   Deritend
- **SH** Smallheath
- **AG** Acocks Green
- **S**   Sheldon

Figure 2.28   *Council-owned and privately owned housing in Birmingham, 1993.*   Source: *Urbanisation* Collins, 1998.

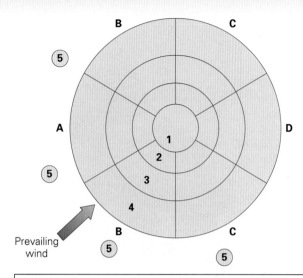

Key

1   Central business district
2   Transitional zone
3   Zone of small terrace houses in sectors C, D; larger by-law
     housing in sector B; large old houses in sector A
4   Post 1918 residential areas, with post 1945 development mainly
     on the periphery
5   Commuting distance 'dormitory' towns
A   Middle-class sector
B   Lower-middle-class sector
C   Working-class sector (and main council estates)
D   Industry and lowest working-class sector

Figure 2.29   *Mann's model of a city in the UK.*
Source: *An Introduction to Urban Sociology* Routledge, 1965.

ACTIVITIES

1 Using Figures 2.23 and 2.24, describe the main features of
   the CBD of UK towns and cities.
2 Study Figure 2.25. The size of the circles and the width of
   the roads show the importance people attach to these
   areas.
   a Which streets are the most important to people in
      Birmingham?
   b Try to explain why some streets and buildings are so
      important.
   c On a copy of Figure 2.25 divide the city centre into the
      following zones:
      • entertainment zone
      • legal zone
      • central shopping zone
      • administrative zone
      • office zone.
   d Why is it difficult to identify some of these zones?
3 What are the main differences in land use between the
   inner-city areas and the suburbs of towns and cities in the
   UK?

Mann's model of urban land use

For many years geographers in MEDCs have tried to
describe the patterns of land use found in towns and
cities. Their aim was to produce a model that summarised
the pattern of land use in most MEDC towns and cities.
Figure 2.29 shows one example, produced in 1965, by P H
Mann, based on a study of land use in Nottingham,
Huddersfield, and Sheffield.

ACTIVITIES

1 Study Figure 2.29.
   a Briefly describe the city shown in Mann's model.
   b Why do you think the industrial sectors in the model
      are in the east of the city?
   c Why do you think that the most expensive residential
      areas are in the west?
2 Study Figures 2.27 and 2.28.
   a How far does Birmingham seem to follow the pattern
      of Mann's model?
   b Try to divide up a copy of Figure 2.27 into the zones
      shown in Mann's model.
   c What are the main problems in trying to apply Mann's
      model to a city like Birmingham?

Land use in towns and cities in LEDCs

Models of land use like that developed by Mann were all
based on towns and cities in MEDCs such as the UK and
the USA. When geographers began to study towns and
cities in LEDCs such as Brazil, they soon found that the
older models were of little use. This is because:

• the growth of towns and cities in LEDCs has been
  much faster than it was in MEDCs
• governments in LEDCs often have a greater say in the
  growth, development, and patterns of land use of
  towns and cities than was the case in MEDCs
• most LEDCs were once MEDC colonies, and this
  influenced the patterns of land use.

New models of urban growth and structure have therefore
been developed for use in LEDCs. One example is shown
in Figure 2.30. Two key points to notice are:

• the large area of squatter settlements around the
  edges of the city
• the concentration of the high-quality, residential area
  in a zone from the city centre out along a main road.

ACTIVITIES

1 Figure 2.31 shows the land use in São Paulo.

a How far does São Paulo seem to have a pattern of land use similar to that shown in the model (Figure 2.30)?

b Suggest how the model might be adapted to include some of the features shown in São Paulo.

c In what ways does the internal land use of São Paulo differ from Birmingham (Figures 2.27 and 2.28)?

Key

CBD Central business district

Commercial/industrial areas

Élite residential sector

Zone of maturity

Zone of new building

Zone of peripheral squatter settlements

Figure 2.30   *A model city in an LEDC.*

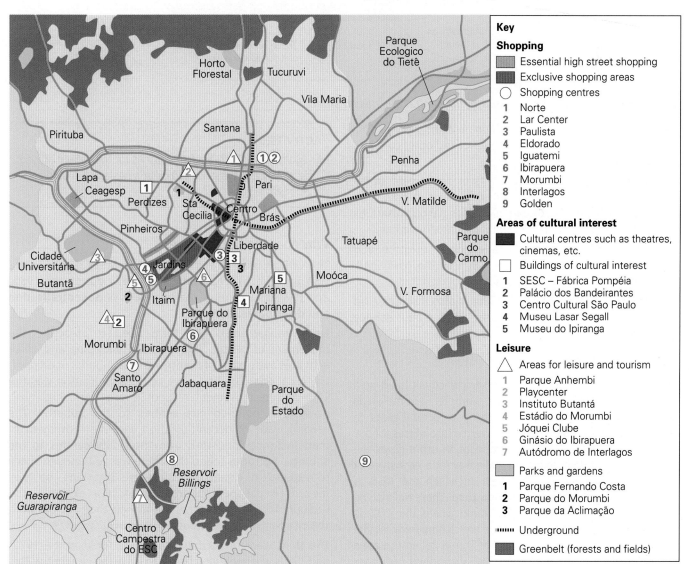

Figure 2.31   *A map of land use in São Paulo.*

Source: *Brazil* Hodder & Stoughton, 1998.

The CBD under pressure

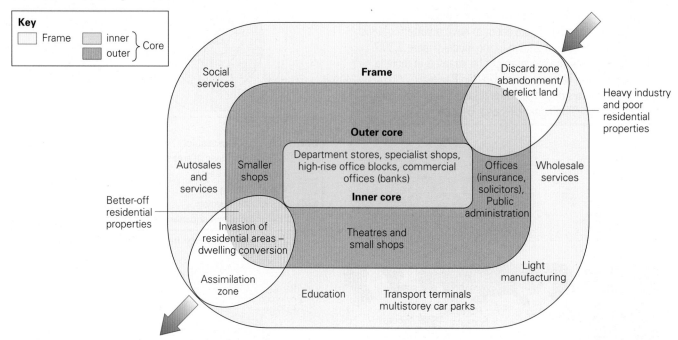

Figure 2.32   *The internal structure of the central business district.*

The CBD of large cities like Birmingham, Paris, or New York can usually be subdivided into an inner and outer core and a frame (Figure 2.32).

The **inner core** of the CBD consists of department stores and specialist shops, and high-rise office blocks. The regional or national headquarters of financial organisations such as banks and insurance companies are found here.

The **outer core** consists of smaller shops, theatres, and public administration buildings, such as the town hall, together with local authority offices.

The **frame** is an area of wholesaling. It also includes road and rail stations and car parks plus some service industries.

The changing CBD

The CBD is not a static part of a town or city. It is an area which expands and contracts. For example, in some areas the CBD will be expanding into nearby residential areas. In some cases the houses may be converted into offices for use by solicitors, accountants or architects. In other cases the houses may be demolished to make way for a new store or car park or warehouse. The area in which the CBD is expanding is called the **assimilation zone.** There will also be places around the edge of the frame where the CBD is retreating, for example where firms are closing because the property is too old or too cramped. This is called the **zone of discard** and is characterised by abandoned buildings awaiting demolition, or derelict land.

ACTIVITIES

1   Study Figure 2.32. Suggest reasons for the pattern of land use shown in the inner and outer cores and the frame of the CBD.

Why does the CBD change?

The CBD in most towns and cities in MEDCs such as the USA and the UK changed dramatically during the 1980s and 1990s as a result of the processes of **decentralisation** and **de-urbanisation**.

Decentralisation is the term used to describe the movement of people, industry, and shopping and office activities away from city centres to the suburbs or edge-of-city locations. The first wave of decentralisation was the 19th-century movement of people away from high-cost, noisy, and polluted city centres to the suburbs. The second wave of decentralisation saw the movement of manufacturing industries away from city centres to the suburbs. Factories found that there was not enough space to expand in expensive city-centre locations, so they moved to cheaper suburban sites. For example, the Cadbury family in Birmingham moved their factory from the city centre to the suburb of Bournville in 1879.

The third wave of decentralisation occurred in the 1970s and 1980s when retailing began to leave the city centre. This was the first really serious blow to the CBD. New shopping centres opened in the suburbs, and then hypermarkets and superstores opened, often on greenfield sites on the edge of the urban area. Soon **out-of-town shopping centres** were built at places like Meadowhall near Sheffield and Merry Hill near Dudley in the West Midlands. These are huge indoor centres with over 100 shops surrounded by large car parks (Figure 2.33).

Figure 2.33 *The Merry Hill Shopping Centre, Dudley, UK.*

Figure 2.34 *Derelict shops in the centre of Dudley.*

ACTIVITIES

1 a Suggest what the local council in Dudley might do to reverse the decline of shopping in its CBD.
   b What problems will successful out-of-town shopping centres like Merry Hill face in the future?
   c Why might some people still prefer to shop in Dudley rather than Merry Hill?

These new developments created real competition for the shops in the CBD. Often rents were lower, parking was easier, access by car was simpler, and the centres were under cover, safe, and air conditioned. The effect of these out-of-town developments led to a loss of trade in nearby city centres, followed by shop closures. For example, in central Dudley there was a 25 per cent fall in retail employment between 1989 and 1995 and a 70 per cent reduction in retail trade as a result of the Merry Hill development. Stores such as Marks and Spencer, Currys, and Littlewoods closed in Dudley and re-opened in Merry Hill. In 1985 Dudley had 190 shops; by 1997 it had 127. Dudley's CBD now has many empty shops (Figure 2.34) and little prospect of attracting more. Even Birmingham's CBD, some 15 km from Merry Hill, suffered from the competition and saw a decline of 12 per cent in retail trade between 1990 and 1995.

The fourth wave of decentralisation saw the movement of offices away from CBDs to office parks on the edge of the urban area. These offices moved because land and rents were lower in new, greenfield-site office parks than in the CBD. It was expensive to expand in the CBD and growing traffic congestion led to long journey times for staff and clients. Parking in the CBD was expensive and difficult and staff costs were often higher in CBD locations than in office parks.

De-urbanisation is the term used to describe the movement of people and employment away from large, dominant cities to smaller, more dispersed towns and cities. Not all the people, industries, shops, and offices which decentralised from traditional city centres stopped in edge-of-city locations. Some moved right away to other, smaller towns where there was more room for expansion, lower rents, and less air pollution and traffic congestion. So, in the case of the West Midlands, some shops and offices left Birmingham's CBD entirely in the 1980s in favour of centres such as Bromsgrove, Redditch, or Solihull.

The CBD fights back

The rapid growth in the number of out-of-town shopping centres during the 1980s led to widespread criticism because of the decline it caused in CBDs. In 1994 the UK government tried to slow the growth of new centres by imposing strict planning regulations on any proposed out-of-town developments. The aims of the policy were to:

- restore a better quality of life to traditional town and city centres
- encourage an improvement in town- and city-centre facilities by introducing pedestrianisation
- reduce dependency on the car
- use the 60,000 ha of derelict land in or near UK town and city centres
- reduce traffic congestion and air pollution.

Cities like Birmingham have taken steps to revitalise their centres, with the aim of re-establishing the attraction and competitiveness of city-centre shopping.

Figure 2.35   *The International Convention Centre, Birmingham.*

Figure 2.36   *The National Indoor Arena, Birmingham.*

Redeveloping central areas in Birmingham

In 1986, Birmingham City Council realised that if the CBD was to survive and grow the council had to:

- develop business tourism, especially the conference trade
- create a new image for the city, based on the centre, which would appeal to international business.

In this way the council planned to create new jobs and a new image for the city to enable it to compete with out-of-town developments and with other cities around the world. The method chosen for the development was the use of **flagship projects**, that is high-profile schemes which attract investment from companies and other institutions.

Birmingham began by building the International Convention Centre (ICC) which opened in 1991 (Figure 2.35). This succeeded in attracting high-profile conferences such as the International Olympic Committee, as well as the G7 world leaders and even the Eurovision Song Contest. The construction of the £38 million Hyatt Regency Hotel, the city's first five-star hotel, was also part of this strategy of making Birmingham known on the international stage.

Other projects included the National Indoor Arena, a multipurpose sports complex opened in 1992 (Figure 2.36), and the Broad Street redevelopment area with its night clubs, hotels, restaurants, and canal-side cafes.

In the mid 1990s, Birmingham extended the pedestrianisation of its shopping area. City-centre stores were encouraged to stay open later for at least one night per week. Special events such as music festivals were used to encourage more people to visit the city centre. The result was a growth in retail trade in the CBD of 5 per cent between 1995 and 1997.

In other MEDCs, the redevelopment of Battery Park City in New York, the La Défense project in Paris, and spectacular office projects in the neglected centres of Houston, Cleveland, and Atlanta in the USA illustrate the same policy. These developments are intended to act as catalysts to kick-start the revival of the city centre. Physically, the projects often bring derelict land back into use and improve existing land uses. They also serve as 'magnets' to attract people, income, and jobs.

ACTIVITIES

1 **a** Identify the main methods used by Birmingham to redevelop its central areas.

   b How far do you think these methods could be applied to other UK cities such as Bradford or Manchester?

2 What other actions might councils take to attract more people to visit the CBD?

The urban doughnut

The centres of cities around the world have had very mixed fortunes. The centres of a small number of global cities such as New York and Baltimore in the USA, and London have boomed. The centres of some former manufacturing cities such as Birmingham and Detroit have been physically transformed by massive investment in hotels, retail, leisure and conference developments. However, other centres, which have failed to compete with out-of-town developments, have declined in importance. In addition, inner-city areas have suffered a huge decline in almost all cities in MEDCs. Worse still, 'inner-city conditions' of poverty, unemployment, and hardship have been found in many housing estates on the edges of cities like Glasgow and Liverpool in the UK.

The effect of these changes is to alter the shape of urban areas. It will no longer be possible to easily identify city centres, suburbs, and countryside. As cities decentralise, more and more new urban areas grow up, often on the edge of one or more existing cities. These new cities are called 'edge cities' or 'stealth cities' and are most apparent in the USA where Los Angeles illustrates this pattern.

The result of the decline of city centres, together with the growth of suburbs and edge cities is to create a pattern of land use called 'urban doughnut', as shown in Figure 2.37. Such a system can only be maintained by an extensive transport system and the growth of telecommunications. It also means that more and more countryside is becoming urban as cities sprawl even further outwards.

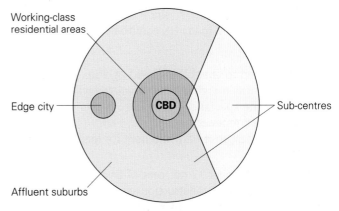

Figure 2.37   *The urban doughnut.*

Pressures on the rural-urban fringe

As towns and cities grow and expand in countries like the UK, there is great pressure for new development on the rural-urban fringe, the area on the edge of the built-up zone.

There is a lot of competition for land on the rural-urban fringe:

- land is generally cheaper than land elsewhere in towns and cities
- rural-urban-fringe land is undeveloped so there is no need for expensive site clearance and clean up-schemes as there is with brownfield sites
- people in cities are attracted by the idea of the clean air, open space, and pleasant countryside of the rural-urban fringe, as an area in which to live and work
- redevelopment schemes in towns and cities have led to the demolition of houses, shops and offices, so people and economic activities try to relocate on cheap sites close to the city.

Many different land uses want to locate in rural-urban fringe areas. The main uses are:

- housing: there is great pressure to build new estates or even new villages or towns on the rural-urban fringe (Figure 2.38)
- retailing: especially hypermarkets and superstores which are attracted by cheaper land and space for large car parks

- office parks and hotels: these are attracted by the clean environment, the landscape, and access to motorways and dual carriageways
- leisure: there is pressure to build new golf courses or riding schools for the town dwellers.

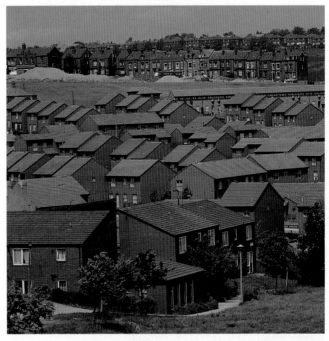

Figure 2.38   *New houses being built on the urban fringe.*

The greenbelt

Planners have realised for a long time that new urban developments might eventually spread and link up with existing towns to create massive urban sprawl. To prevent this, greenbelts were established around cities. Greenbelts are areas of agricultural land or woodland where new urban developments are strictly controlled. The greenbelt around London was designated in the development plan of 1947, since when greenbelts have been created around many UK conurbations.

Greenbelts:

- are designed to check the spread of cities
- prevent towns merging in an urban sprawl
- preserve the special character of towns
- assist urban renewal
- provide an improved environment for recreation and leisure.

Greenbelts now cover 12 per cent of England and Wales, and within them the construction of developments such as new offices, houses, and shopping centres is strictly controlled. However, greenbelts and rural-urban fringe areas face many problems:

- pressure to release land for new housing developments
- land in some greenbelts has been so badly damaged that it is really 'brown belt' and of little environmental value. In these cases, greenbelt land is used for market gardens, sewage works, airfields, hotels, hospitals, and similar developments
- many greenbelts now have motorways or other main roads running through them
- some poor agricultural land in greenbelts has been converted to golf courses, riding schools, and other non-farming uses.

ACTIVITIES

1 Study Figure 2.39.
   a Draw a land-use map of the area using your own symbols.
   b Identify the locations of the main land uses on the map which could create pollution or noise. Which of these do you think are not appropriate for a greenbelt? Give reasons for your conclusions.
2 There is a proposal to build a hypermarket at Chandlers Hill (035833).
   a What arguments would you advance in favour of this development?
   b What arguments would groups and individuals advance against it?

Figure 2.39   *Part of the greenbelt near London. (Ordnance Survey sheet TQ 07/17 1174, 1:25000).*

Quality of life

Quality of life is hard to define. It means different things to different people. The main concern of people in some parts of the world is simply to get a job and a home with basic amenities, together with services such as transport and medical care. Other people are more concerned about issues such as air pollution, noise, and crime.

A study in 1998 of the quality of life in cities in the UK asked people of different ages to rank 20 features of city life in terms of how these features affected the quality of life. The ten features felt to be the most important by people aged over 60 and by people aged between 18 and 24 are shown in Figure 2.40.

Features of cities most important for the quality of life for people over 60

- Violent crime
- Cost of living
- Non-violent crime
- Quality of local health services
- Local shopping facilities
- Cost of private housing
- Public transport
- Cost of public housing
- Leisure facilities
- Pollution

Features of cities most important for the quality of life for people between aged 18 and 24

- Job prospects
- Wage levels
- Violent crime
- Shopping facilities
- Quality of schools
- Cost of living
- Health services
- Sports facilities
- Non-violent crime
- Racial harmony

Overall ranking of the features of cities that affect quality of life

1 Violent crime
2 Non-violent crime
3 Cost of living
4 Job prospects
5 Health services
6 Shopping facilities
7 Wage levels
8 Levels of unemployment
9 Quality of schools
10 Access to public housing
11 Cost of private housing
12 Sports facilities
13 Leisure facilities
14 Pollution
15 Cost of rented housing
16 Racial harmony
17 Quality of council housing
18 Travel to work time
19 Climate and weather
20 Scenic quality

Figure 2.40   *Features of cities that affect the quality of life.*

ACTIVITIES

1 a What are the differences in importance given to the features of quality of life between people over 65 and those aged between 18 and 24?

b Try to explain the differences you highlight.

Problems of 'poor' areas in Manila

'Poor' areas in cities, that is, areas where the quality of life is generally poor, have a number of problems, as the following case study shows.

Tondo, an area of the city of Manila in the Philippines

The Philippines is a country of many islands in the Pacific with a population of over 60 million (Figure 2.41). Nearly 7 million people live in Manila, the capital of the Philippines and its largest city. Manila is growing very, very rapidly with the arrival of migrants from the countryside. Many of these migrants have little money and have to live in shanty towns (Figure 2.42) with no electricity, poor drainage, and no proper sanitation system. About 30 per cent of Manila's population live in these squatter settlements. The district of Tondo, north of the Passig river (Figure 2.43) is an area of shanty settlements, street markets, and some modern buildings. In the dry season when westerly winds sweep across Manila Bay, fires spread quickly, and in 1970 70,000 people lost their homes in savage fires. Disease is a problem, especially in the overcrowded unsanitary conditions, so the infant death-rate is high, and crime remains a big problem.

Figure 2.41   *The Philippines.*

Figure 2.42   *Shanty towns in Manila.*

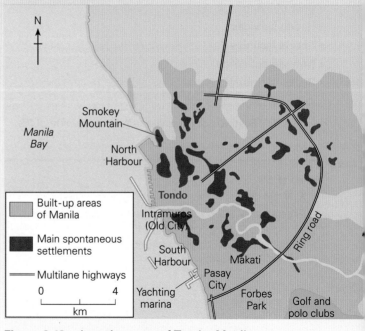

Figure 2.43   *Location map of Tondo, Manila.*
Source: *Urbanization* Collins, 1998.

3 The challenge of managing urban environments

We need to sort out the traffic chaos all over the city. We need a better system of public transport and ways to encourage people to use it.

Mayor of Los Angeles

We need to try to reduce air pollution and provide a safe water supply.

Mayor of Mexico City

We need to be able to provide enough homes for everyone who needs them - in the right part of the country.

Mayor of London

We need to improve access to services such as medical care for the poorest people in the city.

Mayor of Edinburgh

We need to avoid the segregation of people in different parts of cities.

We have to reduce crime in all neighbourhoods in the city.

Mayor of New York

We need to be able to improve the quality of housing available to very poor people.

Mayor of São Paulo

Mayor of Atlanta

Figure 2.44 *Different challenges in different cities.*

Managing the housing stock in MEDCs

Challenge 1: Providing enough homes for everyone

One big problem in managing the housing stock of any large town or city is how to provide enough homes, *at the right price*, for everyone. A government study of 1991 predicted that England would need an extra 4.4 million new homes over the following 25 years. In 1998, this figure was raised to 5.5 million new homes. These new homes are needed because people are living longer, the number of single households is growing, and people are migrating into south-east England. The key question is where should these houses be built? Builders prefer greenfield sites because the land does not need expensive preparation. Environmentalists prefer new homes to be built on brownfield sites, that is land in towns and cities from which derelict factories and houses have been cleared. The amount of brownfield land available in England and Wales, and how it might be used, is shown in Figure 2.45.

The case of Stevenage, UK: greenfield or brownfield?

Hertfordshire County Council has voted to build 10,000 new homes on 800 ha of greenbelt land west of Stevenage (Figure 2.47), a first generation new town. The council claims it needs to build the houses because it has to find 65,000 new homes by 2011 and it can only accommodate 59,000 on brownfield sites.

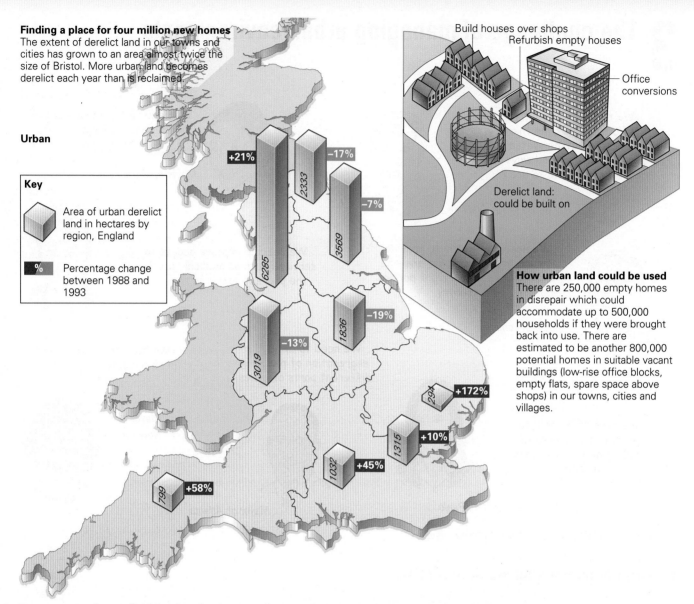

Finding a place for four million new homes
The extent of derelict land in our towns and cities has grown to an area almost twice the size of Bristol. More urban land becomes derelict each year than is reclaimed.

Urban

Key

Area of urban derelict land in hectares by region, England

%   Percentage change between 1988 and 1993

Build houses over shops
Refurbish empty houses
Office conversions

Derelict land: could be built on

How urban land could be used
There are 250,000 empty homes in disrepair which could accommodate up to 500,000 households if they were brought back into use. There are estimated to be another 800,000 potential homes in suitable vacant buildings (low-rise office blocks, empty flats, spare space above shops) in our towns, cities and villages.

+21% 2333 −17%
6285 3569 −7%
3019 −13% 1836 −19%
294 +172%
1315 +10%
1032 +45%
799 +58%

Figure 2.45   *Brownfield land in England.*   Source: Adapted from *The Guardian* 27 January 1988.

	Advantages	Disadvantages
Brownfield land	Less countryside is lost to new housing. Derelict city areas are revived. Existing services such as public transport, water, and electricity are already installed. People do not have to travel long distances to work so commuting is reduced.	Much more expensive than using greenfield sites because land often has to be reclaimed and cleansed of pollution before it can be used. Many brownfield sites are in built-up areas, often surrounded by run-down neighbourhoods in non-prestige locations and so are shunned by the middle classes.
Greenfield sites	Relatively cheap once the site has been purchased, and quick way to build more houses. The whole layout can be planned from scratch, free from existing problems.	Valuable farmland is lost. Attractive, scenic areas are lost. Wildlife and their habitat is lost. Urban sprawl is encouraged.

Figure 2.46   *The advantages and disadvantages of developing brownfield and greenfield sites.*

Greens and Tories unite to oppose new town

Council clears way for homes in Hertfordshire countryside

Alex Bellos

The largest housing development in a greenbelt area since the last generation of new towns looks likely to become reality after it passed its most difficult bureaucratic hurdle this week.

The Hertfordshire county council's environment committee voted to include plans for a town of between 5,000 and 10,000 homes on 800 hectares of countryside west of Stevenage in its general policy which comes into force next year.

Greens and local Tories have criticised the decision, saying it will be an

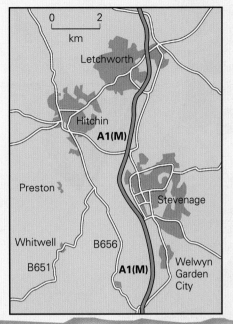

'environmental disaster, wrecking whole swaths of countryside and generating huge amounts of extra traffic'.

Hertfordshire council claims it needs to build the small town – two thirds the size of nearby Hitchin and bigger than Hertford itself – because it has to find 65,000 new homes by 2011. It says it can only accommodate 59,000 by regenerating urban areas.

The battle over the council's plan reflects the national problem of where to build the huge number of homes – forecast to be 4.4 million – needed in Britain over the next 20 years.

Some fear that new developments will encroach on the greenbelt areas created specially to stop urban sprawl.

Figure 2.47 *Expansion in Stevenage, UK.* Source: *The Guardian*, October 1997.

ACTIVITIES

1 Explain carefully how brownfield sites in the UK could be used to provide more homes.
2 Explain the nature of the problem in England and Wales between the supply of brownfield sites and the demand for new homes (Figure 2.45).
3 In what ways will the development in Stevenage:
   a improve the quality of life for local people
   b damage the quality of life for local people?
4 What arguments would you present to Hertfordshire County Council to persuade them to try to find more brownfield sites for new housing?

Challenge 2: Improving housing areas as they grow older

One of the most challenging areas of any city in terms of improving housing conditions is the inner-city area. In the UK these areas are older, usually 19th-century residential and industrial areas located between the CBD and the suburbs. About 4 million people live in UK inner cities. The main challenges facing planners are:

- declining population as more and more people move out

- economic decline as a result of factory closures. Glasgow lost 60,000 jobs between 1961 and 1971. London lost 243,000 over the same period
- physical and environmental decay, leading to dereliction and poor housing
- increasing poverty and social deprivation, with a concentration of poorer, older, unskilled families, often combined with ethnic minorities and homeless people.

Meeting the challenge in the UK

The first attempts to improve housing conditions in inner-city areas were undertaken by local councils who carried out massive **slum clearance** and redevelopment projects. In Birmingham, five comprehensive development areas were built by the council in the 1960s (Figure 2.48).

Later, in the 1960s and 1970s, the UK government began the **urban programme** which tried to bring together central government and local government.

In the 1980s, central government set up city action teams (CATs) which were made up of civil servants and task forces (groups to deal with bigger projects such as garden festivals). Each initiative touched parts of some inner-city areas but progress was very patchy.

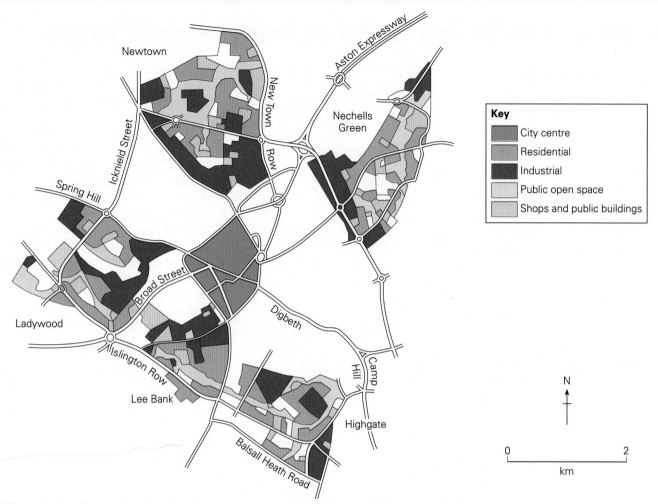

Figure 2.48   *Comprehensive development areas in Birmingham, 1975.*   Source: *Urbanisation* Collins, 1998.

In 1981, enterprise zones (EZs) were established to encourage new industries to locate in some inner-city areas. The hope was that by creating new jobs, people would move back to inner-city areas and private companies could build new houses. By 1990, there were 26 EZs in the UK but not all were in inner-city areas, for example Telford in the West Midlands.

The Action for Cities programme began in 1988 to co-ordinate the role of central government agencies in inner-city areas and so speed up development. In the City Challenge Scheme, launched in 1991, central government invited local authorities to bid for a share of £82 million to spend on projects to improve their area. This scheme was wound up in 1992 as a result of the criticism that redevelopment should not be based on competition.

All these policies for improving housing were essentially based on action by central or local government. Other local government initiatives were pioneered in Leeds which from the 1960s had given grants to improve houses in some parts of the city. This led to a national policy of general improvement areas (GIA) and housing action areas (HAA) which improved houses rather than demolished them.

Leeds has the Partnership Homes Project (set up in 1983), a co-operative venture between the city council and housing associations, which operates in ten urban renewal areas (URA) (Figure 2.49). In this case, the council provides the land, and the housing associations provide the funds for houses and flats. This approach means that local people have a much greater say in the redevelopment of their area.

Urban development corporations (UDC) were property-led. The corporations cleaned up polluted, derelict land and installed an infrastructure. This was intended to attract private investment in houses, offices, and factories. Urban development corporations were government-sponsored agencies whose aim was to regenerate large areas of derelict land in inner cities. They reported to central government and had economic and housing powers similar to new town development corporations. People from business and local government ran UDCs. Their activities can be considered in three phases:

In the 1990s Government funding was made available as **Single Regeneration Budgets** (SRB) in order to attract private investment for broader scale redevelopment in inner-city areas in the UK. Round One began in 1995 when areas like Sandwell in the West Midlands (see pages 237–238) attracted £20 million to promote economic regeneration and to raise educational standards and improve the quality of life. Round Two in 1996 was designed to stimulate activity in the community and voluntary sectors. Round Three, 1997–98, was aimed at improving conditions for young people. Single regeneration budgets have a much broader aim than UDCs, extending the idea of improvement to education, the community and the quality of life.

Another approach to improving inner-city housing conditions is to be found in the process of **gentrification**. In this case, older property in areas like Islington in London became attractive to professional groups such as lawyers and doctors. The attractions are:

- easy access to city-centre jobs and amenities (especially theatres, art galleries, cinemas, and restaurants)
- property with large rooms, and grants to help with improvement
- very much shorter journeys to work
- distinctive houses as opposed to the 'sameness' of suburban housing.

The newcomers improve housing and the area becomes 'desirable', raising property prices and changing the social composition.

Gentrification is one part of the process of **filtering**. Filtering is the process by which social groups move from one part of a town or city to another. As some groups move out to new houses on the edge of a town or city, other groups move into the areas that have been vacated. As a result, the social composition of housing in all areas of cities can change dramatically (Figure 2.50).

Inner-city housing areas are not the only parts of a town or city where redevelopment is necessary. A Civic Trust Report (1999) highlighted the poor state of many UK suburbs where 'houses were rapidly decaying and ill-suited to changing needs, shopping centres were declining and community facilities deteriorating'. This report challenged the policy of massive government spending on inner-city areas. It called for a network of outer city parishes with powers to levy a rate to lead community regeneration.

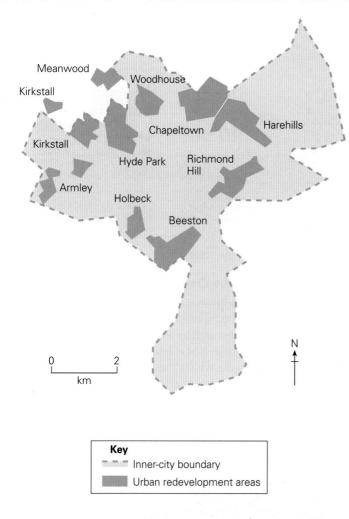

Figure 2.49 *Urban redevelopment areas in Leeds, 1985.*
Source: *A New Geography of Britain* Hodder & Stoughton, 1995.

- 1981: Merseyside and London Docklands Development Corporation established
- 1987: Cardiff Bay, Trafford Park, Tyne and Wear, Black Country, and Teeside Development Corporations established
- After 1988: Leeds, Bristol, Sheffield, and Central Manchester Corporations established.

Urban development corporations were particularly active during the 1980s, but in 1993 there were cutbacks in funding in London and Merseyside, and a freeze on finance in Leeds, Manchester, Bristol, and Tyne and Wear. The funding may have been reduced because UDCs had achieved their aims of regenerating derelict land. However, some people argue that although some UDCs were successful (London Docklands Development Corporation attracted £10 million of private investment for every £1 million of public finance), others were much slower to attract private finance.

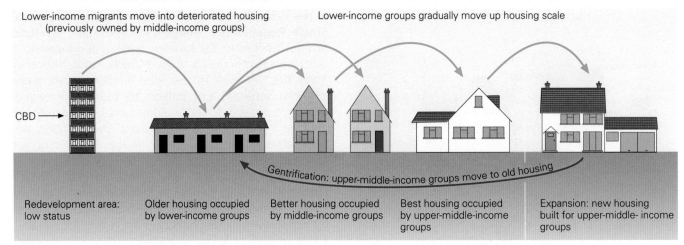

Lower-income migrants move into deteriorated housing (previously owned by middle-income groups)

Lower-income groups gradually move up housing scale

CBD →

Gentrification: upper-middle-income groups move to old housing

| Redevelopment area: low status | Older housing occupied by lower-income groups | Better housing occupied by middle-income groups | Best housing occupied by upper-middle-income groups | Expansion: new housing built for upper-middle- income groups |

Figure 2.50   *Filtering and gentrification.*   Source: *Core Themes in Geography* Oliver & Boyd, 1992.

ACTIVITIES

1   What are the advantages and disadvantages of improving inner-city areas through gentrification compared with improving these areas through redevelopment projects led by central and local government?
2   Why is gentrification not found in all inner-city areas?
3   What arguments would you put forward to persuade local and central governments to spend more on suburbs than inner-city areas?

Housing issues in LEDCs

The very rapid growth of cities in the poorer LEDCs has been very marked in the 1980s and 1990s. For example, São Paulo in Brazil grew from a city with a population of 1 million people in 1930, 5 million in 1967, and 17 million in 1995. This massive growth was larger than the city planners could cope with. The city built low-grade apartment blocks, but there were still more people than homes. Many people had, therefore, to build their own homes in squatter settlements (shanty towns) called *favelas* (Figure 2.19). Many of the *favelas* of São Paulo are islands of shanty housing built on vacant land alongside railway tracks, motorways, or other unwanted areas. Other *favelas* are located on the south and eastern outskirts of the city.

São Paulo's *favelas* have a number of problems:

*   no electricity supply, and bottled gas is expensive
*   clean water is only available from stand-pipes which have to supply hundreds of people
*   sewerage and pit latrines are inadequate
*   the houses are built cheaply and often let in rain
*   it is difficult to maintain hygiene without a proper water supply and sanitation system.

Improving *favelas*: the Cingupura Project

This is the 'Singapore Project', named after the massive slum clearance in Singapore and begun in 1991. The aim is to replace hundreds of São Paulo's *favelas* with low-rise blocks of flats (Figure 2.51). Local people are moved to military-style barracks whilst the flats are built. When they move back, they will have low-interest, 20-year mortgages with which to buy their flat. The aim of the project is to rehouse 92,000 families (500,000 people) from 243 *favelas*. However, whether the families will be able to maintain the mortgage repayments remains a big issue.

Figure 2.51   *New, low-rise flats in São Paulo built as part of the Cingupura Project.*

Self-help schemes

The city planners in São Paulo have also tried to help the people of the *favelas* to help themselves. The city has installed electricity in a few *favelas*, as well as a clean water supply and sewage disposal facilities. Providing these services encourages local people to improve their own homes, for example by making them more weatherproof. This is an example of an **aided self-help scheme**. Another self-help project in São Paulo is the **site and service scheme**. In these areas the council provides the land and the infrastructure, including water, electricity, roads, and sewers. Each family has a plot on which to build its own house, using materials provided cheaply by the council. Rents are low, and in this way local authorities and governments help people to help themselves.

> **ACTIVITIES**
>
> **1** What are the main advantages and disadvantages of:
> **a** the Cingupura Project
> **b** the site and service scheme
> in São Paulo?
> Which is likely to bring the most benefits to the most people?

Figure 2.53 *Traffic in Beijing, China.*

Challenge 3: Managing movement in cities

Figure 2.52 *Nose-to-tail traffic in Los Angeles.*

> **ACTIVITIES**
>
> **1** Study Figures 2.52 and 2.53. They show some aspects of movement in cities around the world. For each Figure:
> **a** identify the nature of the movement problems shown
> **b** suggest ways in which the problems might be overcome.

Public transport in cities

As towns and cities grow larger, so does the volume of traffic. For example, people need to move around in order to get to work, to the shops, or to reach leisure and recreation facilities. This increased mobility, and the volume of traffic generated, is creating serious problems in many towns and cities all over the world.

People prefer to travel by car because cars are more flexible in their usage, providing door-to-door transport and allowing the driver to vary the route and the timing of the journey. However, most cars are about 4m long and in the rush hour often carry only one person. A bus occupies the space of three cars but can carry 30–40 people or more. However, buses are delayed by the volume of car traffic. They also have to follow routes which will gain most income, and this often means travelling along the main radial roads where traffic congestion is at its worst.

Another problem to be overcome when providing public transport is that of distance. Cities have sprawled outwards as a result of:

- the construction of low-density suburbs
- the dispersal of shops and offices to the suburbs and beyond
- the reduced attraction of the city centre.

This city sprawl, combined with greater affluence, has led to an increase in car ownership and a decline in the use of public transport (Figures 2.54 and 2.55). It is increasingly expensive to try to provide public transport to sprawling suburbs with low population densities.

- 72 per cent of households own at least one car.
- There are over 21 million cars on the roads.
- Car travel accounts for 80 per cent of personal travel.
- 90 per cent of business journeys are made by car.
- 80 per cent of shopping journeys over 3km are made by car.
- Between 1965 and 1996 the road network grew by 11 per cent and car traffic increased by 156 per cent.

Figure 2.54   *Traffic facts in the UK, 1998.*

Percentage of all journeys				
Population of city	Public transport	Car	Walk	Other
Over 250,000	16	61	20	3
100,000–249,999	13	62	19	6
50,000–99,999	10	67	17	6
25,000–49,999	9	63	21	7
3,000–24,999	6	67	22	5
Under 3,999	4	72	16	8

Figure 2.55   *Method of travel and city size in the UK (1991).*

Underground systems, such as those operating in London, Berlin, Paris, and New York can be efficient ways of moving large numbers of people around cities. However, such underground systems are very expensive to build, and rarely extend to the outer suburbs because of these construction costs. The London Underground is very overcrowded at peak times and as a result is dirty and decaying on most routes because upgrading lines, stations, and rolling stock is difficult and expensive.

Once public transport begins to suffer competition from car use, a downward spiral of higher fares and lower use often results (Figure 2.56).

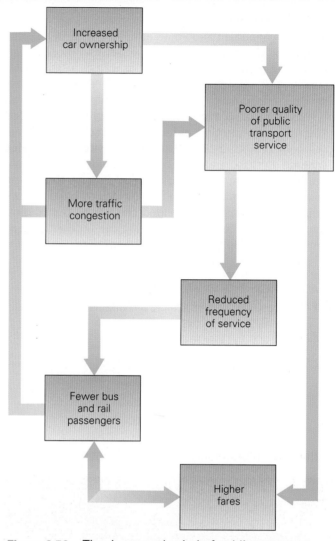

Figure 2.56   *The downward spiral of public transport.*

ACTIVITIES

1 What are the main problems of providing public transport in large towns and cities?
2 Study Figure 2.55.
   a How far is it true to say that the use of public transport increases with city size?
   b Try to explain the relationship between city size and the use of public transport.
3 a Study Figure 2.56. Work in pairs to suggest as many ways as possible to break this downward spiral of public transport. Think about features such as bus lanes, subsidies for public transport, high charges for city-centre car parking, or high charges for cars entering cities.
   b Redraw a copy of Figure 2.56 to show how public transport use might increase as a result of these new features.

Some effects of public transport problems

In MEDCs like the UK, and LEDCs like Mexico it is the wealthier, more mobile elements of the population which can choose where to live. Such groups are usually not interested in public transport and this increases the segregation between the more mobile households and the rest of society. When this segregation is combined with the declining use of public transport it is the young, the old, the disabled, the housebound, and the car-less who are the main losers.

How can public transport be made more attractive?

Public transport cannot compete with the car in terms of comfort and door-to-door service. However, planners have developed a range of strategies to improve the attractiveness of public transport:

- bus lanes exist in many UK cities such as Birmingham and Leeds. These help buses to speed through traffic congestion (Figure 2.57). Some new towns, such as Runcorn (UK), or Almere (Netherlands) have routes solely for buses. In some cases it is possible to have buses that only travel when called, like taxis. This 'dial-a-bus' system is used in Ottawa in Canada where it has been very successful

- supertrams have been introduced in UK cities such as Manchester, Sheffield, and Birmingham. They run on separate lines and pass under or over crossroads. Manchester's supertram (Figure 2.58) makes the journey from Altrincham to the city centre at rush hour in 22 minutes, compared with 52 minutes by car and 64 minutes by bus. Research has shown that the major growth in users of Manchester's supertrams has come from young mothers with prams, disabled people and lone females travelling late at night

- subsidising public transport to make it cheaper might well attract significant numbers of people away from their cars. This would be particularly effective if city-centre car parking were made very expensive as it is in Bremen, Germany. In Leicester and Cambridge motorists wanting to travel into the city centre have to pay a fee, which is deducted electronically from a pre-payment card displayed on the windscreen

- underground systems such as those in Mexico City, Moscow, and London are a more expensive solution to the problem of public transport. The problem is that whilst such systems can cope with large numbers of commuters, in time, even they can become overcrowded. A 1996 survey of the London Underground found massive overcrowding which was encouraging some people to return to using their cars, especially for cross-city journeys.

Geographers' Conference

£1m a mile needed to make bus lanes work

Paul Brown
Environment Correspondent

Plans to get drivers out of their cars and on to public transport will fail unless local authorities spend up to £1 million a mile on a new generation of bus lanes, research has shown.

Cheap lanes increase the speed of buses only marginally and do nothing to change the way people travel, the conference in Leicester of the Royal Geographical Society and Institute of British Geographers was told yesterday.

If the Government's aims embodied in the transport white paper were to be achieved, many millions would have to be spent in each city or town on dedicated lanes, according to Richard Knowles of the University of Salford. Since 1986 when buses outside London were deregulated, passenger numbers outside London had dropped 29 per cent but there was startling evidence this could be reversed where enough money was spent.

On 'Super Route 66' in Ipswich in Suffolk, where £2.3 million was spent on a throughway which only buses with guide wheels could use, passenger numbers increased 42 per cent – one in four being a former car user. In Leeds, on Scott Hall Road, £4 million was spent to produce a 40 per cent increase in bus use.

What was needed was miles of continuous lanes, of which Edinburgh has the best example. Here £7.5 million had been spent on 26 kilometres of lanes, some several kilometres long. Wardens rigorously enforced no parking zones, and the police prosecuted offending drivers. It was too early to assess results, but buses were travelling faster than cars and passenger numbers were rising.

The best example of the switch from road to public transport was Manchester, where 2.6 million passenger journeys a year were made by light rail rather than by car. Traffic on parallel roads between Altrincham and Manchester fell and did not increase on the Bury to Manchester route; on every route not served by the light railway, road traffic has increased.

'What is obvious is that there are no low cost solutions. The first phase of Manchester light rail cost £150 million, the Jubilee line in London is £3 billion, so buses are quite cheap by comparison, and schemes can be delivered quite quickly. But if you spend modestly, you get modest results,' said Dr Knowles.

Figure 2.57 *The cost of bus lanes.*
Source: *The Guardian*, January 1999

ACTIVITIES

1 Outline the main problems involved in the introduction of bus lanes, supertrams, subsidised public transport, and underground systems.

2 Why is it important to have an efficient public transport system in UK cities?

Figure 2.58   *Manchester's supertram.*

Cars, traffic, and commuting

Despite attempts to improve public transport, the major reason for the growth of traffic in cities in MEDCs is the increasing popularity of the motor car (Figure 2.59). The car increases people's mobility (their ability to move around) and improves their access to a range of places for work, recreation, and shopping.

The worst times for traffic in most cities are the morning and evening rush hours, when commuters pour into and out of the city. There are three main aspects of cars which city planners have to deal with:

- keeping cars and public transport moving on overcrowded roads
- providing space for car parks, in or near city centres
- separating pedestrians from cars.

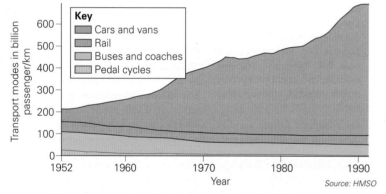

Figure 2.59   *How Britons have switched to the car.*
Source: *The Observer,* 17 October 1993.

Keeping traffic moving

The main measure that cities in Europe, North America, and Japan have taken include:

- Introducing ring roads (inner, outer, and middle) to divert some traffic from city centres and to allow vehicles to travel more easily around the city.
- Introducing **tidal flow schemes**, as in Birmingham where the A38 has four lanes in the peak direction. The peak direction can be easily changed throughout the day.

- Using one-way street systems to help to speed flow in some areas.
- Using schemes such as bus lanes, supertrams, underground systems.
- Using schemes to encourage people to share cars on their journeys to work. In 1999 a trial scheme in Leeds in which vehicles without a passenger are barred from one lane was made permanent when it reduced congestion on the Stanningly Road commuter route. Car occupancy has grown and rush-hour journey times have been cut from 11 to 7 minutes.
- Introducing park-and-ride schemes. Here the aim is to persuade motorists to leave their vehicles on the edges of cities like Bristol and Bath and to take buses into the city centre. These schemes were given a boost by Department of Transport research in 1989. This research predicted a growth in traffic of between 83 per cent and 142 per cent by 2025. Bristol began a shoppers' park-and-ride scheme in 1991 which uses three existing car parks, and which runs on Saturdays throughout the year. In 1993, the first purpose-built car park for a daily service opened at Brislington and in 1996 a second opened at Ashton Vale (Figure 2.60). Plans exist for several more. The Brislington service is used by 6,000 passengers per week and on average people travel 11–13 km to reach the park-and-ride scheme. Most users came from outer parts of the urban area or from surrounding villages. So although 300–400 car trips per day have been removed from the A4 in Bristol, there has been a growth in traffic on the outer roads leading to the park-and-ride schemes. As the popularity of park-and-ride schemes grows (Figure 2.61) they may replace retail and office developments as main land users on the urban fringe.

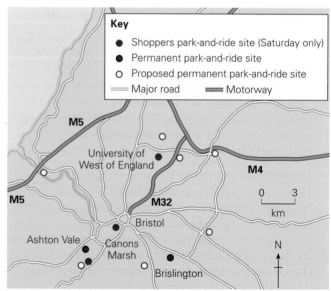

Figure 2.60   *Existing and proposed park-and-ride schemes in Bristol.*

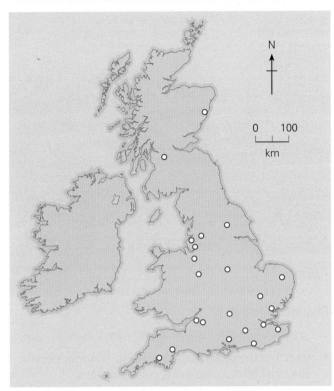

Figure 2.61   *Park-and-ride schemes in the UK.*

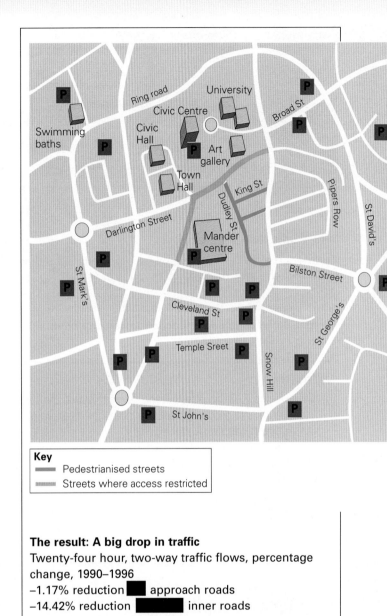

Key

━━━   Pedestrianised streets

▦▦▦   Streets where access restricted

The result: A big drop in traffic
Twenty-four hour, two-way traffic flows, percentage
change, 1990–1996

–1.17% reduction ▉ approach roads

–14.42% reduction ▉▉ inner roads

Figure 2.62   *Redirecting traffic in Wolverhampton, UK.*
Source: *The Guardian*, 12 March 1998.

ACTIVITIES

1   Study Figure 2.60.
    a   Describe the two main types of location of Saturday-
        only park-and-ride schemes in Bristol.
    b   Describe the location of the permanent and proposed
        permanent park-and-ride schemes in Bristol.
    c   Explain the type of locations you describe in **a** and **b**.
2   **a**   Describe the pattern of park-and-ride schemes in the
        UK. (Figure 2.61).
    b   Why do you think these towns and cities have
        developed park-and-ride schemes?

Other measures to keep traffic moving include redirecting
traffic that is excluded from pedestrianised city centres. In
Wolverhampton, a town with a population of 15,000
people, 21km north-west of Birmingham, the town-centre
roads were closed to traffic from 1987 onwards, blocking a
major north–south and a major east–west route. New cycle
ways and traffic-free zones were introduced. The result has
been a big drop in traffic (Figure 2.62). Research suggests
that cross-town traffic:

- goes on another route or at another time
- seeks a different destination (e.g. shopping centre)
- takes bus or train
- consolidates several journeys into one
- is reduced by car sharing.

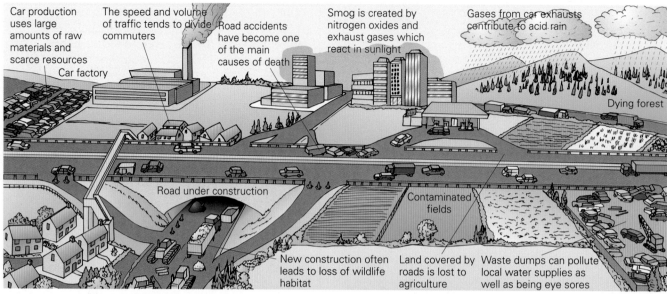

Car production uses large amounts of raw materials and scarce resources

Car factory

The speed and volume of traffic tends to divide commuters

Road accidents have become one of the main causes of death

Smog is created by nitrogen oxides and exhaust gases which react in sunlight

Gases from car exhausts contribute to acid rain

Dying forest

Road under construction

Contaminated fields

New construction often leads to loss of wildlife habitat

Land covered by roads is lost to agriculture

Waste dumps can pollute local water supplies as well as being eye sores

Figure 2.63 *The impact of cars on the environment.*

ACTIVITIES

1 Study Figure 2.63. On a copy of the diagram outline the main benefits to people and the environment if there were a significant reduction in car use.

Changing lifestyles

Car use in cities can also be reduced by:

- fostering the growth of teleworking, whereby people can work from home using computers and telecommunications. They can still retain contact with city-based companies but they are free to work from home and so do not need to commute
- encouraging people to walk or cycle to work. This may necessitate changes in the location of the workplace (shops, offices, schools, etc.) in relation to places where people live. However, the benefits in terms of reduced traffic could be huge.

Challenge 4: Managing environmental problems in the city

Mexico's capital city sinking into the abyss

By Diego Cevallos

Mexico City, Jan. 28 (IPS) – Mexico's capital is nearing the brink of collapse, with the city sinking around nine centimeters per year as its aquifers are tapped to supply more than 20 million people with water, experts warned today.

The city, which was literally a lake until the year 500, will suffer serious water supply problems in ten years'

time. The city's water pipes will become dislocated and roads and buildings could start to crack if the present pattern of water extraction and consumption goes unchanged.

Furthermore, the city, one of the world's biggest, will become more vulnerable to seismic movement and earthquakes, phenomena which could appear with great destructive force at any moment in the next 50 or 100 years.

More than 70 per cent of water consumed in the city comes from 514 aquifers up to 500 metres in

depth, and the rest is piped in from more distant places using various hydraulic systems.

Each inhabitant of the Mexican capital consumes 320 litres per day, an amount higher than that of other large cities like São Paulo or Tokyo, which have levels of below 250 litres, according to official data.

This excessive consumption is compounded by increasing amounts of waste and insufficient waste water treatment capacity, meaning supply sources have already been contaminated.

Figure 2.64 *Water supply problems in Mexico City.*

Source: Online International News, February 1999.

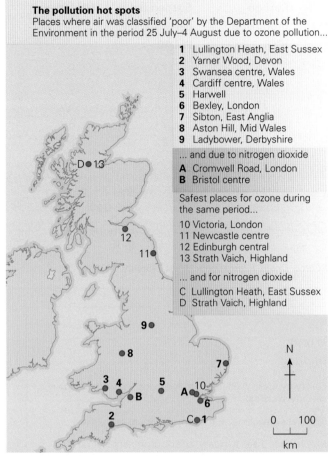

The pollution hot spots
Places where air was classified 'poor' by the Department of the Environment in the period 25 July–4 August due to ozone pollution...

1 Lullington Heath, East Sussex
2 Yarner Wood, Devon
3 Swansea centre, Wales
4 Cardiff centre, Wales
5 Harwell
6 Bexley, London
7 Sibton, East Anglia
8 Aston Hill, Mid Wales
9 Ladybower, Derbyshire

... and due to nitrogen dioxide

A Cromwell Road, London
B Bristol centre

Safest places for ozone during the same period...

10 Victoria, London
11 Newcastle centre
12 Edinburgh central
13 Strath Vaich, Highland

... and for nitrogen dioxide

C Lullington Heath, East Sussex
D Strath Vaich, Highland

Figure 2.65   *Air pollution in Britain.*
Source: *The Observer* 6 August 1995.

nitrogen dioxide. This lethal substance accumulates, especially in cities surrounded by mountains like Mexico City and Los Angeles, to form a **photo-chemical smog**. This is a serious health hazard to people, especially the old, the very young, and those with breathing problems. The gas attacks sensitive tissue in the throat and lungs causing stinging and choking. It is also hazardous to plants and animals. In Mexico City the pollution is so bad that the city disappears from view in the brown smog.

- Ozone: Ozone is created by toxins from vehicle exhausts which react with air in bright sunlight. Ozone sensitises the body to irritants such as pollen or house dust, causing hay fever-like symptoms and asthma.
- Carbon monoxide: Carbon monoxide is produced by the incomplete combustion of fuels. It causes headaches, fatigue, drowsiness, and even death.
- Sulphur dioxide: Sulphur dioxide is produced from car exhausts. It irritates eyes and the respiratory system. It aggravates asthma and bronchitis.
- Suspended particles such as dust, cement, pollen, and organic compounds: Petrol can produce suspended particles which irritate the respiratory system.

Mexico City has some of the worst air pollution in the world. On top of car and industrial pollution the city suffers from a choking dust which blows across the high Mexican plateau.

ACTIVITIES

1 Study Figures 2.64 and 2.65. Each figure illustrates an aspect of the environmental problems facing cities. For each one:
   a outline the nature and likely causes of the problem
   b suggest ways in which the problem could be overcome. In your answer refer to actions by central government, local planners, and individual people.

2 Study Figure 2.66. It shows air pollution in August 1999 in different parts of Mexico City. Study Figure 2.67 which shows land use in different parts of the city.
   a Use Figure 2.66 to draw bar graphs that illustrate the variation in pollution in the different parts of the city.
   b Describe the pattern of pollution shown in your graphs.
   c How far does Figure 2.67 help to explain the patterns of pollution you have described?

Air pollution

The air in many towns and cities around the world is seriously polluted. The main sources of this pollution are:

- vehicle exhausts
- industrial emissions
- emissions from power stations.

The main dangers from air pollution in cities arise from:

- Nitrous oxides: In bright sunshine nitrous oxides undergo a chemical change and are converted into

How do planners and decision makers try to solve air pollution problems?

Planners in Mexico City are trying to reduce air pollution by:

- building a new underground system
- trying to provide funds for spare parts for buses
- introducing the *hoy no circular* (no driving today) by which car use is banned on certain weekdays depending on the car registration numbers. However, rich people simply buy a second or third car.

Zone	Ozone (O₃)	Nitrogen dioxide (NO₂)	Sulphur dioxide (SO₂)	Carbon monoxide (CO)	Suspended particles PM-10	UV Index
North-west	78	17	24	25	23	8
North-east	92	21	21	29	35	8
Downtown	92	37	12	35	32	8
South-west	72	14	7	13	21	8
South-east	110	21	7	25	32	8

Key				
IMECA	Satisfactory 0–99	Not satisfactory 100–149	Not satisfactory 150–199	Bad 200–300
UV index	Low 0–4	Medium 4–7	High 7–9	Extreme 9–15

Figure 2.66   *Air pollution in Mexico City, 9 August 1999.*   Source: *Online International News*, February, 1999.

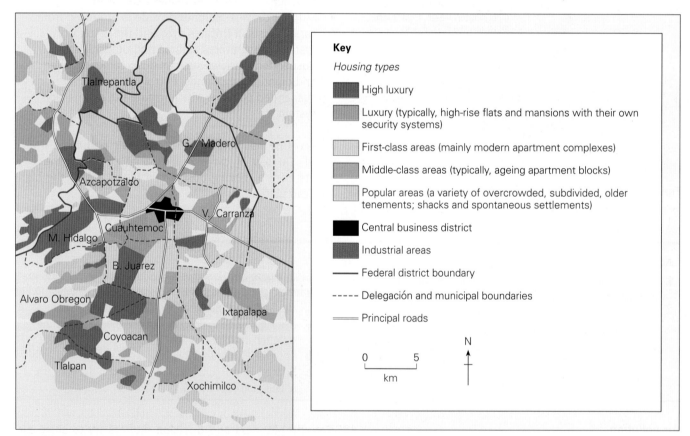

Figure 2.67   *Main land uses in Mexico City.*   Source: *Mexico City* Belhaven Press, 1990.

Solutions in other cities such as Los Angeles that have a similar smog problem include:

- plans by California to introduce 2 per cent of all new passenger cars with zero emissions in 1998 rising to 5 per cent in 2001 and 10 per cent in 2003. However, this plan was suspended in 1995 because technology was not developing fast enough

- cars with a reformulated petrol designed to reduce emissions
- encouraging car sharing, park-and-ride, telecommuting, and staggering work hours.

How successful have air pollution strategies been?

In Mexico City air quality continues to deteriorate due to the rapid expansion in the number of vehicles on the roads. Enforcement of air pollution legislation is difficult and expensive, especially when the government wants even more industrial expansion.

The Los Angeles Air Quality Management Plan of 1989 aims to reduce sulphur dioxide pollution by 62 per cent and nitrogen dioxide by 80 per cent in 20 years. However, although there is strict legislation to reduce vehicle emissions, and new electric cars have been introduced, the rapid growth of people and cars is making it very difficult to improve air quality. The number of vehicles has grown from 2.3 million in 1950 to 10.6 million in 1990. The human population of Los Angeles grew from 4.9 million to 14 million over the same period. So Los Angeles is still the most polluted US city with, in 1993, 63 days when air quality posed a significant danger to human health.

The challenge of waste in cities

Waste disposal is a big problem in cities, and in general terms the bigger the city, the bigger the problem. Mexico City produces 11,000 tonnes of rubbish every day, of which the collection system can only remove 9000 tonnes per day. The rest is dumped on open ground, in waterways, streets, and drains where it clogs the drainage system.

Waste disposal is not just a challenge for cities in LEDCs. New York City has to dispose of 34,000 tonnes of rubbish each day. Half of its rubbish is dumped in Fresh Kills landfill (Figure 2.68). This area of tidal marshland receives 17,000 tonnes of refuse each day, six days per week by barge. The landfill covers 1250ha and its composition is shown in Figure 2.69. The rest of New York City's rubbish goes by road and rail as far as Ohio and Indiana where tipping is much cheaper.

ACTIVITIES

1 What could individual families in New York City do to reduce the mountain of rubbish they generate?

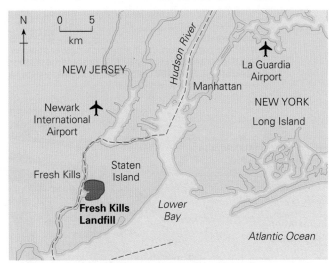

Figure 2.68 *Fresh Kills landfill, New York City.*
Source: *North America*, Hodder & Stoughton, 1997.

Category	% of total	Contents
Paper	50	Newspapers (18%), magazines, telephone directories, mail-order catalogues
Construction and demolition materials	15	Bricks, stone, plaster, timber, mortar
Organic	13	Garden waste (10%), wood, food
Plastics	10	Milk bottles, food containers, bin liners
Metal	6	Aluminium and steel cans for food and drink
Glass	1	Food and drink containers, cosmetic jars
Others	5	Tyres, textiles, disposable nappies

Figure 2.69 *Composition of the landfill debris in Fresh Kills, New York City.*
Source: *North America*, Hodder & Stoughton, 1997.

How do planners try to solve the rubbish problem?

Figure 2.70 shows how MEDCs get rid of their waste. As people continue to produce more and more rubbish, the land, sea, and air are polluted. Most household and industrial waste is a mixture of different materials ranging from harmless organic matter to toxic plastics and poisons. In this form little use can be made of the waste, and so the useful part of the waste is thrown away with the bad.

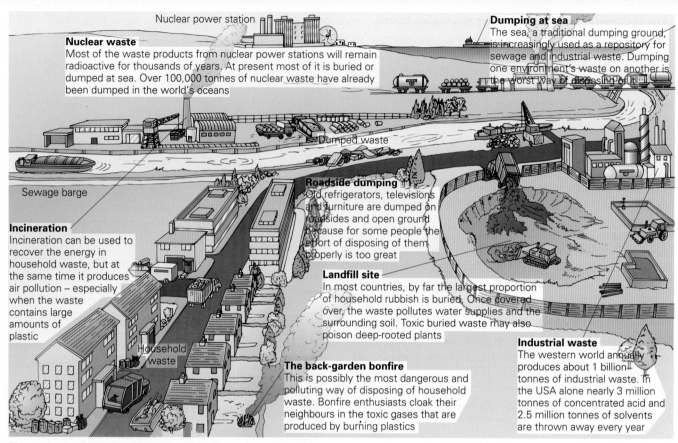

Nuclear power station

Dumping at sea
The sea, a traditional dumping ground, is increasingly used as a repository for sewage and industrial waste. Dumping one environment's waste on another is the worst way of disposing of it.

Nuclear waste
Most of the waste products from nuclear power stations will remain radioactive for thousands of years. At present most of it is buried or dumped at sea. Over 100,000 tonnes of nuclear waste have already been dumped in the world's oceans

Dumped waste

Sewage barge

Roadside dumping
Old refrigerators, televisions and furniture are dumped on roadsides and open ground because for some people the effort of disposing of them properly is too great

Incineration
Incineration can be used to recover the energy in household waste, but at the same time it produces air pollution – especially when the waste contains large amounts of plastic

Household waste

Landfill site
In most countries, by far the largest proportion of household rubbish is buried. Once covered over, the waste pollutes water supplies and the surrounding soil. Toxic buried waste may also poison deep-rooted plants

Industrial waste
The western world annually produces about 1 billion tonnes of industrial waste. In the USA alone nearly 3 million tonnes of concentrated acid and 2.5 million tonnes of solvents are thrown away every year

The back-garden bonfire
This is possibly the most dangerous and polluting way of disposing of household waste. Bonfire enthusiasts cloak their neighbours in the toxic gases that are produced by burning plastics

Figure 2.70 *What happens to waste?*   Source: *Blueprint for a Green Planet* Dorling Kindersley, 1987.

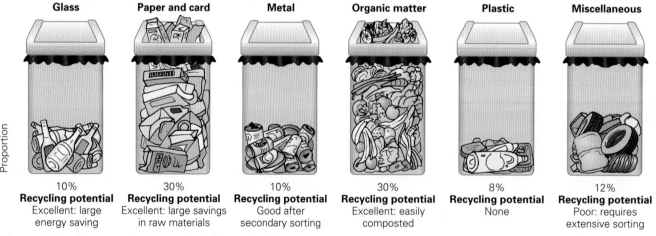

Glass	Paper and card	Metal	Organic matter	Plastic	Miscellaneous
10%	30%	10%	30%	8%	12%
Recycling potential	**Recycling potential**	**Recycling potential**	**Recycling potential**	**Recycling potential**	**Recycling potential**
Excellent: large energy saving	Excellent: large savings in raw materials	Good after secondary sorting	Excellent: easily composted	None	Poor: requires extensive sorting

Proportion

Figure 2.71   *The recycling potential of household waste.*   Source: *Blueprint for a Green Planet* Dorling Kindersley, 1987.

ACTIVITIES

1 **a**   Study Figure 2.70. Explain carefully how land, air, and water become polluted by urban waste.

2   Study Figure 2.71 which shows the recycling potential for household waste. Write a report for a newspaper under the title 'You can save the world'. Point out the recycling potential of household waste and suggest actions that each household could take to recycle its waste.

3   How many of the activities described in the report you wrote in **2** can be carried out by individuals and groups? How many by governments?

4   How successful do you think are the policies of planners and decision makers in removing rubbish from:
   i   Mexico City
   ii   New York City?

Dereliction, noise, pollution, and environmental health in Sandwell, UK

Sandwell is a conurbation of small towns such as West Bromwich and Tipton with a population of 294,100 located in the West Midlands to the west of Birmingham (Figure 2.72).

The challenges in Sandwell

- Large areas of derelict and contaminated land resulting from the decline of manufacturing industry.
- High levels of unemployment. In 1998, 6.8 per cent of the population were unemployed, whilst the UK average was 4.4 per cent.
- Traffic congestion and air pollution.
- Poverty. A survey in 1996 revealed that 50 per cent of households had gross incomes below £10,000 per year.
- High levels of social deprivation. In 1997, Sandwell was the seventh most deprived area in England.
- A lack of green space.
- Poor housing. In 1995, 23 per cent of public housing was unfit for human habitation.
- High levels of illness. In 1997, Sandwell had the third highest rate of heart disease in the UK – 60 per cent above the average.
- Low levels of literacy. In 1997, one in six adults had poor literacy and numeracy skills.

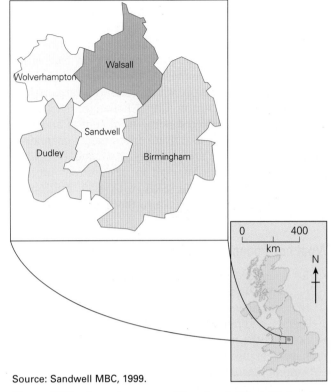

Source: Sandwell MBC, 1999.

Figure 2.72 *Location map of Sandwell, West Midlands.*

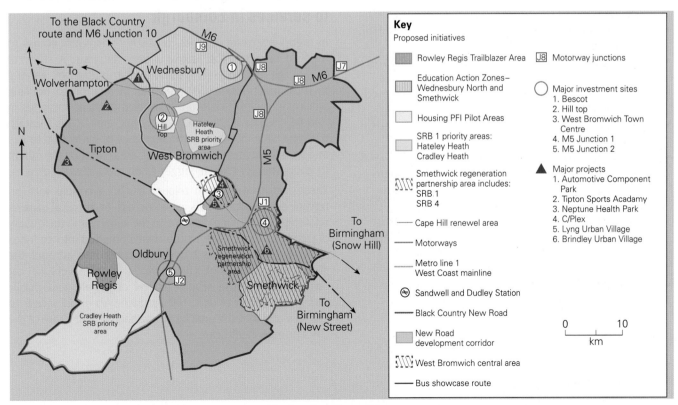

Figure 2.73 *The range of projects used to tackle Sandwell's problems.* Source: Sandwell MBC, 1999.

Figure 2.73 shows the range of projects which have been used to tackle Sandwell's problems of dereliction, pollution, and related social, economic, and environmental issues. Notice that some projects are partnerships between the council and local and national agencies, as well as voluntary organisations and community groups. Sandwell is building on two earlier regeneration programmes, the Black Country Development Corporation, which covered a large part of the borough, and Tipton City Challenge. These two schemes, which involved funding from central and local governments as well as private investment, channelled £1.72 billion into the area between 1987 and 1998 when both schemes ended. Funding for the current projects comes largely from the SRB with £50 million of government investment, plus a further £200 million from the private and public sectors.

What have been the achievements in Sandwell?

- Between 1987 and 1995, 364 ha of land were reclaimed. In many cases this meant cleaning up land that had been severely polluted by mining, heavy metals, and refuse.
- Some of the restored land (typical brownfield sites) have been used for new industry, as in the Automotive Component Park.
- Some of the restored land was used to build new homes. Between 1986 and 1995, 8432 new houses were built and 641 were added each year until 2000.
- New affordable housing for rent was built in Old Hill and Hateley Heath.
- Between 1988 and 1995, 383 new industrial units were opened in Sandwell plus 21,925 m² of retail space.
- Between 1990 and 1998, 6000 new jobs were created in Sandwell.
- Areas of council-owned flats and houses in Cape Hill, Tipton, and Smethwick were renovated.
- 27 km of new road were built between 1990 and 1998. In addition, Sandwell is on the new Midland Metro Line, a light railway scheme which should help to revitalise the centre of West Bromwich.
- New green spaces were created by the British Trust for Conservation Volunteers and Groundwork Black Country who have worked with local people in Hateley Heath.
- Council blocks of flats were refurbished and some transferred to housing associations or to shared ownership with residents. This has often been accompanied by security and crime prevention measures such as CCTV and concierge systems in flats.
- Between 1990 and 1995, two new primary schools were built and high schools were refurbished.

- Sandwell is promoting walking, cycling, and public transport as a means of reducing pollution and encouraging better health.

ACTIVITIES
1 How successful do you think Sandwell has been in meeting the challenges it faced in 1987?
2 What other measures might Sandwell take to improve environmental conditions in the area?

Access to services in cities

Services in cities are things which meet people's needs such as shops, doctor's surgeries, and hospitals. The challenge facing planners, decision makers, and many individuals within cities is that not everyone has equal access to these services. In general, the richer people, living in the more affluent parts of the city, attract more services to their areas and also have easier access to them via their car ownership. At the other end of the socio-economic spectrum, the poor, the elderly, the disabled, and single parents tend to have very poor access to services.

Access to medical care: A study of access to services in Edinburgh

In theory everyone in cities in MEDCs has equal access to medical services. The reality is very different. A study of Edinburgh in 1973 showed the distribution of general medical practitioner (GP) surgeries in relation to housing types (Figure 2.74) reflected a concentration of surgeries in middle class or higher socio-economic areas. This location pattern was reinforced by the tendency of many GPs to live and work in higher socio-economic areas, and by the failure to build premises for GP surgeries on many council estates.

These factors were then related to those people with no private transport. In this case, access to medical care is related to the walking distance to the surgery and the quality of public transport. The results were compiled into an index of accessibility (Figure 2.75) which takes into account the size and location of GP services, local levels of car ownership, and the relative speed of private and public transport. Scores of over 100 indicate very good access to services and that the area has more than its fair share of the city's primary healthcare.

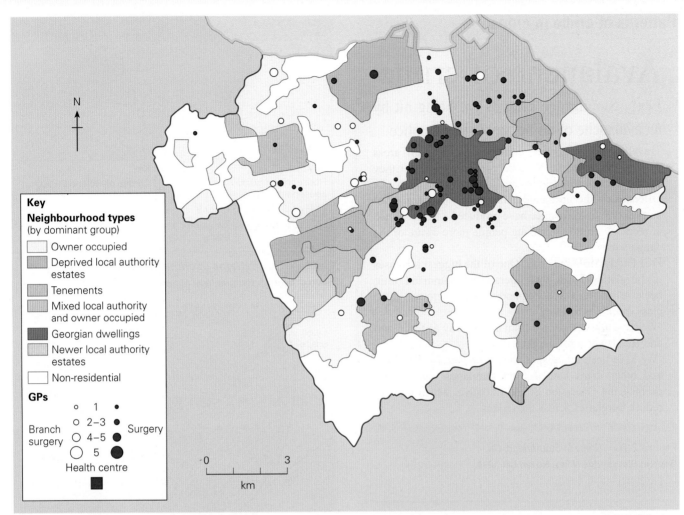

Key

Neighbourhood types
(by dominant group)

- Owner occupied
- Deprived local authority estates
- Tenements
- Mixed local authority and owner occupied
- Georgian dwellings
- Newer local authority estates
- Non-residential

GPs

	1	
Branch surgery	2–3	Surgery
	4–5	
	5	

Health centre

0   3
km

Figure 2.74 *The distribution of general medical practitioners in relation to housing types in Edinburgh, UK in 1973.*

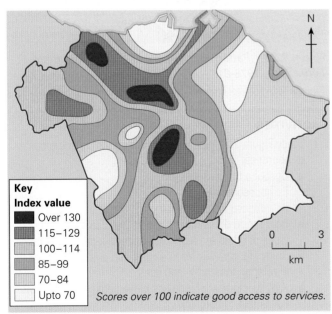

Key
Index value

- Over 130
- 115–129
- 100–114
- 85–99
- 70–84
- Upto 70

Scores over 100 indicate good access to services.

0   3
km

Figure 2.75 *Access to primary medical care in Edinburgh, 1973.*

ACTIVITIES

1 Geographers have identified the inverse care law in which the availability of medical services is inversely proportional to the needs of the people, that is the poorer, older and more fragile elements of the population have poorer access to medical care than the younger, richer elements.

  a Study Figure 2.74. Describe the distribution of GP surgeries in Edinburgh in relation to housing types and ages.

  b Now study Figures 2.74 and 2.75. How far do these maps support or oppose the idea of the inverse care law?

2 Work in pairs to suggest what actions could be taken by:

  a individuals

  b community groups

  c the city council

  d central government

to improve access to primary medical care in cities like Edinburgh.

Patterns of crime in cities

Avalanche of crime

Leafy Stourbridge suburbs are being hit by an avalanche of crime, say worried police.

Travelling criminals are swooping on well-off areas such as Pedmore and Norton. And top cops admit they cannot explain why figures are going through the roof. Offences on the up include burglaries, street robberies and car crime. And police have produced a leaflet aimed at reducing crime by making people more aware of the dangers they face.

DCI Paddy Mulligan said: 'One of the biggest increases in burglaries is in this operational command unit, because of areas like Pedmore where there are good class dwellings.

'We have arrested people from as far away as Erdington and Handsworth for burglaries.

'We have been doing spot checks on cars for jewellery and other items hauled from burglaries and we are pushing the Operation Shield initiative, which aims to reduce burglaries across the region.'

Figure 2.76   *Crime in Stourbridge, UK.*
Source: *Stourbridge News*, November 1999.

ACTIVITIES

1   Study Figure 2.76. Stourbridge is a small town in the West Midlands.
    a What types of crime are associated with the suburbs?
    b What are the police trying to do to reduce this crime?
2   What types of crime do you think might be found in:
    a city centres   **b** inner-city areas?
    Give reasons for your answers.

Research has shown that certain types of crime can be found in certain parts of cities. For example, a study of Seattle in 1995 showed that shoplifting and cheque fraud were concentrated in the CBD whereas burglary was mainly a suburban crime. Inner-city areas of Seattle were a main area of criminal activity, especially car theft, burglary and handbag snatching. Low-income areas – both inner city and outer city – were associated with crimes of violence, especially murder, rape, and assault.

The importance of the micro-environment in relation to patterns of crime was emphasised in a study of Newcastle-under-Lyme, UK (Figure 2.78). The map shows the uneven pattern of burglary in part of the town.

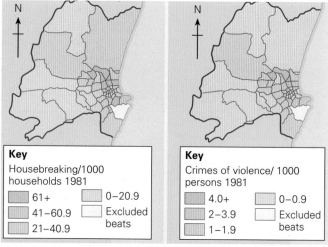

Figure 2.77   *Patterns of crime in Aberdeen, 1981.*
Source: *Scottish Geographical Magazine* 101, 1985.

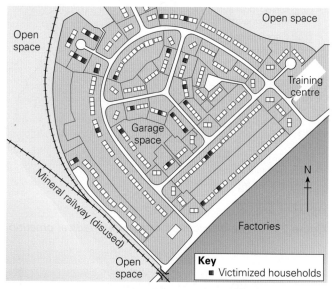

Figure 2.78   *Pattern of burglary in Newcastle-under-Lyme, UK , 1978-81.*
Source: *Tijdschrift voor Economische en Sociale Geografie*, 75, 1984.

ACTIVITIES

1   Study Figure 2.77 which shows the pattern of some crimes in Aberdeen.
    a Describe the pattern of:
        i housebreaking
        ii violence in Aberdeen.
    b How far do these maps support the idea that some types of crime are restricted to certain parts of cities?
2   **a** Study Figure 2.78. Try to explain the pattern of burglary in relation to nearby land uses.
    b Why would these land uses make houses nearby more vulnerable to burglary?

The *causes of crime* are complex. One group of theories links crime to the unequal economic system. It suggests that crime is one way by which poorer groups try to get a share of a country's wealth. Another group of theories links crime to the nature of the social groups in the area, who may be influences for good or bad.

The studies so far have concentrated on the locations of the crimes. However, just as important are the locations of the criminals. In the UK, the location of criminals is often linked to areas of 'problem' housing. These may be inner-city tower blocks or suburban council estates. However, not all crimes are linked to poverty and deprivation. For example, crimes such as fraud are often committed by people living in the wealthier parts of cities.

Residential segregation in cities

Just as different types of housing tend to be found in different parts of cities, so different cultural and ethnic groups tend to be found in particular parts of cities. When this segregation of an ethnic group is very concentrated, the area may become a **ghetto**. The name ghetto comes from the area of Geto in medieval Venice where Jews were forced to live. An example of a ghetto in the city of Kalamazoo, Michigan, USA, is shown in Figures 2.79 and 2.80. There was a massive influx of people into the USA from the Netherlands in the 1890s and early 1900s. The Dutch settlers in Kalamazoo concentrated in two main clusters in 1910, one to the north of the city centre and one to the south. These two clusters were very different. The one to the north contained people from Frisia, the one to the south people from Zealand. Each had its own language and the people could not understand each other.

Why do groups cluster together in ghettos?

The main reasons for groups to cluster seem to be:

- to reduce the feeling of being isolated
- as a defence against attack by other groups
- to avoid contact with the outside world
- to preserve cultural heritage.

Ghettos can perform different functions:

- they can be the means by which groups preserve their sense of identity
- they can be the focus by which groups are dispersed into the host nation.

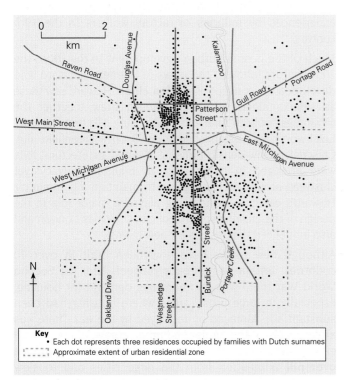

Figure 2.79 *People with Dutch names in Kalamazoo, USA, in 1910.*

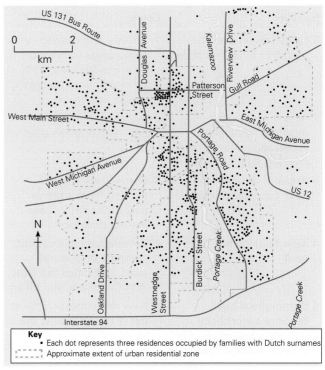

Figure 2.80 *People with Dutch names in Kalamazoo, USA, in 1965.*

227

4 Urban futures

Re-imaging cities: the Birmingham case

Since the 1990s cities have had to market themselves in order to attract investment from around the world. Many older industrial centres like Birmingham, have tried to create a new image (re-imaging) for themselves. Special events such as festivals, trade fairs, and conventions form one part of this re-imaging.

City advertising has to be accompanied by building a new urban landscape, especially in the city centre. Many of these new developments are linked to leisure and entertainment facilities, as well as tourist attractions and business services.

The role of city councils such as Birmingham City Council is vital to this re-imaging. Councils have to be entrepreneurial, that is, be prepared to take risks in order to attract external investment to bring jobs and wealth. Birmingham City Council established a **growth coalition** with other sectors, for example Aston Science Park, and began a series of flagship projects. Birmingham's investment in these schemes grew six-fold between 1981 and 1991, but as a result, less money was available for schools and hospitals (Figure 2.81).

Benefits	Costs
1 Large areas have been rebuilt in attractive styles	1 Poverty and dereliction in some areas increased between 1993 and 1999 as money went to high-profile schemes
2 New business, for example hosting conferences, has grown, creating jobs and income	2 Some new jobs are part time and low paid
3 Areas of derelict land have been redeveloped	3 Some firms are just moving from another part of the city – these are not new jobs
4 New housing has been built	4 Birmingham still cannot compete on a world scale with cities like New York City, Paris, and Milan
5 Birmingham has become a world city and attracted large-scale investment from abroad	5 New developments have not really improved the lot of the poor or the elderly in Birmingham

Figure 2.81 *Benefits and costs of redeveloping Birmingham.*

ACTIVITIES

1 On balance, do you think that the successes of Birmingham's redevelopment outweigh the problems created? Give reasons for your answer.

Are new towns the answer to urban problems?

Building a new town from a 'drawing board design' clearly gives planners the opportunity to create what they perceive to be an ideal environment for people to live and work in. The town can also be sited in a chosen, optimum location. Historically there are examples from Victorian England where philanthropic industrialists such as Lord Lever built settlements for their workers, housing them in healthy, attractive conditions in sites adjacent to what were often model factories in terms of working conditions. Port Sunlight in The Wirral, for workers at Lever Brothers Soap Works, is one of around 20 examples. It is a settlement with low-density housing surrounded by open space and amenities for workers to enjoy. These early examples of planned 'new' towns represented a response to the appalling and unhealthy living conditions experienced by millions of factory workers in the 19th century.

Much of the best suburban development in the UK in the 20th century followed the ideas of Ebenezer Howard who developed the concept of **garden cities**. Howard saw these as self-contained settlements which drew together the advantages of both rural and urban living. His first example, Letchworth, was established in 1903 on a greenfield site. Crescents of low-density housing of varied architectural style were arranged in cul-de-sacs 'to maintain privacy' yet clustered around a village green to maintain a community. Howard's designs and thinking played a major role in the design of the growing suburbs of cities such as London and also influenced the designs for new towns.

Although new towns have now been built in over 70 countries, Britain was an early pioneer. After the Second World War there was an enormous demand for housing, especially in large urban areas where housing had been substantially damaged or destroyed by the war. There was also concern at the unplanned urban sprawl of many large cities. Initially, new towns were designed to house **overspill** population from the large cities and to slow down the suburban sprawl and ribbon development so characteristic of the 1930s.

The New Towns Act of 1946 led to the development of eight new towns in south-east England and others elsewhere (Figure 2.82). The principal planning concepts the new town development corporations aimed to achieve can be summarised as follows:

- the town should grow rapidly to an optimum size (30,000–50,000) from a small initial base population
- the town should be comprehensively planned by a development agency to follow best practice in town planning
- the town should be separate from the 'parent' city and should be self-contained for requirements such as shopping, work, etc.

- a large proportion of the property (80 per cent) should remain in the ownership of the non-profit making development corporation. Initially, only 20 per cent of new town houses could be sold for owner occupation
- new towns should be socially balanced, incorporating a range of age, income and social groups within their neighbourhoods. Balanced communities for working and living was an early marketing slogan.

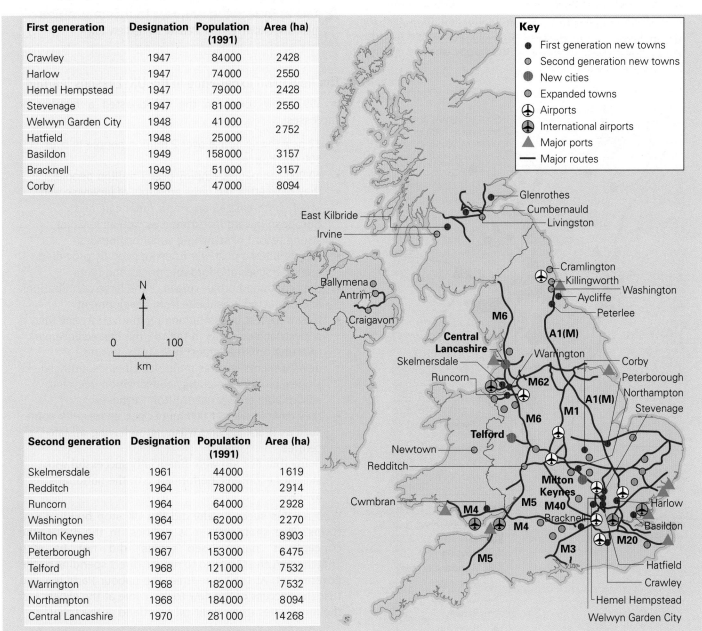

First generation	Designation	Population (1991)	Area (ha)
Crawley	1947	84000	2428
Harlow	1947	74000	2550
Hemel Hempstead	1947	79000	2428
Stevenage	1947	81000	2550
Welwyn Garden City	1948	41000	2752
Hatfield	1948	25000	
Basildon	1949	158000	3157
Bracknell	1949	51000	3157
Corby	1950	47000	8094

Second generation	Designation	Population (1991)	Area (ha)
Skelmersdale	1961	44000	1619
Redditch	1964	78000	2914
Runcorn	1964	64000	2928
Washington	1964	62000	2270
Milton Keynes	1967	153000	8903
Peterborough	1967	153000	6475
Telford	1968	121000	7532
Warrington	1968	182000	7532
Northampton	1968	184000	8094
Central Lancashire	1970	281000	14268

Key
- First generation new towns
- Second generation new towns
- New cities
- Expanded towns
- Airports
- International airports
- Major ports
- Major routes

Figure 2.82 *New towns and cities and expanded towns in the UK, 1996.*

Source: *Commission for New Towns Annual Report 1995-6.*

Whilst the new towns in south-east England were built to house London overspill, other first-generation new towns were built for regional development. The new town at Corby was built to support a steel works (which used local iron ore). Peterlee and Washington new towns were designed to bring new employment to north-east England.

The experiences of the first generation of new towns led to subsequent new towns being designed differently (Figure 2.83). Second-generation new towns such as Northampton and Peterborough were grafted onto existing settlements, resulting in much larger towns. The design changed to reflect the growth of car ownership. Concepts such as social mix and high reliance on rented housing disappeared. Inevitably, car ownership led to a rise in commuting and whilst new towns often provided a wide range of jobs, the dream of all the happy workers cycling to work was not fulfilled.

Milton Keynes and Telford are sometimes referred to as third-generation new towns. They include a number of established settlements, contain very large numbers of people and act as dynamic **industrial growth poles**. They are as important as many cities.

ACTIVITIES

1 Look at Figure 2.82.
   a Describe and explain the distribution of the first-generation new towns.
   b In what ways are the second-generation new towns different in terms of size and location?
2 Look at Figure 2.83. Identify five principles of good urban planning shown on the plan for Irvine new town.

The new town experience in the UK: Lessons learned

In 1997, new towns in the UK boasted a number of successes:

* 32 new towns house over 2 million people in over 500,000 houses
* 50,000 companies employ over 1 million people
* they have attracted large amounts of Japanese and other south-east Asian, north American, and European inward investment as well as having a strong record of spawning small businesses
* they fulfilled a post-war housing need by providing quality houses at affordable prices and rents
* they contained urban sprawl of the large conurbations and protected greenbelts from development
* they were test beds of planning innovation: the first pedestrianised malls in the UK; the first science park (Warrington); the largest innovative leisure developments such as multiplex cinemas, artificial ski slopes; pioneers in energy conservation, recycling, sustainable energy use (Milton Keynes)
* they created over 11,000 ha of open space, with some such as Bracknell and Washington having wildlife centres
* many (but not all) were financially successful with superior economic performance to the national average.

With all this success, why did the UK stop building new towns? The short answer is politics. In the 1980s, the concept of 'nationalised towns' did not fit with Thatcherism and the need to reduce direct spending by the government. At the same time, the Labour Party realised that the success of the new towns came at the expense of the inner cities (their political heartland at the time).

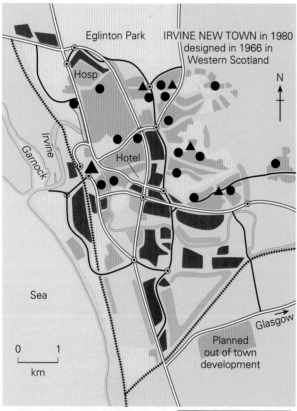

Figure 2.83 *Irvine new town, Scotland, in 1980. It was designed in 1966.*

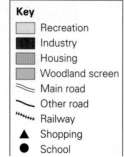

Key

(light)	Recreation
(black)	Industry
(mid grey)	Housing
(grey)	Woodland screen
≈	Main road
⌢	Other road
┼┼┼	Railway
▲	Shopping
●	School

There were also a number of criticisms of new towns:

- Many were built on greenfield sites. Although high-quality agricultural farmland was avoided, many rural dwellers exhibited 'NIMBY' (not in my backyard) symptoms, not wishing to see new towns being built in nearby countryside.
- In the early years, new towns were perceived as boring, with houses which lacked character (toy town/little boxes) and with a lack of community. The media hype was of 'new town blues'.
- New towns never fulfilled their original aims. Early new towns failed to attract a social mix (can you explain?) nor were the new towns in the London area totally self-contained – with commuting at a higher level than first anticipated.
- The new towns might have created half a million new homes, and thousands of new jobs, but how much was at the expense of the inner city?
- New towns were very much a product of their regions and where their regions experienced high unemployment so to a lesser extent did the new towns. In Cwmbran and Skelmersdale for example this was a problem.

Each new town has its problems and its successes. Figure 2.84 contains statements from the chief planners, highlighting issues specific to their own town.

Not only is there a move to re-invent the new town concept in the UK (the over-heated south-east of England will need some giant towns to provide sufficient houses for all those who want to work there) but also the concept of new towns has spread to an enormous number of locations globally.

Stevenage, 1946	'Stevenage provided a fine example of a sustainable community.' 61 per cent of the town's workforce actually live and work in Stevenage.' 'Our neighbourhood planning, our huge amount of open space.' 'We have major problems at present because our 1950s infrastructure is going to cost a huge amount to update.'
Harlow, 1947	'Our neighbourhood system has promoted a very strong sense of community identity in only 50 years.' 'It has been very difficult to match jobs to local people as we have had a lot of hi-tech investment.'
Hemel Hempstead, 1947	'Generally the brick-and-tile development in green, open land looks pleasant.' 'Two big problems are the lack of highways and the long linear town centre.'
East Kilbride, 1947	'Although our road system is excellent, we lack cycle provision and well organised public transport.'
Bracknell, 1948	'Employment and too much of it has been our success.' 'We're M4 corridor here.'
Cwmbran, 1949	'Our problem came with the 1970s recession – suddenly we had to get into the business of job creation for all our workers living here.' 'Although our housing won awards its not liked by most of our residents.'
Skelmersdale, 1961	'We are in an area of endemic unemployment – our battle is to match house construction to job creation.' 'We made mistakes about the design of our walkways.'
Livingston, 1962	'30,000 net jobs created for a town with 45,000 in a beautifully landscaped environment – but our public transport planning was poor.'
Redditch, 1964	'Our urban forest creates a beautiful environment but it was so difficult to plan in terms of population size, household size, traffic generation, etc.'
Irvine, 1966	'We should never have put the major shopping centre for the new town adjacent to the old town centre, it ruined the riverside area.'

Figure 2.84   *Statements by the chief planners on issues specific to individual new towns, 1996.*

New towns around the world

The greatest proliferation of new towns has been in LEDCs where they have been built to cope with expanding population and the urban sprawl which ensues. In large cities such as Bangkok, Delhi, Cairo, or Rio de Janeiro new towns are seen as a way of decentralising economic activity as well as solving the housing problems. In Hong Kong (New Territories) and Singapore, numerous new towns have been built to provide basic houses and services for very large numbers of new migrants (Figure 2.85).

In many European countries new towns are built for a variety of reasons. Paris has a 'ring' of new settlements similar to London. In the Netherlands new towns are built on newly reclaimed land as in Lelystad or Almere where consultants from Peterborough new town were involved.

New towns are built to develop new resources, for example Glenrothes in Scotland was originally built to exploit a new coal seam (which never lived up to expectations). New towns can also 'open up' an outback area for development (Cuidad Guyana in Venezuela) or become the site of a new capital (Brasilia in Brazil; Aruba in Nigeria). Here, consultants from Milton Keynes were involved in the planning.

New towns often became centres of science and technology, with examples such as multifunctional polis (MFP) near Adelaide, Australia, the Technopoli in Japan, or the Cybercities of Malaysia. New towns became the test beds for all kinds of new ideas in urban living. There is even talk of floating new towns in Japan. Although new towns are rare in the USA, Disney is producing 'designer' urban areas – namely Celebration in Florida designed only for the wealthy.

Figure 2.85 *A new town in Singapore.*

ACTIVITIES

1 With reference to a range of named examples, assess the success of new towns as places to live and work. Try to research some of the more exciting futuristic cities to see how urban designs have developed.
2 You can use the computer programme Sim City® to design your own new town.

Sustainable urban development: The way ahead

It is always dangerous to make predictions but one thing is certain – the global level of urbanisation will continue to rise. It is estimated to reach 65 per cent by 2025. Equally significantly, the number of world megacities will grow, and millions of new urban areas will develop. LEDCs will make the greatest contribution to these two global trends.

Sustainability is defined as 'meeting the needs of the present, without compromising the ability of future generations to meet their own needs' (Brundtland Commission, 1987). Figure 2.86 sets out the five implications of the concept of sustainability for urban areas. Sustainability is about resource conservation; respect for environmental quality; achieving equity through social justice; empowerment and community participation in political decision making; and harmonising of built developments with the natural environment.

Why is sustainable urban development so important? Consider these facts and think about issues of equity, resource conservation, environmental quality, and futurity:

- Cities rely on their 'hinterlands' to provide food, water, and energy. They depend on rivers, seas, and the atmosphere to act as their dustbins.
- Cities of the 'south' (LEDCs) are growing at such a pace that they cannot begin to keep pace with the ever-increasing demands made for housing, water, fuel, sanitation, health, etc.
- Cities of the 'north' (MEDCs), which are growing much more slowly, are the real problem. Their citizens are consuming ten times more resources per capita and producing four times more waste than citizens in cities of the 'south'.

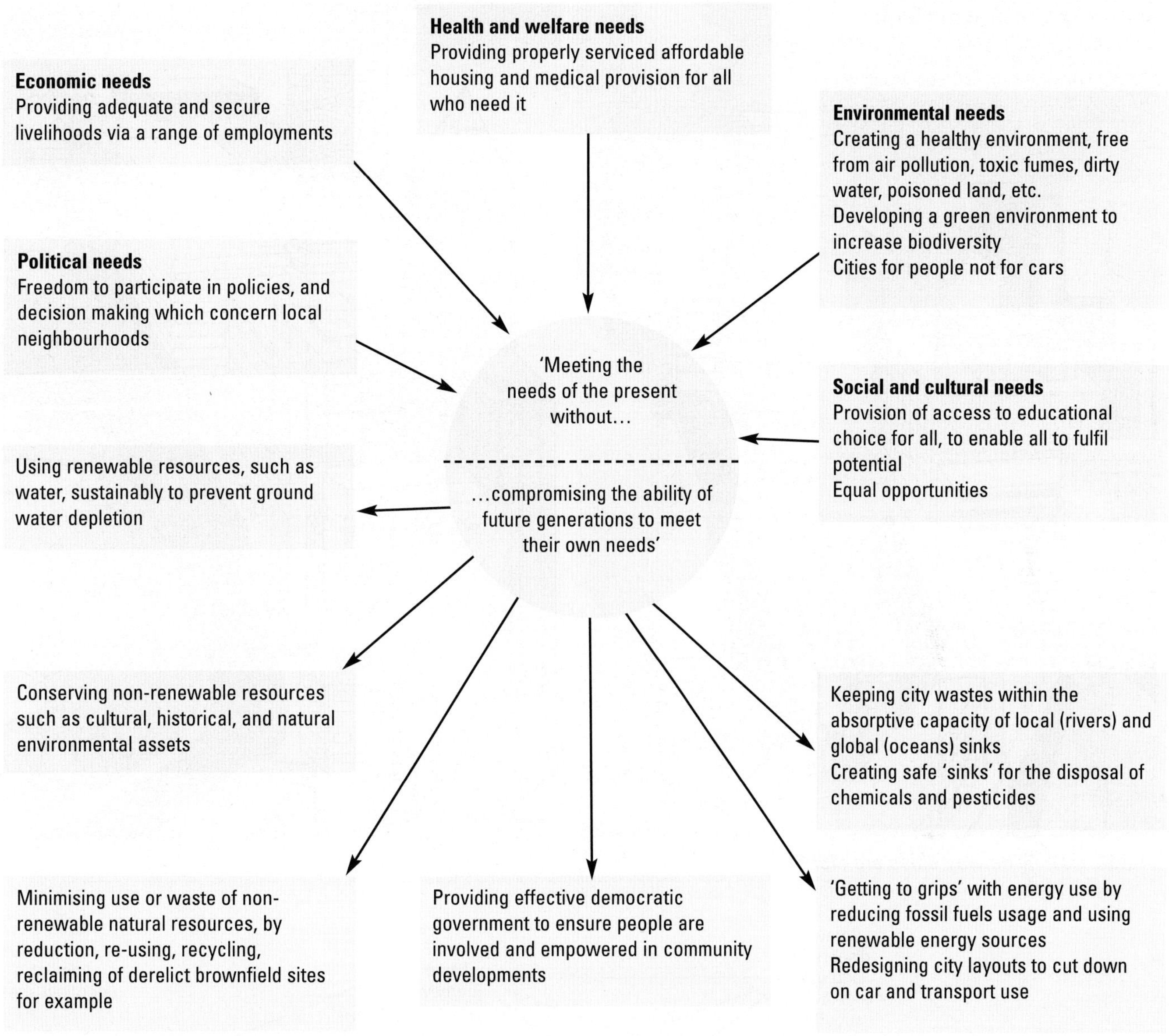
Health and welfare needs
Providing properly serviced affordable housing and medical provision for all who need it
Economic needs
Providing adequate and secure livelihoods via a range of employments
Environmental needs
Creating a healthy environment, free from air pollution, toxic fumes, dirty water, poisoned land, etc.
Developing a green environment to increase biodiversity
Cities for people not for cars
Political needs
Freedom to participate in policies, and decision making which concern local neighbourhoods
'Meeting the needs of the present without...
Social and cultural needs
Provision of access to educational choice for all, to enable all to fulfil potential
Equal opportunities
Using renewable resources, such as water, sustainably to prevent ground water depletion
...compromising the ability of future generations to meet their own needs'
Conserving non-renewable resources such as cultural, historical, and natural environmental assets
Keeping city wastes within the absorptive capacity of local (rivers) and global (oceans) sinks
Creating safe 'sinks' for the disposal of chemicals and pesticides
Minimising use or waste of non-renewable natural resources, by reduction, re-using, recycling, reclaiming of derelict brownfield sites for example
Providing effective democratic government to ensure people are involved and empowered in community developments
'Getting to grips' with energy use by reducing fossil fuels usage and using renewable energy sources
Redesigning city layouts to cut down on car and transport use

Figure 2.86 *The five implications of the concept of sustainability for urban areas.*

ACTIVITIES

1. Study Figure 2.87 which summarises the way cities are at present.
   - **a** Explain how the features shown make them unsustainable.
   - **b** Using the framework supplied, explain how you would redesign the cities to make them more sustainable.

Sustainable development in practice

A clear distinction has to be made between making existing cities more sustainable and designing new developments with 'in-built sustainability'.

Some existing cities begin with much greater advantages of design than others. There is no doubt that compact, high-density cities are much less wasteful in their energy consumption than large, urban, sprawling cities. Figure 2.88 shows the cycle of unsustainability based around the suburbanised land-use pattern seen in many North American and some west European cities.

Half the world's population lives in cities – and the proportion is growing. As cities consume 75 per cent of the world's resources and create most of its pollution, what we do or don't do with our cities is vital not only for citizens but for the planet too.

Food provision   Recycling

Transport strategies

Trees and greening

Sewage and waste disposal

Figure 2.87   *The way cities are (1999).*

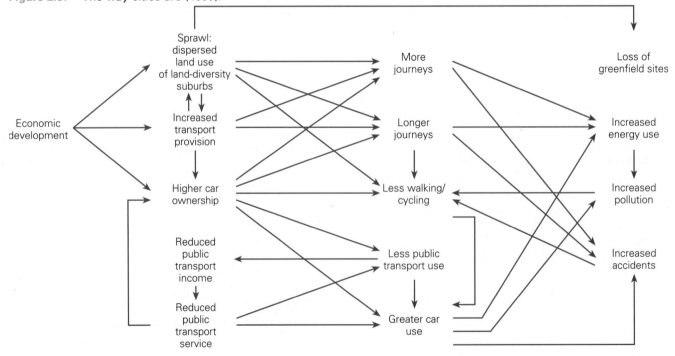

Figure 2.88   *Vicious cycle: Interactions contributing to unsustainability in urban travel.*

Agenda 21 is an agreement set up at the Rio Earth Summit in 1992. Under Agenda 21 national governments were obliged to formulate national plans or strategies for the sustainable development of their cities. Local authorities then developed strategies for applying this agenda at a local scale. A typical local Agenda 21, for example for Birmingham, involves a number of actions:

- provision of effective monitoring of air and water quality
- greening the city by landscaping the environment
- promoting energy efficiency

- establishing effective recycling of waste and litter schemes
- promoting 'green' growth to provide employment
- introducing more efficient forms of public transport, such as trams, or provision of cycle lanes

as well as raising awareness by improving publicity about Agenda 21.

Some strategies would be appropriate citywide, whereas others would be more appropriate for various city zones (Figure 2.89).

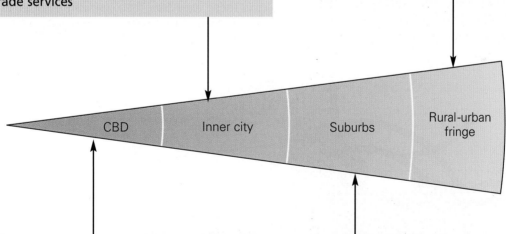

- improve quality of housing – energy efficiency, etc.
- expand and develop green areas – revitalise derelict parks, etc.
- introduce traffic calming and noise abatement schemes to improve inner-city housing areas
- separate incompatible uses to reduce nuisance of mixed zoning
- develop new business and 'tech' parks for new employment
- provide more frequent, reliable, and attractive public transport
- upgrade services

- develop small holding areas and organic farms
- ban out-of-town developments except at public transport routes
- increase water features and reduce water run-off
- improve ecological quality of open spaces
- establish firm controls of sprawl except in development corridors

CBD | Inner city | Suburbs | Rural-urban fringe

- enlarge and develop pedestrian priority areas
- improve public transport – cost, quality, frequency, etc.
- redevelop brownfield areas for new housing, also use 'dead' space above shops as flats
- develop safe pedestrian and cycle routes
- develop energy efficiency programmes for all public buildings
- increase green biomas, and water features
- limit car access to decongest central urban areas

- increase densities in suburban areas but without loss of environmental quality
- improve service provision in suburban centres near public transport
- develop network of roads with public transport priority and parallel networks of cycle lanes
- preserve green spaces and water areas
- establish networks of recycling centres
- develop local industrial poles to provide nearby employment and cut commuting
- develop quality of public transport

Figure 2.89 *Agenda 21 in Birmingham.*

There are numerous examples of successful sustainable developments, especially in European cities, but many of the strategies are not universally popular. Whereas most people will accept technological changes which bring environmental benefits such as catalytic converters, they may only do so if the benefits outweigh the costs or they are forced to do so. Physical curbs, for example on the use of cars, will only succeed if viable alternatives are provided such as high-quality, cheap, fast, and interconnecting public transport systems and even then physical curbs are often very unpopular with voters.

There are a number of 'beacon' cities which have successful, established, sustainable futures. The most well known of these is Curitiba in the state of Parana in Brazil. In spite of an increase in population from 300,000 in 1950 to nearly 2.5 million (2000 est.), Curitiba has managed to address the Brown Agenda (pages 257–260) *and* establish an excellent model for sustainable urban development.

The focus of development in Curitiba has been:

- The utilisation of the environmental setting such as former quarry sites to become landscape features. Curitiba is described 'being rich in visual texture' and has managed to expand rapidly yet retain 52 m² of green area per inhabitant (twice the recommended UN amount).

- The development of cheap, low-technology solutions as opposed to high-technology ones to solve problems. The programme of waste sorting, is an example, where workers are sold rubbish carts at cost price. They collect, recycle and sell the waste to private recycling companies.

- Innovation is developed through the participation of citizens (bottom-up) and incorporated into a wider citywide plan. In Curitiba's health schemes, outpatient posts have been developed for each subregion, and the health units are free to develop plans appropriate to the needs of these subregions.

- The trialling of innovative solutions. The problems of rural-urban migration which have led to development of numerous sprawling satellite areas is tackled by social workers approaching potential migrants at bus stations and offering them free bus tickets to return home (so far 23,000 have been persuaded back). Longer term, the *vila rural* (rural town) idea has been promoted to provide small farms, where the peasants can farm areas around the city between temporary industrial jobs.

- The jewel in the crown is the public transport system which has been promoted at the expense of the private car.

Figure 2.90 is a diagram of Curitiba's transport system. It shows the five main axes which form the main routes for express bus lanes. These are flanked by local roads and high-capacity, one-way streets running into and out of the city. These axes have become centres of commerce and offices. Arterial routes link these radial axes in a 'spider's web design'.

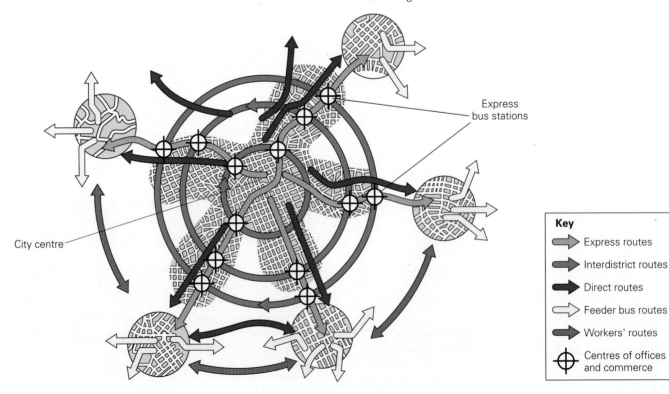

Figure 2.90   *The transport system in Curitiba, Brazil.*

Key
- Express routes
- Interdistrict routes
- Direct routes
- Feeder bus routes
- Workers' routes
- Centres of offices and commerce

Express bus stations

City centre

The transport system is based on 'bendy' buses because it was more economic to establish bus routes than subways. A single fare covers the whole city, to encourage use. The 'patrons' are provided with quality bus shelters, and extra-wide doors ensure speedy loading. With comfortable buses and express routes, journeys are more pleasant than many city bus rides. The bus companies are paid by kilometres of road they serve, not the number of passengers. This encourages them to serve new areas of the city.

The city has even turned its status as an ecocity into tourism, with a tourist trail to show the developments. The Free Environment University provides short courses on environmental management and conservation for the general public, and tailormade courses for companies.

The Brown Agenda

Cities in the developing world are experiencing very rapid rates of growth. Whilst there are parallels with the 19th century urbanisation experienced in MEDCs, there are very significant differences. Urbanisation in the developing world is frequently urbanisation without industrialisation, and it is occurring at ever more rapid rates (rural-urban migration combined with high fertility rates can lead to urban growth rates of up to 10 per cent per year).

In 2000, 1.9 billion people live in urban areas in LEDCs, by 2020 this figure could increase to approximately 4 billion.

In 1992 at the Rio Earth Summit, a broad-based agreement was achieved that pollution problems, environmental hazards, and poverty would be the priorities for action on the urban agenda of the 21st century.

The range of environmental problems experienced by cities in LEDCs is now referred to as the Brown Agenda. Figure 2.91 shows how the nature, range, and mix of environmental problems found in any urban area is clearly influenced by economic development. The Brown Agenda consists of two distinct components:

- Traditional issues associated with environmental health caused by the limited availability of good quality land, shelter, and services such as clean water.
- Problems which have arisen resulting from rapid industrialisation such as toxic/hazardous waste, water, air, and noise pollution, and industrial accidents from poor health and safety standards.

In all cases, it is the low-income groups in the cities that suffer most. Whilst the first set of issues are more dominant and widespread, the two groups of issues are frequently interlinked.

In many LEDC cities such as Jakarta, water is contaminated from sewage discharges, but it also receives discharge from untreated industrial waste which compounds the problem. City managers have to tackle these industrial pollution issues without even having the resources to find effective solutions to traditional pollution issues. The reason for this is that the rapid rate of urbanisation overwhelms the local capacity to provide the necessary environmental infrastructure and services. However, environmental problems are not automatically solved by throwing technology and capital at them. Experiences from initiatives such as the healthy city programme in Bangladesh emphasise the importance of empowering low-income households and communities to organise improvements.

The western image of Calcutta, India, almost certainly includes some aspect of filth or squalor – people living in cardboard boxes and newspapers on the street or people sitting on the top of a bus in a 'people jam' crossing the Hoogly river bridge, or sewage pouring down a side street in a brown river in the monsoon season. These grim images of Calcutta reflect the enormous environmental problems it faces, problems which are a result of both physical and human factors.

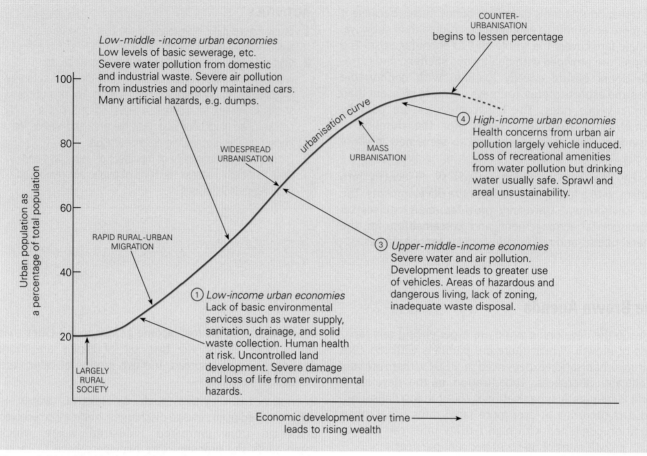

Figure 2.91   *Environmental problems found in urban areas.*

- Population 11.83 million (1990), 14 million (2000 est.)
- India's largest city. Located at the mouth of the Ganges. Highest point of city is only 10 m above sea level – serious frequent flooding problems and sewage disposal issues.
- 45 per cent of residents live in slums/squatter settlements.
- Average population density 7228/km². Squatter settlement density can be as high as 100,000/km². 500,000 people live and sleep on the city's roads.
- Infant death-rate 123 per 1000 live births (largely from diarrhoea, diphtheria, measles).
- No fully operational sewage plants. 60 per cent of people live in structures lacking proper sanitation, 33 per cent have no latrine of any kind so open drains serve as sewers.
- 70 per cent of population have access to piped water – but on average 40 households share a single tap. The 150-year-old water distribution system leaks, and pollutants enter the pipes.
- 95 per cent of rainfall (around 2000 mm) falls in summer – flooding is endemic and leads to water contamination.
- Chemical engineering works and power stations pump out large concentrations of sulphur dioxide. Air quality is now threatened by carbon monoxide, and nitrous oxides because of rising transport-related emissions.
- Many factories produce highly toxic chemicals and many are in densely populated residential areas.
- Noise pollution is city wide (80dB often recorded), human tolerance is around 60–65dB.
- Rapid growth of the city (5–6 per cent per year) resulted in an unplanned city. There is no comprehensive land use zoning policy.
- Financial constraints, shortage of cost-effective technology inhibit progress 'top-down'.
- Communities have more pressing problems of shelter, food, and clothing, i.e. basic survival, than taking part in 'bottom-up' empowerment strategies.

Figure 2.92   *Factfile on Calcutta.*

Calcutta's problems are enormous. However, most researchers argue that if the right management structures can be developed to tackle the overlapping phenomena of 'megacity' with a plethora of brown environmental problems – things can improve significantly.

City-specific solutions are required. Figure 2.93 suggests a management process framework. Sustainability in this case involves the most effective use of limited resources.

Less economically developed cities contain some of the world's safest neighbourhoods. The high-density populations can be seen as an advantage because they allow much lower costs by household for supplying piped water or electricity. The quality of the housing and the issue of who pays for it is the prime problem, not the density of the population itself. Basic programmes can achieve spectacular improvements in LEDC cities. If the city can set out an equitable division of land, many problems can be resolved, for example:

- community work in Orangi, a huge, low-income settlement in Karachi, Pakistan, where 70,000 households dug their own sewers and drains
- the people's housing movement in Johannesburg, South Africa, where new houses have been built for of around £1000 each
- community work in the shanty town of Villa El Salvador.

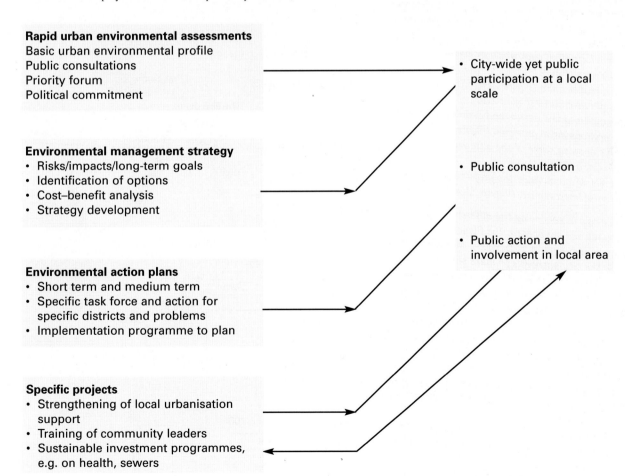

Figure 2.93 *A management process framework.*

Cairo, Egypt

DECISION-MAKING ACTIVITIES

In this exercise, imagine that you have been employed to advise the Greater Cairo City Planning Department on the relative merits of a series of projects which are intended to improve the environment of the city. You have been given a brief by the City Planning Department (Figure 2.94).

Dear Consultant,

As you will be aware, Greater Cairo faces a range of environmental problems which together are called the Brown Agenda. These problems fall into two main groups:

- those traditional environmental health problems which result from a lack of a clean water supply or effective sewage or garbage disposal system
- those problems resulting from industrial growth and the rise in car ownership, for example, the pollution of air, land, and water.

This Planning Department wants to tackle both these groups of problems, though the main priority is to improve conditions for the poorest groups in the city, especially those in the Cities of the Dead and in home-made huts. We enclose an information pack which includes:

- map of the area (Figure 2.95)
- a map of Greater Cairo (Figure 2.96)
- a datafile of basic facts (Figure 2.97)
- a datafile outlining the nature and causes of some of the main environmental problems (Figure 2.98)
- a photo file showing some of the different types of housing in Cairo (Figure 2.99)
- a project file, which outlines the projects for environmental improvement (Figure 2.100).

We need your help in assessing the different projects, which as you will see are costed. The Planning Department has a strict budget limit of £25 million. We have been able to persuade the city authority to make this large, one-off expenditure in order to bring about big improvements in Cairo's environment. Hence we need to ensure that the money is allocated to those projects which meet most of the key criteria listed below. The aim is to bring maximum benefit to the largest number of poorer people in the city. We need to be very clear why we have selected some projects and not others. So we need you to:

- write a brief summary of Cairo's main environmental problems, and use the key criteria to identify those which are a priority for action
- for each project outline its main advantages and disadvantages, and the degree to which it does or does not meet the key criteria
- suggest an allocation for the £25 million between a selection of the projects, giving the reasons for your choices.

The projects have to meet as many of the following criteria as possible. The projects should:

- increase the amount of affordable housing available to poor city dwellers
- reduce death and disease by improving the water supply, sewerage, and rubbish collection to areas inhabited by poorer citizens
- reduce illegal dumping of industrial waste in Cairo's water system
- increase the percentage of waste water that is fully treated before being pumped to the sea
- increase employment for poorer people
- reduce air pollution.

Yours faithfully,
The City Planning Department

Figure 2.94   *Brief from the City Planning Department.*

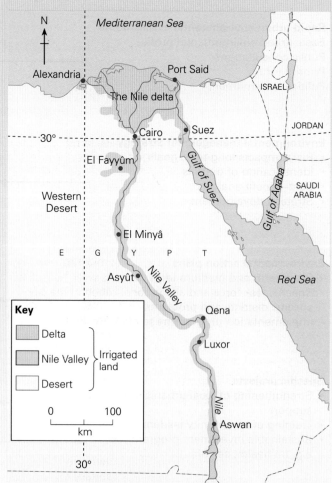

Figure 2.95   *Location map for Cairo, Egypt.*
Source: *Cairo: Urban Problems and Solutions* Stanley Thornes, 1997.

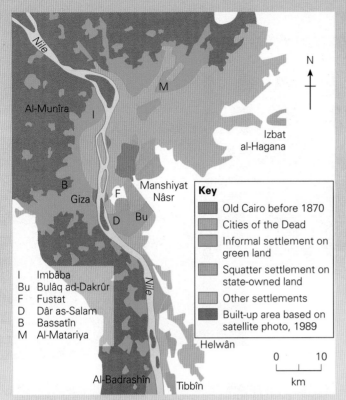

Figure 2.96   *Map of Greater Cairo.*

Key:
- Old Cairo before 1870
- Cities of the Dead
- Informal settlement on green land
- Squatter settlement on state-owned land
- Other settlements
- Built-up area based on satellite photo, 1989

I   Imbâba
Bu Bulâq ad-Dakrûr
F   Fustat
D   Dâr as-Salam
B   Bassatîn
M   Al-Matariya

0 ———— 10 km

Site
An easily defended site on an area of raised land called the Magattam Hills close to the river Nile.

Situation
A strategic position between the rich, fertile farmlands of the Nile delta and the irrigated farmland parallel to the Nile.

Population of Greater Cairo
1995 12 million
2000 13 million

City growth
Old Cairo on the Magattam Hills has narrow alleys and low, flat-roofed houses. However, in the mid-19th century, Parisian-style boulevards and apartments were built closer to the river Nile as part of the modernisation of the city. The most rapid growth took place in the 1960s and 1970s. Between 1968 and 1982 the area of the city doubled. Valuable irrigated land along the banks of the Nile was sold and built on illegally at the rate of 600ha per year.

Population density
32,759/km²

Infant death-rate
105 per 1,000 live births (1991).

Main causes of death
Diarrhoea, tetanus, measles, and diphtheria resulting mostly from overcrowding and poor sanitary conditions.

Figure 2.97   *Datafile of basic facts about Cairo.*

Sanitation
70 per cent of the city is connected to the public sewerage system, but only 15 per cent of the waste water is collected and fully treated. A further 25 per cent is partially treated and 30 per cent is carried untreated in open canals 200 km to Lake Manzalah and then to the sea.

Housing problems
Cairo does not have large areas of spontaneous settlements (shanty towns), but it does have many houses built illegally on irrigated farmland near the river Nile. These 'informal' houses cover 80 per cent of Greater Cairo's 450 km² built-up area.

In other areas, Cairo's people cope with the housing crisis by living in the Cities of the Dead. 2–3 million people live in the tombs of Old Cairo. Yet other people (about 500,000) occupy home-made huts on the rooves of flats and offices in the city centre. Most of these people have no water supply or sewage system. Some landlords illegally add extra storeys to existing blocks of flats thereby making the whole structure more dangerous.

Because rents are fixed at 1950s levels, owners do few repairs, so many houses are on the point of collapse. On average, each person in Cairo has only 13 cm² of space in which to live. The high rates of sickness and death are linked to this overcrowded housing which is poorly built, and has a totally inadequate water supply, and a poor garbage/sewerage disposal system.

Air pollution
High levels of traffic (1.2 million cars in 1991) create exhaust fumes of carbon monoxide (CO) and high levels of lead. Tests in 1995 suggest that these are two thirds higher than in rural Egypt. Fumes from cooking oils add to the air pollution problem creating a toxic smog. Emissions from power stations and many local industries add sulphur dioxide (SO_2) to the atmosphere.

Water pollution
Groundwater is polluted by the illegal dumping of industrial waste from the many backstreet workshops. Leaking sewers add to the problems, and have caused the water table to rise, which in turn rots the foundations of buildings. In 1992, 30,000 of these buildings collapsed in an earthquake.

Rubbish disposal
The Zabbaleen people collect much of Cairo's waste in donkey carts and then sort it and often recycle it. Their work is not encouraged by the government and the Zabbaleen are not able to reach all parts of the city.

Key problem
Lack of financial resources to improve the urban environment.

Figure 2.98   *Datafile of some of Cairo's main environmental problems.*

Figure 2.99   *Different types of housing in Cairo.*

Project 1

This project aims to spend £2 million on purchasing additional carts and donkeys for the Zabbaleen. These people already collect much of the city's rubbish and recycle it. However, with these additional resources they could cover the whole city, especially the poorer areas such as the Cities of the Dead and the roof-top dwellers. Rubbish collection would reduce disease and pollution, it would provide increased employment, and would enable even greater recycling of paper, plastic, and metal in Cairo.

Project 2

This project would build on the existing aid-funded Greater Cairo Sewage Project. The aims are to repair existing sewers and extend the sewerage system to those parts of the city currently not served. This would cost £10 million and would provide some employment for local people.

Project 3

The aim of this project is to reduce air pollution (especially carbon monoxide) by reducing the number of vehicles on the city's roads. Funding of £12 million would allow the construction of additional lines to the underground metro system (which already carries 1 million people per day). There would be some disruption to traffic in the city during construction (3–5 years) but air quality would be greatly improved.

Project 4

This project would provide a simple system to collect and dispose of industrial waste from the many small factories and workshops. In this way, pollution of the water system could be avoided, especially if the service is subsidised by the city and so is cheap to use. It would cost £6 million to install and begin operations, but the results in terms of reduced pollution would be considerable.

Project 5

This project would aim to upgrade the home-made huts currently existing on roof-tops in the city. Building materials such as bricks, concrete and sand would be made available to the inhabitants who would be expected to carry out the work themselves. In addition, the project would take a basic system of water pipes into both the Cities of the Dead and to the areas of the roof-top homes in order to provide a clean, safe supply of drinking water. This project would cost £7 million.

Project 6

This project aims to provide low-cost accommodation in simple flats in new satellite and dormitory towns such as 10th Ramadan and 15 May. This would reduce overcrowding in Cairo, but rents would have to be subsidised, as would the costs of transport between Cairo and the cities. In total the scheme would cost £18 million.

Project 7

The aim of this project would be to reduce air pollution by sulphur dioxide from the power stations of the city. New filters would be fitted to the smoke stacks to remove virtually all the sulphur dioxide, though other sources of this pollutant would not be affected. The filters would have to be purchased from the USA or the UK and would cost £8 million.

Figure 2.100   *Project for environmental improvement in Cairo.*

Unit 2 Reference materials

Chapter 1

Websites

Useful Charity Websites
www.oneworld.org/itdg
www.panda.org/forest
www.actionaid.org.uk
www.charitynet.org/~farmafrica
www.cafod.org.uk
www.christian-aid.org.uk
www.oxfam.org.uk/cod/planet/
www.ontheline.org.uk/index.htm
www.wateraid.org.uk
www.iied.org/resource
www.wwf-uk.org

Rural sites on a number of issues in the UK

CPRE	www.greenchannel.comcpre
NFU	www.nfu.org.uk/educaiton
FAO	www.fao.org/
World Bank	www.worldbank.org/ landpolicy/projects.htm
D of E	www.naturenet.net/
Countryside Agency	www.countryside.org.uk
Environment Agency	www.environment.agency.gov.uk
Rural Development	www.rurdev.usda.gov
Lake District NP	www.lake-district.gov.uk
Yorkshire Dales NP	www.yorkshiredales.org.uk

Sustainable Development
www.oneworld.org/patp/

Articles

- *Rural Issues* and *Countryside Issues* from the Countryside Agency are available free of charge.
- *Tourism Concern* 277-281 Holloway Road, London, N7 8HN provides low cost support materials on issues such as rural Tourism and Eco Tourism.
- *Managing Rural Environments* Heinemann 1999 – provides an introduction.
- *Rural Geography* Arnold 1988; *The Geography of Rural Resources* Oliver & Boyd 1988 – are both quite dated but very good for conceptual ideas.
- *Rural Livelihoods Crises and Responses* Oxford 1992 – provides a sound LEDC focus.
- *Conflict and Change in the Countryside* Wiley 1994 – provides an enormous range of developed world examples.
- A *Geography of Rural Change* Longman 1998 – provides up-to-date information on rural change in N America and Australia as well as Europe.

Additionally most local authorities such as Devon, Norfolk and Kent publish planning materials on issues such as access to services, sustainability and rural tourism. A first starting point is to look for their websites.

The most extensive list of papers in the UK comes from the newly formed countryside agency who publish research papers and free summaries on a wide range of rural issues such as deprivation.

All National Parks publish development plans, as well as a range of Educational materials on countryside issues. The Yorkshire Dales, and Lake District National Parks have some excellent resources on options for the future.

Chapter 2

Websites

www.inhabitat.org/presskit/dp/1790c.htm
www.sustainabledevelopment.org/blp/unchs/
www.urbanobservatory.org/
www.hsd.ait.ac.th/umc/id/ha/ha.html
www.hsd.ait.ac.th/ihsa/si/a131c.html
www.sierraclub.org/

Articles

- *Urban Challenge* Hodder 2000.
- *Urbanisation: Changing Environments* Collins 1998.
- *Urban World/Global City* Routledge 1996 – excellent introduction to Urbanisation and World Cities.
- *The Urban World* Stanley Thornes 1999 – useful parallel text for students.
- *Britain's Cities* Routledge 1997 – useful sections on social inequalities.
- *Urban Social Geography* Longman 1995 – useful sections on Urban Change & Conflict.
- *The Urban Order* Blackwell 1997 – good on race, inequality etc.
- *The Urban Opportunity* Intermediate Technology Publications 1996.
- *The City in the Developing World* Longman 1998 – provides an excellent summary of LEDC issues.
- *An Urbanising World* UN Habital Global Report on Human Settlements 1996 – provides a wide range of statistics and short case studies on world cities.

Unit 2 Glossary

Accessibility   The ease with which people can get to a particular place. Places with good accessibility include city centres, because so many roads and railway lines converge there.

Aided self-help scheme   A method of improving conditions in spontaneous settlements in LEDCs. The government begins the process of improvement by installing electricity, a clean water supply and sewage disposal facilities. This encourages local residents to improve their homes by their own efforts – for example, by using bricks and concrete to create better housing.

Amenity   A facility provided to improve the quality of the environment – for example, a park, a playground or a golf course.

Brown belt   Land lying within a **green belt** that has already been damaged or degraded by activities such as quarrying, landfill and the construction of power stations and sewage works.

Brownfield site   An urban area that used to have old factories and houses, but where these buildings have been demolished prior to redevelopment.

Central business district (CBD)   The central area of a city, dominated by department stores, specialist and variety goods shops, offices, cinemas, theatres and hotels.

Comprehensive Development Area (CDA)   An area, usually in the inner city, where the whole urban landscape was demolished before being rebuilt on a planned basis by the council or city government.

Conurbation   A large urban area formed by the coalescing of several urban centres, or the outward expansion of one major centre.

Core   The centre or focus of an area. It usually contains the largest population cluster (frequently the capital city) and the most developed economic base of a region or country.

Counter-urbanisation   The movement of people away from towns and cities to live in villages and small towns in the countryside.

Cumulative causation   Theoretical process which leads to the formation of core and periphery areas. New economic development in the core often stimulates the local economy and attracts migrants searching for work. The cumulative effect of movements of people and resources increases wealth in the core.

Cycle of deprivation   A sequence of events experienced by disadvantaged people in which one problem leads to other problems and so makes things worse.

De-centralisation   The movement of people, factories, offices and shops away from city centres towards suburban and edge-of-city locations.

Deprivation   The degree to which an individual or an area is deprived of services and amenities. There are many different types and levels of deprivation including poor and overcrowded housing, inadequate diet, inadequate income and lack of opportunity for employment.

Deurbanisation   Terms used to describe the movement of people and/or employment from a small number of large, dominant centres to a more dispersed pattern of location. A policy used frequently by governments to achieve a more balanced distribution of development.

Ecotourism   A form of tourism which aims to conserve fragile ecosystems and market their appeal while providing income for local people.

Enterprise zone   Vacant, and often derelict, land within or near urban areas in which industrial development is encouraged through a series of financial and planning measures.

Externality   An outcome of an activity by an individual, group or institution that affects the welfare of other people. Externalities may be good (see **positive externality**) or bad (see **negative externality**).

Favela   A Brazilian term for a **spontaneous settlement** or slum, where most of the homes are built from scrap materials.

Filtering   A process by which social groups move from one residential area to another, leading to changes in the social nature of residential areas.

Flagship scheme   A high-profile development, designed to encourage investment in an area and to be a model for further developments.

Gentrification   A process by which run-down houses in an inner city or other neglected area are improved by relatively affluent people who move there in order to have easier access to the jobs and services of the city centre.

Ghetto   An urban district containing a high proportion of one particular ethnic group.

Green belt   An area around a city, composed mostly of parkland and farmland, in which development is strictly controlled. Its purpose is to prevent two or more cities from coalescing to form one huge urban area.

Green buffer   An area of open space, composed mostly of parkland and farmland, in which development is strictly controlled. It runs between and around cities to provide most people with access to green space.

Greenfield site   An area, usually on the edge of a city, that has not been developed for housing, industry or transport. The area may still be farmland, which gives it its name.

High-order good/service   A good or service, usually expensive, that people buy only occasionally – for example, furniture, computers and jewellery. High-order services are usually located in larger towns and cities accessible to large numbers of people.

Hinterland   The name given to the area round a settlement which comes under its economic, political and social influence. The same area is also sometimes called the **sphere of influence** or **urban field.**

Inner city   The part of the city centre that includes the central business district and a small area of land immediately surrounding it. In the UK, this area has frequently experienced significant changes in land-use patterns since the 1970s, eg office developments, road improvement schemes, urban renewal and the relocation of established populations.

Less Favoured Areas   Areas in the EC which are given extra funding because they are difficult environments to live and work in.

Multiplier effect   Where development in one activity generates additional employment and wealth in other activities, eg motor vehicle assembly creates a demand for many inputs (lights, tyres, windscreens, brakes, etc).

Negative externality   An unpleasant outcome for other people of an activity by an individual, group or institution – for example, the fumes from a factory or noise from an airport.

New town   A planned urban centre, designed to be freestanding, self-contained and socially balanced.

Out-of-town shopping centre A large group of shops built either on a site at the edge of the urban area or on the site of a former large industrial complex. Such centres usually have large car parks, a pedestrianised, air-conditioned environment and over 100 shops.

Over-urbanisation Over-urbanisation, found in some cities in LEDCs, occurs when the rate of population growth, boosted by in-migration from surrounding rural areas, is more rapid than the growth of the city's economy. The result is that the city is unable to provide sufficient jobs and housing.

Periphery Areas located near the margins of a country or region. They are generally poorly linked to core areas and are less developed regions with problems eg West of Ireland, Mezzogiorno.

Positive externality A beneficial outcome for other people of an activity by an individual, group or institution – for example an individual who endows a city art gallery contributes to the cultural development of local people.

Primate city An urban centre that dominates a country's urban system, with a population much greater than that of the next-largest city.

Redevelopment The rebuilding of parts of a city. Sometimes large areas are completely demolished before being rebuilt; sometimes all or some of the old buildings are retained and modernised to combine the best features of the old and the new.

Re-urbanisation The process whereby towns and cities which have been experiencing a loss of population are able to reverse the decline and begin to grow again. Some form of city centre redevelopment is often the catalyst that starts re-urbanisation.

Rural Areas characterised by low population densities, primary industries and small settlements.

Ruralisation An increase in the proportion of people classified as rural.

Site The land on which a settlement is located. This refers mainly to its local physical setting, eg bridging point, deep-water port.

Site-and-services scheme A method of encouraging housing improvement in poor areas of cities in LEDCs. The government provides the land for a new development and installs services such as water and electricity. Local people can then obtain a plot in the scheme for a low rent and build their own houses.

Situation The locational attributes of a place relative to other non-local places, eg its position relative to international trade routes or proximity to coalfields.

Spontaneous settlement A squatter settlement or shanty town containing self-built houses made of scrap materials such as corrugated iron and plastic; the settlement usually lacks piped water, an electricity supply and sewage disposal facilities. Spontaneous settlements are numerous in cities in LEDCs and are illegal because the residents neither own the land on which the houses are built, nor have permission to build there.

Squatter settlement Another name for a **spontaneous settlement**.

Suburbanisation The process by which people, factories, offices and shops move out of the central areas of cities and into the suburbs.

Transition zone The area around the CBD. It is a zone of mixed land uses, ranging from car parks and derelict buildings to slums, cafés and older houses, often converted to offices or industrial uses.

Urban agglomeration A very large built-up area, with extensive areas of housing, industry, retailing, manufacturing and recreational facilities.

Urban Development Corporation A body set up by the British government to secure the regeneration of designated land within urban areas.

Urban fringe The area at the edge of the built-up part of the city. The fringe is usually a zone of mixed land uses, from shopping malls and golf courses to farmland and motorways.

Urban growth An increase in the absolute number of people living in an urban area.

Urban hierarchy A system of urban centres in a region or country with a size distribution from the largest to the smallest, and a functional distribution from the most specialised to the least specialised.

Urban sprawl An increase in the area covered by urban activities.

Urbanisation The process by which more and more people live in towns and cities. By AD 2000, over half of the world's population will live in urban areas.

Urban morphology The form or shape of a town and the arrangement and layout of its buildings and spaces.

World city A very large city which is important within the world economy, and not just within the economy of one country. World cities include London, Tokyo, New York and Sao Paulo.

Zone in transition The area around the CBD. It is a zone of mixed land uses, ranging from car parks and derelict buildings to slums, cafes and older houses, often converted to offices or industrial uses.

Index